From Realignment to Reform

Thomas Collier Platt (New York Public Library)

From Realignment to Reform

POLITICAL CHANGE IN
NEW YORK STATE,
1893–1910

Richard L. McCormick

Cornell University Press

ITHACA AND LONDON

Winner, New York State Historical Association Manuscript Award, 1979.

Cornell University Press gratefully acknowledges a grant from the Andrew W. Mellon Foundation that aided in bringing this book to publication.

First published 1981 by Cornell University Press.
Published in the United Kingdom by Cornell University Press Ltd.,
Ely House, 37 Dover Street, London W1X 4HQ.

International Standard Book Number 0-8014-1326-5
Library of Congress Catalog Card Number 80-69824
Printed in the United States of America
Librarians: Library of Congress cataloging information appears on the last page of the book.

For KCM, RPM, and CAJ

Contents

Illustrations, Tables, and Figures

Illustrations

Tables

Illustrations, Tables, and Figures

Figures

Preface

Two concepts dominate the interpretative scholarship on late-nine-teenth and early-twentieth-century American politics: realignment and reform. According to the first and more recent of the two, the critical elections of the mid-1890s restructured politics in the United States, not only by altering the balance of power between the parties but also by fixing the distinctive features of the succeeding era. Following the electoral shift to the Republican party, there emerged an early-twentieth-century political order characterized by noncompetitive elections, a demobilized citizenry, and government policies serving a business elite. The second interpretation, which is older, is harder to sum up, both because it has received many more expressions, often in mutual conflict, and because it is inherently less precise. It, too, describes long-lasting political and governmental changes, but here they are associated with what is commonly called progressivism, a reform movement that swept the country well after the political turmoil of the 1890s had settled. Although they patrol the same turf, the proponents of these two theories are not locked in combat, because for the most part they ignore each other. This peacefulness between them deprives the political era they both study of a convincing synthesis.

There are, however, real differences between the two interpretations. The concept of realignment directs our attention to the political system as a whole, while the reform theory concentrates on the historic contexts in which particular men and movements responded to conditions they considered evil. Where the first approach makes important use of social science theory and commonly relies on quantitative evidence, the second places its reliance on more traditional historical methods and sources. Yet both realignment and reform have significantly contributed to describing and explaining some of the same political changes. In particular, both interpretations tell us a good deal, first about the weakening of traditional party politics and the fashioning of alternative means of political participation, and second about the establishment of new governmental policies taking account of the maturation of a complex industrial society. These are the two developments with which this study of New York politics is mainly concerned.

It is not my purpose, however, to merge the two explanations or to mediate between them. Indeed, the reader will discover that I am somewhat skeptical of both theories. In New York, the realignment of the 1890s brought the Republicans to power, but it left most aspects of nineteenth-century politics untouched and is difficult to connect directly to the important changes in participation and policymaking that occurred in the following decade. The reform interpretation, for its part, in focusing on the Progressive movement, diverts attention from the actual political process. Certainly the currently dominant "organizational synthesis" in Progressive-era historiography, while it helps to explain the period's long-term modernizing significance, does not adequately describe the political circumstances that brought forth New York's most decisive changes. Despite my skepticism, however, this book has been heavily influenced by both approaches. It begins with the coming to power of the Republicans in the realignment of the 1890s and ends with reform at a peak as the following decade closed. The interpretation of the intervening years in these pages may contribute to achieving the synthesis of the era's politics which we still lack.

The reader will also find that a third type of political history, even more venerable than the literature of reform, has influenced this book: the study of top political leaders. Out of the many focuses I might have chosen, I decided to scrutinize the leaders of the party in power on the assumption that they had both the position and the motivation to help shape the response of the political system to changing conditions. Their choices were limited, of course, and their power to determine events a good deal less than traditional political history suggests. But within certain bounds, as I will show, New York's Republican leaders decisively contributed to fashioning their state's transition to a new political order.

With the researching and writing of this book behind me, the pleasant task remains of thanking the many people who helped me see it to completion. Over the project's long course, my most exciting moments occurred in the homes of Mr. and Mrs. Collier Platt and Mr. and Mrs. Frank H. Platt, where I was shown and freely allowed to use thousands of previously unexamined manuscripts relating to this book's central figure, Thomas Collier Platt. The Platts, who are descendants of the senator, heartily encouraged and never restrained me, and they extended many personal kindnesses that I will never forget. Collier Platt has generously given the manuscripts in his possession to the Yale University Library. Hamilton Fish allowed me to use the small collection of personal correspondence relating to the career of his father, the Hamilton Fish who served as speaker of the New York Assembly in 1895–96.

All other materials on which this book is based are located in numerous libraries, where I have been treated with genuine consideration. At the New York Public Library, the New-York Historical Society, the New York State Library, the Library of Congress, the Buffalo and Erie County Historical Society, the Buffalo and Erie County Public Library, the Rochester Public Library, the Onondaga County Public Library, the Schoharie County Historical Society, the Connecticut State Library, and the university libraries of Columbia, Cornell, Harvard, Princeton, Rutgers, St. Lawrence, Syracuse, and Yale, librarians and staff members gave me the assistance without which the book could not have been written. I must especially thank those in the various departments of the Sterling Memorial Library at Yale, the Olin Library at Cornell, and the Alexander Library at Rutgers for their unfailing helpfulness.

Portions of Chapter 1 previously appeared in somewhat different form in the *Journal of American History*. Brief passages in several other chapters are drawn from my articles in *New York History* and *The Yale University Library Gazette*. These excerpts are republished here by kind permission of the editors of these three journals.

Several institutions and organizations gave financial support to this project. Yale University was generous while I was a graduate student, just as the Research Council of Rutgers University has been since I joined the faculty there in 1976. A grant from the American Philosophical Society helped finance one final summer of research travel in upstate New York, while a fellowship from the American Council of Learned Societies enabled me to have a year off from teaching to prepare the final draft of my book.

The most indispensable help has come from the many historians who took time to discuss this book with me, to read it in various drafts, and to give me the benefit of their advice—much, but not all, of which I have taken. At the project's inception, I received excellent counsel from Michael F. Holt, Joel H. Silbey, and R. Hal Williams, who encouraged me—not least by communicating the excitement they felt about their own work in political history—and who helped me settle on the scope and nature of the work. In the course of writing, I had the frequent benefit of John M. Blum's sharing with me his own understanding of the era of Theodore Roosevelt. My greatest debt for help at that early stage is to C. Vann Woodward; the scholarly and personal example he set gave me an ideal I can't reach but will always value.

Many other historians also read and commented on part or all of the manuscript. They include Rudolph M. Bell, Paul G. E. Clemens, David C. Hammack, J. Morgan Kousser, Marc W. Kruman, Howard Lamar, Michael McGerr, Samuel T. McSeveney, William L. O'Neill, Albert C. E. Parker, Edward Pessen, Herbert H. Rowen, Neil Viny, and Robert F. Wesser. All put their stamp on this book, but all, I am sure, will still find it lacking in certain respects. Rudy, Paul, Marc, and Sam must be singled out from the rest for being exceptional critics and more generous with their time than I had any right to expect. Herb's editing improved hundreds of my sentences and taught me a great deal about language.

Still others have helped in important ways. Maryann Holtsclaw and Eileen Tyler typed the final manuscript. Bruce Dearstyne put me on to the corporate records of the New York Central and the Delaware and Hudson railroad companies. My sister, Dorothy I. Kelly, prepared for keypunching most of the voting data used here, while John F. Reynolds cheerfully helped me revise and extend the computer work on which my electoral analysis rests. Warren I. Susman encouraged me by his friendship and his confidence.

Finally, Cori Jones assisted this project in countless ways and stuck by me and it. Richard P. McCormick helped the most by being my toughest critic and best example.

RICHARD L. MCCORMICK

New Brunswick, New Jersey

Abbreviations

AAAPSS	*Annals of the American Academy of Political and Social Science*
AEJ	*Albany Evening Journal*
AHR	*American Historical Review*
A.J.	*New York Assembly Journal* (Albany)
APSR	*American Political Science Review*
Auto. TCP	Louis J. Lang, ed. *The Autobiography of Thomas Collier Platt.* New York, 1910.
Barnes v. Roosevelt	Supreme Court, Appellate Division, Fourth Department. *William Barnes, Plaintiff-Appellant, against Theodore Roosevelt, Defendant-Respondent,* 4 vols. Walton, N.Y., 1917.
COHC	Columbia Oral History Collection, Columbia University Libraries
FC	*Fredonia Censor*
GARL	George Arents Research Library for Special Collections at Syracuse University
JAH	*Journal of American History*
LC	Library of Congress
LTR	Elting E. Morison, ed. *The Letters of Theodore Roosevelt,* 8 vols. Cambridge, Mass., 1951–54.
Manual	*Manual for the Use of the Legislature of the State of New York* (Albany)
New York State Men	Frederick S. Hills, compiler and ed. *New York State Men: Biographic Studies and Character Portraits.* Albany, 1910.
NYBTT	New York Board of Trade and Transportation
N-YHS	New-York Historical Society
NYPL	New York Public Library
NYSL	New York State Library
NYT	*New York Times*
P.P.	*Public Papers of . . .* [the] *Governor* (Albany)
PSQ	*Political Science Quarterly*
Red Book	*The New York Red Book* (Albany)
S.J.	*New York Senate Journal* (Albany)
SLP	*St. Lawrence Plaindealer* (Canton, N.Y.)
TDT	*Troy Daily Times*
Trib.	*New York Tribune*

Abbreviations

Trib. Alm.   *The Tribune Almanac and Political Register* (New York)
USS   University Settlement Society of New York City

From Realignment to Reform

1

Nineteenth-Century Politics in Decline

Compared to the breadth and pace of social and economic developments, American political practices and institutions seem relatively unchanging. The same basic constitutional and governmental structures that served an eighteenth-century nation of farmers and small tradesmen still command allegiance from the members of a mass, postindustrial society.[1] A fundamental task of political history is to explain how, through comparatively small adjustments, the old forms were repeatedly enabled to survive amidst new conditions.

It has long been recognized that, far from being evenly spaced across the political past, those adjustments tended to be concentrated during relatively brief spans of time. Considerable evidence suggests that the American political system experienced one such critical period of change between the early 1890s and the end of the first decade of the twentieth century. While the basic constitutional forms and governmental structures persisted, significant modifications in the means of political participation and in the functions of government adapted the old system to new conditions.

This book explores the process of change in a single state, New York. There, as in the nation, urbanization and industrialization created new expectations and demands that altered the methods for constituting government and enlarged its tasks. By focusing on the strategies employed by the leaders of the dominant Republican party for coping with fresh conditions and circumstances, the chapters that follow offer an interpretation of how the American political system met the challenges placed upon it at a critical juncture in our history.

Distinctive patterns of politics and governance characterized the United States from the 1830s to the end of the nineteenth century. Those patterns mark the point of departure for the changes of the

19

1890s and early 1900s and must be described before the changes can be related.

From the Jackson period forward, the major political parties had regularly shaped campaigns and elections into popular spectacles featuring widespread participation and celebration. Three-quarters of the nation's adult male citizens voted in presidential elections and nearly two-thirds participated in off-year contests. Most of those who voted cast a straight ticket conveniently supplied by one of the party organizations. While illicit voting may have swelled the electoral totals and fraudulent counting likely reduced the recorded levels of split ballots, the large majority of electors were probably honest, enthusiastic, and partisan.[2]

In an age when public sources of information and diversion were limited, parties and elections provided crucial forms of education and entertainment. Newspapers were almost uniformly partisan and heavily political in their content. Party speakers were often centers of attraction at community gatherings such as fairs and market days. Once a year or more election campaigns offered drama and aroused emotions. Attending primaries, conventions, and ratification meetings; joining in parades and rallies; hearing speeches; waiting for the returns; and celebrating victories all provided enjoyment and social satisfaction, as well as a feeling of political participation.

Recent studies show that nineteenth-century voting alignments commonly reflected ethno-religious lines and suggest that citizens found parties effective vehicles for the values they learned in their homes and churches. Though not always true to their ideologies, the major parties had distinctive beliefs and characteristic styles that citizens understood and shared. Casting a ballot was an expression of group solidarity. Partisan loyalties typically passed from father to son, just as religion did. Not surprisingly, towns, counties, and states displayed remarkable electoral stability from year to year and decade to decade.[3]

These patterns of political participation helped shape a responsive policy process, especially at the state and local levels. In establishing schools that taught familiar values, enacting slave codes, building roads, and promoting local industries, community authorities routinely met people's expectations for government. The most successful policies were those that helped some citizens without visibly hurting the rest. In practice, of course, these proved easier to achieve in the local arena than in wider ones and in some policy areas than in others.[4]

Where polarizing sectional or cultural issues were at stake, the political system's very responsiveness to diverse local wants endangered policymaking at higher levels of government. Before the Civil War, for example, politicians in both the North and the South vied with one another for supremacy in defending their section's rights. Partly as a result, when territorial expansion forced the slavery issue into the national arena, the political process proved unable to contain the existing emotions, much less to resolve the controversy. In similar fashion, local political leaders championed their constituents' cultural values and sought to preserve them through policies concerning education, leisure, liquor, and social behavior. Beyond the local community, however, ethno-religious groups with contrary beliefs clashed repeatedly over governmental decisions affecting these value-laden subjects. Both sectional and cultural differences thus gave rise to divisive issues that resisted compromise in larger arenas of government. Their political irresolvability probably helps to explain why such questions so significantly shaped long-term partisan loyalties.[5]

On economic policy matters, nineteenth-century political authorities had more success in containing conflict and satisfying diverse constituencies than on sectional or cultural questions. It is important to see how and why this was so, both because certain economic policies formed the most characteristic type of nineteenth-century government action and also because much of the impetus for political change at the end of the century came from new economic demands on government.

Throughout the century, the most pervasive economic role of government was the promotion of development by distributing riches and privileges to individuals and small groups. Land was one such resource, and for almost the whole century federal and state officials allocated and sold it. Charters and franchises for banking, transportation, and manufacturing likewise were given away, especially by the states. Special privileges of every kind came from government: the right of eminent domain, the privilege of charging tolls on roads and bridges, the right to dam or channel streams and rivers, to name only a few. The federal government's tariff also represented a kind of public gift to the individuals and corporations whose products received protection. Public authorities at every level distributed aid by constructing or subsidizing highways, canals, railways, bridges, and harbors.[6]

To be sure, policies of economic promotion often fed political conflict, just as sectional and cultural questions did. There were never enough of the choicest resources and privileges to go around. Battles at every level of government were fought for the best land, the most lucrative charters, and the finest transportation facilities. Those who lost called into question the legitimacy of bestowing "special privileges" on some and not others. From the 1830s, politics echoed with the Jacksonian complaint that virtually everything the government did helped only a few. That accusation in turn aroused the historic American distrust of public power and brought forth recurring efforts to scale down the authority of government.[7]

For most of the century, however, countervailing influences dampened conflict and distrust sufficiently to permit the continuance of a policy structure based on the bestowal of government goods. Land and natural resources remained relatively abundant, while new communities offering charters and privileges to entrepreneurs continually opened up. These favorable conditions, deriving from the extent and richness of the national domain and from the spread of population, mitigated scarcity, or at least disguised it.

The policy process itself and the inherent qualities of nineteenth-century distributive goods encouraged this pattern. At every level of government, the dominant legislative branch threw open its doors to special, local interests demanding assistance and decrying restraints. The very nature of the benefits being sought facilitated legislative acquiescence in constituent demands. While public revenues were limited and heavily taxed citizens sometimes insisted on the reduction of spending, some distributive policies, land sales in particular, conveniently generated the revenue to support others. Of equal importance, distributive policies were almost infinitely divisible. Voting tariff protection for one commodity did not preclude protecting others; aiding one canal company was no bar to helping a second and a third. Thus, if there was not something for everyone, nearly everyone could plausibly hope for something.[8]

Finally, government allocation was facilitated by an ideological counterweight to the dread of public authority. As a general principle, nineteenth-century citizens accepted government assistance to business and commerce, and they possessed only an imprecise conception of the distinction between what was public and what was private. Robert Lively remarks how regularly "official vision and public resources" were "associated . . . with private skill and individual desire." That association was possible, according to Carter Goodrich, because "Americans did not feel themselves bound by any permanent and unalterable demarcation of the spheres of state action and private enterprise."[9]

Forever giving things away, governments were laggard in regulating the economic activities they subsidized. In the states, where regulation was considered a basic function of government, the form it took often reflected developmental purposes more than restrictive ones. Administration also proved difficult to accomplish for nineteenth-century governments. According to Leonard White, federal administrative practices remained as rudimentary at the end of the century as they had been in the 1830s. Historians of state politics have similarly observed the limits of administration there, including the unwillingness of the states to rely on independent commissions for policy formation, fact-finding, and day-to-day regulation. The paucity of planning also characterized nineteenth-century American government. According to Willard Hurst, "We often made policy piecemeal and in disconnected efforts and areas, where a more rational practicality would have told us to link our efforts, fill in gaps, and move on a broad front." Government "policy" was little more than the accumulation of isolated, individual choices, usually of a distributive nature.[10]

It seems pointless and present-minded to blame nineteenth-century authorities for these "failures." From everything we know, the American people got roughly the economic policies they wanted. Given a choice between governmental promotion and restraint, they clearly preferred the former. Except for the abolition of slavery, the distribution of economic benefits probably represents the outstanding accomplishment of nineteenth-century American government. Certainly it was the most characteristic achievement.

Balanced and fairly stable, though by no means placid or consensual, the nineteenth-century political system generally fit the conditions and ambitions of the people. Impatient for material progress, they welcomed the government's assistance to their profit-making enterprises, but felt little need to weigh all the costs against the benefits. Individualistic and upwardly mobile by aspiration, they readily identified with their community and its beliefs but resisted thinking in the class terms that might have led to sterner demands for calculation in government policymaking. Distrustful of power and jealous of their liberties, the people restricted the authority of public officials. But citizens relished joining and participating and expressing group values, and they bestowed on parties a degree of devotion they never would have given to government itself.

The old order was not to endure, however. Within a comparatively brief span of years at the end of the nineteenth century, social and economic changes significantly altered the existing political system. Several groups in the population tested forms of politics outside the major parties. In some cases the experiments failed and led to a withdrawal from politics entirely. As a result, the high voter turnout characteristic of the nineteenth century waned. Other groups succeeded in winning shares of power and influencing government without benefit

23

of party politics. Both the losers and the winners contributed to a transformation in the means of political participation at the beginning of the twentieth century.

At the same time that some elements lost confidence in the parties, divisive demands for enlarging governmental functions endangered an economic policy structure based on distributive benefits. Where nineteenth-century conditions had tended to disguise the inequalities resulting from government allocation, the scarcities and complexities of an urban-industrial society now made it plain that government actions helping one group often hurt another. These developments compelled public authorities to recognize the clash of interests and to adopt what Willard Hurst calls "a new disposition of calculation."[11] That in turn required new and expanded methods of governance, including regulation, administration, and planning.

In their broad outlines, these developments are familiar to historians of the 1890s and early 1900s. But considerable differences of opinion remain concerning the origins of political change, its precise nature, and its significance. This book addresses these problems of causation and interpretation through a study of how New York's political leaders handled the challenges that new conditions posed to nineteenth-century politics.

In politics and governance, late-nineteenth-century New York exemplified the practices characteristic of the nation as a whole. Closely contested, party-oriented elections involved the great majority of adult males and were the main means of political participation. State government was geared to assist but not to supervise commerce, industry, and agriculture. Already by the 1880s, however, social and economic developments capable of transforming the nineteenth-century political system were well under way. Especially in the state's large cities, but also in the countryside, the new conditions fostered discontent with existing politics. Throughout the 1880s, the leaders of the major parties in New York were able to dampen dissent and keep to the old political ways. The relative ease with which they did so may have prepared them badly for the following decade, when the forces for political change became stronger.

Stalemate, stability, and partisanship characterized New York State voting behavior in the 1880s. So close was the balance between the Republicans and Democrats that only once in the decade, in 1882, did either major party's percentage of the total vote exceed the other's by more than 3 percent. (See Table 1.) Statewide, except for 1882 and 1887, both parties maintained their strength almost identically from

Table 1. New York State vote for president or highest state office, by party, 1880–89

Year and office	Republican candidate	Democratic candidate	Other	Estimated turnout*
1880				
President	50.3%	48.4%	1.3%	92.1%
1881				
Secretary of state	49.6	48.0	2.4	68.6
1882				
Governor	37.4	58.5	4.1	73.1
1883				
Secretary of state	49.6	47.5	2.9	70.2
1884				
President	48.2	48.2	3.6	89.0
1885				
Governor	47.8	48.9	3.3	76.4
1886				
Associate judge	47.5	48.3	4.2	70.8
1887				
Secretary of state	43.4	45.0	11.6	74.4
1888				
President	49.2	48.1	2.7	92.2
1889				
Secretary of state	47.6	49.7	2.7	69.4

*The Appendix discusses the estimation of voter turnout.
Source: Trib. Alm. (1881–90).

year to year. Below the state level, too, there was little fluctuation in the basic structure of party support, as the high interelection correlations of the county-level Democratic vote suggest. (See Table 2.) Approximately 90 percent of those eligible to do so participated in presidential elections, while about 70 percent voted in the off-years.

Table 2. New York State Democratic vote, 1880–89: Pearson correlations

	1881	1882	1883	1885	1886	1887	1888	1889
1880	.96	.90	.88	.92	.88	.85	.93	.89
1881		.90	.82	.90	.87	.82	.92	.88
1882			.77	.88	.84	.75	.91	.87
1883				.81	.85	.75	.81	.80
1885					.91	.88	.96	.93
1886						.86	.91	.90
1887							.88	.89
1888								.94

Source: Lee Benson, Joel H. Silbey, and Phyllis F. Field, "Toward a Theory of Stability and Change in American Voting Patterns: New York State, 1792–1970," in Joel H. Silbey, Allan G. Bogue, and William H. Flanigan, eds., *The History of American Electoral Behavior* (Princeton, 1978), p. 93.

Even when the highest office contested was secretary of state, two-thirds or more of the potential electorate went to the polls. As Table 1 shows, almost all of them voted for the candidate of one of the major parties. For most electors, the choice of which party to support seems to have been shaped by ethnocultural identifications. According to a recent study of New York voting patterns from 1860 to 1892, English immigrants and their descendants, French Canadians, and the descendants of New Englanders supported the Republicans. The Democratic party enjoyed the allegiance of the Dutch, Germans, and Irish.[12]

With the opposing coalitions so balanced and stable, success depended upon reinforcing the voters' existing loyalties and getting them to the polls on election day. For these tasks, both the Republicans and Democrats possessed well-organized hierarchies of committees extending from the election districts up to the state level. Following a period of intense factionalism between competing leaders at the beginning of the 1880s, both party organizations became moderately harmonious for the rest of the decade. Former United States Senator Thomas Collier Platt achieved a position of recognized leadership among the Republicans, while Governor David Bennett Hill—in uneasy alliance with the leaders of the great urban machines—gave direction to the Democrats. For the time being, both men, with their organizations, were able to sustain the long-term loyalties of the mass of voters and to capitalize on the partisanship that still underlay political culture in the United States.[13]

In economic policymaking, as in electoral behavior, New York in the 1880s generally typified the nineteenth-century nation. The Erie Canal, which the state had constructed during the 1820s and had maintained and improved thereafter, represented the kind of public policy that government carried out best. Abolition of all tolls on the canal in 1882 was but the latest example of New York's practice of assisting the transport of products to market. The government's largesse toward canal users was duplicated in policies toward other groups. Farmers were helped through state aid for agricultural societies and experiment stations. Merchants and small manufacturers had the benefit of a diversity of transportation improvements. Large corporate interests were encouraged through generous charters and low rates of taxation.

While it assisted numerous producer groups, the state government was less active in regulating them. The Board of Railroad Commissioners began its work in 1882 but had limited powers. A comprehensive factory act was passed in 1886, but until the twentieth century the few inspectors appointed under it did little to enforce the law's provisions. Some regulatory policies were chiefly promotional. Much of the little work done by the Insurance Department and the Dairy Commission, for example, was intended to advance their respective industries. Most citizens of New York probably took moderate levels of governmental assistance for granted, rarely calculated its differential effects on various groups, and would have resented significant state supervision of their enterprises.[14]

Even as politics-as-usual persisted in New York, demographic and industrial changes were taking place which threatened nineteenth-century patterns of participation and governance. In the 1880s, these developments led to a series of protests against existing politics; over the course of the following two decades they produced a more far-reaching political transformation.

The urbanization of New York State, particularly the concentration of people in very large cities, provided one of the most significant forces for political change. In 1880 almost half of the five million people of the state lived outside of cities, in rural areas or towns of under ten thousand people. (See Fig. 1.) Forty years later, while New

Figure 1. Population of New York State, 1880–1920, by size of place of residence

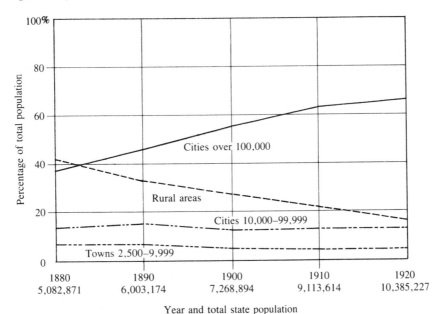

Year and total state population

Sources: Bruce L. Melvin, *Rural Population of New York, 1885 to 1925* (Ithaca, 1927); *Manual* (1886, 1925).

York's overall population had doubled, many rural counties actually had fewer people than in 1880. Now only about a fifth of the state's residents lived in places with fewer than ten thousand people. Most of the population gains were concentrated in the largest cities. In 1880 a little more than a third of the people lived in New York City, Brooklyn, and Buffalo, the three places with over one hundred thousand inhabitants. By 1920 almost two-thirds lived in cities of that size, a group that now also included Yonkers, Albany, Syracuse, and Rochester. Despite the efforts of rural and town politicians to prevent the state from being dominated by its great urban centers, the large cities and their problems achieved a commanding influence on New York politics.[15]

While much of the increase in city population was due to the migration of rural New Yorkers, many of the urban newcomers were immigrants. Between 1890 and 1910 alone, well over a million foreign-born people settled in New York State, and the proportion of foreign-born residents in the population rose from 26 to 30 percent. Before 1890, most immigrants had come from the British Isles and Western Europe, especially Ireland and Germany; now they increasingly migrated from the Slavic and Latin nations of Eastern Europe. The vast majority of them settled in the state's cities, especially those on the main Hudson River–Erie Canal axis, where the great cities of New York, Albany, Rochester, and Buffalo lay. Here the concentration of foreign-born residents was much greater than elsewhere in the state. In 1910 40 percent of the people of New York City had been born outside the United States.[16]

New York City formed the state's nucleus of population and power. In 1880 it already had 1.2 million people. Consolidated with Brooklyn, Queens, and Staten Island in 1898, the downstate metropolis included half the state's residents. Throughout the period studied here, the accessibility of raw materials and markets, thanks to a combination of natural advantages and man-made means of transportation, enabled New York City to maintain its position as the country's largest center of manufacturing and commerce. Especially in the production of non-durable consumer goods, like clothing and printed materials, and in foreign trade, the city remained the national leader. Yet in both manufacturing and commerce, New York experienced a relative decline from its mid-nineteenth-century position of dominance while it was achieving increasing importance as a center of financial and technical services and as the headquarters for large industrial corporations. In the age of giant business combinations, no other city could match the markets, capital, information, and expertise that New York provided. The city's sheer size and diversity created problems of governance that

28

nineteenth-century politics-as-usual could not solve; its great wealth and population forced the rest of the state to pay attention to those problems.[17]

Despite New York City's comparative decline as a manufacturing center, it was still by and large manufacturing that drew increased millions of people to the state's large cities. In the forty years after 1880, the number of wage earners in manufacturing more than doubled, while the dollar value of the state's manufactured products grew by a factor of eight. (See Fig. 2.) All of the largest manufacturing districts in the state turned out a great diversity of products. Rochester, for example, which had once specialized in flour milling, now also produced textiles, optics, cameras, and other photographic equipment. Syracuse factories made chemicals, steel, shoes, farm machinery, and pottery. Particularly after 1890, electrification encouraged manufacturing growth. In 1881 the first generator was installed at Niagara Falls, and the electricity it produced supplied power for much of western New York. Niagara Falls itself became an important manufacturing center. The city's population rose from seven thousand in 1880 to over fifty

Figure 2. Manufacturing activity in New York State, 1879–1919

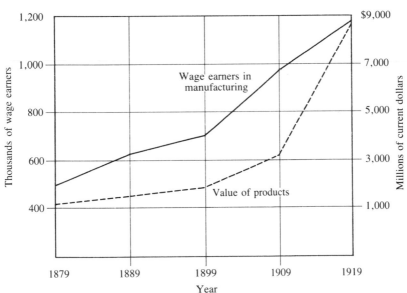

Source: Richard A. Easterlin, "Estimates of Manufacturing Activity," in Simon Kuznets and Dorothy Swain Thomas, eds., *Population Redistribution and Economic Growth: United States, 1870–1950,* 3 vols. (Philadelphia, 1957–64), 1: 635–701, Tables M-2 and M-7.

thousand in 1920. Schenectady, where Edison established his electric plant in 1886, became a city of almost ninety thousand by 1920, as the home of the General Electric Company.[18]

While factories multiplied, farms declined in number and area. The ones that survived, however, established or maintained New York's national leadership in the production of a considerable variety of agricultural products. From 1880 to 1920 the number of farms in the state fell from 241,000 to 193,000 while the acreage of improved land declined from over seventeen million to thirteen million. The percentage of the state's labor force in agriculture dropped from 23 to 7. Behind the pattern of decline lay a shift from grain production to dairying and horticulture that was already well under way by 1880. Milk production rose rapidly to supply the growing cities, as the dairy region of the state spread west and north. Especially in western New York, fruit and vegetable growing became major industries, while grape production for wine thrived in the Finger Lakes region and in far western Chautauqua County. This was an unusually diverse pattern of agriculture. Fewer farmers than in 1880, working relatively small farms (averaging about one hundred acres), produced a surprising variety and amount of food for market.[19]

The pathways leading from these social and economic developments to the political and governmental responses were long and twisted. They took several decades to become well traveled. In the most general terms, the changes in demography, industry, and agriculture brought forth new needs for political expression not satisfied by party-oriented electoral participation and encouraged expectations for government not met through existing policies. Often organized groups whose members considered themselves socially, culturally, or economically distinct from the general population first voiced the new demands.

These trends were especially pronounced in large cities. Amidst a highly concentrated and diverse population, most people had occasion to feel that others with values and interests unlike their own had excessive political influence. This consciousness encouraged groups to devise new forms of participation for themselves and to seek restraints on the participation of others. Urban conditions also gave rise to demands that government carry out the housekeeping and regulatory tasks that crowded citizens could not practically perform for themselves but upon which decent life depended. Each group naturally had its own conception of which policies to carry out and how to do it.

Like urbanization, industrialization also enhanced the consciousness of social and economic distinctions and led to new means of political participation and new government policies. The growth of manufacturing and trade made it increasingly evident that the separate economic interests of a mature industrial society may have been intertwined but were far from harmonious. Workers and employers, producers and transporters, customers and vendors each frankly wanted and needed things that hurt the other. To an increasing degree, each sought ways of influencing government authorities and of getting the desired policies.

Agricultural developments had less pronounced implications for politics and governance. Rural citizens tended to be satisfied with party politics and to make relatively few demands on public authorities.[20] Only reluctantly, in response to outside conditions, did farmers give up these traditions. Faced with a declining voice in government and with the organized might of those who transported and purchased their goods, farmers slowly recognized the need to enlarge their own political influence and obtain more official protection.

In the 1880s several groups of New Yorkers voiced their discontent with existing forms of politics and governance. While their achievements were limited, they introduced most of the complaints and tried out many of the methods that would bring lasting political changes in the following two decades.

Municipal reformers, drawn from an old, upper middle class and from among young professionals, expressed one type of dissatisfaction with politics-as-usual. Unhappy with city governance by bossed party machines, which seemed vicious in their methods and representative only of the dangerous, immigrant classes, the reformers sought structural changes instituting efficient, nonpartisan municipal administration. Through civil service reforms, the concentration of executive responsibility, the separation of local elections from state and national ones, and municipal home rule, they hoped to bring about their ideal of businesslike city government. Especially in New York's largest cities, municipal reformers achieved some successes in the 1880s. A new city charter for Brooklyn, approved by the legislature in 1881, gave the reformers the strong mayoralty they wanted, and they filled the office that same year with one of their own, Seth Low. During the following four years, Low carried out the reformers' ideal of responsible, nonpartisan administration. When an 1883 state law allowed the cities to institute civil service regulations, Low's Brooklyn, as well as New York City and Buffalo, quickly inaugurated merit systems of appointment.

Particularly in the late 1880s, however, municipal reformers met more setbacks than successes. Low's two terms as mayor of Brooklyn were followed by the return to power of an invigorated Democratic machine under boss Hugh McLaughlin. Across the East River in New

York City, Tammany Hall, which had previously shared power with rival, reform-oriented Democratic organizations, now consolidated its citywide authority. In no large city in the state did civil service regulations actually deprive the machines of the spoils of office. The reformers remained a small elite of wealthy and well-educated citizens. They established clubs, wrote magazine articles, and supported charter reforms and new election laws. But they showed little capacity to enlarge their ranks or to confront the social and economic problems of their cities.[21]

Although most city voters of the 1880s ignored reform, one issue caused particular discontent among all classes of urban residents: the performance of public utility companies. In typical nineteenth-century fashion, most cities granted gas, electric, and street railway franchises with few restrictions attached and no provision for payments to the public treasury. Rates and fares, often low at first because of the competition between rival companies, rose sharply when the competitors merged, as they frequently did. Customers also complained of poor service and the utilities' reluctance to extend their lines into less settled areas.

In response to these conditions, patterns of protest developed in the cities of New York. Citizens held mass meetings, voted against "boodle" councilmen, boycotted the offending utilities, and occasionally sought help from the state government. The results were mixed. Sometimes political pressure forced the companies to agree to new terms with the city. Occasionally the state legislature acted, as in 1886, when it established $1.25/thousand cubic feet as the maximum rate for gas in New York City. But often little could be done to regulate utility companies already holding long-term franchises. Only in small cities and towns did municipal ownership materialize as a real alternative. Jamestown (population 16,000), for instance, built its own electric plant in 1891 after two years of turmoil over the utility issue, but the state's largest cities continued to have their essential services provided by untamed private companies.[22]

Particularly in the cities, outright conflict between labor and capital was another source of political unrest in the 1880s. From 1885 to 1891 there were over twenty thousand strikes involving almost one-half million workers in New York. Many of the strikes were successful, but in many other cases workers felt that the government contributed to their defeat. Workingmen tried several means of expressing their grievances through politics. One approach involved putting pressure on the legislature for measures protecting labor's rights. Three organizations were active in this cause by the end of the 1880s, but they were less effective than one might have been. With the voices of labor divided, the legislative results were usually more symbolic than substantive.

Electoral politics provided labor with a more potent weapon. In 1886 the Central Labor Union of New York City nominated the famed single-taxer Henry George for mayor and ran an inspired campaign on his behalf. George won tens of thousands of normally Democratic votes and finished second, ahead of the Republican candidate, Theodore Roosevelt. The next year, under the banner of the newly organized United Labor Party, George conducted a statewide race for secretary of state. Although he received more third-party votes than any other candidate of the decade, George's New York City vote dropped well below its level in 1886, and the United Labor Party withered within a year.[23]

While labor strove to influence legislation and elect candidates, several economic groups undertook a political campaign to bring about government regulation of the railroads. Well before the 1880s, merchants and farmers had voiced complaints about the high cost of rail transportation, especially on the great trunklines. Downstate merchants pointed to statistics showing that one reason for New York City's relative commercial decline lay in discriminatory railroad charges. Upstate farmers believed that Western producers shipping their goods across New York paid lower rates than did rail customers from within the state. Late in the 1870s organizations representing the aggrieved interests undertook an alliance to agitate for railroad regulation. They were greatly helped in 1879 by a sensational legislative investigation that disclosed the railroads' sordid business practices and brought about an intense, if brief, public interest in the railroad issue. In response, both political parties endorsed regulation, and, following several years of delay, the legislature established a Railroad Commission in 1882. In the gubernatorial election that year, public agitation over the railroads remained sufficient to contribute to a Democratic landslide, an unusual occurrence in closely contested New York. (See Table 1.) The upheaval was shortlived, however, and its results were limited. Electoral stalemate returned in 1883, while the Railroad Commission soon proved its harmlessness to the supervised interests. Disappointed merchants and farmers turned their attention to the national scene, where in 1887 they assisted in the establishment of the Interstate Commerce Commission.[24]

Besides railroad regulation, one other cause significantly mobilized upstate New Yorkers against the dominant political forces of the 1880s: prohibition. Concentrated in the upstate rural districts where immigrants were few and native-born Protestants predominated, the antiliquor forces drew support away from the Republican party. Indeed, throughout the middle and late 1880s, when the Democrats were narrowly carrying state elections, the Prohibitionist vote repeatedly exceeded the victors' plurality over the Republicans. While even at their peak in 1886 and 1887 the drys captured only 4 percent of the statewide electorate, they fared far better than that in many upstate counties and in several won over 10 percent of the vote.

In 1887 and 1888 Republican legislators tried to win back the Prohibitionists by increasing saloon license fees, but Democratic Governor Hill vetoed the measures. Following the second veto, the Republicans nominated a gubernatorial candidate with special appeal for the drys, and he made liquor his main issue. The ploy halted the Prohibitionists' gains and reduced the antiliquor party to just over 2 percent of the statewide vote for governor in 1888. Unfortunately for the Republicans, however, that was still enough to give the Democrats victory. (See Table 1.) Ironically, the Prohibition party continued to be a factor in New York politics precisely because the vast majority of voters divided evenly between the major parties.[25]

Why did such varied movements of protest and demand leave the existing political system in New York relatively unchanged in the 1880s? Part of the answer lies in the ability of Republican and Democratic leaders to provide symbols reinforcing the electorate's traditional loyalties. Republicans pointed to their party's achievements in winning the Civil War, abolishing slavery, and fostering industrial growth. These were considerable accomplishments, none the less important to Republican voters in the 1880s because they were skillfully put to partisan use and then labeled "bloody shirt" tactics by opponents and historians. Democrats, for their part, reminded New Yorkers of their party's record in standing for the people's personal liberties, especially those of immigrants and their descendants, whose habits and values were menaced by crusading native-born citizens. These achievements seemed quite real to most Democrats. In trying to persuade New York voters to abandon their old parties, city reformers, United Laborites, and Prohibitionists faced an extremely difficult task. Traditional partisanship remained strong, for good reasons.[26]

A second part of the explanation lies in the party leaders' success in portraying the existing economic policy structure as beneficial to everyone. Democrats as well as Republicans supported the allocation of aid to diverse producer groups and treated their interests as fundamentally harmonious.[27] It is understandable that the party leaders felt more comfortable with distributive policies than with regulation. Because the recipients were usually small, geographically based groups, distributive benefits (like patronage) helped the parties maintain the support of disparate constituencies. Unlike regulation, allocative decisions seldom intruded where fundamental consensus was lacking or risked unmanageable divisions in the party coalition. The leaders' claim that government aid brought prosperity to a society of harmonious producer groups was far from implausible. With upward (and downward) mobility sufficient to suggest that class lines were neither impassable nor permanent, many must have believed the promise of prosperity. On the face of things, distributive benefits opened up possibilities rather than foreclosed them, and they had the appearance of benefiting almost every interest.[28] In attempting to persuade a majority of New Yorkers that government authorities should restrain industry, as well as promote it, the special interests favoring regulation had no easy job.

Faced with skillful opponents who had many advantages on their side, those seeking political changes in the 1880s were further weakened by their own backwardness and narrowness. Except for the merchants and farmers whose demands for railroad regulation captured attention between 1879 and 1882, none of the protesting groups was adept at reaching out to others or engaging the public's imagination. Elite urban reformers sometimes talked about appealing to those in the "tenement districts" but seldom did so, except in a condescending way. The party of labor did well only in 1886 when Henry George put the popular single-tax issue ahead of working-class issues. The Prohibitionists distinguished themselves for the narrowness of their concerns and the exclusiveness of their constituency. Almost none of the discontented groups seemed to want an alliance with the others or to know how to interest a larger public in its causes.[29]

Over the course of the next two decades this would change. The dissenters learned the advantages of cooperation across group lines and sometimes worked together for reforms from which they expected different results. Particularly in the early 1900s, when new conditions were increasingly weakening the party leaders' ability to control political participation and shape expectations for government, the discontented groups found ways of engaging the interest and support of the unorganized public. When these things happened, the nineteenth century's old and durable patterns of politics and governance were transformed.

The leaders of the party in power from 1895 to 1910, the Republicans, had a key vantage point from which to assess the forces changing politics. Wishing to stay in power, they had to find ways of dealing with those forces. Their options were scarcely unlimited, of course, for social and economic developments bore relentlessly upon party politics. But within certain bounds, Republican leaders fashioned strategies and made key choices that determined the precise forms assumed by new political and governmental practices.

In several respects, the Republican party of the 1890s was well fitted to respond to new conditions. While the Democrats were badly split into factions and their historic ideology of localism and limited government was becoming outmoded, the Republicans remained comparatively unified and doctrinally relevant. The party's activist national ideology, grounded in a conception of interdependent producer groups, still seemed plausible for a nation of growing cities and growing factories. Republican leaders of the early 1890s worked to dispel their party's image as the preserve of native-born, Protestant voters and open it to all ethno-religious groups. Amidst the depression that began in 1893, voters throughout the East and Midwest registered their confidence in the Republican party's ability to solve the problems posed by immigration, urbanization, and industrialization. Within a decade, Republican ideology would be under attack, much as Democratic doctrines already were, but in the mid-1890s the old party and its beliefs seemed to suit a plural, industrial society.[30]

In New York, as in the nation, the Republicans were well positioned to govern. Controlling all branches of the state government from 1895 through 1910, they had the full array of executive, legislative, and judicial techniques at their disposal. Having imaginative and skillful leaders, New York Republicans were often fortunate enough to find themselves facing a foolish and divided Democratic enemy. Perhaps of most importance, the party had the incalculable benefit of favorable national circumstances. In the age of Bryan, New York was sure to be Republican in presidential years. That made it far easier than it otherwise would have been to keep the state in line between the national contests and gave New York Republicans a degree of leeway they had done nothing to deserve.

Against all the advantages possessed by New York's Republican leadership stood a great disadvantage. Many of the changes at work struck directly at the parties' traditional dominance of the political system. An increasingly independent electorate, together with an array of new rules making it more difficult to keep the machine in order or to get out the vote, decreased party control over political participation. Divisive economic policy demands and the creation of new government agencies that assumed power from the partisan legislature weakened party management of the policy process. To win elections, Republican leaders worked to accommodate their party to the new conditions. But the very process of accommodation undermined the old political system and the party organizations that had dominated it.

The decline of parties should not be exaggerated, of course. Like other politicians of the day and others since, New York's Republican leaders were resourceful in coping with adversity. The concept of *party strategy* is useful in analyzing how they did it. By party strategy I mean the combination of official government action and political rhetoric which the leaders adopt in order to gain and maintain the voters' allegiance and to fulfill other commitments upon which party success depends. It includes both style and substance, symbols and policies.

A party's history sets limits upon its strategy. New York Republican leaders could not adopt a plan that included blatant appeals to newer immigrant groups, defense of liberalized liquor policies, attacks upon agricultural interests, or a renunciation of the social and economic functions of government. The party's tradition of government activism on both moral and economic issues and its identification with native-born, Protestant voters, particularly in the farming regions of the state, precluded all these approaches. The party's past shaped its present.

A party's degree of responsibility for government also determines its methods. Before 1893 the New York Republican party, being out of office, enjoyed the luxury of fashioning a party strategy entirely out of symbols and rhetoric. Then in 1893 and 1894 the Republicans won every state office as well as control of the legislature, and by the beginning of 1895 they were in full charge of state government. Retaining power, unlike winning it, meant passing laws as well as making speeches, and the party's strategy for the next sixteen years became vastly more complicated than it had been before.

Commitments to other organizations also restrict a party's options. For example, Republicans in New York felt an obligation to protect the industrial and transportation interests whose campaign contributions made election victories possible. Regardless of demands for stringent regulatory laws, the promises of party leaders and the need for future contributions militated against their passage and enforcement. Within the confines imposed by past strategies, by the party's responsibility for governance, and by its commitments to groups outside the party, Republican leaders devised strategies to maintain their electoral majority and keep the benefits of official power.

Government policies provided an essential component of the party's strategy. To preserve their coalition, Republicans had to reward various groups: a ballot reform law for the city independents, stricter liquor legislation for the prohibitionists, reduced property taxes for the farmers, and so forth. In addition, the organization rewarded itself through laws creating patronage and extending the party's control over government. But state policies alone could not satisfy the Republican majority. For one thing, the goals of different elements in the party conflicted. On liquor legislation, upstate moral reformers wanted measures that contradicted those the party's German-American supporters demanded. With respect to taxation, farmers urged policies that clashed with what industrial interests wanted. While some government decisions split the party, many others held no interest at all for the majority of voters. The value of much that the state did rarely proved direct or obvious to ordinary citizens. Laws that no one understood or cared about hardly advanced the party's electoral goals. Thus for two reasons policy programs alone proved unequal to the task of building support for the Republicans: some questions divided the party, while others interested too few citizens to provide it with any strategic advantage.

With the tangible policy components of their strategy inadequate, Republican leaders adopted rhetorical and stylistic techniques that probably outweighed policies in importance to the electorate. Speeches, platforms, and candidates all provided political symbolism. What party leaders said, the values they seemed to endorse, and the nominees they named attracted and held support, regardless of what the government did on particular issues. Laws, too, could have expressive qualities that made them valuable symbols, whatever their substantive effects. An election law might have one purpose on its face and another intention in fact. A liquor statute could enunciate one standard of behavior and be enforced according to a contrary one. The Republican strategy included such stylistic elements because policies alone could not satisfy everyone and because the electorate was accustomed to symbolic rewards.[31]

From the mid-1890s to 1910, the Republican strategy in New York changed when the leadership changed. Different party bosses had their own perceptions of what was required to keep the organization in power, unique commitments to special interests in the coalition, and selfish purposes that were unrelated to party success. Each major leader of the era exploited a combination of programmatic and symbolic techniques through which to enhance his own power and the party's. Conflicts between competing leaders and their strategies were a major factor in the state's politics.

At the beginning of the period, Thomas Collier Platt offered the party a strategy based on relatively traditional nineteenth-century political practices. By the late 1890s, Platt himself was reluctantly taking account of changing conditions, but more significant revisions in strategy came from three other major leaders: Theodore Roosevelt, who was elected governor in 1898 and became president in 1901; Benjamin B. Odell, Jr., who followed Roosevelt as governor and Platt as boss; and Charles Evans Hughes, who became governor in 1907. In response to the pressures on politics-as-usual, all four men took steps to keep their party in power by meeting the crises at hand. To be sure, the leaders differed in their degrees of loyalty to the existing political system and in their openness to change. But all four searched for political innovations to preserve their party by accommodating it to the forces changing politics and governance as nineteenth-century Americans had known them.

2

Democratic Crisis and Republican Ascendancy, 1893–1894

Periodically in American history, political upheavals have shifted the balance of power between the parties and established new and enduring voting alignments. One such shift, ending an era of electoral stalemate and bringing the Republicans into power for more than a generation, took place across the country in the 1890s. New York was not immune to the upheaval. Yet while national factors, especially those arising from the economic depression that began in 1893, help explain the surge to the Republicans in New York, local circumstances defined the peculiar character and composition of the now-dominant party there and shaped its behavior in the coming years. Since these were years in which politics and government underwent considerable transformation, the critical elections that brought the Republicans to power in New York require close scrutiny if the political changes of the late nineteenth and early twentieth centuries are to be understood. In itself, however, the realignment of the mid-1890s did not mark an immediate departure from most aspects of nineteenth-century American politics. The upheaval was narrowly electoral. Only over the course of time did more fundamental changes occur in the means of political participation and the process of governance.[1]

It took four years (from 1893 to 1896), and two crises (one economic, the other urban-political), plus the climactic Battle of the Standards, for the Republicans to complete their ascent to power in New York.[2] Until relatively recently, political historians studying the realignment of the 1890s focused almost all their attention on the election of 1896. Even in more recent works, the McKinley-Bryan contest properly occupies a central position.[3] Yet, critical as the 1896 election was in the state and the nation, the new Republican majority in New York had been substantially formed in 1893 and 1894. Out of office in all branches of government in the early 1890s, the Republicans began

Table 3. New York State vote for president or highest state office, by party, 1891–96

Year and office	Republican candidate	Democratic candidate	Other	Estimated turnout
1891				
Governor	46.0%	50.1%	3.9%	75.9%
1892				
President	45.6	49.0	5.4	85.6
1893				
Secretary of state	47.9	45.8	6.3	71.4
1894				
Governor	53.1	40.8	6.1	78.1
1895				
Secretary of state	51.6	43.8	4.6	70.3
1896				
President	57.6	38.7	3.7	84.2

Source: Trib. Alm. (1892–97).

their drive to power in 1893 by capturing both houses of the legislature, winning several state offices, and electing most delegates to an upcoming constitutional convention. The next year, they won the remaining statewide positions, including the governorship, by a greatly increased margin of victory. (See Table 3.) At the beginning of 1895, the Republicans were already in a position to govern New York, and they did so for the next sixteen years.

To understand how the events of 1893–94 shaped the way the party used its power in the following decade and a half, it is important to study not only which voting groups shifted toward the Republicans but also how the party's leaders in government handled the economic and political problems causing the upheaval. Such analysis reveals that their responses were fairly limited. Indeed, despite the magnitude of the political forces at work during the mid-1890s and the attention they have received from historians, neither the economic nor the urban-political crises of these years decisively transformed politics and governance in New York State. Of the two, the economic depression had the less pronounced effect on traditional behavior.

Seeds of the Republicans' triumph in New York lay in their decisive losses in the gubernatorial election of 1891 and the presidential contest of 1892. (See Table 3.) Strengthened and emboldened by victories in these elections, the leaders of the Democratic party's dominant faction, especially the large-city bosses among them, arrogantly flexed their political muscles. The excesses they committed on behalf of the party organization not only split the Democracy and aided the Republicans but also revitalized the tradition of independent reform by causing many voters to ask whether partisanship was relevant to city politics. Their doubts about parties placed such men in the vanguard of a movement that would eventually undermine a nineteenth-century partisan political culture.

Late in 1891, Governor-boss David B. Hill established the aggressive pattern that other Democratic leaders would soon follow when he engineered what came to be called the "steal of the senate." In his seven years as governor, Hill had never had the advantage of Democratic control of both legislative houses. Now, with his successor, Roswell P. Flower, just elected and his party apparently only three senate seats away from complete domination of the state government, Hill devised and carried out a plan involving contested returns and court challenges that eventually gave the Democrats the three seats they needed. Not everyone in the party approved of Hill or applauded his tactics, but with one of their own, Grover Cleveland, again the candidate for president in 1892, most New York Democrats remained loyal to the party. During the two years that followed, however, the Democratic party became a battleground, especially in the cities.[4]

At one level, the Democratic divisions of 1893 and 1894 represented only the latest outgrowth of the long-standing factional rivalry between the forces of Hill and Cleveland. The president, with his aura of political independence, had won the devotion of many native-born upper- and middle-class Democrats whose culture, inclination, and self-interest led them to oppose the party machine and its methods. Twice, in 1888 and again in 1892, Cleveland's national reputation for political honesty and morality helped him defeat Hill for their party's presidential nomination. Despite his losses at the national level, Hill could depend on the loyalty of most of the still-numerous Democrats living in the towns and villages of upstate New York, while, at the same time, he maintained his alliance with the leaders of the immigrant-backed Democratic organizations in the largest cities. He and Cleveland cooperated warily in the successful general election campaign of 1892, but the next year they resumed their outright hostility.[5]

While the president used federal appointments to strengthen his supporters in the state, Hill, who was now a U.S. senator, and his followers tightened their control of the regular party organization by purging Clevelandites from positions of state and local leadership in the Democracy. Despite warnings that he was unnecessarily risking damage to the party, Hill laid plans with Tammany Hall boss Richard Croker to elect Edward M. Murphy, Jr., as New York's other senator. Murphy was the master of Troy's Democratic machine and a personal enemy of the president. To compound these affronts to Cleveland Democrats, the party's state convention in 1893 nominated Isaac H. Maynard for judge of the Court of Appeals. Two years before, when he was deputy attorney general, Maynard had been instrumental in the "steal of the senate." Now, supporters of Cleveland joined with the Republicans in denouncing Maynard's candidacy for the court. Though Hill privately urged Maynard to decline the nomination for the good of the party, organization leaders publicly defended him and, by implication, the excesses of partisanship he represented.[6]

The factional division between Cleveland and Hill was mirrored in the large cities. There Democratic leaders, seeking to make the most of the victories of 1891 and 1892, just as Hill had done at the state level, virtually read the Cleveland elements out of the party. In New York City, Croker's Tammany organization established its undisputed dominance. Where Cleveland men had once held a share of power in the party through the rival County Democracy, they now found that a network of local district organizations had enabled Tammany to consolidate citywide control over nominations, patronage, and public officials. In 1892 Tammany elected all thirty aldermen and all but one of the city's state assemblymen. Similar developments occurred in Murphy's Troy, Hugh McLaughlin's Brooklyn, and William F. Sheehan's Buffalo. In each, a disciplined machine achieved dominance in the Democratic party and extended its authority over the city by election victories in the early 1890s. Each machine, moreover, was led by a man bold enough to take all measures necessary to keep control of elections and appointments, even if these actions further alienated the Cleveland wing of the party. In consequence, the state's largest Democratic cities all exploded in 1893 and 1894 with accusations of dishonest political methods.[7]

At issue was a desperate effort by the Cleveland Democrats to avoid exclusion from their own party, but it soon became something more. The threats of Hill, Croker, and the others to the Cleveland Democracy also rejuvenated an independent reform tradition destined to be a decisive political force. Led by businessmen and professionals, and informed by an ideology of political independence, the antimachine movement became more powerful in 1893 and 1894 than it had ever been before. A combination of circumstances was needed to bring this about. First were the series of Democratic election victories giving the leaders of the party's dominant faction the means and the will to solidify their hold on power. Second was an urban reform tradition with a historic doctrine of efficient, nonpartisan municipal government which suddenly took on new relevance amidst the events of 1893 and 1894.

Third was an economic depression that encouraged discontent with those in power and gave elite reformers the opportunity to broaden their base of support. Finally, as we shall see, there was an opposition political party peculiarly fitted to assist in the revitalization of independent reform and to profit by it. One by one the large cities of the state felt the movement's effects.

Buffalo and Brooklyn, at opposite ends of the state, came first and established the pattern that Albany, Troy, and New York would later follow. Early in 1893, "Blue-Eyed Billy" Sheehan, lieutenant governor of New York and boss of Buffalo, obtained legislative passage and gubernatorial approval of a charter amendment transferring the power to appoint his city's police and excise commissioners from the mayor, whom he could not dominate, to the comptroller, whom he could. In response, members of the Merchants' Association and the Real Estate Exchange organized mass meetings to protest what they considered to be outrageous state interference in Buffalo's municipal affairs. Workingmen's groups, medical societies, and bar associations soon added their voices of opposition to Sheehan's maneuver. In the spring, dissident Buffalo Democrats formed an independent party organization, called the Erie County Home Rule Democracy, to enroll voters and contest Sheehan's control at the upcoming fall elections. Successful in reorganizing the police, however, Sheehan was soon reported to be employing them to "colonize" closely contested wards with fraudulently registered voters. Sheehan's tactics focused wide attention on Buffalo. Down the state, the Cleveland Democratic *New York Times* reported that "even the police have taken a hand in the colonization scheme, and are running all the tramps they can find to the lodging house [at 133 Main Street, Buffalo] for the purpose of having them vote."[8]

In Brooklyn, a slightly different scenario shaped the enactment of a similar political drama. There independent Democrats refused to support the reelection of Mayor David A. Boody, said to be the tool of boss Hugh McLaughlin. According to the dissidents' leader, Edward M. Shepard, Boody "has permitted himself to be completely and unutterably effaced as mayor of the City of Brooklyn." Reluctantly Shepard and his allies in the Brooklyn Democratic Club, the German Democratic Union, the Young Men's Democratic Club, and the Citizens' Union endorsed Charles A. Schieren, the Republican candidate for mayor. What the reformers began as an antimachine campaign soon became an effort to prevent the electoral corruption allegedly being committed by McLaughlin's organization. In nearby Gravesend (an independent town in Kings County), 6,218 voters were discovered to be registered out of a total population of 8,418. When reformers tried to investigate, McLaughlin's ally John Y. McKane had them forcibly rebuffed. The day before the election the nearby *New York Tribune* reported the story under the headline "Gravesend in Rebellion/ A Crisis in This State." Just as in Erie, events in Kings County disgraced the regular Democratic organization and gave independent reform new life.[9]

The 1893 election results suggest that allegations of bossism and corruption, rather than economic depression, caused the Democrats' greatest setbacks that year. Across most of the state, the shift to the Republicans was modest. Excluding the results in Buffalo and Brooklyn, the successful Republican candidate for secretary of state (the highest office contested) ran only 0.4 percent ahead of Benjamin Harrison's losing vote for president in 1892. (See Table 4.) In Albany and Troy, the Democrats actually gained strength over the previous year; in New York City the party balance remained almost unchanged. Only Isaac Maynard, the Democrats' controversial judicial candidate, trailed considerably behind the rest of the state ticket. Buffalo and Brooklyn, by contrast, shifted strongly away from the Democrats for all offices. In Buffalo, Sheehan's local candidates were trounced. In Brooklyn, a similar upheaval brought about the election of the Republican, Schieren, as mayor. Significantly, in both cities opposition to the local Democratic machine was transferred to the party's state ticket. In Buffalo, the Republican nominee for secretary of state ran 9.1 percent ahead of Harrison's percentage in 1892, while in Brooklyn he gained 11.2 percent. Maynard's decisive defeat and the sharp Democratic

Table 4. Republican percentage of total vote in New York State, Brooklyn, and Buffalo, 1892 and 1893

Year and office	Entire state	State except Brooklyn and Buffalo	Brooklyn	Buffalo
1892				
President	45.6%	46.3%	40.7%	46.7%
1893				
Secretary of state	47.9	46.7	51.9	55.8
Judge	51.4	50.2	55.9	58.7
Republican gain for secretary of state	2.3	0.4	11.2	9.1
Republican gain for judge	5.8	3.9	15.2	12.0 ·

Sources: Trib. Alm. (1893, 1894); *Manual* (1893, 1894); *Buffalo Morning Express,* November 8, 1893.

losses in Brooklyn and Buffalo indicate that the party fared badly where voters had reason to rebuke its machine methods. Elsewhere, even amidst depression, the voters of New York shifted but slightly away from the Democratic party.[10]

What Buffalo and Brooklyn began in 1893, other Democratic cities continued the following year. In Albany, alleged frauds had marred the elections of 1893 and, according to popular opinion, given the Democrats an undeserved victory. Angry citizens formed the Committee of Fifty to insure the punishment of those responsible for the corruption of the ballot and to oppose the Democratic machine in the municipal elections scheduled for the spring of 1894. Running as the Honest Election party, the combined forces of independent Democrats, Republicans, and nonpartisans carried the city and elected a Republican mayor.[11]

Similar if more extreme events occurred in Troy. Reported ballot-box fraud by Murphy's victorious Democratic machine in the fall of 1893 made "honest elections" the main issue in the local campaign the following spring. Proclaiming that "partisanship gives place to patriotism," antimachine Democrats joined with Republicans to oppose Murphy. In an election marked by further intimidation and violence, including the murder of a Republican poll-watcher by a notorious Democrat named "Bat" Shea, Murphy's forces won again. In response, aroused citizens formed the Committee of Public Safety. The *Troy Daily Times* announced one mass meeting under the headline "Awakened! By a Bullet! Troy's Voice" and compared the murder to the firing on Fort Sumter. "The moral sentiment of the city is solidified as never before," said the paper. "Good people, without regard to politics, are united in a common purpose."[12]

Last of all, New York City, too, had a wave of antimachine feeling. By far the largest and richest of the state's cities, with over a quarter of its people, almost half its real and personal property, and with government expenditures four times those of the state itself, New York City occupied a position of crucial political importance. Reform was, of course, not new to the great downstate metropolis. Within the memory of many men still living, Boss Tweed had been brought down by a coalition of independent Democrats and Republicans in 1871, and since then a succession of reform organizations had intermittently battled the dominant Tammany Hall machine. But their achievements were seldom large and had seemed smaller than usual in recent years.[13]

Now in 1894 New York City's antimachine tradition was renewed and transformed. Just as in Albany and Troy, the Democrats' sizable victory in 1893 led reformers and Republicans to level charges that their opponents had fraudulently registered men, voted repeaters, mis-counted ballots, intimidated Republicans, and assaulted poll-watchers. Thirty-nine Democratic election inspectors were eventually convicted of fraud. Sensing Tammany's vulnerability, a number of new indepen-dent Democratic organizations formed in late 1893 and 1894. Some, to be sure, reflected only the calculated aspirations of those shut out from the spoils of office, but some were less self-interested, and all proved adept at employing the rhetoric of opposition to bosses and machines.[14]

The man most responsible for establishing the tone and content of this rhetoric was the Reverend Charles H. Parkhurst of the Madison Square Presbyterian Church. Since February 1892, Parkhurst had preached Sunday after Sunday against the protection of criminals by the Tammany police. "I had supposed," Parkhurst said, that the police department "existed for the purpose of repressing crime, [but] it now began to dawn upon me . . . [that] its principal object . . . [was] to protect and foster crime and make capital out of it." Working through the City Vigilance League, an organization of citizens formed in each assembly district to gather data on police corruption, Parkhurst and his co-workers slowly gained attention. By early 1894, they had brought about considerable public revulsion against police wrongdoing under Tammany. In response, the Republican state senate named a commit-tee, chaired by Clarence Lexow, to investigate New York City's police department. Beginning in March 1894, and continuing for the rest of the year, the Lexow Committee took ten thousand pages of testimony from 678 witnesses that corroborated Parkhurst's charges in extensive and sensational detail. Never before had New Yorkers had so much grimy information about their police department and the Democratic officials behind it.[15]

As a result of the disclosures, and through the unusual cooperation of a number of disparate organizations, Tammany, which had never been stronger than it was in 1892 and 1893, met decisive defeat in the fall elections of 1894. The anti-Tammany campaign was coordinated by a nonpartisan Committee of Seventy, named and patterned after the group that had broken Tweed's power in 1871 and drawn from the city's commercial, financial, and legal elite. Independent Democrats, Republicans, and nonpartisans joined together and agreed on a fusion ticket headed by the Republican merchant, William L. Strong. In November, Tammany, which had elected every alderman in the city in 1892, carried only five of thirty assembly districts for its mayoral nominee and was reduced to 40 percent of the total vote.[16]

While there were circumstances unique to each city, common themes shaped the movements against the regular Democratic organizations of

Buffalo, Brooklyn, Albany, Troy, and New York. In each case, the dominant machine, seeking to maintain its position, committed acts that opened it to charges of municipal mismanagement and electoral dishonesty. Everywhere independent Democrats joined with Republicans and nonpartisans in local election campaigns against the entrenched Democratic organizations. Like all political alliances among "out" groups, this one was undertaken because each of the participants saw gains to be won by defeating those in power. But the antimachine coalitions forged in 1893 and 1894 hold special significance not simply because they triumphed, but also because they voiced and applied a persuasive body of thought about municipal government destined to affect all levels of politics in the coming years.

The heart of the doctrine was that partisanship had no place in city politics because national party ideologies were irrelevant to the tasks of municipal government. By harping on national issues and appealing to habitual party loyalties in local elections, politicians obscured the real problems of city government and perpetuated an artificial line of division between citizens who actually had common interests. The solution lay in choosing men for municipal office solely on the basis of their ability to provide efficient, economical government, without regard to party. Antimachine Democrats and Republicans as well as thoroughgoing independents all saw advantages in nonpartisan municipal government. And while they differed on details, these groups increasingly concurred on a number of political reforms to bring about their goal: the separation of local elections from state and national contests, city home rule without legislative interference, civil service reform, ballot reform, and a series of structural changes strengthening the mayor and weakening district councilmen.[17]

To advance these reforms, a considerable number of nonpartisan municipal organizations sprang into existence in 1893 and 1894. In New York, the exclusive City Club established more than twenty local Good Government Clubs with a mostly middle-class membership numbering about six thousand. These groups investigated municipal questions, publicized their findings, spread the gospel of nonpartisan city government, and endorsed candidates who shared their beliefs. Independent organizations also formed in the other large Democratic cities: the Citizens' Union in Brooklyn, the Committee of Fifty in Albany, and the Committee of Public Safety in Troy. Partly in imitation and partly in response to their own problems, additional large and small cities also boasted the establishment of nonpartisan clubs and associations in 1894: the Municipal Club of Rochester, the Municipal Reform Club of Syracuse, the Good Government Club of Yonkers, the

Municipal League of Schenectady, and the Citizens' League of New Rochelle. These independent associations devoted their attention exclusively to municipal affairs. Said the Yonkers group: "It is not the business, nor is it the desire, of this Club to weaken any man's allegiance to his State and national party, but it is one of the chief aims of the Club to weaken the influence of partizan politics in the government of the city of Yonkers."[18]

Behind the independents' ideology of municipal nonpartisanship stood particular men and interests seeking to benefit from a new form of city government. But these interests were far from monolithic. Unquestionably the movement's leadership came from businessmen and professionals. In Buffalo, merchants and real estate men originated the call for mass protests against Sheehan. In New York, the Committee of Seventy, consisting of bankers, lawyers, and merchants, directed the fall campaign from the Chamber of Commerce building. Everywhere, reform drew its leaders from the ranks of those businessmen who looked to city government for cleanliness, peace, and order rather than for special favors and franchises. Even the men at the head of the movement, however, were not always in agreement on what city government ought to be and do. While many voiced a desire for a "businesslike" polity, others recognized that business corporations were themselves often responsible for political abuses. On questions involving taxation, regulation, and city services, the leaders of reform, even the businessmen among them, were often divided.[19]

While it was led by businessmen, reform also attracted certain middle- and lower-class city elements. To some, reform meant weakening the preponderant influence that Irish Catholics exercised through the Democratic party. Thus the German-American Reform Union opposed Tammany, just as the German Democratic Union joined the enemies of McLaughlin's machine in Brooklyn. In Buffalo, too, middle-class citizens of German descent supported the drive against Sheehan. Compared to city reform movements of the 1880s, those of the 1890s made greater efforts to appeal to lower-class voters. Antimachine elites were beginning to recognize that party organizations provided benefits for their supporters and that the government would have to offer corresponding forms of assistance if reform was to prevail. New York's Committee of Seventy observed that "all classes of citizens, rich and poor alike, suffer" under Tammany misgovernment and devoted about half its platform to calling for expanded municipal services. The same city's Good Government Clubs investigated and exposed foul tenements, dirty streets, inadequate means of transportation, and poor schools. Depression conditions undoubtedly helped persuade lower-class voters that existing city government added to their suffering. In consequence, tenement wards, as well as brownstone districts, shifted against the Democrats at the municipal elections of 1893 and 1894.[20]

The independents nonetheless remained a minority having a firm base only among businessmen and professionals. They were a growing minority, to be sure, and one large enough to encompass divergent views on economic and social questions. Startling public events had confirmed their diagnosis of political ills and generated fresh interest in their proposed remedies. But while more people than ever before listened to the independents' message, the great majority of voters continued to be firm partisans. Even most independents, while rejecting local party machines, still identified with, if they did not always vote for, one or the other of the great national parties. The historic significance of the independents of 1893 and 1894 lies in their persuasive expression of doubts about party loyalties and practices at the outset of an era destined to see important changes in the nature of political participation. Their immediate significance lay in the successful revolt they led against the particular party machines that offended them most.

The Democrats' state leader, David B. Hill, saw what was happening to his party as a result of crises and blunders in the largest cities. Writing to a close adviser in March 1894, Hill observed that "the recent election troubles, beginning at Gravesend and terminating in Troy, . . . hurt the party. . . . It is very evident that the Republicans are seeking to make party capital over our misfortunes. . . . These citizens associations are nothing more or less than Republican associations in disguise."[21] Hill was not quite accurate in calling the new nonpartisan leagues Republican, but his worry was understandable, for the Republicans indeed attracted antimachine support. Their inclusion of the urban independents and their assent to many of the things the independents believed had important implications for the course of New York politics. For no element of the Republican majority now mobilizing would so vigorously press its demands or spread its ideology in the coming years as the city independents who gained new life and new members in 1893 and 1894.

The New York State Republican party of the mid-1890s was historically and ideologically well suited to the task of attracting the strategic minority of urban citizens who were questioning the value of partisanship. From the time of their party's founding, the Republicans, like the Whigs before them, had included more than their share of men who remained skeptical of parties and their divisiveness. In the 1850s, idealists who wanted above all to crush slavery had allied hesitantly with others more firmly committed to party-building. After the Civil War tensions rose between Republicans with different measures of loyalty to the party organization. Twice, in 1872 and again in 1884, independent Republicans in New York, as elsewhere in the Northeast and Midwest, broke toward the Democracy. Indeed, for almost a decade after Cleveland's first election to the White House, his party seemed to be more receptive than the Republicans to criticism of party machines. As late as the winter of 1893, a nominally Republican independent like Seth Low could still think of becoming a Democrat if only "the elements now in control of the Democratic state machinery" could be destroyed. But instead of meeting destruction, those elements claimed the whole party, and so independent Republicans like Low came home to the G.O.P. Trooping with them, for the time being, were many independent Democrats as well as genuine nonpartisans.[22]

Winning them over was not an especially difficult feat for the Republicans. The Democrats themselves did most of the work. As party boss Thomas Collier Platt told an associate in mid-1893, "It will be the policy of the [Republican] State Committee and the Republican leaders in this State to keep quiet and await developments in the Democratic Party." Nonetheless, the Republicans did what they could to capitalize on Democratic divisions and mistakes. Unashamedly they fashioned their rhetoric to fit what the independents wanted to hear. In Buffalo, Republican newspapers appropriated the antimachine Democrats' very name by calling the Republican candidates for local and legislative office "Home Rulers." Promising purer and cleaner politics, the *Morning Express* declared it "the duty of every friend of good government to vote the entire Republican ticket this year." The party's state platform of 1893 made Isaac Maynard's "connection with the conspiracy to steal the Senate" its main issue. "Five men," it declared with ominous reference to Hill, Croker, Murphy, Sheehan, and McLaughlin, "constitute the Democratic machine and seek the mastery of the Commonwealth."[23]

In the following year, the Republicans' control of the state legislature gave them added means to expose the opposition's misdeeds. Besides the Lexow investigation of the New York police, the senate also conducted a similar, if smaller, inquiry into Troy's election methods. Throughout the spring and early summer, during the same months when "Bat" Shea's trial and conviction received wide attention, one hundred witnesses paraded to the stand and offered testimony in support of the senate committee's later conclusion that "what is known as Murphyism" caused the "revolting" conditions in Troy. Nonpartisans as well as antimachine Democrats criticized the Republican partisanship that plainly lay behind these investigations. But the resulting disclosures, especially about New York, caused a number of independent journals to judge the Lexow investigation eminently worthwhile. It was "unexpectedly successful" according to *Harper's Weekly.* "Whatever motives actuated the appointment of that Committee," said the *New York Times,* "it is already clear and incontestable that . . . [it] has performed an enormous public service."[24]

Effective as these investigations were, the real key to the alliance of Republicans and independents lay in their joint efforts to retool the electoral machinery. Historically this was a good Republican issue, since southern and urban elections had often brought forth the party's attempts to adjust the voting process in the name of reform. Each for their own reasons, Republicans and independents now agreed on measures to regulate voting, especially in the Democratic cities of the state. In session from May to September 1894, a constitutional convention gave the Republicans the opportunity to embed the reforms in fundamental law.

Every twenty years, according to a provision dating from 1846, the voters of New York had the opportunity to decide whether to call a constitutional convention. A referendum on the question was overwhelmingly approved in 1886, but seven years of interparty squabbling over delegate-selection procedures intervened before the Democrats were able to enact plans for a convention they expected their party to control. To the surprise of almost everyone, the election results of 1893 gave the Republicans a solid majority in the convention. When it opened, they organized it as if it were a legislative body. They elected one of their number as president and appointed committees, each with a Republican chairman and a Republican majority.[25]

While some independent as well as Democratic journals criticized this drawing of party lines, circumstances mitigated the conclave's apparent partisanship and enabled the Republicans to satisfy the independents. Not expecting to win the 1893 elections, Republican leaders had dressed up their slate of fifteen delegates-at-large by nominating men distinguished for their professional activities rather than for close association with the party organization. Two of them, Joseph H. Choate, the convention's president, and Elihu Root, chairman of the judiciary committee and Republican floor leader, became the convention's most influential members. Many of the party's district delegates (chosen in groups of five from the state's thirty-two senate districts) were similarly free of strong organizational ties. Compared with the state legislators sitting that year, the convention members were more professional (four-fifths were lawyers), more highly educated, and less politically experienced. Fewer than one-fifth of them had previously served in as high an office as state legislator. The delegates exemplified the old assumption that constitution writing was a task for the learned lawyer, standing above partisanship. As Dorman B. Eaton expressed it in the language of an upper-middle-class independent, the members of the convention "represented the best public opinion, rather than the mere party opinion, of the State." The delegates, he judged, were "both morally and mentally much superior to the members of the New York Legislature."[26]

The convention's agenda, like its membership, suited it to the task of winning independents over to the Republicans. Most of the conclave's work related to governmental procedures: the rules for filling offices, locating authority, and organizing the different branches. These were the very problems that most concerned the city independents. While it is not surprising that a constitutional convention devoted most of its time and effort to procedures for constituting government, these were the only issues on which the delegates made significant innovations. They debated many economic and social questions but did not undertake a single major policy departure in these areas. Instead suffrage requirements, legislative apportionment, judicial reorganization, and city government provided the largest issues before the convention and formed its major accomplishments.[27]

Frederick W. Holls, a delegate-at-large who shared the independence of Choate and Root, recognized the valuable opportunity the convention presented the Republicans, "and all the greater, the more merely partisan points of view are ignored." By using their power temperately, Holls told a fellow delegate before the convention opened, the Republicans would "do more to rehabilitate us with the independent and cultured class of the state than anything else." In Holls's opinion, the convention succeeded. "There is a spirit of patriotism [among the delegates] which is very inspiring," Holls informed another independent Republican, Andrew D. White. "In fact, I have never been in any body where party lines were held so lightly." In significant measure, as we shall see, nonpartisans and independent Democrats concurred in Holls's view and approved the convention's work.[28]

Several constitutional changes regulating the voting process, especially in the cities, received nearly unanimous support from Republican delegates and won the approval of independents across the state. One amendment mandated secrecy in voting and allowed the legislature to authorize the use of voting machines in place of the traditional paper ballot. These provisions constituted a sort of literacy test, since secret voting by ballot or machine required each citizen to read for himself the names of the candidates, offices, and parties. Another change obliged a naturalized citizen to wait ninety days after attaining citizenship before becoming eligible to vote. A third amendment required voter registration by personal application in cities and villages of over five thousand population, while it exempted the small towns and country districts. All three amendments increased the difficulty of mobilizing recent urban immigrants to vote. The advantage to the Republicans was that most of these voters were Democrats. The advantage to the independents was the limitation placed upon the ability of city bosses to control elections by bringing to the polls, through corrupt means or fair ones, what the nonpartisan New York *Evening Post* called "large bodies of ignorant foreigners."[29]

However much the independents welcomed these amendments, they considered measures insulating city government from partisan politics to be even more important. Led by the City Club of New York, independent organizations from around the state formed the Committee of Twenty-One to frame amendments in the interest of cities. Highest among the committee's priorities were the separation of city elections from partisan state and national contests and the enlargement of municipal home rule by reserving certain city functions entirely to local determination. On the first of these issues, the independents got substantially what they wanted because their goals complemented those of the Republicans. On the second question, the reformers fell short of their aims because it was not in the interest of the Republican party to give up legislative authority over Democratic cities.[30]

Regular Republicans had good reasons for agreeing to divorce local contests from state and national elections. With the governorship or the presidency at stake when city elections occurred, there was little probability of persuading Democratic voters to support Republican or fusion candidates for municipal office. Moreover, because Democratic organizations characteristically reserved their greatest efforts for local campaigns, the Republicans stood to benefit in state and national contests by separating them from municipal elections. Finally, the Republicans knew that city politics had first priority with most independents and anticipated that the isolation of municipal elections would discourage the nomination of independent candidates for state offices. Thus, for strikingly different and, indeed, partially contradictory, reasons, Republicans and independents agreed on the separation of municipal elections. Almost every Republican member of the constitutional convention thus joined with a minority of Democratic delegates in voting for an amendment scheduling state elections in even-numbered years and requiring cities of fifty thousand or more to elect local officials in the odd years.[31]

Municipal home rule found less favor among the convention's majority members. After defeating the Committee of Twenty-One's proposal for home rule, the convention voted along party lines to adopt a weaker amendment dividing the state's cities into three population classes and providing for the enactment of general laws applicable to all cities of the same class. Local authorities were permitted to reject measures affecting only their city, but the legislature could override such vetoes by a simple majority vote. Democratic delegates criticized the modified home rule amendment. One member protested against including "such trash as this" in the constitution. Another labeled it "a spurious measure of home rule."[32]

Outside the convention, independents as well as Democrats lamented the delegates' substantial failure to shield the cities from state interference. At the same time, however, many reformers and their journals made it clear that they regarded the separation of elections as more important than home rule. "If you secure separate elections," Edward M. Shepard, leader of the independent Democrats in Brooklyn, had told the chairman of the convention's committee on cities, "you have secured . . . by far the most important part of the reform." The *New York Times* agreed that "there is one amendment . . . that overtops all the others in importance. It is that which provides for separate municipal elections." "Give us that and the rest will come in time."[33]

When they surveyed the convention's work after its adjournment, the independents found other constitutional changes that also pleased them: a provision for bipartisan election boards, a recognition of the principles of civil service reform, and a thorough overhaul of the state's judicial system. Even the plainly partisan legislative apportionment article found favor with many independents because of the limitations it placed upon the representation accorded to the Democratic machine's largest strongholds, New York City and Brooklyn. When the amendments came before the voters in the form of three referenda in November, prominent independents visibly supported the successful campaign for the new constitution. The *Nation,* whose militantly nonpartisan editor, E. L. Godkin, confessed to voting for even the partisan apportionment article, declared that the constitution's adoption "gives this state at one stroke so long a list of beneficent reforms that such good fortune seems incredible."[34]

In the years after 1894, Republicans and independents kept up their cooperation in large part because they continued to agree on changes in the methods for constituting government. Frequently the two sides had somewhat different reasons for favoring the same measure, as in the case of the separation of municipal elections. Sometimes they both disguised their real intentions behind rhetorical facades. Often the actual consequences of reform proved unexpected to everyone. These complexities, while increasing the difficulty of interpreting changes in the electoral machinery, place them among the most expressive political achievements of the era.

Having behind them a state party organization evidently committed to measures the independents wanted, Republican leaders in the largest cities took steps in 1894 to cement the alliance with the reformers. Efficient-looking "business" candidates were named for local office, and "good government," as the independents defined it, was promised. In New York City, where the Republican machine had frequently cooperated with Tammany Hall in return for a share of the considerable municipal patronage, the party now underwent a thorough reorganization apparently designed to free it from Tammany's grasp and restore control to rank-and-file Republicans. Put forward by George Bliss, Elihu Root, Joseph H. Choate, and other "heavy respectables" in the exclusive Union League Club, the new plan of organization established eleven hundred local election-district associations, each of which was to enroll any Republican who met a loose test of party affiliation. Believers in nonpartisan municipal politics were to be welcomed, not excluded. While observers noted that these reforms did not prevent boss Thomas Collier Platt from keeping control of the party machine in New York City, the Republican reorganization there, in combination with the party's participation in the fusion campaign against Tammany, encouraged independents to believe that the Republicans had become more open and honest by far than their Democratic opponents.[35]

It was an impression that reformers across the state widely shared in 1894. By supporting specific reform measures as well as simply by being the Democrats' enemy, the Republican party had won the confidence of many independents. Despite their distaste for Platt, they concurred with Godkin that the Republican organization was "saintly" compared to the Democratic machine and significantly concluded that "a Republican Legislature as well as Governor" were needed to enact further measures reforming city government. With varying degrees of reluctance, independents of all stripes, including antimachine Republicans, nonpartisans, and many Cleveland Democrats, seemed prepared to give the Republican party a chance to bring about their vision of what politics and government ought to be.[36]

Compared to the urban political upheaval of 1893–94, the contemporaneous economic depression, beginning in the spring of 1893 and deepening over the course of the next several years, resulted in a far more painful social crisis affecting the lives of many more people. Unemployment reached staggering proportions, especially in the large cities where relief efforts were greatly inadequate. While political corruption aroused mainly an established elite, the economic collapse took its most severe toll on the numerous urban poor. As a result, the depression probably shifted more votes to the Republicans than did the bad behavior of the Democratic machines. Yet, of the two crises contributing to the partisan realignment of 1893–94, the depression had the less enduring impact on politics and governance in New York State.[37]

In control of the state government when hard times struck, Democratic officials compounded a refusal to act with political blunders. Late in the summer of 1893, the president of the American Federation of Labor, Samuel Gompers, wrote to request a meeting with Governor Roswell P. Flower to discuss public-works employment for the growing ranks of jobless. The governor's secretary replied to Gompers that Flower, whose receipt of the letter had been delayed because he was vacationing in the Adirondacks, planned to leave immediately for the Chicago World's Fair and afterward would make his usual tour of upstate county fairs. The governor therefore could not possibly see Gompers until October; in any event, Flower preferred to have Gompers's message in writing. Labor leaders naturally howled at Flower's insensitivity and were not appeased when the governor declared his sympathy for workers but strongly argued against new state undertakings for unemployment relief. "In America," Flower proclaimed, "the people support the government; it is not the province of the government to support the people. Once recognize the principle that the government must supply public work for the unemployed, and there will be no end of official paternalism."[38]

While Flower's attitude had relaxed a bit by the next year, his administration's most significant policy response to the demand for public-works employment occasioned more political embarrassment. In February 1894, Flower signed a bill authorizing the New York City park department to spend up to $1 million employing men on park improvements. From the outset, the experiment provoked controversy. Park officials quarreled with the city's Board of Estimate and with the mayor over the use of the money; Democratic aldermen threatened an investigation of the project when their patronage demands were not met. Late in the summer, the Central Labor Union began an inquiry into the expenditure of the $1 million and eventually concluded that most of it had been wasted. In a sense, Flower had predicted such an outcome. In his attack on public-works expenditures the previous year, the governor had asked, "What public works would be authorized?

Where would they be located? What should they cost?" Such legislation, he said, would produce "large apples of discord. They would lead to log-rolling and combinations." A conventional nineteenth-century politician, Flower doubted that party politics could cope with class legislation, and he feared the consequences of explicitly making policy to assist a particular economic group.[39]

The Republicans, for their part, pointed to the Democrats' insensitivity and corruptness but made no significant departure from Flower's governmental philosophy. Almost all the attention they gave to the depression concerned the Democratic national administration's responsibility for hard times and the promise that their own party's tariff policy would restore prosperity. At the state level, the depression was a practically invisible political topic. Frugality in government provided the Republicans' leading state economic issue. Party leaders pointed to high taxes and expenditures under the Democrats and, in 1894, lauded their own legislators' success in reducing both. Like the Democrats, the Republicans argued that state government should cost less and do less. Neither party felt the state could do anything about hard times.[40]

The constitutional convention of 1894 gave the Republicans another opportunity to respond to the depression. Distant from the political fray, the convention saw more serious thought and expression about the government and the economy than the legislative halls or political stump permitted. The convention received for consideration numerous far-reaching economic and social amendments providing for stringent corporate regulation, pensions for older citizens, meals for school children, and other endeavors considerably extending the bounds of government. Most of these amendments died in committee; none came before the whole convention for debate. Instead the delegates' labors on economic issues were contained within familiar limits and the majority party's members held down demands and compromised conflicts. Their work suggests how little impact the depression had on governance in New York.[41]

Organized labor proposed to the convention a number of amendments, including an increase in employers' liability for injuries to workers, recognition of labor's right to organize, relief from tenement work, guarantees of home rule for cities, and a system of direct legislation. None of these or other measures sought by labor would have drastically altered the state's economic system; none specifically addressed depression conditions; some were not even intended exclusively for the benefit of workers. Nevertheless the sole labor article adopted was one shielding workers from competition with convicts by prohibiting the commercial use of prison labor or the sale of its products. This article served as something of a symbol for larger labor questions. One delegate called it a way of forestalling working-class unrest; another suggested that the sweating system would be impossible if competition between convicts and free workers did not keep wages so low. Useful as it may have been in good times, the prison labor article contained the seeds of a serious side effect in a period of depression by explicitly permitting prisoners to do government work in competition with the jobless.[42]

The convention's decision on the controversial issue of enlarging the Erie Canal further demonstrated the delegates' inclination to avoid significant new economic policies and their aptitude for compromise between conflicting interests. Upstate farmers and merchants who relied on the canal to transport their products to market, together with spokesmen for commercial interests in New York City and Buffalo, pressured the delegates to adopt a specific plan of enlargement. Others, including the trunkline railroad interests, as well as those who lived too distant from the waterways to benefit from them, strongly opposed such an amendment. As a compromise, the convention approved an article permitting the legislature to enlarge the canals and finance the improvements either through annual revenues or, if the voters approved, by borrowing. In effect, the delegates favored the canal interests with an amendment accepting the principle of improvement but evaded a specific plan of enlargement and placed upon the voters the responsibility for authorizing any project that was large enough to necessitate the creation of a state debt. This was a compromise for which neither side had aimed. A pro-canal Buffalo newspaper called it "harmless humbug," while opponents declared the canals "good enough" and unsuccessfully urged voters to defeat the amendment when it was submitted to them in November.[43]

In an era of slowly mounting anxiety about the power of large corporate interests, the convention adopted only one amendment specifically affecting relations between business and government, a prohibition on the then-common acceptance of free transportation passes by public officials. The details of that article, moreover, suggest that the delegates largely faulted the politicians, not the corporations, for any impropriety resulting from the distribution of free passes. While the amendment made both the public official who received the pass and the company agent who offered it guilty of a misdemeanor, it required corporation employees to testify about passes they offered and guaranteed them immunity from prosecution on the basis of such testimony. Expressing the assumption behind that provision, one delegate said "we should put the offense where it properly belongs, on the public officer receiving the pass, and we should leave the corporations as our witnesses to be called against the public officer."[44]

When the convention closed, eight leading Republican members issued an "Address" to the people in which they praised the conclave's avoidance of "undue experiments." That was an accurate description of the delegates' work on economic matters. Professional and established, they were personally wary of expanding the government or adding to its functions. Meeting at a time when, after several years of industrial unrest, labor organizations had fallen to a low point in influence and numbers, the delegates safely assumed they could ignore most of the workers' requests. Finally, as good Republicans, they were willing to adopt bold measures helping their party, such as the new legislative apportionment article, but were inclined to compromise wherever conflicting economic interests threatened Republican unity. All these influences restrained the delegates from adopting new policies and encouraged what one sympathetic observer called their sturdy refusal "to depart from the old and well-tried principles of government."[45]

The convention's work, together with the prevailing acceptance of Governor Flower's philosophy and the politicians' avoidance of hard times as a state political issue, suggests that the depression of the 1890s did not significantly affect expectations for government in New York State. To be sure, a small number of scholars and social reformers responded to the depression by beginning to recast their ideas about the government's responsibility for poverty, unemployment, and business conditions. But their new thoughts scarcely reached the political arena at all. Changing the government's relationship to the economy was too difficult and complex a task to be faced at a moment when all classes of people were shaken by misery or fear or both. Undoubtedly, the hard times of the 1890s made a permanent impression upon many and helped forge a determination to confront difficult problems of political economy. But not until several more years had passed and good times had returned was that determination distinctly and widely visible in New York.[46]

Compared to the dense and troublesome questions raised by depression, the restoration of decent municipal government seemed far simpler. While no one really understood the most difficult economic problems, an articulate urban elite was suggesting seemingly straightforward solutions to the ills of partisan city administration. Facing two crises, the political community gave more of its energy to the less difficult and threatening one. Indeed, by appearing solvable, the urban political problems of 1893 and 1894 may have provided a kind of catharsis for a people anxious about the divisive and damaging issues presented by the maturation of an industrial economy, but not quite ready to confront them. In the mid-1890s the conditions that would soon encourage people to face those issues were just beginning to form.

Despite a significant increase of independence from party machines, as well as the existence of a depression which suggested that fundamental problems of political economy soon required attention, the state election campaign of 1894 was conducted within the bounds of the basically partisan political culture that still pervaded New York. The election results, correspondingly, while they completed the transfer of state power from the Democrats to the Republicans, revealed the fundamental continuance of nineteenth-century electoral behavior. Not for about another decade, for reasons that had little directly to do with the realignment, would these patterns significantly change.

Hoping to unify their divided coalition, Democratic leaders in 1894 relied heavily on their party's familiar appeals to ethno-religious groups, especially Irish Catholics and Germans of both the Catholic and Protestant faiths. Party speakers repeatedly reminded voters of the Republicans' illiberal tendencies—particularly toward the Sunday closing of saloons, a policy the Germans dreaded—and pledged to avoid interfering with "the personal liberty or reasonable customs of the people." An even more emotional issue concerned the anti-Catholic American Protective Association, an organization alleged by the Democrats to enjoy the full support of the Republican party. Indeed, the Democrats so fiercely attacked their opponents' "religious intolerance" that one leading Republican felt constrained to remind Senator David B. Hill, the Democratic candidate for governor, that "this is a political campaign and not a religious crusade." But Hill, who knew what he was about, believed that only by crusading for the votes of the Democrats' traditional ethno-religious constituencies did his party have a chance to overcome the extreme political disadvantages of a depressed economy and a discredited organization.[47]

To oppose Hill for governor, the Republicans confidently nominated Levi P. Morton, a wealthy banker and party fund-raiser who had served as ambassador to France in the 1880s and as vice-president from 1889 to 1893. With wide acquaintance among the social and economic elite of New York City, Morton found acceptance in the same circles from which the independents drew their leadership. Boss Thomas Collier Platt also found the former vice-president acceptable. In anticipation of the nomination, Morton, who was seventy years old, wrote to Platt in July to ask, "Wd the position of Govr be a laborious one for me & cd I pass a good portion of the summer season at Rhinebeck [Morton's home]?" Platt replied that as governor Morton would have to be present in Albany only during the legislative session and, even then, only four days a week. With a good private secretary, Platt continued, Morton could make his own labors "very light."[48]

Following a harmonious convention, the Republican organization ran an efficient campaign made easier by the likelihood of victory. Wealthy men and corporations were persuaded to contribute money; party officeholders and candidates generally did so without persuasion. The state committee made up a roster of willing speakers and dispatched them to rally special constituencies in the coalition. To the offices of loyal newspapers, especially upstate weeklies, the committee sent boiler-plate editorials praising the Republican candidates and reminding voters of the Democrats' misdeeds. The party's emphasis continued to be upon national economic issues, especially the Democratic depression and the Republican remedy, tariff protection. To counter their opponents' appeals to ethno-religious groups, the Republicans fashioned their own. Native-born Protestant voters were reminded of the party's historic identification with their values and beliefs, while Morton's public letter accepting the nomination took the other tack by welcoming "the liberty loving of all lands" and pledging to support "the fullest freedom in the worship of Almighty God." To Catholics, Republicans spoke with pride of a compromise, adopted by the constitutional convention, permitting state aid to sectarian charitable institutions in return for a prohibition on assistance to religious schools. Since the basic nature, if not the details, of all these methods and appeals were familiar, the Republican campaign of 1894 did not fundamentally differ from those the party had often conducted before.[49]

In a campaign dominated by economic and cultural issues, the state topic to which the Republicans gave the most attention was Democratic corruption, especially in the cities. "No decent platform could possibly tell the truth about Democratic government," declared the *New York Tribune*. "Of its shamelessness, of its corruption, of its crime, of its open dependence upon all that is rotten and lewd and criminal, no platform could give more than a hint without passing the limits." The *Tribune*'s understanding of corruption was the conventional one, embracing bribery, election fraud, and the protection of criminals by policemen. If the Democrats took campaign money from business corporations and afterward protected the generous interests, the Republicans made nothing of it, for their party commonly did it too, and, besides, there was almost no public recognition of this form of misgovernment.[50]

When the election returns came in, the size of the Republican majority astonished even the party's leaders. Platt, who had predicted a plurality of between 40,000 and 140,000, now found that Morton's actual margin of victory exceeded his most optimistic projection by 16,000 votes. Winning every contested state office, the Republicans also captured 105 out of 128 assembly seats. All the constitutional amendments were comfortably approved, including the frankly partisan apportionment plan.[51]

Just as they traditionally had, the town and country districts of upstate New York provided the Republicans' firmest base of support. Voters there gave the party over 57 percent of the total vote. (See Table 5.) Only in pockets of the Hudson River valley and in the two little counties of Chemung, in the southern tier, and Schoharie, west of Albany, did the rural and small-town Democracy retain political dominance. At the state's northern and western extremities were several counties in which the Republican vote approached or exceeded a re-

Table 5. Geographical distribution of New York State Republican vote, presidential election of 1892 and gubernatorial election of 1894

Geographical area	1892		1894		
	Republican percentage of the total vote	Percentage contributed to the state-wide Republican total	Republican percentage of the total vote	Percentage contributed to the state-wide Republican total	Percentage of the state's total population, 1890
Downstate metropolitan area (New York, Kings, Queens, and Richmond counties)	37.0%	30.4%	48.0%	34.1%	42.2%
Five large upstate cities (Albany, Buffalo, Rochester, Syracuse, and Troy)	47.1	10.8	53.2	10.9	10.6
Twenty-five small upstate cities (Population 10,000–49,999)	48.4	9.3	54.5	9.3	8.3
Rural areas and small towns	52.0	49.5	57.3	45.7	38.9
Entire state	45.6	100.0	53.1	100.0	100.0

Sources: Trib. Alm. (1893, 1895); *Manual* (1893, 1895); U.S. Department of the Interior, Census Office, *Compendium of the Eleventh Census: Population* (Washington, D.C., 1892), pt. 1, pp. 442–52.

markable two-thirds of the total. Elsewhere in the north and west, landslide majorities of lesser dimensions were registered almost everywhere. This was a resounding victory for the party in its usual areas of strength, but the extent of the triumph should not be exaggerated. In the Republican landslide of 1894, the town and country districts were, on the whole, only 5 percent more Republican than they had been in the banner Democratic year of 1892.

While the party's base lay in the country, its largest gains came in the cities. Just as Brooklyn and Buffalo had provided the Republicans' heaviest increases in 1893, now in 1894 the party registered its most sizable advances in New York City, Albany, and Troy. In New York, Morton added 12.8 percent to the party's vote for secretary of state in 1893, while in Albany and Troy the Republicans gained 11.1 percent and 15.6 percent, respectively. Outside these three cities, Morton ran only 2.6 percent ahead of the Republican vote the previous year. Brooklyn and Buffalo both remained approximately as Republican as they had become in 1893. Together these five "Democratic" cities—especially New York and Brooklyn—had shifted much more decisively toward the Republicans since 1892 than had the rest of the state, and they provided the bulk of the gains that brought the party into office. (See Table 6.) Large-city votes, including those in traditionally Republican Rochester and Syracuse where the party's gains were more modest, contributed fully 45 percent of Morton's total vote. Since long-range population patterns were adding to the large cities' electoral strength at the expense of the country districts, the Republicans' gains there represented good signs for the party's future. Yet it remained to be seen whether a party oriented in many respects toward its rural and town base could keep the support of the big-city voters who had put it in power.[52]

Table 6. Republican percentage of total vote in large New York cities, presidential election of 1892 and gubernatorial election of 1894

Cities	1892	1894	Republican gain
Two downstate cities (New York and Brooklyn)	36.9%	47.7%	10.8%
Three upstate Democratic cities (Albany, Buffalo, Troy)	45.2	52.3	7.1
Two upstate Republican cities (Rochester and Syracuse)	50.5	55.0	4.5

Source: Trib. Alm. (1893, 1895).

Except in Albany, where the Republicans had run unexpectedly well in 1892, every ward (or, in the case of New York City, every assembly district) in the state's five large "Democratic" cities shared in the shift toward the Republicans between 1892 and 1894. In Irish Catholic districts as well as in old-stock ones, in tenement wards as well as in brownstone neighborhoods, the Democrats lost support to the Republicans. The party's urban gains were pervasive enough that no single economic or cultural factor can account for them. According to Samuel T. McSeveney's insightful analysis of the shifts, especially those in New York City and Brooklyn, two separate anti-Democratic trends may have been at work: one based on depression-related economic issues and another based on antimachine reform appeals. Separating the two trends is difficult, however, and, indeed, it seems likely that they interacted and reinforced one another. Certainly it is clear that the combination of depression and independent reform experienced in Buffalo, Brooklyn, Albany, Troy, and New York City produced significantly greater shifts there than in other cities or in the state at large.[53]

The sequence of the Republicans' urban gains suggests the special role played by independent reform movements in establishing the party's majority. In all five cities, the shift to the Republicans coincided with or followed a municipal election at which Republicans and independents allied against Democratic machines accused of corruption. In Buffalo and Brooklyn this happened in 1893 and the Republican gains came that year; in the other three cities, the same scenario was played out in 1894. Not only did urban political crises weaken the Democrats locally, but by inspiring municipal fusion campaigns those crises brought many voters all the way into the Republican state coalition.

Contemporaries of various political persuasions had little doubt about the independents' contribution to the Republican majority. Edward M. Shepard, the leader of the dissident Democrats in Brooklyn, lamented that his group's independent candidate for governor received such a small vote and concluded that "a large number of men really belonging to us in politics voted the whole Republican ticket." Other observers thought they detected a permanent change in the character of the electorate. "Great numbers of voters appear . . . to have belonged to one party two years ago and to belong now to the other," declared the *Nation*. "Two years from now they may change their party again." Lincoln Steffens estimated that in New York City alone "at least 45,000 intelligent men, once strong partisans, are today neither Republican nor Democratic. . . . They will swing from side to side, and where they go victory will follow."[54]

Urban independents there were, but it is doubtful that the election of

65

Table 7. New York State Republican vote, 1892–1910: Pearson correlations

	1894	1896	1898	1900	1902	1904	1906	1908	1910
1892	.88	.81	.91	.90	.88	.91	.88	.89	.81
1894		.88	.86	.89	.83	.86	.83	.84	.78
1896			.76	.88	.75	.77	.72	.77	.65
1898				.90	.84	.91	.88	.90	.82
1900					.85	.91	.86	.89	.82
1902						.91	.90	.86	.82
1904							.91	.95	.86
1906								.91	.79
1908									.88

Source: The Appendix describes the electoral data from which these correlations were computed.

1894 actually produced an enduring transformation of the electorate. In several key respects, its character remained partisan and traditional. First, as McSeveney has shown, the Republican majority of the mid-1890s did not come about because of "any dramatic re-shuffling of the bases of support for the rival parties." Gaining among almost all voting groups and in nearly every county, the Republicans generally remained strongest in those areas and among those cultural groups where the party had traditionally established its base. Nor, to judge from county-level correlations, did any profound "re-shuffling" occur during the following sixteen-year period while the party remained in power. (See Table 7.)[55]

Second, the vast majority of voters continued to cast their ballots for major-party candidates for statewide office. In 1894 the minor-party vote for governor reached 6.1 percent, a bit higher than the average for the 1880s, but in succeeding years the percentage dropped back. (See Table 3.) At the assembly level, independent candidacies played a somewhat greater role in 1894, especially in the large cities. In New York City, 17 percent of the assembly vote was cast for other than Republican or Democratic candidates; in Brooklyn, the figure was 15 percent. In the years to come, independent candidates, especially those nominated by nonpartisan "citizens'" groups, continued to contest for assembly seats. Often, however, they did so with the endorsement of one of the major parties.

Voter participation rates also point to the traditional character of the 1894 electorate. Seventy-eight percent of those eligible to do so cast ballots for governor and the other state officers; about 3 percent fewer did so for Congress and assembly. These turnout figures compare favorably with those for gubernatorial elections in the 1880s. While there was a modest tendency for less populated counties to have higher rates of participation (turnout and size of electorate correlate at − .52), there were no dramatic geographic or urban-rural differences in voter turnout. Every upstate county having a large city (over 50,000) equaled or exceeded the statewide turnout level; Brooklyn fell below it by 0.5 percent, while New York City was five points lower with a voter participation rate of 73 percent. Observers generally agreed that the election of 1894 was conducted honestly, certainly more so than elections in New York, Albany, and Troy were said to have been a year earlier. If contemporary opinion can be believed, the recorded levels of voter turnout were not significantly inflated or deflated by dishonesty at the polling place. In succeeding years, those levels would decline, but in 1894 the New York electorate participated as actively as ever.[56]

Finally, the election returns suggest that most voters cast straight and complete tickets for one party or the other. In the great majority of counties, the Republican state candidates, as well as those for assembly and Congress, received very similar votes. The least popular Republican candidate fell behind the party's most successful nominee by a county mean (weighted according to size of the electorate) of only 5.1 percent, a figure almost identical to that registered in the last previous gubernatorial election in 1891. In two-thirds of the counties, the Republican who trailed the ticket fell less than 3 percent short of the ticket-leader's vote. Only downstate, where there were independent assembly candidates, and in three upstate counties, where an independent ran for Congress, did county electorates significantly exceed the mean level of Republican ticket-splitting. The Democrats had somewhat greater difficulty in mustering support for their entire slate of candidates. In almost every county, the party's congressional and assembly nominees ran well behind the state candidates, mainly through Democratic abstentions rather than ticket-splitting. On the average, the least popular Democrat fell 15.4 percent behind the leader's vote. This figure represented an unusually high degree of party failure to obtain support for the whole ticket. In time, such failure would become less unusual.

The election of 1894 brought to a close two years of political and economic crises that placed the Republicans in control of the state government where they would remain for the next sixteen years. Ending an era of electoral stalemate, the Republicans' triumph gave unfettered authority to a party whose traditional activist ideology, together with a newly enlarged urban base, seemed to fit it well to govern an urban-industrial state. In many important respects, however, the political system of New York State was not significantly transformed by the realignment of the mid-1890s. Despite the challenge to party machines brought by an organized minority of urban independents, the campaign and election of 1894 showed how much of the older partisan political culture still persisted. In the face of an economic depression indicating that existing methods of governance were inadequate to meet the needs of a developed industrial society, the political upheaval of 1893–94 by no means produced an immediate adjustment of policy-making to the new economic order. What the realignment years had done, above all, was to reveal the increasing challenges to the tradition-al structure of New York State politics and to bring to power a party whose task it now became to face them.

3

Thomas Collier Platt's
Party Strategy, 1895–1900

In New York State, the electoral realignment of the 1890s trans-ferred power from the Democrats to the Republicans but did not im-mediately bring about new kinds of politics and policies. Considering the political and economic crises through which the system had passed and the forces for reform that had joined the new majority, one might have expected to see a changed political order in the aftermath of the upheaval. But the old order endured, presided over now by a Republi-can boss, Thomas Collier Platt, whose politics were thoroughly grounded in the beliefs and practices that Americans had known since the 1830s and still followed.

Confident that he understood how the Republicans had come into control of the state government in 1893 and 1894, Platt fashioned a strategy for keeping them there. He knew that small-town and rural voters formed the core of the party's support, and he resolved to avoid measures they found objectionable. Platt also felt indebted to the busi-ness and financial interests who had paid for the campaign, and he promised to protect them. In the boss's view, the Republicans' national economic program, centered upon tariff protection, had played a cru-cial role in winning votes, and he believed that national issues should continue to receive the heaviest emphasis at election time. Of most importance, Platt felt, was the Republican machine, which had to be strengthened by added state patronage and a greater role in governing the large cities.

Since the boss never explicitly put these ideas forward as a strategy, the elements of his plan must be deduced from the study of scattered evidence and events. In correspondence with fellow leaders, Platt dis-cussed his methods and hinted at the assumptions behind them. So did the columns and editorials of loyal newspapers. Despite the absence of an articulated party plan, the logic, the completeness, and the coherence of Platt's tactics suggest that they merit the label of party strategy.[1]

For all its strengths, however, Platt's plan for continued Republican success failed to deal with many of the forces already challenging traditional politics and governance in New York. Well suited to an electoral universe in which nearly every voter was a firm partisan, the boss's strategy took little initial account of the urban independents who had contributed to the Republican victory. To be sure, Platt did not ignore the large cities. They were important to him for their wealth and patronage, but he gave scant attention to the changing needs of city voters and the inability of traditional party politics to fill those needs. Nor did Platt significantly acknowledge new economic demands on government. Committed to the nineteenth-century system of government aid to presumably harmonious producer groups, Platt did not recognize the need for policies taking explicit account of the clash of interests. Old-fashioned and traditional, his strategy was intended solely to advance the Republican party, whose strength he deemed a sufficient solution for the political and governmental problems New Yorkers faced. While these limitations were apparent to many people in and out of the party, Platt's approach to politics was far from dead in the last years of the nineteenth century. Indeed, his Republican strategy decisively shaped politics and policy in New York from 1895 to 1900.

Lacking both energy and public appeal, reluctant to speak publicly, and seldom an inspirer of innovative government policies, Thomas Collier Platt did not look like a party leader. Close observers attributed his authority variously to the Republican party's chaotic political situation at the time Platt rose to power in the 1880s, to his unceasing efforts at harmonizing local Republican machines with the state organization, to his straightforward honesty with political associates, and, not least, to his connections with business and financial interests. These elements were critical to Platt's success, but his chief asset was an ability to make the most of the sentiments and techniques of partisanship in an age when many political developments threatened parties.[2]

An early convert to the Republicans, Platt had cast his first vote—for John C. Frémont—in 1856, led torchlight parades for Lincoln, and by the late 1860s had risen to the party chairmanship in his home county of Tioga. Tying his political career closely to the party's leader, U.S. Senator Roscoe Conkling, Platt served two uneventful terms in Congress during the 1870s and afterward won a promotion to the chairmanship of the Republican state committee. A shadowy figure who operated best behind the scenes, Platt kept Conkling's favor, made private peace with Conkling's enemies, and played his role as chairman so deftly that legislators elected him to the U.S. Senate in 1881. Only a few months later, however, Platt and Conkling together resigned from the Senate during a patronage dispute with President James Garfield. Both men sought and failed to win the vindication of reelection. For Conkling, the affair marked the end of a political career and, for Platt, a period of humiliation and seclusion.[3]

Platt soon renewed his political activity, and by the late 1880s he had become the recognized leader of the Republican party in the state. Just how he did it remains what an observer called "one of the marvels of American politics." Conkling's demise had left the Republicans boss-less, disoriented, and frequently beaten at the polls. Platt, who wanted the leadership more than anyone else, took on the hard, hidden work of putting the machine in order and restoring harmony to its divergent elements. Well before the Republicans came to power in the 1890s, he had helped the party put behind it the divisiveness of the 1870s and the disorganization of the early 1880s. Though Platt could take little personal credit for the Republican victories of 1893 and 1894, his leadership had prepared the party organization to make the most of its new electoral majority.[4]

As a loyal Republican, Platt believed in his party's public policies, but above all he stood for the party organization. "Were I asked why I became a Republican," Platt wrote, "I might reply that I could not be a Democrat. Early in life I became a believer in the Hamiltonian theory of politics. From that time I have held consistently to the doctrine of government by party, and rule of the party by the regular organization." That non sequitur, composed late in life, suggests that Platt's Republicanism was simply an article of faith. He could hardly put it into words, but it was nevertheless his deepest conviction. Phrasing his appeals in the language of party loyalty, Platt asked for and received support from local leaders, campaign funds from wealthy men, and votes from the faithful on the grounds of commitment to Republican success. In all honesty he could write that "the main consideration with me in . . . all . . . matters during the whole period of my activity in politics, was what I considered to be the welfare of the Republican party, which I have never discriminated from the welfare of the State and the nation."[5]

To his strong personal partisanship, Platt added considerable skill in the familiar methods of late-nineteenth-century politics. He was a master at managing the hierarchy of party committees and at calling and running harmonious conventions. When the nominations were made, Platt knew how to mold the hundreds of party newspapers into an efficient propaganda machine, to send the right speakers to the right places, and to rouse the voters' enthusiasm. On election day his organization spread the campaign funds judiciously, got the Republicans to the polls, and frustrated Democratic attempts at fraud. When Republicans won office, Platt made the most of the patronage their positions brought and strengthened the party for the next election. These practices were the stock-in-trade of bosses, and Platt performed them well, both before the mid-1890s and afterward.[6] To impose his strategy on the party and the state, however, Platt needed more than an efficient machine. For that, he relied on his particular ability to influence the other leading Republican politicians and to dominate the men who held state office, especially the legislators and governors.

Always an "easy boss," Platt made it a practice to find out where the other leaders would go before he led them there. By letter and telephone he frequently consulted legislators and local bosses on party questions. On Sundays he called them down to meetings at the Fifth Avenue Hotel in New York and sought their advice. Dubbed Platt's "Sunday School," these sessions provided occasion for the give-and-take of leadership opinion on legislation, patronage, and other important matters. In accord with his own style and his position as the leader of the "respectable" Republican party, Platt spoke softly and behaved decorously at these meetings. While his views did not always prevail, he was usually able to reconcile antagonistic leaders and send them back home with firm commitments to a common program.[7]

Twenty men, including Platt, can be identified as having held significant power at the highest levels of Republican politics between 1895 and 1900. (See Table 8.) They included legislative leaders like Senate President Timothy E. Ellsworth of Lockport and Assembly Speaker S. Fred Nixon of Westfield in Chautauqua County; upstate city bosses like William Barnes, Jr., of Albany, Francis Hendricks of Syracuse, George Washington Aldridge of Rochester, and John Hazel of Buffalo; as well as such long-standing Platt confidants as Benjamin F. Tracy and Lou Payn. Most of the twenty leaders stood at the head of their local party machines, and nearly all held public office at some time during their careers.[8]

Local political prominence had come early in life to many of the leaders. Aldridge chaired Rochester's Executive Board and controlled most of its patronage at age twenty-eight. Barnes owned both of Albany's leading Republican newspapers at age twenty-three and began service on the Republican state committee at twenty-six. Nixon became town supervisor at twenty-six and a year later advanced to his county's Republican leadership and to the assembly. J. Sloat Fassett owned a daily newspaper in Elmira when he was twenty-six and reached the state senate at thirty. These were ambitious men; most

Four members of Platt's organization (*from left*): Michael J. Dady, Louis F. Payn, Timothy L. Woodruff, and George W. Aldridge (Library of Congress)

Table 8. A profile of twenty New York State Republican leaders

Leader	Residence*	Birthplace†	Age in 1895	College attended	Primary field of occupation	Highest public office, 1895–1900
G. W. Aldridge	Rochester	Michigan City, Ind.	39	none	manufacturing	state superintendent of public works
J. P. Allds	Chenango County	Claremont, N.H.	30	Colgate	law	assemblyman
W. Barnes, Jr.	Albany	Albany	29	Harvard	publishing	surveyor of customs, Albany
C. M. Depew	New York City	Peekskill	61	Yale	railroads	U.S. senator
G. W. Dunn	Binghamton	Castle Creek	55	none	banking, manufacturing	state railroad commissioner
T. E. Ellsworth	Lockport	East Windsor, Conn.	59	Rochester	law	state senator
J. S. Fassett	Elmira	Elmira	42	Rochester	law	none
J. R. Hazel	Buffalo	Buffalo	35	none	law	U.S. district court judge
F. Hendricks	Syracuse	Kingston	61	none	photo supply	state superintendent of insurance
O. Kelsey	Livingston County	Rochester	43	none	law	assemblyman
E. Lauterbach	New York City	New York City	51	CCNY	law	none
S. F. Nixon	Chautauqua County	Westfield	35	Hamilton	farming, manufacturing	assembly speaker
B. B. Odell, Jr.	Newburgh	Newburgh	41	Columbia††	banking, utilities	congressman
L. F. Payn	Columbia County	Chatham	60	none	business	state superintendent of insurance
T. C. Platt	New York City	Owego	62	Yale††	business	U.S. senator
L. E. Quigg	New York City	Cecil County, Md.	32	none	journalism	congressman
J. Raines	Ontario County	Canandaigua	55	Union Law	law	state senator
B. F. Tracy	New York City	Owego	65	none	law	president, New York City charter commission
C. P. Vedder	Cattaraugus County	Ellicottville	57	none	law	none
T. L. Woodruff	Brooklyn	New Haven, Conn.	37	Yale	business	lieutenant governor

*City or county.
†New York State, unless otherwise noted.
††Attended but did not graduate.

S. Fred Nixon (*Red Book*, 1905)

William Barnes, Jr. (*New York State Men*)

John Raines (*New York State Men*)

dreamed of the governorship, and one or two thought of the White House. Any of them would have been pleased to replace Platt as state leader; soon after 1900 one of them, Benjamin B. Odell, Jr., did.

In 1895 the twenty party leaders averaged forty-eight years of age. All were native-born, fourteen in upstate New York. Half of them still had for their political base the very town or county of their birth. Eight of the twenty had graduated from college, and one had a law school education; two others, Platt and his successor-to-be as state leader, Odell, had attended college without graduating. The remaining leaders received their education in the common schools, high schools, and academies.

Virtually all twenty carried on successful careers outside politics, though only Chauncey Depew, as chairman of the board of the New York Central Railroad, was a truly eminent businessman. Eleven of the leaders chiefly followed commercial, financial, or manufacturing pursuits, while nine were lawyers. Almost all had "interests" in a wide range of businesses. Platt was involved in banking, railroads, and lumbering, in addition to his main business as president of the United States Express Company. Edward Lauterbach, a lawyer, specialized in organizing railroads and served several lines as an officer. Newspaper writer and editor Lemuel E. Quigg had substantial utility and street railway interests, while George Washington Dunn of Binghamton managed that city's leading newspaper and served various manufacturing and banking concerns. Many of the leaders mixed business and politics. Platt's express company for many years held a lucrative federal contract to transport the government's bullion and securities. Barnes's publishing company won numerous state printing jobs. Depew's usefulness to the Vanderbilt family, who owned the New York Central Railroad, substantially depended on his political connections. According to prevailing standards, most of these men were not dishonest, though at least three of them apparently took a bribe at least once.[9]

If "conservative" means acceptance of special privileges for the business class and of rule by party machines, then these twenty men all qualified as conservatives. In another sense, it is a misleading term, for they were not ideologues, except perhaps in later years when challenged by "progressives." Ambitious for political influence, these men saw the path to power through support for existing standards of public policy and through the regular party organization. Few of them crusaded for innovative legislation, and none dealt with political ideas. Like Platt, they supported their party's policies, but mostly they supported the party organization.

While Platt dominated the Republican machine through his close

Chauncey M. Depew (Library of Congress)

relations with other leaders, it was the boss's influence in the legislature that gave him his handle on the state. Despite growing sentiment for curtailing its powers, the legislature remained the most powerful branch of government. Unlike congressmen whose sphere of action the federal constitution restricted to particular subjects, New York legislators had the power to make law on any topic not expressly excluded from their province. With its latitude so broad, the legislature held the key to making the policies Platt's strategy called for.

The boss's influence in the legislature began with his oversight of nominations. "I want to ask you," Platt characteristically wrote to an upstate leader, "what has been done or what is being done to secure strong nominations from your [assembly] districts?" Once trustworthy candidates were named, Platt distributed the campaign funds among them. Party leaders from around the state appealed to him for support in their districts. One year Barnes of Albany asked "if something additional could be done for . . . Nussbaum in the third district and Foster in the second." If so, Barnes promised, "their election can be made certain."[10]

After the election, Platt exercised considerable power to choose the legislative officers and, with their help, to determine committee assignments. For purposes of party unity in 1895, Platt acquiesced in the selection of his onetime opponent, Hamilton Fish, for assembly speaker, but only after Fish had promised "I am with the machine now. I am going to be a part of it." Two years later, the stalwart James M. E. O'Grady of Rochester replaced Fish, and in 1899 the honor fell to S. Fred Nixon. Serving as speaker until his death in 1905, Nixon established records both for longevity in that office and for sheer power over legislation. He became a powerful ally of Platt.[11]

During the session the boss kept in careful touch with the legislators, by letter and telephone and in person. He visited Albany and conferred privately with the leaders. More frequently, they came down to visit him at the Fifth Avenue Hotel. In ordering Speaker Fish to kill one particular measure, the boss pointedly added, "I cannot explain by letter but will when I see you on Sunday when I hope you will be here [in New York City] without fail."[12]

The legislators whom Platt controlled in the late 1890s were, like the party leaders, mostly unexceptional men of native birth and middle-class occupations. Roughly one-third of the Republican assemblymen were professionals, most of them lawyers. Another one-sixth farmed, while the remaining half followed commercial or manufacturing pursuits. Many were merchants; others sold real estate and insurance or worked as brokers, clerks, and agents. Some were middle-class jacksof-all-trade and moved from job to job. Relatively few assembly members earned livings as craftsmen; fewer still performed semiskilled or unskilled labor. Not many lived in either poverty or great wealth. Virtually none had a distinguished career outside politics.[13]

The Republicans always had majorities in the senate and assembly during these years, and upstate members dominated the party's delegations. Usually the Republicans achieved or approached majorities in both houses even without the votes of their downstate members. Upstate legislators chaired most of the important committees. While spokesmen for New York City and Brooklyn frequently complained that their concerns were placed "in the hands of country assemblymen," small-town and rural New Yorkers proudly took note of their own section's potency in the lawmaking body. "Really western New York was 'right in it' this year," a newspaper in Nixon's county observed in commenting on legislative assignments, "and mighty near 'the whole thing.' "[14]

A look at the 1899 legislature provides further understanding of the institution upon which Platt's influence in government depended. The Republicans controlled the senate by twenty-seven to twenty-three and were even more dominant in the assembly, which they led eighty-seven to sixty-three. In both chambers, upstate party members fell just short of a majority without the help of downstate Republicans. While every Republican senator chaired a committee, upstaters headed the most powerful committees, including finance, judiciary, canals, railroads, and taxation. Brooklyn and New York senators led lesser ones on revision, printed and engrossed bills, and military affairs. All four downstate members sat on the important cities committee, but its chairman came from Fulton, population 5,281. In the assembly, New York and Brooklyn members filled five of thirty-six chairmanships, including taxation and cities.[15]

New York's legislature was not yet sufficiently "institutionalized" for seniority automatically to determine positions of leadership. Platt, together with the assembly speaker and senate president, made committee appointments according to their estimates of the members' reliability. But because few legislators served more than two or three terms in Albany, those who did so acquired considerable authority. In 1899 the two most senior Republican assemblymen, Nixon and Otto Kelsey, each in his sixth consecutive one-year term, served respectively as speaker and judiciary committee chairman. Among the thirteen Republicans who were serving at least their third term in the assembly, all but one had chairmanships. Of the forty-four Republican assemblymen who had not sat in the 1898 legislature—half the party's total delegation—only four headed committees. With so few assemblymen having more than two years' seniority, power tended to be concentrated in the hands of a small number of men who were known to be reliable.[16]

The lawmakers of 1899 were not, however, new to politics. Since prior service in the assembly was normally necessary to reach the senate, fully 81 percent of the Republican senators boasted legislative experience, compared to only 54 percent of the assemblymen. Even the legislative newcomers were not political neophytes. Each of the five senate Republicans serving in Albany for the first time had held local office or run previously for the legislature. Of the forty assembly Republicans with no previous legislative service, twenty had held local office, seventeen others had been active party workers or convention delegates, while only three had seen little political activity before 1899.

Experienced in politics, the legislators were not generally powerful men. Few could claim to lead the Republican party in their home counties; only a handful had worked intimately with Platt in the Republican state organization. Most had loyally done enough political work to earn a term or two in Albany, but few had the stature to dare defy Platt there. They would roll logs to build bridges and monuments for their home towns, work hard for the party's interests as others defined them, and vote as they were told by the man who seemed to have a strategy for keeping the Republicans in power.[17]

The lawmakers' relative lack of distinction and their submission to Platt fueled criticism of the legislature and led to efforts to curtail its authority. Discontent with legislative government was, of course, a historic American theme. For a century, a slow trend had taken its toll on the power of state lawmakers by shortening their sessions, forbidding them to pass certain kinds of laws, and burdening them with procedural limitations. Now in the 1890s these pressures continued from those who distrusted the legislature to deal with increasingly specialized matters of governance. Every state executive of the period sought in a different way to lessen legislative powers. Governor Levi P. Morton supported procedural reforms; his successor, Frank S. Black, proposed biennial instead of annual sessions; while Governor Theodore Roosevelt chose critical moments to rally public opinion against the legislature. Although these efforts generally failed, they helped prepare for a real weakening of the lawmakers' role in the following decade. For the time being, however, the legislature remained a potent governmental tool in Platt's hands.[18]

In 1897 its members elected him U.S. senator. A month before the balloting Platt had informed Lemuel E. Quigg, "I shall not announce myself as a candidate or attempt to make any personal contest for the position. Somebody will touch the button and the Republicans will do the rest." When the button was touched, Platt received 142 out of 149 votes in the Republican caucus. Election by the whole legislature rapidly followed. Hundreds of letters of congratulation poured in upon Platt. Many cited the contrast between his present triumph and the humiliation of his resignation from the Senate in 1881. Others simply assured Platt of support for his party strategy. As one assemblyman put it, "I am an advocate of your methods, for the advancement of Republican principles and their ultimate success."[19]

If there was a weak link in the chain of factors that made it possible for Platt to carry out his strategy, it was his relationship to the governor. A prestigious office, with numerous constitutional and ceremonial functions, the governorship inevitably encouraged anyone who attained it to distance himself from the boss. By the 1890s, moreover, the tradition of executive subservience to the legislature was weakening, and governors became increasingly inclined to propose, as well as execute, a program of government. While these factors limited Platt's influence over the state executive, other circumstances strengthened his hand. New York's administrative system was sufficiently decentralized so that the governor lacked authority over most department heads, many of whom Platt controlled. With only a two-year term, moreover, the governor soon found himself dependent on the boss for renomination or advancement. Men who reached the governorship of New York usually aspired to the U.S. Senate or even to the presidency. This was true of Levi P. Morton, Frank S. Black, and Theodore Roosevelt, all of whom Platt influenced.[20]

Morton, who was elected governor in 1894, wanted to be president and curiously placed his faith in Platt to secure that office for him in 1896. At crucial moments, Platt dangled the presidency before the governor as an incentive to follow the boss's program. When gubernatorial action was required, Platt stayed in constant touch with Morton and kept the pressure on him. "I received your messages over the telephone and by telegram yesterday," the governor responded to Platt one time. "Late last evening your three special delivery letters arrived and all have been fully considered." On appointments and legislation Morton sought the boss's advice and normally took it, but occasionally he showed resentment of Platt's domination. Morton's most significant act of defiance, the promulgation of new civil service rules, significantly came late in 1896, by which time the presidency has passed him by.[21]

Black, who served as governor in 1897 and 1898, aspired to a seat in the U.S. Senate, and Platt played on that ambition. Like Morton, Black usually gratified the boss where patronage and policies were concerned, but he was less inclined to consult Platt regularly. During the spring of 1897, the governor made a brief effort to build up a machine of his own. Adeptly distributing state patronage, Black seems for a time to have enhanced his own power at Platt's expense. By the next year, however, the governor had resubmitted to Platt's authority in hope of renomination.[22]

Even the most independent of Platt's three governors, Theodore Roosevelt, accepted the need to consult the boss. Their frequent breakfast meetings in New York City during 1899 and 1900 often resulted in appointments or laws Platt wanted. In several celebrated instances Roosevelt defied the boss, but only after trying to find common ground with him. Their relationship, to be considered in the following chapter, did not, on balance, weaken Platt.[23]

Through his influence on legislators and governors, Platt exercised a significant impact on state policies from 1895 to 1900. His ties to appointed officials additionally allowed Platt to say a good deal about the administration and enforcement of government decisions. The policies he chose provided critical elements of his strategy for keeping the Republicans in power.

But the boss did not decide everything the state did. Many measures did not concern Platt or interested him only for the patronage they provided rather than for the programs they established. Most state functions reflected pressures and trends that antedated 1895 and continued beyond 1900. It is important to distinguish those undertakings and decisions that were intrinsic to Platt's strategy from those that would probably have come about if another leader, or another political party, had held the reins of power.

One starting point for policy analysis is the examination of categories of legislation. Each year during the Platt era, the lawmakers wrote between 747 and 1,048 new statutes, more than two-thirds of which affected special subjects, such as single individuals, businesses, or places. The remaining laws concerned general topics, including government itself, state services and institutions, and economic activities regulated by the state. From 1894 to 1900, the distribution of general laws by subject underwent little change. The percentage of statutes on corporations, for instance, varied from a low of 10.6 percent (in 1899) to a high of 17.9 percent (in 1896), but there was no trend. The proportion of legislative attention devoted to other subjects also remained fairly steady.[24]

A more meaningful measure of policy than the number of laws on different topics is the level of expenditures for government functions and services. From 1894 to 1900, state costs rose from $15.8 million to $22.9 million, a growth of 45 percent. While the average yearly increases somewhat exceeded those during the previous thirteen years of Democratic administration, only a small number of new expenditures reflected distinct Republican choices.[25]

Several categories of expenditure rose only slowly, at about the same rate as did total state costs. (See Fig. 3.) The expenses for all branches of the government itself, as well as those for charitable institutions, roughly followed this pattern. Certain other governmental expenditures changed little during this period and, as overall costs rose, came to account for smaller fractions of the total. This was true of educational

Figure 3. Growth of New York State expenditures, 1894–1900: percentage increases for selected major categories of government expenditures

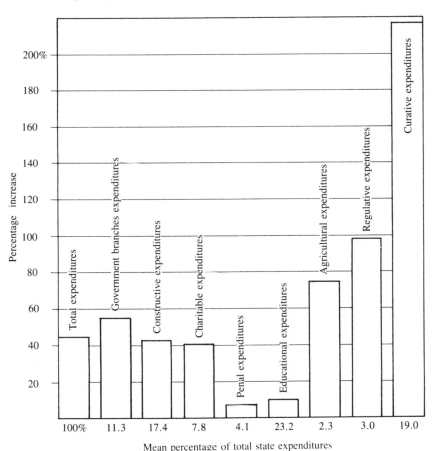

and penal expenses. In general, expenditures for the government's most traditional tasks and services rose incrementally year by year or remained fairly steady. Shaped by long-term demographic and economic factors, these costs would almost certainly have been about the same with another boss or another party in power.[26]

Expenditures for major constructive undertakings, such as the state capitol, the Erie Canal, and highways, followed irregular patterns from 1894 to 1900. While the Republican administration controlled these costs, it is highly possible they would have been quite similar under the Democrats. The new capitol, in construction since the 1860s, had received funding at the hands of both parties. Canal and road improvements were managed by the Republicans, but, to judge from legislative roll calls and popular referenda, were most enthusiastically received in the large Democratic cities. There is no reason to suppose the Democrats would not have undertaken these projects.[27]

Agricultural, regulative, and curative expenditures all rose more steeply than overall state costs. Under the Republicans, the government expanded its payments to local agricultural societies, enlarged the Agriculture Department's duties, and created a state veterinary college, a college of forestry, and an experiment station at Cornell University. While the cost of most established regulatory functions rose only slowly year by year, the initiation of state supervision of the liquor traffic and of elections in the New York City metropolitan area added considerably to the state's regulative expenditures. Curative costs for care of the insane increased more than any other class of expenses, as the state gradually took over from county governments the burden of support for insane asylums. Under a policy begun before the Republicans came into office, these institutions became the state's second most costly undertaking, only narrowly surpassed by schools.[28]

Many of New York State's expenses in the late 1890s were thus beyond the Republicans' sole control. Of the two largest classes of expenditure, education and care of the insane, one remained little changed and the other increased because of a policy supported by both parties. Only a few expenditures reflected innovations for which Platt and his party bore direct responsibility. These included regulation of the liquor traffic and of downstate elections, increased agricultural services, canal improvement, and road construction. All were important policies, but they were far from comprising the whole of the state's duties and costs.

A third way to analyze the government's policies is by examining broad trends in its activities. In the late 1890s, three related developments were enlarging the state's tasks: the centralization of government services and institutions, the regulation of private undertakings, and the control of local governments. Since all three trends antedated the Republican era, it becomes necessary to identify the handful of policies for which Platt's party was actually responsible.[29]

Prisons, charities, and insane asylums headed the list of institutions that came under centralized control. For all three, however, the changes began prior to 1895 and occurred without significant partisan controversy. The 1894 constitutional convention had mandated the establishment of a Commission of Prisons, and a year later the legislature created such a board. Empowered to oversee both state and local jails, the new commission collected data, required reports, and ordered the improvement of conditions. The convention of 1894 also gave constitutional recognition and increased authority to the State Board of Charities. Laws adopted in 1895 and 1896 confirmed the convention's mandate by giving the board powers of inspection and supervision over all public and private charitable institutions. The state's assumption of responsibility for the indigent insane, noted above, began in 1893 under the jurisdiction of the Commission in Lunacy. Recognized by the new constitution, the commission expanded its duties in 1895 and 1896 when asylums in the counties of Kings and New York finally came under the state system.[30]

The ongoing trend toward the supervision of private undertakings inspired only minor policy changes during the Platt era. Banking, railroad, and insurance companies continued to be mildly supervised by the state, but no other large classes of business came under regulation. The Board of Factory Inspectors doubled its force of deputies, and the Forest, Fish, and Game Commission centralized the regulation of certain forest and fish interests. In 1895 the State Racing Commission was given authority to supervise horse racing. But otherwise the Republicans initiated no new policies of regulation in the 1890s.[31]

The party's most innovative measures fell in the third broad policy area, state control of local governments. Such supervision was scarcely unprecedented, however. In the 1850s and 1860s the state had briefly taken over the departments of fire, police, and health in the downstate cities.[32] More recently, various state boards and officials had been assuming increased authority to oversee local governmental functions. Schools, charities, prisons, hospitals, civil service appointments, highways, and tax collection all were under state regulation, to greater or lesser degrees. In the 1890s the Republicans accelerated this trend. Beginning in 1896, a new Department of Excise took control of the liquor traffic out of local hands. Two years later the state government began supervising downstate elections. The most dramatic case of interference in local government came when the state consolidated New York, Brooklyn, and the surrounding towns into Greater New York City. These measures clearly bore Platt's imprint. He found the continuing trend toward state control over local governments well suited to his party's needs.

Despite the party's grip on all branches of government and Platt's grip on the party, much of what New York State did in the late 1890s bore no relation to the boss's strategy. The unchanged distribution of general legislation, the incremental growth of many state expenditures, and the continuation of earlier policy trends all suggest that most state policies would have been carried out even if another man had led the Republicans or if the Democrats had been in power. Certain governmental decisions plainly reflected Republican purposes, however, particularly state intervention in the affairs of cities and regulation of the liquor traffic.

In the New York legislature, policy concerning cities drew a line between the parties as did no other subject. While most legislative roll calls were unanimous, and most of the rest failed to produce a clear division along party lines, the subject of cities proved uniquely capable of eliciting partisan votes. In 1899 the state senate voted along party lines (that is, at least 90 percent of the members of each party voted together against the other party) forty-seven times. Nineteen of those votes (40 percent) concerned Greater New York City and nine (19 percent) affected other cities in the state. In the assembly, the percentages were even higher. Forty-five (48 percent) of ninety-three party votes there concerned New York City, while twenty (22 percent) pertained to other cities. The number of partisan roll calls on economic subjects was strikingly small. Each house divided along party lines only seven times with an economic measure at stake. The relative rarity of party votes in 1899, as well as the distribution of the few there were, suggests that on most matters the Republican majority did not make policy. But when issues arose that involved the cities, the party had a program.[33]

Because the cities' charters, their boundaries, and, indeed, their very existence depended on the government at Albany, the party in power had access to any number of devices for increasing its share of patronage and authority in the great Democratic cities. Some of the measures succeeded and fulfilled Platt's purposes, while others fell to the vetoes of governors who were less tied to the boss than the legislature was. One device was the legislative investigation. On the pretext of gathering information necessary to lawmaking, legislators took testimony calculated to embarrass and discredit local Democratic officials. In

1899 an assembly committee chaired by Robert Mazet made a full-scale investigation of the government of Greater New York City, then under Tammany control. Sitting from April until December, the Mazet committee uncovered sensational evidence of corruption and personal profiteering that compared with the revelations of the Lexow investigation of 1894. Platt supported the Mazet inquiry from the beginning. He used his influence to insure its full funding by the legislature and to stifle the investigation when it threatened to trespass on Republican interests.[34]

Another tactic was tinkering with city charters. Sometimes called "ripper bills," such measures had the purpose of putting one group out of office and another in. One of them, in 1895, would have replaced the three-member charities commission of Brooklyn with a single commissioner appointed by a board composed of the supervisor-at-large, the sheriff, and the county clerk. Known to be a device to give Platt's local henchman (who controlled the sheriff and the clerk) authority over public charities in Brooklyn, the bill excited public opposition and, to Platt's dismay and disgust, received Governor Morton's veto.[35]

Allegations of electoral fraud in the Democratic cities inspired several successful Republican measures. In 1898 the Metropolitan Election District law established state supervision over elections in New York City and some nearby towns. Headed by a superintendent of elections and staffed by seven hundred deputies, the new bureaucracy possessed considerable powers of investigation and enforcement. The following year another measure expanded the state's oversight of New York City elections.[36]

The most common device Platt used to control the Democratic cities was the bipartisan police board. The immense power of the police over the lives of urban citizens, the value and prestige of appointments to the department, the potential for graft, and the police's authority to supervise elections all lent weight to the Republicans' claim on a share of police power. Platt's party framed police bills carefully in accord with local circumstances and adjusted the provisions to assure the appointment of reliable Republicans to the board. Evaluating an 1895 police bill for Staten Island, Platt told Speaker Fish that modifications were needed to "make it more palatable as a Republican measure."[37]

On straight party votes, the legislature revamped the police force of West Troy in 1895 and the next year overhauled the Albany department. The West Troy law provided for the election of two police commissioners to a four-member board and for the automatic appointment of the two losing candidates. Win or lose, the Republicans would have two members. The Albany law transferred the power to name police board members from the mayor to the common council. In doing so, it precisely reflected the city's political situation since a Democrat had won the mayoralty the year before while the Republicans retained control of the council. Platt's party defended these measures on the grounds of the need to protect the purity of elections, but most Democrats, as well as independents, agreed with the New York *Evening Post* in regarding them as part of "a general raid upon the cities of the state."[38]

The best place to "raid" was New York City. Early in 1895, the Lexow investigating committee's final report aided Platt's design by advising the creation of a four-man, bipartisan police board, for which the county committees of the two major parties would virtually name the members. The Lexow committee also recommended that the governor be empowered to appoint three commissioners to "reorganize" the New York City police. With regular Republican membership on the police board written into law and with "reform" in the hands of a friendly governor, the most important agency of government in the state's largest city would belong at least partly to the Republican machine. Once again, however, Morton succumbed to public protests and, in the end, Platt got his bipartisan board but not the gubernatorial commission.[39] Two further devices for controlling the police in Democratic cities interested Platt: a metropolitan police agency covering the entire New York City region and a state constabulary, or central police force, covering all the cities of the state. From 1897 on, the boss tried but failed to obtain one or the other of these systems.[40]

The most ambitious and successful expression of Platt's strategy toward the cities came in 1896 and 1897 when the legislature consolidated Brooklyn and New York and approved a charter for the unified metropolis. With roots as early as the 1830s, the movement to join the two cities had become more compelling as they grew larger and more interdependent. Commercial and real estate interests that favored economic and social advancement on a metropolitan scale pressed continually for union. So did upper-class reformers who saw in consolidation an opportunity to improve New York City's ungainly government and divorce administration from politics. While the movement met resistance from many in Brooklyn who valued their political autonomy, even across the East River consolidation won support from those who saw that unification with New York would enhance Brooklyn's growth and lower its tax rate. For all the dreams and calculations of two-thirds of a century, the drive to join the cities succeeded when it did because the leader of the Republicans believed it to be in his organization's interest.[41]

In the aftermath of an 1894 referendum showing that consolidation had overwhelming support in New York while it evenly divided the citizens of Brooklyn, Governor Morton's annual message of January 1895 treated unification as practically a fait accompli. "The people of the cities involved . . . have declared by popular vote in favor of this consolidation," he said, "and it now becomes the duty of the Legislature . . . to carry their wishes into effect." Upon the governor's recommendation, and with Platt's support, the assembly voted to create a commission to frame a charter for the unified city. In the senate, Brooklyn legislators, who knew their constituents to be divided on consolidation, demanded a provision for submitting the charter to the voters. Platt opposed such a referendum, perhaps because he doubted the kind of charter he wanted could win approval, and senators loyal to him defeated it. The standoff on the question of popular submission killed the unification bill for 1895. As Morton's private secretary told Platt, "It would undoubtedly have passed if the referendum amendment had been suitable to yourself and your friends."[42]

The resistance to unification came from several sources. Many up-state people instinctively opposed enlarging a metropolis made up of social and cultural elements they considered alien. In Brooklyn, a similar sentiment prevailed among those who were attached to the old city's middle-class, Protestant traditions and who feared the consequences of joining with Manhattan, which was more Catholic and Jewish. The danger of Tammanyizing Brooklyn particularly aroused critics of unification. The worst result of consolidation, said one, "lies in the loss of good government threatened thereby. . . . Would we not, in all fairness, simply be putting ourselves into the power of a city whose people have governed themselves very, very ill?" Republican leaders in Brooklyn worried that their city, which had gone against the Democrats in 1893, 1894, and 1895, would now, as Mayor Frederick W. Wurster warned Morton, "vote against the Republican party that forced . . . [consolidation] upon her."[43]

Morton sympathized with these apparently sincere views, so many of which came from Republicans, and, to Platt's dismay, encouraged a full debate on unification. Unlike his 1895 message, Morton's 1896 address did not take consolidation for granted but instead recommended its "earnest and careful consideration." The governor wrote to the boss's close friend Benjamin F. Tracy that he was "alarmed as to the possible effect upon the interests of the party of disregarding the strongly expressed views of many leading citizens of Brooklyn." After the "struggle to establish the ascendancy of the Republican party in that hitherto Democratic stronghold," Morton felt Brooklyn could only "be held as a Republican city if treated with consideration by our own people."[44]

Although the governor had asked Tracy to discuss the matter with Platt, he was probably not prepared for the boss's withering response. "I was disgusted and disheartened when General Tracy handed me . . . your letter," Platt wrote. The boss berated Morton for backing away from settled party policy and for the governor's message, which Platt called "weak as dishwater." He went on cruelly to raise the matter of Morton's presidential prospects. "This whole business utterly discourages and demoralizes me," Platt said, "and it makes me wonder what would be the result if you succeeded in becoming President of the United States and had to meet such issues as are involved in the questions of the present hour, for instance, the Venezuelan question and the Bond question." If the Greater New York measure failed, Platt threatened, "I will not feel like taking off my coat and doing the work I contemplated doing in the Presidential matter."[45]

Several considerations underlay Platt's support for a policy that leading Republican officeholders believed dangerous for their party. For one thing, it was far from clear that Tammany would control the unified city. In 1894 the Republican state ticket had carried the combined area that would form Greater New York. A year later the Democrats had won a plurality there, but in 1896 the Republicans had a majority. Some Republican spokesmen believed that consolidation would actually help rather than hurt the party that accomplished it. The Republicans' recent gains in the metropolitan region, plus the popularity of unification, might permanently shift the consolidated city against the Democrats.[46]

Even short of electoral success, Platt had other possibilities in mind for Greater New York. A politically unified, uniquely large metropolitan region provided a strong case for state interference in local affairs. The boss planned to supplement consolidation by creating state commissions to run New York's police, health, fire, and public works departments until the greater city's new charter took effect, or perhaps even permanently. Morton's opposition, as well as hostility from the civic and commercial interests behind consolidation, killed the chances for commissions in 1896, but the possibility remained that conditions in the unified city would "demand" state intervention in the future. At the very least, unification gave a state-appointed board the opportunity to frame a city charter favorable to the Republicans.[47]

Consolidation also strengthened Platt's hand in dealing with rival political interests in the metropolitan region, especially independents and Democrats. Mayor William L. Strong's fusion administration in

New York City had deeply disappointed Platt by failing to give adequate recognition to regular Republicans. Consolidation offered the boss the opportunity either to legislate Strong out of office or at least to confuse and preoccupy his independent supporters by creating uncertainty about the future of their city's government. The same uncertainties helped Platt in his dealings with Tammany boss Richard Croker. While there is no surviving evidence of a deal between Platt and Croker, the possibility that the consolidated city would have a Republican majority plus the heightened threat of state interference may well have persuaded Croker to agree to share the spoils whether Greater New York was Democratic or Republican, locally controlled or state run.[48]

With some help from Croker, Platt forced consolidation through the legislature in 1896. In the assembly, sixty-three Republicans favored unification, while thirty-seven, including all eleven of the party's representatives from Brooklyn, opposed it. In the senate, twenty-eight Republicans voted for the bill, while five, including two of three from Kings County, disapproved it. A majority of Democrats favored the measure in both houses. Providing for the unification on January 1, 1898, of New York, Kings, and Richmond counties, Long Island City, Newtown, Flushing, and Jamaica, the bill established a fifteen-member commission to write a charter for the consolidated city and present it to the legislature by February 1, 1897.[49]

Opposition to the measure arose from predictable quarters. Even many who favored consolidation in principle distrusted a law that unified the cities without spelling out the terms of union or the form of government. Critics also complained that the charter commission could not possibly complete its task by early 1897 and that Platt intended such a failure to justify governing the city from Albany. Sharing these concerns, Mayors Strong and Wurster returned the bill without approval and thus brought it again before the legislature. Despite the defection of Tammany assemblymen, who now apparently feared that the Republicans might actually succeed in governing the city through state boards, the consolidation measure was repassed and sent to Morton. Using his usual form of persuasion, Platt told the governor, "I am exceedingly anxious to have this out of the way, . . . so I can devote all my energies to the national campaign." On May 11, 1896, Morton signed the law.[50]

The next year, the charter commission, on which regular Republicans formed the largest but by no means the sole element, reported a plan of government for the unified city. An immense, rambling document, admitted even by its framers to contain incongruities and repetitions, the proposed charter reflected a series of compromises among the different interests favoring consolidation and aroused little enthusiasm from any of them. Some of its features, such as new provisions for the regulation of public service franchises and for an expansion of home rule on fiscal matters, found favor among city reformers. Other provisions, including the dispersal of power among five borough governments and the multiplicity of new offices met criticism. Opponents especially attacked the bipartisan police board with its continued power to supervise elections. The *New York Times* called the document a "machine-made charter" designed to prevent nonpartisan government. Theorists of municipal government, such as Dorman B. Eaton, Albert Shaw, and Frank Goodnow, also criticized the plan.[51]

Braving these assaults, Platt called for the charter's passage without the "dotting of an i or the crossing of a t," and he continued to entertain the possibility of establishing temporary commissions to govern the soon-to-be-consolidated city. To his ally George Washington Aldridge, Platt wrote, "I hope you will take hold and help urge the Greater New York bill through promptly, so that if necessary supplementary legislation can be had by the present Legislature." The party's assemblymen and senators overwhelmingly complied with Platt's wishes, while Democrats in both houses opposed the charter by two-to-one margins. When Strong's veto sent the bill before the legislature a second time, the Republicans repassed it without debate. Governor Black held perfunctory hearings on the measure, and he approved it early in May 1897. Accepting the pen Black used to sign the charter, Platt felt hope that New York City now had a Republican plan of government.[52]

While Greater New York was perhaps Platt's most lasting legislative achievement, no act was more central to his strategy than the Raines liquor law of 1896. Establishing the state regulation and taxation of traffic in alcoholic beverages, the Raines law provided multiple benefits for the Republican organization. It took the troublesome liquor issue out of politics, gave the party new offices to fill, deprived the Democrats of an alliance with the liquor interests, and created a major new source of state revenue. Harshly criticized but also highly successful, the law represented the most original policy initiative ever taken by a boss not generally known for imaginative government programs.[53]

From the early 1880s until 1896, the liquor issue had injected more volatility into New York State politics than any other local question. Fueled by the desire to impose Protestant standards of behavior on the community, temperance sentiment flourished in northern and western New York where in the early 1890s the Prohibition party ran well ahead of its statewide average of 2.5 percent of the total vote. To prevent the drys from defecting, the Republicans had flirted with a number of policies to satisfy them: local option, high license fees for saloons, and even a prohibitory constitutional amendment. The enactment of any of these, however, would almost certainly have produced a backlash among voters concerned with "personal liberty."[54]

In New York City, the liquor question had another face that also proved dangerous to the Republicans: the Sunday closing of saloons. While Tammany administrations had applied the Sunday law only against saloon keepers who refused to subsidize the Democratic machine, in 1895, Theodore Roosevelt, one of the fusion administration's new police commissioners, began rigorously enforcing the rule. Roosevelt's policy alienated Germans who had supported the anti-Tammany coalition in 1894 but who preferred the Democrats' "liberal" Sunday. The police commissioner's actions also disturbed Republican leaders who feared a voter reaction against the closings. Against the advice of Platt, who hoped to avoid so divisive an issue, the rural-dominated Republican state convention of 1895 endorsed the Sunday rule, while in New York City the party virtually repudiated it. At the local election that fall, many German voters evidently returned to the Democrats, and observers blamed Roosevelt.[55] The next year Platt sought and found a way to remove the liquor issue from politics.

In his annual message of 1896, Governor Morton dealt cautiously with the problem. He cited figures showing that New York State had one saloon for every 150 people, compared to a nationwide ratio of 278. Without mentioning other facets of the liquor issue or proposing any particular plan, Morton vaguely called for a law reducing the number of saloons.[56]

Within days after the governor's message, Senator John Raines introduced a bill that went far beyond Morton's limited goal. Abolishing the local excise boards in whose hands liquor regulation rested, Raines's bill, as finally passed, established in their place a State Department of Excise to be staffed by a commissioner, deputy commissioners, and sixty special agents. The measure taxed saloons at graduated rates according to local population. One-third of the revenue would go to the state, two-thirds to local governments. Raines's bill also laid down restrictions on where, when, and by whom liquor could be sold.[57]

The outcry against the measure came swiftly, particularly from those who considered it a Republican ploy for added patronage and further state control of the cities. Critics noted that the bill perversely set high liquor taxes in urban areas where little demand existed for such regulation and low rates where the temperance movement flourished. The bill further rankled city residents by continuing the ban on Sunday sales except in hotels, and by such petty interference with local drinking customs as a ban upon free lunches in bars. While the measure took account of upstate sentiment by allowing local option on prohibiting liquor sales altogether, it did not permit city voters any comparable choice on the question that troubled them, Sunday closing. Urban complaints were not confined to the great downstate cities, for the mayors of Albany, Buffalo, Rochester, Syracuse, Troy, and Ithaca all objected to the bill at a hearing before Governor Morton.[58]

Platt nonetheless demanded the bill's passage. He penned letters to newspaper editors and twisted legislative arms. While some Republican lawmakers dreaded popular reaction to the measure, especially in the cities, the great majority of them went along with Platt and passed it over the unanimous opposition of the Democrats in both houses. Morton seemed genuinely uncertain whether to sign the bill. He reminded Platt that the party platform had simply pledged Republicans to support Sunday closing and that the governor's message had cited only the need to reduce the number of saloons. "Had legislation been confined to those two principles, . . ." said Morton, "I am sure we should have been on safer ground." But pressured by Platt, the governor signed the Raines bill into law.[59]

Not everything went according to the boss's plans, however. The liquor statute had designated sixty excise inspectors as "confidential agents," and it was well known that the Republican organization intended that this status should exempt them from competitive examinations under the civil service system. Ignoring legal advice to the contrary, Morton did as Platt wished and placed the agents in the noncompetitive class, subject only to "pass" examinations. Civil service reformers howled, and independent Republicans joined in. "It's a Whiskey Machine," headlined the *New York Tribune*. "Governor Morton Weakly Yields to the Politicians." When a majority of the men whom Platt nominated to take the noncompetitive examination failed it, the boss called the test "farcical" and complained to Morton that "there is not one in four of those questions that either you or I or those Civil Service Commissioners themselves could answer when called upon without any preparation to consider."[60]

As events unfolded, the farce became more ridiculous. Comptroller James A. Roberts refused to pay the salaries of agents appointed, as he saw it, unconstitutionally, and Governor Morton began to rethink his decision placing them in the noncompetitive class. At this juncture, Platt's ally Senator Timothy E. Ellsworth conferred with both Morton and the members of the Civil Service Commission and persuaded them that any reclassification of the excise agents would also affect hundreds of other state employees in the noncompetitive class. Thinking he had convinced them to delay action, Ellsworth soon discovered that he had actually provided the commissioners with a rationale for the entire suspension of the noncompetitive civil service grades. The reclassification struck a severe blow to the machine's patronage power. "How could they have done anything more damaging?" Platt asked Ellsworth. "While this indiscriminate dynamiting was going on, what was there left of the Republican Party and the Republican Organization?" In July 1896, Henry H. Lyman, the new excise commissioner, finally chose his agents on the basis of a competitive examination. While Platt retained considerable influence over the selection process, he had lost the battle for the right to name the agents solely on partisan grounds.[61]

Even with the boss's authority over patronage weakened, the liquor law created lasting resentment. Critics pointed to the heavy proportion of excise taxation that fell on the cities and noted that in 1896 Brooklyn and New York City alone provided two-thirds of the revenue. The law suffered added condemnation for promoting vice. Saloon owners evaded the Sunday ban by adding ten "guest" rooms and calling their establishments hotels, which in many instances became houses of prostitution. "No brain," said one reformer, "could devise a plan better adapted to corrupt neighborhoods."[62]

Urban complaints notwithstanding, Republican leaders considered the Raines law a success. By August 1, 1896, the new Department of Excise had overseen the abolition of 950 local boards, licensed some 27,000 liquor dealers, and collected nearly $11 million in taxes. The state's one-third share became a huge new source of revenue and permitted the reduction of property taxes. Despite fears, the Raines tax did not rob local governments of needed revenue. Indeed, their two-thirds share greatly surpassed the total receipts from excise fees under the old system.[63]

Of greatest political significance, the Raines law dampened all aspects of the liquor issue. In the cities, the hotel provision effectively allowed Sunday sales in any saloon having rooms upstairs and keeping a sandwich visible as evidence that meals were being served to guests. With liquor regulation in the hands of the state, local authorities like Roosevelt were relieved of—Platt would have said prevented from— enforcing the law and costing Republican votes. In the rural areas, the statute also benefited the party by curtailing the electoral activity of the drys. Moderate temperance advocates were satisfied by the increase in license fees and the widespread reduction in the number of saloons. For those who demanded total prohibition, the law offered the opportunity to conduct "no license" campaigns under the local option provision. Many who had previously engaged in partisan politics evidently redirected their efforts, for within several years about three hundred towns, mostly in northern and western New York, had voted to become dry. In 1896 the Prohibition vote fell to 1.1 percent, and it failed to reach as high as 2 percent for the rest of the Republicans' years in office. As the New York *Sun* boasted in 1899: "The rural Prohibitionists . . . are now refraining from attempts to secure radical legislation in their favor and to extend their party organization in the State. Reasonable temperance men are acknowledging the practical advantages of the present law."[64]

The Raines law combined all the vital features of Platt's party strategy. It appealed to rural voters while it provided yet another means of control over Democratic cities. It compelled the liquor interests to deal with the Republicans and gave the party organization new patronage. Above all, the law removed a complex and damaging issue from state politics. For Platt, it illustrated more completely than any other measure of his career how the Republican party of New York State ought to govern.[65]

Platt's strategy for keeping the Republicans in power included campaign appeals as well as legislative programs. Through party platforms and nominating addresses, newspaper editorials, and stump speeches, the leaders reminded the electorate of the party's policies and sought to provide attractive symbols for those whom the programs left unsatisfied. By selectively explaining and interpreting the Republicans' public record, campaign appeals served purposes that policies alone could not fulfill.

In 1896, 1898, and 1900 the party rested its campaigns on national issues, including current ones like the tariff and money questions, as well as older ones like the Republicans' triumphant defense of freedom and the union. More than a quarter of the 1896 state platform attacked the "hopeless and absurd" silver heresy. While the tariff issue received somewhat less platform space, local party spokesmen emphasized the benefits conferred by policies based on the "cardinal principle" of protection. Two years later, the Republicans continued to run on the national economic topics of 1896. A lengthy section of the platform explicitly argued that with the silver threat still alive, national issues ought to predominate even in a nonpresidential year. "We are ready to meet the Democrats on all State issues," the Republican address proclaimed, "but in a larger sense this campaign is a National campaign." In 1900 the Republicans encompassed their national economic issues in the slogan "prosperity." The party's prescription for a healthy economy had worked and the Democratic predictions had been wrong. In both presidential years, party newspapers lauded McKinley and excoriated Bryan but scarcely mentioned the gubernatorial candidates, Frank S. Black in 1896 or Benjamin B. Odell, Jr., in 1900. Only in the midterm campaign of 1898 was significant attention focused on the state candidate, in this case Theodore Roosevelt, fresh from his heroic exploits in Cuba.[66]

It is not hard to understand why New York Republicans stressed national questions. Since most voters identified with a national party and its program, such issues provided the surest way to reinforce the electors' long-term loyalties and get them out to vote. The lingering depression, and then the memory of it; the fear of Bryan; and the widespread confidence in tariff protection and gold currency all offered the opportunity to draw disparate groups together on the basis of the Republicans' inclusive national doctrines.

As time passed, however, an emphasis on national questions became less satisfactory. While depression and the Spanish war had boosted the Republicans in 1896 and 1898, by 1900 the party found itself on the defensive against Democratic attacks on "trusts" and "imperalism." The Republicans praised McKinley's overseas policy and worked both sides of the trust issue by lauding "the tremendous industrial results which have been won by Republican policies" and by denouncing "all combinations seeking to control prices and to prevent competition." But having no decisive issue of their own in 1900, the Republicans spent more than the usual amount of time discussing state affairs.[67]

Selectivity rather than comprehensiveness characterized the Republicans' treatment of state issues from 1896 through 1900. No overriding state topic dominated the elections; nor did the leaders seem to be in search of such an issue. Three state subjects received mention in every Republican platform of the period: the Raines law, the improvement of roads, and the virtues of the outgoing governor. Since the latter two issues were treated but cursorily, only the liquor statute gave the platforms continuity on state questions. The issues the Republicans omitted and the constituencies they neglected disclose as much about their party strategy as those they included.[68]

Each year the party praised the Raines law. In 1896 the Republicans made it their leading state issue and devoted more than a quarter of the platform to its triumphs. In 1898 and 1900 the liquor law filled less platform space but, unlike any other state policy, the Raines law received consistent mention by name and became a political byword. In 1896 the Republicans treated the measure both as a tax law and as a liquor-control statute. They cited the revenues it generated and the efficacy with which it closed saloons, enhanced public order, and removed the liquor business from politics. That year the platform even cited the Sunday-closing requirement. In 1898 and 1900 the Republican address handled the Raines law solely as a tax measure. Even then, however, upstate party weeklies featured detailed charts, sent out by the state committee, showing the law's impact on both local revenues and the number of saloons.[69]

Except for the mention of Sunday closing in 1896, Republican platforms said nothing on sensitive ethnic and religious issues. At the local level, however, party leaders took quiet steps to bring Irish, German, and Italian Catholics, as well as Jews, into the coalition by promising "liberal" enforcement of the Sunday law, nominating them to office, and including them in the distribution of funds for party work on election day. Barnes in Albany, Aldridge in Rochester, and Lauterbach—himself a Jew—in New York all took special care to appeal in these ways to foreign-born and non-Protestant voters.[70]

While the responsibility for Catholics and Jews normally lay with local Republican leaders, Platt himself made sure to appease the native-born Protestants, even the bigots. During the 1898 campaign, members of the anti-Catholic American Protective Association charged that gubernatorial candidate Theodore Roosevelt had spoken against their organization several years before. James Coote of the A.P.A. wrote to Platt that "these things are remembered," and he offered to make a speaking tour to bring association members "into line" behind the Republican party. At first Platt resisted Coote's suggestion, but finally the boss paid for a tour in which Coote explicitly advised American-born Protestants to vote for the Republican ticket. The party evidently cooperated with the A.P.A. in other campaigns as well.[71]

Just as the Republican platform omitted mention of ethno-religious groups who supported the party, the address generally failed to recognize agricultural and business interests in the coalition. Hailed locally in speeches and newspapers, farmers went unmentioned in Republican platforms, except in 1900 when the address briefly noted appropriations for agricultural purposes. Business interests, too, were largely ignored in the campaigns. While farmers and businessmen got little explicit recognition, workingmen got a great deal. In 1898 labor legislation received more platform space than any other state subject. Since the Republicans had actually taken few policy initiatives for workingmen, campaign talk gave them their only chance to reach laborers. "The Republican Legislatures of 1897 and 1898 were occupied largely with . . . [labor] legislation," said the 1898 platform. That was untrue, but by saying it at election time the Republicans compensated a bit for its falsity.[72]

There were several reasons why the party's appeals failed to mirror its constituency. For one thing, since different groups conflicted and competed, the leaders avoided appeals to one element which would alienate another. The explicit recognition of business interests might have repelled many middle-class Republicans; the direct appeal to any ethno-religious group would have offended the others. Moreover, the neglected constituencies were not totally ignored. Appeals based on national issues reinforced the party loyalties of traditional Republican groups like farmers and native Protestants. Special local appeals supplemented the national ones. Workingmen formed a special case, since election rhetoric alone gave the party what little chance it had to enlist significant numbers of them.

Just as the party's constituency was only imprecisely reflected in its appeals, so the Republicans' policy programs were aired only incompletely at election time. Except in 1896 when the platform lauded the creation of Greater New York City, the party said nothing of its policies toward the large cities. Even that year, the platform coupled its praise of consolidation with a statement of support for home rule. Like the party's campaign attention to labor legislation, the home rule plank compensated for, rather than described, the Republicans' actual policies. Until 1900, campaign appeals also neglected the subjects of expenditure and taxation. Although most citizens experienced their contact with government through its institutions and services, almost nothing in the platforms of 1896 and 1898 concerned schools, hospitals, canals, insane asylums, or recreational areas.

Republican campaign rhetoric thus complemented the party's policies by giving only an imprecise accounting of them. Most of what the state government did usually received no mention in the platform and little discussion on the campaign trail. Even when state policies were discussed, their relative prominence in the campaign often proved disproportionate to the attention the party really paid them.

Finally, in 1900, the Republicans issued a platform that accounted in some detail for their management of the state. Schools, hospitals, orphanages, roads, fairs, parks, timber lands, and even battle monuments all received praise. Terms such as "liberally provided," "greatly extended," and "firmly established" marked the party's account of the government's growing functions. The 1900 address also included a data-laden discussion of state revenues. Their dearth of new national issues partly explains the Republicans' greater attention to state topics in 1900. So does the popularity of the outgoing governor, Theodore Roosevelt, whose scandal-free administration the Republicans capitalized on. The increasing influence in party counsels of Benjamin B.

Odell, Jr., also helps account for the new campaign orientation. Soon to take the reins of leadership from Platt, Odell would make state finance and the efficient provision of government services the leading issues during his two terms as governor. The campaign of 1900 did not, however, entirely follow the pattern marked out by the platform. In editorials and stump speeches, party leaders fell back on the old tactic of stressing national topics such as the tariff. In his last campaign as the undisputed party boss, Platt himself evidently favored the continued neglect of divisive state subjects, the reliance on local appeals to particular cultural and economic groups, and the emphasis on national issues.[73]

Election rhetoric misleadingly implied that the Republicans and Democrats significantly disagreed on state questions. Despite their dramatic tariff and currency differences in the 1890s, the parties clashed far less decisively below the national level. To be sure, each party assaulted the other's honesty, competence to govern, and past performance. Each disagreed with the other over which issues had priority, but they scarcely offered alternative agendas for state action.[74]

Campaign appeals provided a critically important element of the Republican strategy. By focusing voters on the party's strengths, selectively interpreting its record, and trying to recognize groups not otherwise satisfied, election rhetoric helped bridge the gap between party policies and party supporters. But campaign appeals did not accurately reflect either the party's constituency or its program; nor did they shape elections into sharp contests for conflicting state policies. Instead those appeals balanced the party's legislative programs by creating images that had strategic value because they were partly false.

Platt's programs and appeals carried on the traditional political ways that still flourished in New York in the late 1890s. Merely by upholding the Republican organization and encouraging the loyalty of those who were content to express themselves through it on election day, Platt and the other leaders filled the political needs felt by great numbers of men. For the minority who were not satisfied just to vote, the Republican organization offered the same regularized means to political advancement that adult male citizens had known since Clay's day. Men who successfully performed local political work might sit briefly in the legislature at Albany. For the few who reached the top of the party hierarchy, there was the reward of Sunday summonses to the Fifth Avenue Hotel.

There decisions were reached about the best means for using government to benefit the Republican party. While population growth and economic progress silently dictated the slow, steady expansion of the state's traditional functions, Platt's party undertook a handful of selected policy initiatives to help particular elements in the coalition and strengthen the organization. For the most part, the measures the leaders decided on satisfied Republican voters, especially those in the town and country districts who demanded relatively little from government. Republican officials boosted appropriations for agricultural services and fashioned a liquor law that appealed to native-born Protestants. But above all, Platt's organization avoided measures disliked by these voters and counted on their historic loyalties to the party.

Much more effort and attention were required to satisfy urban elements in the coalition and to build up the party in the cities. Many of Platt's most characteristic policy measures were designed to win city votes and patronage, especially in the great downstate metropolis. Utilizing multiple techniques of state control, Platt sometimes failed but often succeeded in harnessing urban wealth and power to fuel the Republican machine. The very attention Platt paid to the large cities and his success, to be studied below, in finding accommodation with the powerful industrial interests located there testify to his considerable imagination and flexibility. Applying them from 1895 to 1900, he helped keep alive the partisan political culture that had persisted since the 1830s, when Platt was born.

Soon that culture would die because of forces largely generated in the same cities to which Platt devoted so much attention. There urban citizens experienced new political conditions curtailing their partisanship and enlarging their demands on government. Dissatisfaction with Platt's approach to city politics inspired the most potent challenges to his party strategy. There also, economic developments presented political and governmental problems not solvable by Platt's methods. These difficulties, too, inspired assaults upon his strategy. Already by the late 1890s other Republican leaders were beginning to recognize and deal with the decline of partisanship and the emergence of new social and economic demands on government. Their rivalry with Platt and their competing party strategies ultimately helped redirect the course of politics and governance in New York.

4

Independence from the Party Machine, 1895–1901

The strongest challenge to Thomas Collier Platt's Republican strategy came from the movement of urban independents against party machines. Platt symbolized to them the worst features of the existing political system. "The mugwumps look upon him as a man with a cloven hoof," observed a Rochester newspaper in 1894, "a man who spends his waking hours arranging 'deals' with Tammany and all other kinds of political crookedness."[1] All of Platt's most important policy initiatives of the late 1890s, including the Raines law, the creation of Greater New York, and his numerous other city ventures, aroused independent opposition, both for what they were in themselves and because of the kind of politics and governance they represented. Having different political expectations than strict partisans, New York's urban independents in these years voiced the most influential "opposition" ideas in state politics, ideas destined to have a major part in reshaping the political system. Because most independents had supported the Republicans in 1893 and 1894, this opposition was expressed most vigorously within Platt's own party.

In providing the main voice for political innovation, as they did, the independents played a role often taken by the minority party, but which the Democrats of Platt's era did not fill.[2] Badly split in 1893 and 1894, the Democrats continued to be paralyzed by division for the remainder of the decade. After the loss in 1894, the party's warring factions briefly made peace, but William Jennings Bryan's nomination for president in 1896 interrupted the reunion. While Bryan won the formal, if unenthusiastic, support of Tammany Hall in New York City, he got only silence from David B. Hill and active opposition from the waning Cleveland Democracy. Under these conditions, a new party cleavage replaced the old one. Richard Croker's support for Bryan greatly enhanced the Tammany leader's authority in the Democratic party, and two years afterward he took control of the state organization. Ironically, Hill now became the symbol of unbossed Democracy; demoralized upstate Democrats, as well as old Clevelandites, looked to him to lead the battle against Tammany. The party's divisions helped prevent the Democrats from fashioning a unified policy program and so lessened interparty conflict on state issues. The two parties differed, to be sure, on national topics, as well as on questions involving the large cities, but in no sense did they present coherent, competing programs for the government of New York.[3]

In the absence of significant policy differences between the divided Democrats and the dominant Republicans, the renewal of close electoral competition between them after 1896 enabled fresh ideas, largely emanating from the Republican camp, to become potent in state politics. To beat the Democrats, Platt reluctantly recognized the city independents who had joined his coalition in 1893–94. He thus enabled them to bring about political innovations, including measures reforming city politics, new election laws, civil service reforms, and the elevation to high office of men who were independent from the party machine. Perhaps the most important concession the independents wrested from the Republicans was the party's adoption of their language and its lip service to their beliefs. In consequence, principles critical of traditional party politics were legitimized and spread across New York.

The doctrine of independence from party machines originated, as we have seen, in the demand by urban elites that municipal government and politics be divorced from partisanship. The independents had varying motives for opposing the party machines and competing conceptions of what nonpartisan city government ought to do. Some advocated "structural" changes, others "social" reforms; even in the 1890s, a few were already concentrating their attention on the administrative methods and bureaucratic techniques of city government, regardless of who filled its offices or what its functions were. Like their machine rivals, the independents were led by serious politicians, who were wholeheartedly committed to political work. They formed and maintained a diversity of organizations, including municipal parties and issue-oriented interest groups, through which they competed for office and pressured those who attained it. Far from united in their policy aims, the urban independents nonetheless drew together in opposing bossed party machines and in finding ways of placing their demands on the political agenda of New York State.

Everywhere the organized independents drew their leaders and most of their members from the business and professional classes. In New York City, the Citizens' Union was founded in 1897 by 165 men, of whom about 90 percent were businessmen, merchants, bankers, manufacturers, and lawyers or other professionals. In Rochester, a Committee of Sixty-Five named to direct the Good Government movement was similarly constituted, although there middle-class citizens and skilled workers made up a slightly larger minority of the whole. When they presented candidates for city office, as the Citizens' Union did in 1897, these organizations sometimes received significant support in working-class wards, but the men who fashioned the independents' ideology and determined their policy proposals came from the wealthier districts.[4]

Well-to-do and established as they were, the independents did not speak for a unified urban elite. Nor, during these years of tremendous changes in the functions of municipal government, did they all stand together for particular social or economic policy programs. Indeed, in a span of only a little more than a decade beginning in the mid-1890s, four distinctive strands of urban reform successively emerged in the cities of New York, all with the visible support of upper-class independents. First was an older, mugwumpish approach, stressing businesslike economy and efficiency, together with structural changes strengthening the mayor at the expense of district councilmen. In 1894, New York City's Committee of Seventy basically stood in this tradition. Second was what may be termed conservative social reform. Practiced by William L. Strong's mayoral administration in New York City from 1895 to 1897, this approach moved beyond economy and efficiency to improving services that contributed to the health and cleanliness of the city: public baths and parks, sanitation measures, and, above all, clean streets. A more advanced variety of social reform, begun during Mayor Seth Low's administration in 1902 and 1903, embraced substantive social and economic changes, including tax reform, utility regulation, and the expansion of city services for poorer citizens. A fourth expression of reform, represented by the founding of the Bureau of Municipal Research in 1907, concentrated on improving techniques for administering and evaluating the newly enlarged functions of city government. While an emphasis on one manner of reform successively gave way to the next, these four approaches (as well as related variations not enumerated here) were closely intertwined. None provided a stark alternative to the others. All four continuously found supporters among the independents, whose political activity cannot be viewed as the unified expression of any particular vision of city government.[5]

Indeed, independence from party machines brought together men who disagreed on sensitive social and economic issues. Although some independents hoped to lessen the political influence of immigrants and

Catholics through restrictive election-law reforms, the movement as a whole did not find its basis in such sentiment. The independent organizations generally appealed for the support of foreign ethnic and religious groups, endorsed their demands for less restrictive liquor laws, and, as time passed, supported city services they wanted.[6] While certain independents opposed party bosses to further particular economic goals, the antimachine urban reformers actually disagreed on such subjects. As city services, public franchises, and municipal ownership came up for debate and decision, independents showed themselves to be of far from one mind.[7] Despite their differences, however, the independents' assault on party bosses and machines became a force for political innovation in its own right, capable of uniting a growing and diverse constituency.

Finding the existing parties unwilling to promote reform, as the independents variously defined it, they established nonpartisan organizations to fill their needs. Throughout New York's large cities, they formed municipal parties to nominate and elect men to city office or, if the terms were right, to ally with one of the major parties. Increasingly as time passed, the independents looked beyond the goal of electing city officials and concentrated their efforts through interest organizations that put pressure on whomever filled the offices. No matter which strategy they adopted, the urban independents proved willing to do hard political work. Far from being the "mornin' glories" George Washington Plunkitt called them, they were activists with surprising energy and tenacity.[8]

What they shared, and what made their diverse movement ultimately so influential, was their articulate expression of the doctrine of independence from bossed party machines at a time when many social and economic circumstances were creating a receptive environment for an assault on parties. However they defined reform, the independents found partisan city governments to be selfish, particularistic, and corrupt, and hence incapable of making policy in the interest of the whole community. Whichever social or economic programs they favored, the independents believed that only nonpartisan city administration could bring them about.

In consequence, a series of political reforms designed to take power from the parties united the independents. They welcomed the progress toward municipal nonpartisanship made by the 1894 constitutional convention, especially the separation of city elections and the beginnings of urban home rule, though in practice both amendments failed to meet the independents' expectations. They also pressed demands for changes in the rules governing elections and appointments: ballot legislation to encourage ticket-splitting, primary-election laws to assure fair nominations, and civil service reforms to place merit above partisanship in the selection of government employees. By persuasively voicing these demands in the late 1890s and compelling the Republican party to adopt many of them, the urban independents put themselves at the front of a much broader movement that soon would weaken the partisanship of individuals and interests everywhere.[9]

The doctrine of municipal independence united not only those who disagreed in their prescriptions for reform but also men who were divided in their national party loyalties. For while they opposed partisanship locally, few independents in the 1890s envisioned any alternative to it nationally. The Citizens' Union of New York City declared itself "by no means opposed to the national parties; it asks no citizen to abandon his party. . . . In national elections we must have national issues." Some independents occasionally expressed the hope that nonpartisan government, once established at the city level, might extend upward. But generally they accepted state and national parties, and, indeed, most of them retained allegiance to such organizations.[10]

While some independents were Republicans, some Democrats, and a few genuinely renounced both parties, they often proved indistinguishable from one another locally. This was especially true on those occasions when the independents were most numerous: at city elections in which nonpartisan candidates opposed the nominees of the regular organizations. Contemporaries often failed to distinguish the different antimachine groups. They used the terms "mugwump," "independent," and "nonpartisan" interchangeably and left the historian little choice except to do so too.

At the leadership level, however, the independents need not be homogenized. Indeed, to understand how their doctrine acquired such influence in state politics, it is necessary to scrutinize the Republican independents who challenged Platt's party strategy. The boss and his intraparty critics disagreed on how the Republicans had won power and how to keep it. Where Platt credited national issues, loyal upstate voters, and a strong party machine—and shaped his strategy accordingly—antimachine Republicans emphasized the sizable contribution of urban voters and advanced a party strategy of concessions to the independents, greater attention to state and local issues, and special efforts to keep large-city voters, not just city spoils, in the party.

Almost from the moment the 1894 election returns were known, independent Republicans criticized Platt's plans for taking advantage of the party's victory and offered plans of their own instead. Assailing the boss's evident intention to control the legislature, to dominate Governor Morton, and to place his henchmen in prominent positions, the *New York Tribune* and other antimachine newspapers warned Platt that such tactics would "be repudiated by the conscience-voters, who were in the majority at the November polls." Platt's critics had a point. Many of the gains that put the party in power had come from large-city voters who supported the Republican state ticket in order to complete the downfall of bossed Democratic machines, and they would not tolerate bossism in the Republican party either. To reward and reassure these voters, Platt's critics demanded the passage of specific city-reform measures recommended by urban independents, the selection of an assembly speaker from one of the large cities, and the adoption of a reformed ballot law. If New York was to become "a sure Republican State," warned the *Tribune*, ". . . it is absolutely necessary that both Governor and Legislature should lift their vision above mere partisan considerations." To achieve that, it was necessary to model the state Republican party on what the *Buffalo Commercial* called "the new and better spirit of republicanism that has accomplished much for the cause of good government in Buffalo, in Brooklyn, and in New York."[11]

Platt and his allies rejected the strategy of renouncing partisanship in order to appease the urban independents. Republican state officials need not apologize for their Republicanism or "shape their course in deference to the theories of Democrats and Mugwumps" declared Lemuel E. Quigg's New York *Press* early in 1895. "If ever the Republican party came into power with a mandate to carry forward Republican methods and principles, the Republicans of the State of New York have that mandate today."[12]

For as long as Platt remained Republican leader of the state, he and his enemies kept up their dispute over party strategy. Independent Republicans objected to most of the boss's important policies, while he, in turn, killed, amended, or delayed most of the reform measures they favored. The conflict essentially concerned the large cities, whose growing power both Platt and his critics recognized, but to which they had different political responses. What made those differences so significant was their capacity to arouse a broad debate about whether partisanship was valuable to governance.

Sixteen leading Republicans who frequently opposed Platt may be compared with the twenty regulars sketched in the preceding chapter. (See Table 9.) Some of them, including William Brookfield, Frank D. Pavey, and Elihu Root, worked to reform the Republican organization of New York City. Others led similar movements elsewhere: Seth Low in Brooklyn, Oren E. Wilson in Albany, Harvey F. Remington in Rochester, James J. Belden in Syracuse, and William H. Hotchkiss in

Whitelaw Reid (*New York State Men*)

Table 9. A profile of sixteen New York State independent Republican leaders

Leader	Residence*	Birthplace†	Age in 1895	College attended	Primary field of occupation	Highest public office, 1895–1900
J. J. Belden	Syracuse	Fabius	70	none	banking	congressman
W. Brookfield	New York City	Greenbank, N.J.	51	none	manufacturing	New York City commissioner of public works
J. H. Choate	New York City	Salem, Mass.	63	Harvard	law	ambassador to England
W. H. Hotchkiss	Buffalo	Whitehall	31	Hamilton	law	none
S. Low	Brooklyn	Brooklyn	45	Columbia	merchandising	New York City charter commissioner
W. Miller	Herkimer County	Hannibal	57	Union	manufacturing	none
F. D. Pavey	New York City	Washington Court House, Ohio	35	Yale	law	state senator
W. Reid	New York City	Xenia, Ohio	58	Miami University	journalism	none
H. F. Remington	Rochester	Henrietta	32	Union Law	law	municipal court judge
J. A. Roberts	Buffalo	Waterboro, Me.	48	Bowdoin	law	state comptroller
T. Roosevelt	New York City	New York City	37	Harvard	writing, politics	governor
E. Root	New York City	Clinton	50	Hamilton	law	secretary of war
C. T. Saxton	Wayne County	Clyde	49	none	law	lieutenant governor
J. W. Wadsworth	Livingston County	Philadelphia, Pa.	49	none	farming	congressman
A. D. White	Tompkins County	Homer	63	Yale	university administration	ambassador to Germany
O. E. Wilson	Albany	Boston, Mass.	51	Columbia	business	mayor of Albany

*City or county.
†New York State, unless otherwise noted.

Buffalo. Joseph H. Choate became an anti-Platt symbol in 1897 when he opposed the boss for the U.S. Senate seat filled by the legislature that year. In a somewhat different category were several leaders who had learned their opposition to Platt amidst the party factionalism of the 1870s and 1880s, including Whitelaw Reid, Warner Miller, and James W. Wadsworth.[13]

These were not men who grew up alienated from party politics or who proposed to sacrifice their careers on the altar of independence. Virtually every one of them was a lifelong Republican, and all, at one time or another, received appointments or nominations from the party's hands. The most prominent of them, Theodore Roosevelt, spent his whole career as a professional, Republican politician. While the sixteen opposition leaders held fewer state offices between 1895 and 1900 than did their regular counterparts, they had the compensation of somewhat greater success in winning federal positions, including cabinet offices and prestigious ambassadorships.[14]

Yet in the late 1890s all of them voiced the doctrine of independence from the party machine and championed a strategy of appealing to municipal nonpartisans. Many of the sixteen naturally hoped to advance their own political careers by opposing the regular organization. But that helps explain their motivation; it does not disprove their sincerity. It is difficult to read the correspondence of Low, Roosevelt, Root, or even Reid—the editor of the *New York Tribune* and, in a real sense, the behind-the-scenes coordinator of the opposition to Platt—without feeling they believed what they espoused. There was, of course, nothing unusual about dissenting members of the majority party attacking bosses and machines. But the Reids and the Roosevelts who did so in the 1890s got hold of the doctrine just when it was taking on new meaning and importance. It was through their sometimes self-serving efforts that ideas of independence entered and helped transform New York State politics.[15]

Like the pro-Platt leaders, the dissidents were ambitious, talented men. In age, birth, education, and occupation, little distinguished the two sets of politicians. Most of the independent leaders followed business or professional careers, as did their regular counterparts, though the antimachine leaders achieved somewhat greater prominence outside politics than did the Platt men. Root and Choate were among the foremost members of the New York bar; Andrew D. White and Seth Low achieved distinction as presidents respectively of Cornell and Columbia universities; Reid occupied one of the nation's most prestigious editorial chairs. Scarcely poor or unsuccessful or opposed to the capitalist system, most antimachine leaders were among the social and

Elihu Root (Library of Congress)

economic elite of the day. All seven from New York City and Brooklyn were listed in the *Social Register*.[16]

What chiefly separated the antimachine leaders from their opponents was the tendency to crusade, to identify with causes, and to break party discipline. Charles Saxton fought for ballot reform, Hotchkiss and Pavey for a new primary-election law, and James A. Roberts for extension of the civil service system. Roosevelt and Miller crusaded for the Sunday closing of saloons, as Low later did on behalf of the National Civic Federation. All sixteen antimachine politicians prominently participated in battles for reform as they defined it. Some of them won labels for their ideological positions: Choate, Wadsworth, and Root as "conservatives"; Roosevelt and Low as "progressives." In the late 1890s, the opposition leaders crusaded mainly against party bossism. Within a few years, some of them began to apply their cause-oriented style of politics to economic and social questions too.

Over the course of the Republicans' first seven years in office, the dissidents' influence on the party's strategy grew considerably. At first, especially during 1895 and 1896, Platt pressed his own program with only minimal regard for the urban independents. Many of their demands for legal changes in the means for constituting government were ignored; others were adopted only in emasculated form. Then in 1896 and 1897, first national, and then local, events greatly strengthened the independents at the expense of the regular Republicans. Platt shrewdly modified his strategy and remained state leader, but he paid a price in the considerable recognition of the independents and their doctrine. These developments must be considered in detail because they marked a crucial stage in the passage from a nineteenth-century partisan political culture.

Two of the independents' major concerns were ballot legislation and civil service. On both issues they found the Republicans' first years in office disappointing. Ever since the 1880s, when the reformers had learned of the efficacy of the so-called Australian ballot in preventing bribery at elections, ballot reform had been an issue in New York State. In place of the distinctive, party-printed, publicly cast tickets which wardheelers traditionally distributed to the voters at the polls, supporters of the Australian system favored a secret, official ballot containing the name of every candidate for all offices. Already by 1895, considerable progress had been made toward the new way of voting. A law passed in 1890 provided for the public printing and secret casting of ballots, but it permitted the voter to bring with him to the polls a partially or completely marked ticket called a "paster," which he could affix to the official ballot. The law also required separate tickets for each party and each independent slate of candidates. In 1894 the constitutional convention had confirmed the secrecy of voting, but New York still remained without the Australian ballot, already adopted by the majority of states.[17]

Like the several electoral reforms enacted by the constitutional convention, an Australian ballot appealed to both independents and Republicans. From the reformers' perspective, the ballot deterred vote buying. If every elector cast an identical-looking secret ballot, the purchaser of votes could never be sure the goods he was buying had been delivered. To Republicans, the ballot's benefits were partisan. A secret, official ballot was a kind of test in English literacy and therefore likely to disfranchise many of those who made up the large, urban majorities of the Democratic party.[18]

But the ballot issue was not quite that simple. In the years since the issue was introduced, independents had discovered new purposes to which an Australian ballot, if adopted, might be put. Where reformers had initially favored ballot-law change chiefly to purify elections by checking venal voting, most of which they assumed was done by poor immigrants, they increasingly recognized that such legislation could permit genuinely independent electoral behavior. For one thing, a blanket ballot, containing the names of every party's candidates, facilitated ticket-splitting. For another, an official ballot made it as simple to vote for nonpartisan as partisan candidates. Here were possibilities for independent electoral behavior that transcended the narrow aim of "pure" elections. Properly framed, an Australian-ballot law would not simply make voting honest, but could substantially transform the existing partisan electoral process.[19]

Regular Republicans of course had no intention of allowing such a development. In his legislative message of 1895, Governor Levi P. Morton noted "an imperative public demand" for a new ballot law, and Platt made known his support for such a measure. With little dissent, the legislature passed, and Morton signed, New York's first Australian-ballot law. It provided for a single, blanket ballot listing candidates in party columns headed by identifying pictoral emblems; independents nominated by petition would be listed in separate columns. (See Fig. 4.) A voter could cast a straight ticket by making a single mark in the circle under his party's emblem, but to split his ticket he had to make multiple marks according to precise rules. Some reformers naturally complained about the incentives to pure partisanship in these provisions. "If it becomes law," a representative of New York City's Good Government Clubs predicted before the measure's final approv-

Figure 4. The Australian ballot, Essex County, New York, 1895

TO VOTE A STRAIGHT TICKET MAKE A CROSS (x) MARK WITHIN THE CIRCLE ABOVE ONE OF THE PARTY COLUMNS.

TO VOTE FOR AN INDIVIDUAL CANDIDATE MAKE A CROSS (x) MARK IN THE SPACE BEFORE HIS NAME.

TO VOTE FOR A PERSON NOT ON THE TICKET, WRITE THE NAME OF SUCH PERSON UNDER THE TITLE OF THE OFFICE IN THE COLUMN ON THE RIGHT AND MAKE A CROSS (x) MARK IN THE SPACE BEFORE THE NAME.

ANY MARK OR ERASURE MADE ON THIS BALLOT EXCEPT AS ABOVE INDICATED MAKES THE BALLOT VOID AND IT CANNOT BE COUNTED. USE ONLY A PENCIL HAVING BLACK LEAD.

REPUBLICAN TICKET.	DEMOCRATIC TICKET.	DEMOCRATIC PARTY REFORM ORGANIZATION TICKET.	PROHIBITION TICKET.	SOCIALIST LABOR TICKET.	PEOPLE'S TICKET.	INDEPENDENT NOMINATIONS.	
For Secretary of State, JOHN PALMER.	For Secretary of State, HORATIO C. KING.	For Secretary of State, HORATIO C. KING.	For Secretary of State, WILLIAM W. SMITH.	For Secretary of State, ERASMUS PELLENZ.	For Secretary of State, THADDEUS B. WAKEMAN.		For Secretary of State
For Comptroller, JAMES A. ROBERTS.	For Comptroller, JOHN B. JUDSON.	For Comptroller, JOHN B. JUDSON.	For Comptroller, FREDERICK B. DEVENDORF.	For Comptroller, PATRICK MURPHY.	For Comptroller, DAVID ROUSSEAU.		For Comptroller
For Treasurer, ADDISON B. COLVIN.	For Treasurer, DEWITT CLINTON DOW.	For Treasurer, DEWITT CLINTON DOW.	For Treasurer, WILLIAM R. RATHBUN.	For Treasurer, WILLIAM F. STEER.	For Treasurer, HERBERT L. CASE.		For Treasurer
For Attorney-General, THEODORE E. HANCOCK.	For Attorney General, MORTON CHASE.	For Attorney-General, MORTON CHASE.	For Attorney-General, ELIAS ROOT.	For Attorney General, JOHN H. MOORE.	For Attorney General, LAWRENCE J. McFARLIN.		For Attorney General
For State Engineer and Surveyor, CAMPBELL W. ADAMS.	For State Engineer and Surveyor, RUSSELL R. STUART.	For State Engineer and Surveyor, RUSSELL R. STUART.	For State Engineer and Surveyor, WALTER A. MILES.	For State Engineer and Surveyor, MORRIS BERMAN.	For State Engineer and Surveyor, ELIAS H. BORDEN.		For State Engineer and Surveyor
For Associate Judge of the Court of Appeals, CELORA E. MARTIN.	For Associate Judge of the Court of Appeals, JOHN D. TELLER.	For Associate Judge of the Court of Appeals, JOHN D. TELLER.	For Associate Judge of the Court of Appeals, EDWIN C. ENGLISH.	For Associate Judge of the Court of Appeals, HENRY P. GRAY.	For Associate Judge of the Court of Appeals, CHARLES WARD.		For Associate Judge of the Court of Appeals
For Justice of the Supreme Court, CHESTER B. McLAUGHLIN	For Justice of the Supreme Court, CHESTER B. McLAUGHLIN	For Justice of the Supreme Court,	For Justice of the Supreme Court,	For Justice of the Supreme Court,	For Justice of the Supreme Court,		For Justice of Supreme Court
For Senator, GEORGE CHAHOON	For Senator, HIRAM WALWORTH.	For Senator,	For Senator,	For Senator,	For Senator,		For Senator
For Member of Assembly, ALBERT O. WEED	For Member of Assembly, JAMES E. TRIMBLE	For Member of Assembly,	For Member of Assembly,	For Member of Assembly,	For Member of Assembly,		For Member of Assembly
For Coroner, K. J. DUNN	For Coroner, H. H. KNAPP.	For Coroner,	For Coroner,	For Coroner,	For Coroner,		For Coroner

THE VOTER MAY WRITE IN THE COLUMN BELOW UNDER THE TITLE OF THE OFFICE THE NAME OF ANY PERSON WHOSE NAME IS NOT PRINTED ON THE BALLOT FOR WHOM HE DESIRES TO VOTE.

Source: Essex County Republican, October 24, 1895.

al, "the 'Machine vote' will be even more powerful than under the present law, and the 'Independent voter' will find it doubly difficult to express his will at the polls." But to most citizens, such complaints must have seemed petty. The Republicans could plausibly claim that they had enacted a long-sought reform.[20]

The following year, the Republicans amended the ballot law along lines that left little doubt of their intention to limit nonparty voting. Making what they termed minor changes to eliminate imperfections, the legislators doubled (to six thousand) the number of signatures required for statewide independent nominations and instituted a requirement for at least fifty petitioners in each county. The City Club of New York bitterly observed that the 1896 amendments "are constructed upon the theory that public policy requires that the freedom of citizens to act outside of political party lines in elections ought to be further limited than at present." Even regular Republicans admitted that the measure would cut off "buncombe independent nominations" and curtail political action outside the regular parties.[21]

Thus while the ballot statutes of 1895 and 1896 made bribery at elections more difficult, the measures also delayed the achievement of other goals that had become at least as important to the independents: ticket-splitting and nonpartisan nominations. Both sides recognized the new laws' deterrence to ticket-splitting. After passage of the measures, illustrated explanations of how to vote a straight ticket regularly appeared in party newspapers at election time. While Republican editors sometimes explained how a right-thinking Democrat could mark his ballot for the Republican presidential candidate and still support his own party for state and local offices, spokesmen usually advised voters to cast a straight ticket in order to avoid invalidating an improperly cast ballot. For their part, the independents began a long campaign to abolish the premium on straight-ticket voting by listing candidates according to office rather than party. In the *Nation*'s view, "That there should be any element of truth in the cry 'Vote Straight: it is the only way to get your ballot counted,' is itself the deepest reproach."[22]

Aggregate election returns suggest that the adoption of the Australian ballot did not significantly increase ticket-splitting among New Yorkers. Figure 5 displays the mean percentages (weighted according to county size) by which the Republican party's least popular candidate fell short of the ticket leader's vote in gubernatorial-election years from 1891 to 1902. While ticket-splitting appears to have risen somewhat in 1896, the first year after the adoption of the new ballot, such behavior seems more readily attributable to the unique national circumstances of 1896 than to the ballot law. William McKinley led the Republican ticket in more than three-quarters of the state's counties, suggesting

Figure 5. Ticket-splitting, 1891–1902: mean percentage by which Republican party's trailing candidate fell behind vote of ticket leader

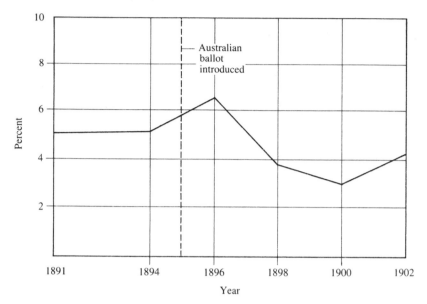

that many Democrats deserted Bryan but remained loyal to the rest of the party's candidates. For many who did so, the ticket-splitting habit was evidently not lasting. In 1898, 1900, and 1902 aggregate returns point to an even lower level of split tickets than in the pre-Australian ballot years. Beginning in 1904, and especially in 1906 and 1908, ticket-splitting significantly rose, for reasons to be considered below. But while the new ballot law undoubtedly facilitated the increase when it came, it is clear that ballot reform did not solely or directly cause ticket-splitting to rise. The Republicans who framed the law of course intended it that way.[23]

In time, some independents came to regard the adoption of the Australian ballot as a loss for their movement. Not only did it encourage straight-ticket voting, but it also discouraged independent nominations by making the requirements so stringent. Far from transforming the electoral process, the Australian ballot simply pointed the way to the next reform needed: changes in the rules governing nominations. Thus in the aftermath of the Australian ballot's adoption, serious debate began in New York about primary-election laws. As the independents now knew, however, the regular Republicans were experts in making partisan use of an apparent reform.[24]

The civil service system was of even more long-standing concern to the independents than the ballot. Here the Republicans first pleased and then disappointed the reformers. Urged on by well-organized civil service advocates who frequently sent delegations to see him in Albany, Governor Morton worked to extend the merit system even while he abided by Platt's wishes on most day-to-day patronage matters. The sight of his governor listening to the dissenters worried Platt. Upon learning of one audience Morton gave them, the boss grumbled that "every man in official position is always pestered by these same people; and, let him do his best, he can never satisfy them, except he adopts their ultra views and acts accordingly." Platt's worry was justified, for in December 1896, Morton's last month in office, the governor, now aged seventy-two and beyond further political ambition, issued an executive order establishing a new, more comprehensive code of civil service regulations. Their implementation threatened Platt's control of patronage and gratified those whom he now termed "fanatical 'reformers' of the Evening Post school."[25]

Morton's new rules did not last long, however. Within weeks, his successor, Frank S. Black, called for civil service with "less starch" and chided reformers who championed "ideas so delicate as to be worthless in actual practice." Black urged that appointing officers have wide latitude in determining applicants' qualifications, regardless of the results of competitive examinations. In an act that pleased Republican partisans and appalled independents, the 1897 legislature approved Black's proposals.[26] Once again, the Republicans had defeated a reform the independents considered crucial. Only if they acquired much greater political strength could the antimachine elements reverse their setbacks at the hands of state government and compel the Republicans to recognize their doctrines. Controversial national political events came to the independents' aid in 1896; so, to an even greater degree, did city politics the following year.

The presidential election of 1896 assisted the independents in several ways. First, with Platt boosting Morton's presidential candidacy, his enemies rallied around McKinley, whose widespread popularity they used as a weapon against the boss. They formed McKinley clubs and threatened Platt's hold on New York's delegation to the national convention. While the boss survived the challenge and was eventually "recognized" by McKinley's manager, Mark Hanna, as having full control of the national campaign in New York, he was humiliated by his failure on the national scene and by his rivals' success in gaining the prestige of backing the winner first.[27]

With McKinley nominated, the tumultuous campaign and election that followed served to loosen the traditional party loyalties upon which Platt's kind of politics depended. Republicans and Democrats alike argued that the polarizing monetary and tariff issues of 1896 transcended partisanship. "In this campaign," Governor Morton proclaimed, "party lines are largely obliterated . . . in the higher purpose of maintaining the honor of the nation." Many who joined the Republican bandwagon that year did so on the basis of issues rather than habitual party loyalties. The result was a landslide for Platt's party, but not one constructed along lines that encouraged traditional partisanship. The election of 1896 had one further implication for the Republicans' intraparty struggle in New York. With McKinley in the White House and the country protected from Bryan's heresies for at least four years, it became safe for dissenting Republicans to desert their party in municipal elections without fear of imperiling the gold standard or hurting the national party. This they now did. Ironically, McKinley's huge victory thus helped make possible the Republicans' shattering defeat the following year.[28]

Even before the election of 1896, the Republican-independent alliances of 1893–94 had been in trouble. Despite their shared interest in defeating local Democratic machines, several problems weakened the bonds of cooperation that regulars and reformers had forged in the large cities of the state. One was municipal administration. Having worked together to elect mayors in Albany, Buffalo, Brooklyn, and New York, they afterward found it difficult to cooperate in governing the cities. Sometimes they divided over policy questions, such as the level of spending or the regulation of public service corporations; always they divided over patronage. "Home rule" also drew a line between the former allies. While the regulars supported state legislation to fasten Republican control on the cities, the independents disapproved such measures and pressed continually for laws further separating state and local politics. Competition for control of local Republican organizations provided a third source of disagreement. At the heart of the trouble was deciding who was entitled to participate in party primaries and conducting a fair enrollment of such persons.[29]

While these sores were festering, two developments placed the independents in a stronger position than ever before to abandon their uncooperative allies and form separate municipal parties in local elections. The Raines law of 1896, by taking liquor regulation entirely out of city hands, removed an issue that had often undercut political reform movements. Relieved of having to enforce the Sunday-closing law if they won control of city government, the independents now had the opportunity to attract immigrant voters who opposed the machines but rightly feared the puritanical streak in upper-class reformism. Of perhaps greater importance, the separation of city elections from state and national contests made it easier to persuade many voters, who would never desert their party with the presidency or the governorship at stake, to support nonpartisan local candidates. Not intended by the Republicans to have these effects, the Raines law and the elections amendment increased the independents' opportunity to establish separate municipal parties likely to draw significant support.[30]

Already by 1895, local problems had alienated the independents from the regulars in Albany, Rochester, and Syracuse where mayoral elections were scheduled for the fall. Only one year after the Republicans' capture of the state, their differences with the reformers cost the party control of these cities. By 1897, the passage of the Raines law, McKinley's victory, and the full application of the separation-of-elections amendment (under which all the large cities were holding mayoral elections) together helped swell the independents' ranks to perhaps two hundred thousand or more. That year, the culmination of these developments was the defeat of the Republicans in every large city and the loss of the party's statewide majority as well.

In Albany, where regulars and independents had joined forces under the Honest Election party banner in 1894, they soon parted company. Quarreling with Mayor Oren Wilson over appointments, as well as over the city's electric lighting contract, William Barnes, Jr.'s regular Republican organization declined to support Wilson for reelection in 1895. The mayor ran defiantly as an independent and took 20 percent of the total vote, just enough to deprive Barnes's man of victory. Two years later, a similar result occurred, except that the independent candidate's share of the vote now increased to 27 percent and virtually equaled that of the regular Republican nominee.[31]

In Rochester, a slightly different pattern of events also resulted in the election of a Democratic mayor in 1895 and 1897. Finding fault with the incumbent Republican administration for high taxes, inferior services, and the usual patronage improprieties, a group of leading merchants, lawyers, and clergymen organized the Good Government movement in every ward and enrolled seven thousand members. In 1895, they nominated a bipartisan slate of municipal candidates and persuaded the Democrats to endorse them all. Only the mayoral nominee, himself a Democrat, won, but that alone was an impressive achievement for the independents in a Republican city in a Republican year. In 1897 the same alliance persisted, but now the Good Government–Democratic forces won overwhelmingly and controlled the city council as well as the mayoralty.[32]

Syracuse Republicans and independents also quarreled during the same years. In 1895 the dissidents nominated a nonpartisan slate of city candidates that received six thousand votes under the Citizens' Municipal Reform party emblem and deprived the Republicans of victory. At issue in Syracuse was the problem of enrollment. Antimachine Republicans charged that Francis Hendricks's regular organization kept control by corruptly manipulating the lists of those eligible to participate in party primaries. In 1897 the dissident Republicans combined with other Syracuse independents in a Citizens' Union to nominate municipal candidates. Though the regulars eventually joined the coalition, independent-Republican animosities were sufficiently deep to keep Syracuse, like Rochester, a Republican city with a Democratic mayor.[33]

The same causes of dissension that divided upstate regulars and reformers also operated in New York City where more organizations practiced independent politics than anywhere else. The Committee of Seventy went out of existence in mid-1895, but the City Club and the Good Government Clubs carried on, as did numerous commercial and trade associations—headed by the Chamber of Commerce and the New York Board of Trade and Transportation—each pressing policy demands they believed only a nonpartisan city administration could fulfill. Within both political parties, moreover, well-organized factions opposed the dominant machines and voiced, with varying degrees of calculation and sincerity, the doctrine of independence.[34]

While they had joined with regular Republicans to elect Mayor Strong in 1894, the members of these organizations soon found that they disagreed with Platt, and to a lesser extent with each other, on what a "reform" administration meant. All could agree, at a minimum, that Tammany officials should be replaced, but in appointing new men Strong was torn between the nonpartisan ideal his campaign had voiced and the pressures put upon him by the different factions that had supported him for mayor. Almost inevitably, Platt was disappointed with the share of jobs allotted to his organization. He complained to Governor Morton that Strong and his public works commissioner, William Brookfield, an anti-Platt Republican, "have been filling all the offices in the gift of the local Administration here with their partisans. . . . There is no end to the places which they have given and have to give." In retaliation, Platt delayed or watered down a series of legislative measures that the reformers believed essential to the success of Strong's administration. They in turn organized rallies and protest meetings to oppose the boss's bills, including the bipartisan police-board measures of 1895 and the charter for Greater New York City adopted in 1897.[35]

Besides being distressed with Platt's "war" on Strong, independent Republicans also regretted the behavior of their party's regular organization, headed first by Edward Lauterbach and then by Lemuel E. Quigg, both loyal to the boss. The dissident elements were strongest in the assembly districts of mid-Manhattan and the upper West Side where properous, native-born professionals, like young Henry Stimson, drafted circulars, called meetings, and manned the primaries in order to defeat the machine. The issue of party enrollment provided the most constant source of conflict. Independents repeatedly charged the regulars with purging party dissidents and filling the rolls with cooperative Democrats. One prominent committee of antimachine Republicans reported early in 1896 that the enrollment was padded by as much as 44 percent in some assembly districts and that 25,000 of the party's 77,000 members in New York City were illegitimate.[36]

In 1897, the year of the first municipal elections for the consolidated city of New York, these accumulated grievances fueled an explosion of independence, astutely channeled by the Citizens' Union's fresh approach to nonpartisan politics. Instead of "fusing" the different anti-Tammany factions, the newly formed C.U. enrolled voters, collected over one hundred thousand signatures in support of Seth Low for mayor, and afterward nominated him. Other political organizations were welcomed to endorse Low, but they were not promised a share of the patronage or other concessions in return. While it was dominated by businessmen and professionals, the Citizens' Union made a determined effort to attract working-class and foreign-born voters through promises of social reform and cultural tolerance. But the heart of the new organization's appeal was nonpartisan municipal administration. The consolidation of Greater New York, and the large powers and responsibilities its first mayor would have, gave special cogency to the argument that national partisanship had no place in city government. In support of this doctrine, antimachine Republicans, dissenting Democratic organizations, thoroughgoing nonpartisans, and even some party regulars all endorsed Low.[37]

Platt did not, for, as he explained later, "I was not willing to put the Republican organization behind a man who, in advance, repudiated all obligation to the Republican party." Instead, the Republicans nominated the stalwart Benjamin F. Tracy and issued on his behalf one of the most ringing defenses of partisanship ever heard in American politics. Repeatedly they made two arguments. The first was that party meant principle. "The Republican party was founded upon principles," declared Lieutenant Governor Timothy Woodruff, the Republican leader of Brooklyn. "It has always subordinated everything to its convictions." The argument was not simply that Republicans deserved support because they had defended right principles; the point was that without party there could be no principles in politics. Or, as Governor Black put it, "A non-partisan is an unbeliever." The second argument was that party meant responsibility. In Black's words, "The claim that a candidate may be responsible to no political party, but directly to all the people is a vain delusion. . . . If a candidate owes no allegiance to any party, he owes none to the people." To ask whether Platt, Woodruff, and Black believed their two arguments is to miss the point. They were Republicans first and political theorists last, if at all. Without a doubt they considered their party a responsible vehicle of coherent principles and had no qualms about so arguing. But to these men partisanship was intrinsic; its defense was an afterthought, voiced most vigorously just at the moment when the independents were winning the power to force the partisans to recant.[38]

The 1897 election results gave proof of the independents' strength in the city and the state. Low captured 150,000 votes and ran second to Tammany's mayoral nominee, Robert A. Van Wyck. The Republican Tracy, finishing a distant third, managed only to assure Low's defeat. Low won votes everywhere in the consolidated city, but he ran best in areas with a high concentration of middle- and upper-class native-born citizens. In seven such assembly districts running up the spine of Manhattan and along the upper West Side, Low averaged 42 percent of the vote and beat both Tracy and Van Wyck in all but one. On the lower East Side, where poor East European Jews were highly concentrated, Low averaged 24 percent of the vote and beat Tracy in four of six districts. In the Irish enclaves of lower Manhattan and the West Side, where Van Wyck won overwhelmingly, Low received an average of only 18 percent of the vote. Here even Tracy beat him in five of eight districts.[39]

The Greater New York mayoral election strongly affected the results for the single state office contested in 1897, chief judge of the Court of Appeals. In place of McKinley's majorities the year before, William Wallace, the Republican judicial candidate, now won only 29 percent of the vote in New York and 36 percent in Brooklyn. With no judicial candidate on the Citizens' Union ticket, most Low supporters evidently declined to vote at all for judge. In Manhattan and the Bronx, where there were 55,000 fewer votes for judge than for mayor, support for Low correlates at + .87 with the percentage of ballots that were blank or defective for chief judge. Since Wallace lost to the Democrat, Alton B. Parker, by approximately the number of blank judicial ballots in the greater city, the desertion of Low supporters may have cost Wallace the election.[40]

Republican losses in 1897 were not confined to New York and Brooklyn. Throughout the state, urban voters, turning in force to the Democracy, reversed the process that had made the cities, and the state, Republican in 1893 and 1894. In Rochester, where the Good Government forces again allied with the Democrats, Wallace's share of the vote dropped to 52 percent, compared to McKinley's 60 percent. In Buffalo, where a dispute over party enrollment divided independents from regulars, the Republican vote fell from 61 percent for McKinley to 49 for Wallace. In Syracuse, the party's loss was similar, from 63 to 51 percent. A number of smaller cities, including Binghamton, Jamestown, Amsterdam, Kingston, and Schenectady, chose independent-sounding Democrats for mayor and gave Wallace, on the average, 10 percent less than they had given McKinley a year before.[41]

Just as in 1893–94, the most pronounced electoral shocks of 1897 were felt in the cities, while the town and country districts remained relatively stable. In one respect, however, electoral behavior outside the cities was unusual: voter turnout fell sharply, to well below its normal off-year levels. Statewide, only 63 percent of the eligible electorate cast ballots for chief judge, compared to about 70 percent who had voted in 1893 and 1895. The decline was steepest in strongly Republican northern and western New York where the rate of participation fell to 50 percent or less in eleven counties. Some observers believed the turnout losses occurred because rural Republicans were made "sick at heart and indifferent to their duty at the polls" by seeing their party foolishly allow Tammany Hall to take control of Greater New York City. A more persuasive explanation, recognized at the time, was the amendment separating state and city elections. While the cities were choosing mayors, voters in the towns (where local officials were elected in the spring) had only the judicial contest, plus county and assembly races, to draw them to the polls. Party leaders there had little incentive to encourage a high turnout since there were no vital state contests for which Republican votes were needed. The pattern established in 1897 continued: off-year elections in upstate New York never regained their previous rates of participation.[42]

Rural and town electors who abstained in 1897 did so for reasons different from those that moved city voters to act independently of the party organizations. Where there were no vigorous local governments performing a variety of police and social-service functions, citizens were much slower to adopt the doctrine of independence. Yet there was a kinship between the two developments, for both represented departures from nineteenth-century partisan electoral behavior. Both were encouraged by the constitutional amendment separating elections, and both established habits that proved long lasting. Upstate Republicans recognized the dangers of off-year apathy. "It is not by laxness that so vast a political organization is maintained in good effective working order," warned one loyal newspaper. By the next year it was evident that many rural and town citizens were becoming familiar with the antimachine doctrines of the city and learning to apply them. In the spring elections of 1898, an unusually large number of "independent" and "citizens'" candidates challenged the regular-party nominees for local office, and some of them won. This trend away from partisan behavior continued, encouraged by the recognition the Republicans were now compelled to accord the doctrine of independence.[43]

Seeing the losses that befell the party only one year after McKinley's great victory, regular Republicans took various steps to restore their majority.[44] While Platt, disgraced by his part in causing Tammany's triumph over Low, at first remained behind the scenes, Governor Black marked out the road to reunion with the independents by championing measures of reform they favored, especially a primary-election law passed in the spring of 1898. Then Platt reemerged during the summer and fall to bring about the nomination and election of Theodore Roosevelt as governor of New York. Roosevelt's subsequent administration, conventional as it was in many respects, restored the Republican-independent alliance and brought the dissidents' doctrines at last into the mainstream of state politics.

In the months before Roosevelt's nomination, the Republicans fashioned a number of reforms to pacify the independents. For one, the cities were exempted from the hated civil service law of 1897. For another, a long-delayed uniform charter was adopted for the state's second-class cities (that is, those with between 50,000 and 250,000 people), Albany, Troy, Syracuse, and Rochester. Based on the National Municipal League's model city charter, the new plan of government, which had failed of enactment in 1896 and 1897, replaced the separate charters then operative in each of the four cities and removed the occasion for continuous legislative interference in their local affairs. Most city independents welcomed the uniform charter, as the measure's sponsor, Senator Horace White of Syracuse, intended they should. The year before, White had pointedly reminded Rochester's Republican boss, George Washington Aldridge, that the new charter "will at once appeal to the independent voters, and will be a strong evidence of our genuine desire to accomplish progressive legislation for the cities of the second class." "We cannot elect a mayor in Syracuse," White told Aldridge, "and I suppose it is doubtful if you can in Rochester, without the help of the people of independent tendencies." In signing the new charter, Governor Black, who had vetoed it in 1897, recognized the strength of those very people by virtually renouncing his party's accustomed practice of interfering in the local affairs of the state's medium-sized cities.[45]

The most important reform adopted for the independents' benefit in 1898 was a primary-election law establishing thorough state regulation of nominating procedures. In every large city, the long-standing problems of defining party membership and conducting primary elections presented barriers to reuniting regular and antimachine Republicans and called forth various proposed solutions. Early in 1898, a group of independent Republicans in New York City, constituting themselves as the Committee of Fifty-Three, drew up new party rules that explicitly allowed those who supported nonpartisan local candidates to participate in Republican primaries. If adopted by the city's Republican organization, the committee proposal meant recognizing the regularity of Republicans who had voted for Seth Low and placing the party formally in support of municipal nonpartisanship. In Buffalo, where the Republicans had already extensively experimented with new party rules in recent years, the independent Buffalo Republican League supported a different approach: legal regulation. "There is but one way to heal the existing breach in the Republican party in this state," concluded William H. Hotchkiss, a leading member of the League, ". . . a new law controlling on the test of party membership and regulating the machinery of political committees, primaries and conventions." Before long, Republicans everywhere were recognizing the advantages of such a statute.[46]

Governor Black took charge of making sure the measure satisfied both regulars and dissidents. "We want a fair, liberal, honest primary law, one against which no complaint can be made by a Mugwump or anybody else," he told Lemuel E. Quigg. "We can afford to be liberal in the matter, and those of us who are pretty strong partisans and sensible at the same time, can perform a great service by yielding a little wherever necessary." The task of drafting the law fell to two prominent antimachine Republicans from New York City, Elihu Root and Paul D. Cravath. Conferring with the Committee of Fifty-Three, the Buffalo Republican League, and the governor, as well as with other independents and regulars, Root and Cravath obtained substantial agreement on a bill in March. Some rural and town Republicans registered skepticism of the measure. "Those fellows in New York . . . will get up an independent ticket, primary law or no primary law," grumbled Senator John Raines of Canandaigua. "You can't satisfy them." Even Raines went along, however, for the bill won unanimous approval in both legislative houses and received Black's signature.[47]

The primary law of 1898 showed by its contents, as well as by the consultation that had produced it, that regulars and independents had rediscovered election-law reform as a basis for cooperation. Taking from political parties in the large cities the authority to determine many of their own rules, the new law prescribed the manner of enrolling party members, constituting party committees, and holding conventions. It provided for the conduct of primaries by the regular election inspectors at public expense. Like the rules the Committee of Fifty-Three had proposed, the new statute permitted party members to join nonpartisan organizations, such as the Citizens' Union, whose field of action was municipal politics alone. But by denying such associations the right to nominate candidates for state office (except under stringent conditions), the statute reserved the state political arena to the parties. In agreeing to the law, the regulars accepted the permanence of municipal nonpartisanship, while, for their part, the independents foreswore the opportunity to contest state elections.[48]

Republicans on both sides expressed confidence that the new law paved the way for harmony. "I am sanguine," Low told Black, "that . . . its passage will re-unite the Republican party in this State for the contests of the future." Timothy Woodruff, Platt's ally in Brooklyn, praised the law for "what it has accomplished toward closing the breach which divided the ranks of our party." Even the nonpartisan *Nation* expressed approval of what it called a "decidedly revolutionary measure" that entirely did away with "the old style of primary."[49]

Of course, no revolution really occurred. In the spring primaries of 1898, the machine's opponents found themselves outnumbered in most districts of Greater New York. In Rochester, the story was similar. As one of boss Aldridge's lieutenants reported to him, "I don't think I am premature in congratulating you on the results of the enrollment. . . . Good hard work was done by our boys, while that done by the opposition is notable only in a few instances." When the primaries were held in June, Aldridge's boys indeed won. Despite their losses, independent Republicans admired the new system's adherence to their principles. As Whitelaw Reid's *New York Tribune* observed, those who voted for Low "are not only welcomed back [into the party], but occupy the pulpit, and their doctrine of municipal non-partisanship is not only accepted as an edifying text, but is incorporated into the canon of party law." State law, too, Reid might have added.[50]

Although he had led the way in achieving reforms the independents wanted, Governor Black found that several things stood in the way of his renomination for governor in 1898: the memory of his excessive partisanship the year before, the suspicion that he was still scheming to take away Platt's leadership, and the recent disclosure that much of a $9 million canal-improvement fund had been misused by officials in his administration. From Platt's point of view, all of Black's weaknesses could be overcome if the party nominated someone conspicuously free of close ties to the regular organization. Such a man would reassure the independents and restore the party's scandal-tarnished image but would lack the organizational base needed to unseat the boss. Theodore Roosevelt was the perfect choice.[51]

Roosevelt had always stood, in Mark Sullivan's phrase, "at the outer edge of party regularity." If he had never completely broken with the machine, he had never been part of it either. At each point in his political career, by now nearly two decades old, Roosevelt had taken actions that regular Republicans found objectionable. As an opponent of Blaine's nomination in 1884, as a crusading civil service commissioner, as the enforcer of Sunday closing in New York, and as a supporter of Low, Roosevelt had repeatedly infuriated Republican leaders. Yet his freedom from the machine, in combination with his recent heroic record at San Juan Hill, was exactly what the machine now needed.[52]

Indeed, politicians from around the state who wrote to Platt on Roosevelt's behalf late in the summer of 1898 cited his independence more frequently than they mentioned his heroism. "His nomination would solidify the Republican party," wrote one correspondent. "'Independent' and 'Machine' Republicans would work shoulder to shoulder, and the internal dissensions in the party would be healed up." According to another writer, "many Democrats and Mugwumps, (Independents as they are more politely termed) have said to me that they would vote for him." Still another told Platt that "a large class who call themselves 'Independents' will vote for the Rough Rider, but not for the present Governor."[53]

Members of Platt's inner circle, including Odell and Quigg, brought him the same message. Before committing himself, however, Platt took the precaution of sounding out Roosevelt. Their negotiations, conducted through the intermediation of Quigg, demonstrated the subtle, painful process through which independents and partisans were reconciled. Quigg asked Roosevelt if, as governor, he would regularly

Theodore Roosevelt (Library of Congress)

consult the party leaders on both appointments and policy, and the Rough Rider said he would but reserved the right to confer with independents too. Roosevelt and Quigg exchanged several lengthy statements in which each of them tried to express the essence of what Governor Roosevelt's relationship to the organization would be. Finally, Roosevelt met with Platt himself, and together they went over the ground Roosevelt had covered with Quigg. In the end, Platt took a chance on Roosevelt's expressions of willingness to consult the party leaders. "He will undoubtedly disappoint us," Platt told an upstate ally, "but I think he is and means to remain a Republican."[54]

Most observers interpreted Roosevelt's nomination as proof that the Republicans had recognized the independents. His candidacy "appeals directly for the support of men who are really independent in politics," said the *Buffalo Commercial*. Regular and antimachine leaders both affirmed their intention to unite behind Roosevelt. "It is very important," the candidate told Quigg, "that we should get the idea firmly established that the forces which were divided last year, are united this year." Quigg agreed. To James B. Reynolds of the Citizens' Union Quigg wrote, "I think that we ought to act on the assumption throughout this campaign, that we are not going to break away from one another hereafter."[55]

Roosevelt's narrow election (by 18,000 votes compared to McKinley's margin of 270,000 in 1896) reunited the independents and Republicans of Greater New York City. There the party recovered many of its losses from the year before, especially in the districts where Low had run most strongly. In Greater New York as a whole, the Republican vote exceeded its 1897 total by 74,000, while the Democrats added but 19,000. Among the large upstate cities, however, only Syracuse followed the downstate pattern; in Buffalo, Rochester, and Albany, Roosevelt ran behind Wallace's vote. There the independents and Republicans remained disunited. As governor, Roosevelt would have the opportunity to provide what Quigg termed "the argument for union" between them. That he should do so, after all, was the intention behind his nomination.[56]

During 1899 and 1900, Governor Roosevelt succeeded in the trying task of avoiding either "a split with the Machine or a smashup with the independents." He consulted Platt, as he promised he would, but he also consulted the reformers. Roosevelt championed specific laws, as well as appointments, that they favored, and he influenced the regulars to cooperate with them in city politics. Perhaps above all, Roosevelt articulately phrased a qualified endorsement of party government which rejected partisanship's excessive claims. "It is only through the party system that free governments are now successfully carried on," he said in his inaugural address, "and yet . . . the usefulness of a party is strictly limited by its usefulness to the State." Spread by Roosevelt and his supporters, that idea soon became the conventional wisdom in New York politics.[57]

Although Roosevelt's frequent meetings with Platt rankled some independents, the governor defended his course. "I want results," he told Seth Low. "I am only too glad to call on Mr. Platt, or to have him to dinner, or take breakfast with him, and to discuss with him first and at length all projects, provided, in the end, I have my way about these same projects." Low understood, but a vocal minority of nonpartisans, to whose opinions the *Nation* and the *Evening Post* gave voice, did not. They excoriated Roosevelt for truckling to Platt and serving the organization. In denouncing these "ultra independents," as he called them, the governor was merciless. "The Goo-Goo and Mugwump idiots are quite as potent forces for evil as the most corrupt politicians," he told one correspondent. Yet in his policies, Roosevelt usually pleased the majority of independents, whose doctrines he shared.[58]

This was especially true in the areas of civil service and municipal reform. Labeling Black's "starchless" civil service a "farce," Roosevelt proposed a new system harmonizing the methods of appointment used in different parts of the state and extending the use of competitive examinations. The governor cooperated closely with the members of the Civil Service Reform Association in framing the new law, which later received the association's praise as "superior to any civil service statute heretofore secured in America." Where the large cities were concerned, Roosevelt did not pursue the partisan tactics that had characterized Republican policy from 1895 to 1897. He opposed Platt's metropolitan police plan for downstate New York and, after initially favoring it, withdrew his support for a state police constabulary covering all the large cities. In appointing a commission to revise the charter of Greater New York in 1900, Roosevelt explicitly took the part of the independents against Platt. While the boss wanted a Republican for chairman, the governor insisted on George L. Rives, an independent Democrat. "Nothing . . . would damage us more in New York . . . than to have them [the independents] get the idea that the charter commission was being managed as a republican adjunct," Roosevelt told Platt. "It seemed to me that the Charter Commission was eminently a body in which I could afford to recognize the independent element."[59]

While Roosevelt and Platt sometimes disagreed on specific laws or appointments, the boss approved the governor's efforts to keep up cooperation between the independents and the regulars. "I expected you to have consideration of the views and wishes of our independent friends," Platt told Roosevelt in May 1899, "and, indeed, wished you to take that course in the hope that you would succeed in uniting the party."[60]

City politics continued to be the most critical arena for Republican-independent relations, and there Roosevelt successfully encouraged party regulars to cooperate with the reformers and recognize their doctrines. In Greater New York, where a mayor would next be elected in 1901, the legislative and judicial contests of 1899 provided a trial run for the renewal of harmony among the anti-Tammany forces. Led by Quigg, who felt it important "not simply to avoid a split with the Independents but actually to maintain the same harmonious relations that we had with them last year," Republican regulars took Roosevelt's advice and joined with the independents in nominating a fusion ticket.[61]

The same cooperation was practiced in the large upstate cities where the Republicans adopted the language of nonpartisan city government and, in consequence, now recovered from the disaster of 1897. In Albany, Barnes's Republican organization named a municipal ticket acceptable to most independents and conducted a campaign pointedly free of partisan appeals. When the returns were in, an independent splinter ticket had been reduced to 1.5 percent of the vote, compared with 27 percent in 1897. Barnes's *Evening Journal* declared it a victory for businesslike government, not for the Republican party. In Rochester, where the Good Government forces had allied with the Democrats in 1895 and 1897, Aldridge now picked a city ticket in consultation with the leading independents and returned Rochester to the Republican fold. In Buffalo, where the Republicans explicitly appealed for independent support, the party's entire local ticket swept to victory. Even in Troy, the Republicans forged an alliance with independent Democrats and won. Among the large upstate cities, only Syracuse, where a popular Democrat won a third term as mayor, remained in Democratic hands. There the alliance of Republicans and independents was not reestablished until 1901.[62]

That year, with Roosevelt in the White House, the cooperation that his election to the governorship had fostered in 1898 pervaded politics in all the largest cities of New York. Syracuse reentered the Republican camp, while Albany, Troy, Rochester, and Buffalo remained there. The most significant triumph came in New York City where the Republicans joined with the Citizens' Union, as well as with other anti-Tammany groups, to elect Seth Low as mayor. The circumstances of Low's election contrasted strikingly with the conditions under which he met defeat in 1897.[63]

Both the Citizens' Union and the Republicans had become more amenable to fusion. Most C.U. leaders recognized that it was unrealistic to expect all the different anti-Tammany elements to coalesce without previously coming to some understanding about policies and patronage in the upcoming administration. For their part, the Republicans also were more prepared to cooperate than they had been in 1897. The blame he suffered that year and the consequences of that election made Platt wary of seeming to help Tammany again. Moreover, with his own leadership threatened by the new governor, Benjamin B. Odell, Jr., Platt was in no position to take the unpopular position of naming a separate Republican ticket.

After months of discussion, the Citizens' Union, the Republicans, and numerous groups of Democrats and ethnics chose Low for mayor and nominated a balanced slate of candidates for the other local offices. In the campaign that followed, the Republicans' position differed entirely from the one they took in 1897. "In the deliberations of National and State conventions partisanship has a proper place," declared Timothy Woodruff, ". . . but in the government of the municipality, . . . non-partisanship should be the dominant idea." The Republican organization appears to have worked loyally for Low, and the results suggest that the fusion ticket received the full Republican and independent vote.[64]

Encouraged by Roosevelt, Low and Platt met soon after the election to talk about the Republican party's relationship to the new administration. Though frictions later developed between them, Platt promised to give Low's regime a fair chance. When the mayor-elect and his victorious running mates spoke publicly of their hopes for the coming administration, they conveyed a commitment to solving the city's problems and bringing its diverse people together without regard to party purposes. In standing with Low at that moment, the considerable forces of Platt Republicanism had become a part of something quite different from the quest for city spoils the boss had begun seven years before.[65]

"Is it not undeniable," Robert Fulton Cutting, the president of the Citizens' Union, asked in 1901, "that the Republican party has felt the chastening influence of the movement of '97, and relinquishing the lust for city plunder, purified its intentions and its practices?"[66] It *was* undeniable that the "movement of '97" had changed Republican behavior. The party had curtailed its political interference in the cities and approved measures of municipal reform the independents wanted. New election laws had given the government responsibility for running the primaries and printing the ballots, both of which had previously been

Seth Low (Library of Congress)

unfettered party functions. Theodore Roosevelt and Seth Low had been elevated to the two highest offices in the state, and their qualified language of independence had become a common element of political rhetoric. All these things had happened through the influence of the urban independents, unquestionably the most dynamic element in the political system during the Platt era.

The independents' impact depended upon their demonstrated freedom from partisan restraints on election day. Having swung heavily toward the Republicans in 1893 and 1894, they continued to behave independently during the following years. Their volatility, their propensity to name independent candidates, and their tendency to vote split tickets or abstain compelled the Republicans to adopt measures the dissidents demanded. Some of those measures, while not automatically weakening the party machines, made easier the independents' nonpartisan voting practices and led other elements in the state to experiment with them also. Already the separation-of-elections amendment was encouraging nonpartisan nominations in the cities and discouraging off-year turnout in the town and country districts. Soon ticket-splitting would be on the rise, made easier by the Australian ballot. These legal changes plainly facilitated independent ways of voting, but they did not cause them. For behind the new laws stood urban attitudes of independence which, in the long run, provided a more fundamental source of changed electoral behavior than did the new legal machinery.

It is important not to exaggerate the gains made by independence at the expense of partisanship during the 1890s. Turnout losses and ticket-splitting remained small compared to their levels in the following decade. Many of the seeming triumphs over partisanship were rhetorical and symbolic and reflected the capacity of shrewd party leaders to fashion concessions that did not affect the structure of politics. Most of the advances toward independence, moreover, were made by men who in state and national politics considered themselves good Republicans. Their battle with the regulars was in some respects a family squabble, shaped by self-interest on both sides. Indeed, the independents' dynamic influence on the political system was possible only because many of them *were* Republicans, with a party strategy of their own for keeping control of New York.

Yet the independence they voiced presented a real threat to the old-style, nineteenth-century partisan politics. Maintaining a party coalition with men who rejected municipal partisanship and were skeptical of partisan claims at any political level proved difficult and dangerous. In order to appease such men, the regular party leaders accommodated to the symbols and language of independence, yet in so doing they inadvertently permitted the new words and new laws to become available for use against themselves if the occasion arose, as it did toward the middle of the new century's first decade. In 1900 one observer of New York politics accurately noted a considerable "confusion of thought among the people on the question of party government."[67] The established party system was entering a period of flux, whose outcome was far from certain. Independence had not triumphed, but it was challenging the partisan political culture, and it was gaining.

5

Republicans and Economic Policies, 1895–1900

As the nineteenth century neared its end, the New York State political system stood on the verge of a major transformation, barely discernable at the time. Independence from parties was already changing both electoral behavior and the conduct of politics. Industrial developments were simultaneously beginning to move the government toward policies that recognized and mitigated conflicts of economic interest. Not for a few more years, however, would independence and the demand for new economic policies become closely entwined with one another and work a significant restructuring of the traditional system.

In its basic thrust, economic policymaking under Platt followed an accustomed nineteenth-century pattern. Government excelled in distributing benefits to promote commerce and industry, while it gave less attention to regulating, administering, and planning for the enterprises it assisted.[1] In carrying out promotional policies, public officials cooperated closely with the businessmen being benefited. Behind such a policy process lay the assumption, sincerely stated by Republicans and implicitly shared by many Democrats, that distributive benefits directly or indirectly assisted almost everyone, because the different producer groups in society had fundamentally harmonious interests. So long as social and economic conditions lent plausibility to the belief in harmony, officials furthered promotional policies and discouraged regulatory and administrative measures which were inherently more divisive. By the late 1890s, however, growth and change were forcing the party in power to begin to acknowledge the existence of conflicts of economic interest and to move toward new ways of governance on material questions.

Two broad developments were responsible for the emergence of a new structure of economic policy. The first and most visible source of change lay in the increasing organization of producer groups to bring about government actions that would help them even at others' expense. Farmers, workers, merchants, manufacturers, and owners of public utilities, each becoming more aware of their own special interests, opposed measures that assisted rival groups and banded together to demand specific public protections for their own endeavors. Their efforts not only succeeded in establishing many of the desired policies but also served to discredit distributive benefits based on the assumption of harmony. A second, less tangible, impetus for change came from the unorganized public's dawning sense of unease, fear, and anger about the transformations wrought by large corporations. Favorable to "industry," ordinary New Yorkers distrusted "big business." Sometimes the people's inchoate feelings focused on the ill-understood "trusts"; at other times, their negative emotions found more tangible local targets in street-railway or electric power companies.

New York's Republican leaders responded reluctantly to both sorts of pressure. They found existing policies congenial and their personal interests made them unsympathetic to antibusiness feelings. Many of them no doubt genuinely believed that the distribution of resources and privileges to businessmen brought prosperity to the whole society. Of more importance, distributive benefits strengthened the party by providing the policy equivalent of patronage, while the recognition of economic interests through regulation or administration seemed sure to invite division in a coalition that extended across class lines. To these political purposes were added personal ones: many Republican leaders enjoyed close financial relations with the businessmen who benefited from government allocation. At first, Platt's party stubbornly withstood the pressure for new policies or responded symbolically by instituting regulations but not enforcing them. Then, in 1899 and 1900, Governor Theodore Roosevelt cautiously began moving the Republicans toward twentieth-century methods of governance on economic matters.

There was nothing unusual in public assistance to economic interests. In allocating franchises, constructing transportation facilities, and maintaining generous tax policies, New York Republicans of the 1890s promoted business interests, just as government officials in America traditionally had. What made Platt's policies somewhat distinctive, however, was the regular system he established of exchanging government assistance for campaign contributions. Only dimly perceived by New York citizens in the 1890s, this system ultimately did great damage to Platt's reputation and to that of his party.

Public actions supporting business were not, of course, inherently corrupt. A staple of policymaking, these measures often provided a source of pride for those responsible for them. Party platforms, gubernatorial messages, and local newspapers called attention to such achievements, just as individual politicians eagerly sought the distinction of assisting their districts' industries. John C. Davies of Oneida County, state attorney general from 1899 to 1902, informed one constituent that he had "done considerable by way of promoting the interests of . . . [Utica's] business men." He told another that "I have not hesitated to attempt to find a market for the products of some of the manufacturers of our county, whenever it was thought that a suggestion from me would help along." Davies claimed never to have received "so much as a cigar" for his efforts.[2] But other helpful officeholders got cigars, and more, for themselves and for the Republican organization.

Many leading Republicans sought government benefits for their private business concerns. Some pleaded for and received state contracts, such as the printing jobs that newspaper publisher William Barnes, Jr., often performed for the government. Others applied pressure to have the state purchase products in whose manufacture they had a financial interest, as George E. Green and George Washington Dunn did when they asked Public Works Superintendent George Washington Aldridge to favor the Bundy Time Recorder. Most characteristically, they used their influence to protect and extend the privileges held by utility and transportation companies in which they were interested. Chauncey M. Depew frankly spent most of his political career keeping a friendly eye on the New York Central Railroad. Edward Lauterbach did the same for New York City's Third Avenue railway line.[3]

Platt sympathized with his allies' projects, for the boss and his family also enjoyed governmental largesse. Noting in 1897 that President William McKinley and Mark Hanna had approved Platt's nominee for chief clerk of the United States Treasury Department, an envious observer exclaimed, "Now please stand off and watch the U.S. Express Co. [of which Platt was president] get contracts at liberal rates for the transportation of currency and Government funds." Platt's company indeed received such contracts. Two of the boss's sons, Frank H. and Henry B., benefited from a state law passed in 1895 that legalized the bonds of out-of-state surety companies, such as the Fidelity and Deposit Company of Maryland in which they had large holdings. Passed with the support of their father, who privately labeled the measure "the only legislation in which . . . [I have] felt any personal interest," the law allowed the Platt brothers' company to bond liquor dealers, canal contractors, and others from whom the state demanded surety. Sellers of liquor, who were required by the Raines law the next year to post bonds equaling twice their yearly tax, perceived the advantages of dealing with the boss's sons, and, incidentally, with Senator Raines's son, who also worked for the Fidelity. Henry B. Platt acknowledged that their company "was fortunate enough to secure more [of the liquor bonding business] than others."[4]

Of greater significance than such personal dealings were the established arrangements between Republican leaders and big businessmen. Sharing similar values as well as interests, the two elites mutually thrived through the interchangeability of political and economic power. Their relations, while far from entirely harmonious in the late 1890s, gave certain classes of large corporations, alone among the state's economic groups, regular access to political representation.[5]

Considering the secrecy with which the politico-business alliance was naturally shrouded, a surprising amount of evidence documents its operation under Platt. A number of legislative investigations conducted between 1905 and 1913, as well as a stunning libel suit that Barnes brought against Roosevelt in 1915, provide convincing testimony by many leading participants in the alliance, including businessmen and Platt himself. Interviews, newspaper probes, and considerable correspondence add detail to the picture.[6]

What the sources show is that when the Republicans came to power in 1895, Platt put into operation a centralized system of collecting campaign funds from big companies and afterward protecting their interests through the government. "He received contributions from all the large corporations," confided Benjamin B. Odell, Jr., in 1922. "That was the way that things were done in those days. . . . The money for campaigns had to be raised from somewhere and the corporations which sought legislative favors began to contribute." Roosevelt recalled how Platt had told him of taking campaign funds from businessmen and feeling an "honorable obligation" to defend their interests afterward. Asked during the legislative life insurance investigation of 1905 whether "the use of these contributions in the election of candidates to office puts the candidates under . . . moral obligation not to attack the interests supporting," Platt admitted, "That is what would naturally be involved."[7]

The elements of Platt's system were not unknown in American politics before the 1890s, but the extent and success of its operation were new to that decade. Forced by civil service reforms to find fresh sources for the election funds that political appointees had once provided, party leaders increasingly tapped corporate wealth. In national politics, Hanna perfected the collection system in 1896, while leaders like Platt in New York and Matthew Quay in Pennsylvania were doing the same at the state level. Especially from that year on, with the

Democratic party Bryanized, corporate executives found it prudent, in Chauncey Depew's words, to "contribute [to the Republicans] like taking out an insurance policy, for the benefit of the general interests in which they were involved."[8]

Platt was proud of the centralized method of collection, not simply because it enhanced his status as the harmonizer of business and politics in the Empire State, but also because, as one contemporary claimed, it worked "a great improvement" by reducing "the corruption of the individual legislator." From descriptions later given, it is certain that Platt's election fund from corporate sources amounted to tens of thousands of dollars each year. The largest life insurance companies alone evidently contributed ten thousand dollars each on a regular basis. Delivered to Platt in cash by secret messengers, the contributions came without strings attached.[9]

In return, Platt used his influence with the legislature to shape policy in accordance with what the contributing interests wanted. Often this meant killing harmful measures. "There is a bill which was introduced by Wieman in the Assembly, reducing telegraph tolls," Platt wrote to Speaker Hamilton Fish in 1895. "It is in the Committee of Electricity and Gas. There are various reasons why this should not get out of Committee." The boss similarly guided Speaker S. Fred Nixon. Writing of two measures harmful to the racing interests, Platt told him, "The influences back of these bills are bad and some of our good friends are seriously opposed to them." Frequently Platt acted positively in support of measures his business allies favored. He asked Governor Morton to approve a bill permitting the Niagara Falls Hydraulic Power and Manufacturing Company to continue to use the falls to generate electricity. It was important, the boss said, that the Republicans not deny the company power. One assemblyman later recalled how the party organization had often supported bills originating with industrial or financial interests. "We'd know that some business group had ordered it," he said. "We'd never heard of it. It would go through just the same."[10]

Among the most complex business measures for which thorough documentation of Platt's role survives was the Pennsylvania Railroad tunnel bill of 1902. On January 20, Platt informed Governor Odell and the legislative leaders that he had "just had an interview with President Cassatt, of the Pennsylvania Railway Company, at which he has disclosed to me his plans with reference to their entrance into the City of New York [from New Jersey] via an underground tunnel. I will disclose to you, at the proper time, the legislation they desire." A few days later, Cassatt sent Platt a draft of the bill the company wanted, and

Platt forwarded it to the governor and the legislators. Taking the form of an amendment to the New York City charter, the bill permitted local authorities to grant the railroad a perpetual franchise for its tunnel in return for "reasonable" annual compensation.

Within a week, railroad officials had apparently changed their minds concerning some details of the tunnel bill, for Cassatt sent amended legislation to Platt, who, in turn, passed it on to the Republican members of the assembly and senate. After another week, Cassatt again informed Platt of "defects" in the bill, and the boss helpfully supported another revised measure. In more than one instance, Platt adopted Cassatt's exact words in telling legislative leaders about the bill. Throughout the winter, Platt kept in close touch with both Cassatt and the lawmakers. Writing to Nixon late in February, the boss said he hoped there would be no hesitation on the part of the assembly about the tunnel bill because it was "just and right." Platt's wish was fulfilled, and when the measure passed Cassatt told him, "You have placed us under an obligation which it will be a pleasure to acknowledge when ever an opportunity offers."[11]

Effective as Platt's system was, it did not preclude some of the favor-seeking corporations from carrying on their own extensive legislative relations, usually conducted by agents stationed in Albany. The Mutual Life Insurance Company, for instance, employed one Andrew C. Fields, who kept up a house, known as the "House of Mirth," for the entertainment of the lawmakers. During one winter session, two members of the senate insurance committee actually made Fields's place their residence. The steam railway companies also cultivated Albany connections, perhaps none more extensively than the New York Central Railroad, which plainly persuaded some legislators to do its bidding. "We are interested in this bill and would like to have it pushed through and become a law before May 20th," the company's general counsel told Senator Joseph Mullin of the railroad committee on one occasion in the spring of 1895. On another matter, the railroad's lawyer informed Mullin, "I think that we are much opposed to this bill. Will you please see that it is not progressed until you hear from me further?" In 1899 the Delaware and Hudson Railroad Company used comparable legislative muscle to obtain a vital revision of its corporate charter.[12]

Despite Platt's progress in centralizing the transfer of monies from business to politics, individual lawmakers were often paid for their services to large corporations. Besides cash, they frequently received transportation passes, usually given in the name of a man's wife to circumvent the constitutional ban on free passes for public officials. Sometimes, the legislators demanded payment in return for killing harmful "strike" bills that had been introduced for the sole purpose of fleecing the threatened companies. According to later testimony by leading businessmen, these measures were common and could only be stopped by bribery. But the weight of evidence suggests that, in general, it was affirmative action, benefiting their interests, that the corporations wanted and paid for.[13]

Among the more elaborate arrangements for paying off legislators were the ones devised by G. Tracy Rogers of Binghamton, president of the Street Railway Association of the State of New York. Representing traction corporations in most of the state's large cities, Rogers's organization levied yearly assessments, totaling $20,000 or more, on its member companies and distributed the funds to friendly lawmakers, as well as to county and state committees of the Republican party. A legislative investigation in 1910 disclosed that Rogers operated through the brokerage firm of Ellingwood and Cunningham in New York City. There he had quietly established a series of joint accounts, each in his own name and the name of a key legislator, usually a member of the railroad committee. By paying the association's money into the accounts, Rogers secretly transferred it to the helpful lawmakers.[14]

As these illustrations suggest, the men who bought the government's favors either from Platt, or directly from members of the legislature, or both, tended to come from certain sectors of the business community. In general, the heads of transportation and communication corporations, gas and electric power companies, and insurance concerns worked closely with the Republican leadership. Such businesses required public franchises and privileges in order to prosper, and all were nominally regulated by the state. They depended on the government to maintain their existing privileges, to grant new ones as required, and to avoid instituting harmful regulations. To these classes of business may be added several others—especially liquor and horse racing—that operated in the face of moral disapproval by a significant segment of the population and thus felt a special need for the protection of those in power.[15]

On the other side were the manufacturing and mercantile concerns that asked relatively little from the state or demanded things the Republicans resisted giving. Such companies felt small need to fill Platt's coffers. Manufacturers naturally wanted federal tariff protection for their products, but from state government they craved mainly neglect. The merchants likewise needed few benefits from Albany, or at least few the Republicans could easily grant. What large-city merchants increasingly demanded was the stricter regulation of transportation, communication, and utility corporations, as well as large appropriations to improve the Erie Canal system, but Republican leaders were wary of supporting either. Regulation was likely to harm the parties' existing business allies, while canal improvement deeply divided upstate Republican voters. Organized in chambers of commerce and boards of trade, the merchants of the large cities generally pressed their demands for new economic policies by opposing Platt, rather than by purchasing his help.[16]

In the 1890s, New York citizens had only a rudimentary understanding of the politico-business alliance. Most criticism of Platt's machine concerned narrowly political evils such as election fraud, spoilsmanship, or deals with Tammany Hall. Occasionally, the Democrats attacked their opponents' corporate connections, as a Buffalo newspaper editor did in 1897, when he observed that if the Republican mayoral candidate were elected, the city "would undoubtedly have a great 'business administration.' We admit that. But the corporations would do the business." More often, those who grasped the connection between politics and business openly sympathized with the businessmen. One critic accurately described Platt's centralized system of collecting funds and protecting the corporations but reasoned that businessmen contributed solely in order to buy "peace" from corrupt and hostile politicians. Theodore Roosevelt later recalled that "'Big Business' was back of . . . [Platt]; yet at the time this, the most important element in his strength, was only imperfectly understood. It was not until I was elected governor that I myself came to understand it. We were still accustomed to talking of the 'machine' as if it were something merely political, with which business had nothing to do."[17]

Still less understood in the 1890s was how an economic-policy tradition based on discrete, distributive benefits, little checked by regulation, encouraged the corrupt alliance of business and politics. Corporations that needed privileges but abhorred effective state regulations offered to buy the policies they wanted. Those in power sold them willingly and secretly, while at the same time they forestalled measures of regulation and administration through which the government might have recognized an industrial society's conflicts of interest. Other economic groups, having less access to government, generally failed to monitor the transactions and were just beginning to perceive how their own interests were being hurt. Not until the following decade was the connection between the nature of policy and the corruption of government widely seen in New York.

While it quietly assisted certain business interests, Platt's party resisted adopting new public policies on economic subjects. Almost any noteworthy government decision—whether concerning labor, taxation, regulation, or transportation—meant explicitly recognizing the claims of some groups at the expense of others. Leading Republicans were wary of doing this. Their party's traditional ideology affirmed the harmony of interests; divisive policies would inevitably endanger a heterogeneous coalition; and innovations might hurt the party's existing business allies. Thus during their first years in office, the Republican party largely avoided new economic policies or, failing that, enforced the measures only weakly.

On labor issues, the depression conditions of the mid-1890s strengthened the Republicans' disinclination to take significant action benefiting workers. Middle- and upper-class aversion to organized labor had been aroused by the violent strikes of 1894 and remained strong in the following years. As hard times hurt labor's position, union membership fell. Labor's weakened legislative voice remained divided between the Workingmen's Assembly, the State Federation of Labor, and the State Assembly of the Knights of Labor. The years 1895–98 consequently brought little that was new in the way of labor policy.[18]

On the two issues of most importance to organized labor, the eight-hour day and employers' liability, the Republicans took no action. The state's eight-hour law, permitting workers to "contract" for overtime work, remained a dead letter, while existing practices continued to allow employers to evade liability for accidents causing injury and death to their workers. Where labor by women and children was concerned, New York maintained its relatively advanced position by adopting several new measures that further extended the state's official oversight of hours and conditions. But where the labor of adult males was involved, the Republicans' record was thinner. Some measures actually took away gains won in earlier years. One law exempted railroads from the requirement that wages be paid weekly; another modified the previously enacted limitation upon hours for brickyard workers. In 1897 the legislature approved an entire revision of the labor law but made almost no substantive changes.[19]

Even where new rules were enacted, enforcement was designedly lax. The child-labor laws, for instance, included phraseology that practically insured their ineffectiveness. An 1896 statute regulating the work of women and children in department stores gave the responsibility for enforcement to local boards of health, sure to be influenced by the store owners. The office of the Factory Inspector, which was charged with investigating the conditions of work in every manufacturing establishment in New York, steadily grew in size but could not possibly complete its assigned task. Under the Republicans, it almost seemed to stop trying. Daniel O'Leary of Glens Falls became inspector in 1896, and during his three-year regime the enforcement of factory laws—which had never been strenuous—practically came to a halt. The fines imposed by the bureau for all violations averaged less than $300 a year under O'Leary, compared to over $2,000 from 1893 to 1895; the average number of prosecutions fell to 22 a year, compared with 136 before. Blaming O'Leary seems pointless. New York State had no previous tradition of continuously overseeing labor and industry, and it is not surprising that nothing the Republicans did during their first years in office helped establish one.[20]

In small, local ways, the party took steps on behalf of laborers, especially those employed on public-works projects. Republicans in Albany defended the interests of construction workers completing the new state capitol; when funds for the building ran out, Barnes demanded more. Public Works Superintendent Aldridge similarly protected laborers on the Erie Canal. By supporting an hourly wage of at least fifteen cents, enforcing the eight-hour law and the ban on alien labor, and settling local disputes along the waterway, Aldridge used his position to strengthen the party and himself among canal workers. But where the interests of purely private employers were at stake, the Republicans did much less.[21]

In defense of this policy, party leaders maintained that the true interests of workers fundamentally corresponded with those of other economic groups. As Governor Black put it in his annual message of 1897, "There is no natural antagonism between labor and capital. They are the same. Capital is nothing but labor turned into money." Already, however, that postion was becoming difficult to maintain. Some years later, Timothy Woodruff indiscreetly disclosed another reason why his party had ignored the special needs of labor when he acknowledged that "in the past the Republican party in the state had received 95% of its campaign contributions from corporations and, therefore, had been unable to listen to the workingmen's side."[22]

Since each economic group had a stake in reducing its own taxes at the expense of others, tax policy, like labor questions, brought politicians face-to-face with conflicting interests. Indeed, there was a growing recognition in New York in the 1890s that the existing system of taxation, based on the general property tax, was defective and inequitable. Real-estate levies varied unfairly from one place to another; personal property was difficult to assess, especially in the newer, intangible forms it was assuming due to the growth of big business; and corporations, taxed haphazardly, frequently evaded their payments on a massive scale. Yet, with the important exception of the Raines liquor-tax law of 1896, the Republicans maintained the state's existing taxation system during their first years in office. Governors Morton and Black declined to recommend new levies or the revision of old ones, while party campaign statements essentially avoided the tax issue.[23]

"Great care should be taken," Morton warned in 1895, "that the [tax] burdens placed upon business enterprise are not too heavy." Levied according to different formulas for different classes of business, corporation taxes remained largely unchanged in the 1890s. Although the number of taxed companies more than doubled from 1893 to 1898, most of those added to the rolls were small. Indeed, the proportion of state revenues furnished by corporations declined between 1894 and 1900, from about 15 percent to 12 percent.[24]

In 1897 Comptroller James A. Roberts proposed a graduated inheritance tax in place of the uniform assessment then made against every estate. Designed to tap personal wealth which otherwise escaped taxation, as well as to compensate for the "special privileges conferred by government . . . [which provide] the foundation of most of the great fortunes," the proposed tax enjoyed widespread support. It "will be a popular measure with all who are not millionaires," declared one upstate weekly newspaper. The assembly unanimously approved a bill embodying Roberts's suggestion, and an overwhelming, bipartisan majority of senators concurred. But Platt considered a progressive inheritance tax "vicious" and prevailed on Black to veto it. In doing so, the governor took the occasion to denounce the assault on wealthy interests. "The claim that the rich are growing richer and the poor poorer is not true," he said, "and would have no bearing here if it were."[25]

The unpopularity of Black's veto and the evident demand among Republican voters for tax reform suggested that soon the party in power would have to face the need to overhaul the state's revenue system. Yet doing so was difficult because of the clashes of locales and groups that the question inevitably inspired. Reducing direct property taxes on farmers and middle-class city dwellers meant increasing the so-called "indirect" taxes on personal and corporate wealth. In 1898 Roberts declared that state costs could be met entirely from indirect sources, but his advice went unheeded. Not willing to increase the burden on their business allies or to risk inciting the group conflicts that tax-policy changes invited, party leaders stilled discussion of what an equitable tax structure would be.[26]

The supervision of business corporations posed a policy problem as sensitive as that of taxation. Yet regulation was more argued about than practiced in the 1890s. While the state prescribed the manner of organizing corporations and played minor supervisory roles from inspecting gas meters to certifying surgeons, only a few classes of business were much affected by regulation, and none encountered continuous government involvement in their affairs. Instead, like distributive benefits, regulatory policies were discrete and piecemeal; they were usually undertaken to solve particular problems, sometimes brought to the authorities' attention by consumers but more often by the affected businesses themselves. Nothing accomplished during the first six years of Republican rule in New York altered the existing haphazard quality of business regulation.[27]

Railroad, insurance, and gas policies illustrate the state's unsystematic approaches to supervising business. Created in 1882, the Board of Railroad Commissioners possessed a range of investigatory and advisory functions but exercised them weakly. Without enforcement powers, but with three prized posts for deserving politicians, the board had more political than economic significance. A letter from Governor Black to Platt casts light on how casually Republican leaders regarded the commission. It could be expanded from three members to five, Black suggested, by assigning them "some little extra work to do," such as regulating gas, telephones, or electricity. "Giving the Railroad Commission one or more of the above subjects would be our excuse for increasing the Board" and creating added patronage. Black's proposal was not adopted. By 1900 the failure of the partisan commission to lay down reliable policy was frustrating even the railroads themselves, as well as the shippers who wanted good service and fair rates.[28]

Insurance regulation proved more helpful to the affected industry than railroad regulation. Ignoring the internal management of the business or the handling of policyholders' funds, the Insurance Department restricted its attention to the companies' solvency. Such regulation was so safe that firms sometimes asked for an investigation into their business, just to obtain the department's stamp of approval. In 1897 Henry B. Hyde, president of the Equitable Life Assurance Society, suggested to Louis F. Payn, superintendent of insurance, that "it seems to me desirable that your Department should make a fresh examination of our affairs." Payn quickly assured Hyde he would "take pleasure in complying with this request."[29]

State supervision of the gas industry was entirely by statute, rather than through a board or department. In 1897 the legislature met complaints about the cost of gas in New York City by reducing the legal price of one thousand cubic feet by $.05 per year for five years. Denounced as a surrender to the corporations because it failed to meet the public demand for an immediate price reduction from $1.25 to $1.00, the law exposed the majority party's lawmakers to unbearable cross-pressures between companies and customers. Whether by partisan commission, an industry-oriented department, or the legislature, existing methods of state regulation increasingly failed to insure continuing, acceptable relations among the corporations, the public, and the government. Soon the Republicans would have to address the problem.[30]

The issue of state support for improvements on the Erie Canal system also troubled the party leaders by causing deep division in their coalition. Despite the prosperity it had fostered during the second and third quarters of the century, the shallow and ill-maintained waterway was now steadily losing business to the cheaper, quicker railroads, which operated the year round. Yet merchants in New York City and Brooklyn believed that a thriving canal system was essential to holding down railway rates and to reversing the relative commercial decline of their metropolis. Together with mercantile interests along the waterway, especially at Buffalo, the downstate merchants waged a strong campaign for state improvement of the canals. Their most numerous opponents were small-town and country citizens who lived too far from the waterways to benefit from them and resented subsidizing the transportation of western agricultural products to market. Joining the opposition and probably bankrolling it were the trunkline railroads, particularly the New York Central and the Erie, which opposed any threat to their growing monopoly on freight transportation.[31]

The division of opinion on the canal issue placed Republican leaders in a difficult position. On one side stood many of their rural and small-town supporters, while on the other were most large-city voters and many business groups, with the significant exception of the railroads. The Democrats' strong advocacy of canal improvements added to the pressure the Republicans felt. Fortunately, the 1894 canal amendment to the state constitution provided a convenient way of avoiding accountability. Since the creation of a debt for canal purposes required popular approval, the electorate rather than the party would have the final say. As a Rochester newspaper observed, the Republicans "will gladly turn the question of the expenditure over to the people, and then escape from it by claiming that it should not be supported as a party measure."[32]

That is what the Republicans did. With Platt's behind-the-scenes support, a $9-million bond issue for deepening the canals and lengthening the locks passed the legislature early in 1895. Democrats voted for the measure with near unanimity, while Republican lawmakers divided along predictable geographic lines. In November, the electorate endorsed the bond issue by a highly polarized vote. In many counties distant from the waterways, a quarter or fewer of the voters approved, while in New York City and Buffalo over 75 percent favored the expenditure. Even though the Republican leadership had allowed the measure to come before the people and quietly supported it, thirty-two out of thirty-three anticanal counties remained in the party's column. Platt had maneuvered onto the winning side of the canal question without alienating those in the party who felt differently.[33]

Bad luck and bad management soon imperiled the Republicans' best efforts to keep the canal issue out of politics. In 1896 and 1897 construction contracts were let and the authorized improvements begun. By early the next year, however, the $9 million had proved insufficient to complete the planned work, and the state officials most directly involved were accused of inefficiency and corruption. The canal project's failure angered those on both sides of the question. Opponents saw state money wasted, while canal advocates believed that irresponsible political management had doomed prospects for revitalizing the waterways. Although the party organization had managed to avoid accountability for the original decision to fund improvements, the apparent culpability of Republican officials now made the canal a party issue. The political damage done must have reinforced Platt's inclination to leave divisive policy problems alone if he could.[34]

During their first years in office, the Republicans grappled uneasily with economic questions. On labor, taxation, and regulatory issues, the leaders' avoidance of group conflicts, as well as their commitments to business interests, prevented significant innovations. On canal improvements, the party acted more decisively, but only after making a strong effort to prevent the issue from damaging the coalition. Leading Republicans outwardly took the position that all was well since the interests of different groups generally coincided. But, in reality, the rise to power of organized economic interests, each voicing divisive demands, was making that argument increasingly unrealistic and pushing the party toward new ways of handling material questions.

Economic-group conflict had not, of course, been absent from politics before the 1890s. Its large presence was recognized by those who established American governmental institutions in the 1770s and 1780s, and it formed a familiar element in political ideology and practice throughout the 1800s. But while it had always been present, group conflict assumed a new political form at the end of the nineteenth century that contributed heavily to reshaping the policy process. To a greater degree than at any time previously, the diverse producer groups in society became conscious of their distinct economic positions and began organizing intensely to influence politics and government in their own interests. This development of functional specialization, of rising group consciousness, and of increasing organization is familiar to students of modernization. The process was scarcely sudden, yet in New York State its coming to new political significance can be dated rather precisely—at the time the depression lifted in the late 1890s.

The large increase of labor-union membership and the adoption of stronger political tactics by workingmen were indicative of the trend toward the organization of economic interests. Between March 1897 and September 1900, the number of labor organizations in the state rose by 76 percent to over sixteen hundred, and the number of union members increased by a similar percentage to nearly a quarter million. While most of the growth came in the state's largest cities, especially New York, Buffalo, Rochester, and Albany, organized workers became more numerous in the smaller towns as well. In both 1899 and 1900, the roll of towns having at least one labor union rose by twenty-four, bringing the total to one hundred thirty-five. To capitalize on organized labor's numerical strength, a new legislative pressure group, the Workingmen's Federation, arose in place of the old Workingmen's Assembly and the State Federation of Labor. More unified than before, those represented by the new organization put pressure on both parties to adopt labor's goals, including the eight-hour day, employers' liability, and the enforcement of existing laws. The perceptible increase in legislative attention to workingmen at the end of the 1890s has led labor historians of New York to identify these years as a real turning point in the unions' political position.[35]

Compared to labor, mercantile interests had been well organized politically for several decades. In the late 1890s, however, large-city merchants intensified their efforts to influence state government through a series of organizational innovations and educational devices. Of most importance to them were the canals, and despite the disillusionment that had followed the misuse of the $9-million bond issue, the merchants succeeded in forming new organizations that revitalized the campaign to improve the state's waterway system. Led by existing mercantile associations in the largest cities, commercial groups from across New York held a State Commerce Convention at Utica in 1899 and there planned the strategy which would culminate four years later in the state's decision to build a thousand-ton barge canal costing $101 million. In 1900 downstate commercial organizations formed the Canal Association of Greater New York, and in that year and the next the second and third annual State Commerce Conventions met in Syracuse and Buffalo, respectively. The pro-canal mercantile organizations dispatched speakers, sent out newspaper boiler-plate, and put pressure on politicians. Remarkable enthusiasm was thus engendered for improving a worn-out waterway that recently had seemed more productive of corruption than commerce.[36]

Farmers in New York State were slower than either workers or merchants to organize for political purposes. Generally satisfied that their interests were represented in the state government, farmers tended not to put much confidence in new laws or new programs. As Roosevelt observed in 1899, the farmers "do not look for aid from the State to carry on their ordinary avocations. Indeed, it is doubtful if they would approve any special legislation in their favor." Yet while they were less demanding than some other groups, by the end of the century, dairymen, fruit growers, and livestock raisers all were beginning to acknowledge the necessity of organizing politically to protect their interests against transporters, middlemen, and wholesalers. A number of large agricultural organizations thus came into being during these years, including the New York State Fruit Growers Association and the Western New York Milk Producers Association. One student of rural life, who intensely examined sources from six "typical" agricultural communities in New York, concluded that the farmer now "began to realize that politics had more to do with his economic prosperity than before" and that he acted accordingly. Reluctant as they were to organize, farmers, too, increasingly felt the need to "'get together'" in associations formed along producer lines to influence state government.[37]

Other economic groups, including real estate interests, trade associations, and professionals of every sort, also began or intensified their political organizing. Transportation and utility corporations, though they already had the ears of those in power, nonetheless expanded both their lobbying and their campaign-giving late in the 1890s and early in the 1900s. Within a few years, more interests than ever before became organized to press their demands on New York State government.

In doing so, they presented real challenges to the traditional economic-policy process. Coming to consciousness of their own distinct needs and of their differences with other groups, the newly organized interests increasingly questioned distributive benefits predicated on the assumption of harmony and asked for policies that openly recognized the clash of interests. Each group wanted regulatory measures restraining its rivals and tax policies shifting the burden to others. Labor demanded a stricter employers' liability law that took account of the conflict between boss and worker. Merchants supported railroad regulation recognizing the different interests of shipper and transporter. In itself, the appearance of conflict was not new, but the emergence of so many organized groups, committed to calling political attention to it, compelled those in office to take more explicit account of disharmony than ever before.

Whether party politicians were capable of making decisions that openly and carefully weighed the needs of conflicting economic interests remained to be seen. Explicitly or implicitly, the new organizations registered skepticism of partisan policymaking. The New York Board of Trade and Transportation was explicit. Observing that "the average Legislature consists of a large number of untried men," often controlled ". . . by 'orders' from the Party machine," the board's executive committee noted that such conditions "are not ideal for the handling of intricate state problems" and recommended the establishment of "permanent organizations of business men . . . whose sole object is to watch and study legislative measures and methods." Besides criticizing the inadequate manner in which partisan bodies formulated policy, the new groups doubted whether their own specialized needs could be met by parties that also served rival economic interests. As one labor spokesman in New York City saw it, "the corporations are superior to both parties, and until the workingmen take the power into their own hands they will get nothing."[38]

Skeptical of the regular parties, the new economic groups channeled some of their energy into independent politics. In every large city, organized merchants took the initiative in the formation of separate municipal parties. Often labor groups joined in, and sometimes they established their own local parties, as in New York City in 1899. The independent organizations characteristically went to considerable lengths to identify and recognize the economic needs of different groups, and they frequently discovered how difficult it was to satisfy conflicting interests. In 1901 the Citizens' Union of New York was accused, with some justification, of conducting a "two-faced campaign" on behalf of Seth Low. C.U. speakers stumped East Side working-class districts with promises of municipal ownership and social progress, while uptown they stressed efficient, businesslike administration. Yet while they lacked the means to resolve economic conflicts, leading independents at least acknowledged and addressed the clash of interests, which was something the regular parties rarely did.[39]

Formed to exert pressure on the men who controlled the existing policy machinery, the new interest-group organizations actually behaved in ways tending to restructure the traditional policy process. Their demands for inherently divisive measures, their criticism of partisan legislative methods, their efforts to mobilize public opinion, and their involvement in nonpartisan politics all suggested that more was involved here than whether or not to pass certain laws. At issue was whether the state's established manner of making authoritative allocations suited an industrial society of clashing, demanding interests.

While different groups were organizing to influence state government, the middle-class public's growing anxiety about "big business" provided a related, if less sharp, impetus for economic-policy change. One cause of unease were "trusts," the large industrial combinations that proliferated in the post-depression years, with presumably harmful implications for the cost of living and the economic opportunity of ordinary people.[40] Another source of anxiety closer to home was public utility corporations, about whose service and rates city dwellers increasingly complained. These were potentially explosive issues, but so long as the unorganized public failed to crystallize its demands for particular remedies or to recognize the corrupt alliance between big corporations and partisan politics, those in power were able to still the outcry by means of legislative investigations and weak laws. During the 1890s, these responses generally sufficed.

The loudest furor over the trusts arose in 1896 and 1897 when rising coal prices focused popular attention on the presumed monopolistic practices of several large companies engaged in hauling coal from the minefields of Pennsylvania and selling it in New York. Over the objections of Platt, whose son's law firm represented the coal interests, the legislature responded to public concern in the winter of 1896 by passing two bills authorizing the attorney general to investigate the companies and bring action. Little came of the measures, however, for Governor Morton let one die without his signature, while the other was repealed in 1897.[41]

That year, with Platt's consent, the lawmakers cautiously took account of the trust issue through the familiar device of a legislative investigation. For most of February, a joint committee took testimony from the officers of leading corporations and gathered a wealth of unfavorable information about various industries, including coal, but also sugar and rubber. Finding nothing to justify the familiar claim that trusts lowered prices or produced superior products, the committee drew the conclusion that such combinations overcapitalized stock, fixed high prices, reduced employment opportunities, and stifled competition. Although the committee's report declared that the trusts should be restrained in the interest of public welfare, it pessimistically called attention to numerous legal and practical reasons why New York State could not, or should not, do so. Two fairly weak antitrust measures became law as a result of the inquiry, but when the attorney general tried to use them against the coal companies, the courts voided his actions on a technicality, much to the satisfaction of the corporations involved. Remote from daily life and not very well understood, trusts provided the Republicans with an occasion to air public grievances, but not for the most part to make public policy.[42]

The behavior of transportation and utility corporations also aroused popular concern in the 1890s. In most large cities, street-railway, gas, and electric companies had been granted perpetual franchises with few restrictions, in return for little or no compensation to the public treasury. State regulation by commission offered one approach to the problem, but, while occasionally suggested, it was not seriously considered by the legislature. What the state instead did was curtail the franchise-granting power of the large cities. The Greater New York charter of 1897 restricted new franchises for use of the city's streets to a term of twenty-five years, plus a twenty-five year renewal, to be awarded in return for reasonable payment to the city. The uniform charter for second-class cities similarly set a fifty-year limit and provided for the equitable determination of compensation. With their privileges already in hand, however, most utility and transportation companies escaped the new restrictions. One authority compared the limitations to "locking the stable door after the horse is stolen."[43]

Municipal ownership of utilities offered another approach. Though widely condemned as socialistic, it was far from rare in New York. By 1897, local governments held and operated fully half of the state's 342 water works, including those in most of the large cities. While there were fewer public lighting plants, by 1902, twenty-eight municipalities had acquired electric stations. Most such towns were small ones located in northern and western New York. Their average population was less than 2,400, and the mean worth of their plants was below $30,000.[44]

Where big-city interests were at stake, municipal ownership of power and transportation was more controversial. In 1894 voters in New York City had decisively approved a referendum calling for the construction of a city-owned rapid transit subway line, but public ownership made little further progress in the large cities in the 1890s. In recognition of the growing interest in it, however, the assembly of 1896 named a committee of six members to study the question of municipally owned street railways. Taking testimony in the state's eight largest cities, the assemblymen uncovered evidence of watered stock, excessive fares, and callousness toward the public by private railway companies. Their final report reflected surprising openness to advanced opinion; it advised the adoption of regulatory measures to meet the abuses and treated municipal ownership as a serious possibility. But the legislators, supported by the opinions of well-known authorities, recommended against it in the end. "As an abstract proposition," they concluded, "we believe that no government . . . should embark in a business that can be as well conducted by private enterprise."[45]

By investigating trusts and municipal ownership, the Republican legislature showed its sensitivity to the growing anxiety about large corporations. The resulting legislative reports, moreover, offered thoughtful, honest appraisals of difficult economic questions. But the net result for public policy was practically nil. In the late 1890s, the people's concern about big business was real, but it was uninformed and unfocused, and it had not yet settled on any particular remedies. Thus, while the party in power was obliged to make *some* response to the problem, its response did not have to be very much more than a symbolic one.

Even so, the public's anxiety about business was ominous for the Republicans. From its founding, the party had proudly made governmental assistance to industry and enterprise its central tenet and based its policies upon that principle. Any explosion of public antipathy to business could discredit those policies and hurt the party. If the leaders' close relations with the corporations came to light, the explosion might be even greater.

While these dangers had not yet crystallized in the 1890s, the opposition party was working to solidify them. Under Bryan, the Democrats had begun to pay increasing attention to the ill effects of industrial growth, and in New York, Bryan's party was picking up the theme. Group conflict was also becoming a more prominent feature of Democratic rhetoric; the silver issue explicitly divided debtor from creditor, farmer from banker, and Democrats pointed out the divisions. In New York City, the party's press, especially Hearst's *Journal* and Pulitzer's *World*, shrilly distinguished the interests of workingmen from those of capitalists. As anxieties about big business intensified and interest-group divisions became more politically salient, it was understandable that the Democrats, out of power, took rhetorical advantage of the new issues. For the Republicans, in power and charged with making economic policy, those issues posed enormous problems, for they brought almost to hand the necessity not just for new measures, but for new ways of deciding material questions.

As governor in 1899 and 1900, Theodore Roosevelt took moderate but creative steps toward the adjustment of economic policymaking in accordance with new demands and new conditions. In response to the outcry against big business, he scrutinized the distribution of privileges to corporations and, on several matters, used his authority in ways that outraged his party's business allies. Where economic issues split the Republican coalition and caused Platt and the legislative leaders to avoid policy decisions, Roosevelt worked to facilitate action by removing the issues from party politics or, in a few cases, by firmly taking one side or the other. Above all, he sought out and recognized the representatives of different economic classes and frankly acknowledged that they did not share the same interests. Innovative as he was, Roosevelt's most important contributions lay less in new policies—of which there were only a few—than in his language, his identification of issues, and his preparation of public opinion for a new approach to policymaking. Essentially conservative and far from completely successful, his management of economic issues notably anticipated—though it did not inaugurate—twentieth-century methods of governance.

In his handling of politico-business relations, Roosevelt broke from the past, but not so decisively as his own rhetoric sometimes suggested. For, while he took no personal part in the corrupt alliance, it clearly continued during his administration. Roosevelt refused free transportation passes when they were proffered, and he declined to give unquestioning support for measures helping business. Even allowing for a self-serving aspect in his language, Roosevelt could legitimately boast that "it is idle even to propose anything to me on behalf of a corporation merely to benefit that corporation." But he did very little to prevent Platt and the legislative leaders from maintaining their close relations with businessmen, relations of which Roosevelt plainly had more than a dim awareness, though probably not a full understanding. While he sometimes vetoed business measures the party leaders wanted, Roosevelt approved others. In one highly controversial case, he went along with the sale of sixteen acres of underwater land in New York City to a gas company for $3,506, despite one official's estimate that it was worth $3 million. Roosevelt took the position that his decision was right precisely because it was consistent with the state's past policy of generosity to business corporations.[46]

In public statements, the governor typically mixed defense and denunciation of big business. "Much of the outcry against wealth, against the men who acquire wealth, and against the means by which it is acquired, is blind, unreasoning, and unjust," he declared in his annual message of 1900, "but in too many cases it has a basis in real abuses." His remedy for trusts was publicity: by publicizing information on company assets, debts, and profits, the government would reduce the opportunity for wrongdoing and make direct action against the trusts unnecessary. Conservative in its approach, Roosevelt's policy nonetheless addressed a widely feared industrial condition on which his party had substantially avoided action. The legislature declined to enact the proposal.[47]

The governor's qualified criticism of corporate abuses suggested that he recognized the clash of economic-group interests. Where Republicans traditionally asserted that industrial prosperity provided universal benefits, the governor disagreed. "While under normal conditions the acquirement of wealth by an individual is necessarily of great incidental benefit to the community as a whole," Roosevelt declared, *"yet this is by no means always the case."* That observation and its implications provided him with an important new orientation toward material issues.[48]

Roosevelt publicly and repeatedly acknowledged that economic groups were not alike in their wants and conditions, and he affirmed the legitimacy of their diverging demands. "We must recognize the fact that, aside from their general interest as citizens, special groups of citizens have special interests," Roosevelt declared. "Different sections of the community have different needs," he maintained. The new doctrine made evident political sense. With group consciousness rising, Roosevelt's stand corresponded with the growing reality that almost every government action helped some organized classes and hurt others. To bury that truth was certainly to risk a disaster.[49]

Despite its value, the tactic of acknowledging economic diversity also carried a risk that terrified politicians: party realignment along class lines. Roosevelt understood the danger, and for every recognition of separate interests, he issued a clear call for unity across economic and social barriers. "While sometimes it is necessary, from both a legislative and social standpoint, to consider men as a class," in the long run, he said, ". . . it is impossible for a democracy to endure if the political lines are drawn to coincide with class lines."[50]

His fears of class politics thus made plain, Governor Roosevelt went ahead with a conscious effort to consult the representatives of different groups where their interests were at stake. When a bill came before the legislature concerning the permissible investments of savings banks, Roosevelt sought to enlist the advice and support of those affected. "We ought to get the leading representatives of the savings banks committed in favor of the bill," he told Benjamin B. Odell, Jr. In considering a measure limiting the hours of work for drug clerks, Roosevelt asked opinions from those touched by it. "Take the bill," he urged Jacob Riis, and ". . . go to some small druggists . . . and find out

159

if you can what . . . [they] really think about it, and what they believe its effects really would be." By accepting the legitimacy of organized interest groups, Roosevelt anticipated the role of "honest broker" he later played as president. "I should very much like to get . . . in touch with the best labor men," he characteristically told an associate, "and the best employers, and thereby get the two classes in touch also."[51]

Roosevelt's labor policies reflected his openness to group action and to special-interest legislation. Devoting one-fifth of his first annual message to issues affecting workingmen, the governor praised the "organization and association . . . of the trade unions and labor federations" and affirmed the need for "legislation in the interest of labor." Not wishing to foster class politics, Roosevelt quickly added that such "legislation is not necessarily against the interest of capital," but his language made plain he recognized the conflict. During his two years as governor, Roosevelt proposed, and the legislature approved, an increase in the number of factory inspectors, enforcement of the eight-hour day for state workers, added protection for women and children in factories, the inspection of tenements used for manufacturing, and limitations upon drug clerks' hours. At the insistence of Republican leaders, however, the lawmakers rejected the governor's most advanced proposal, an employers' liability bill. Willing to enact conservative measures stabilizing industrial conditions or strengthening the enforcement of existing regulations, party leaders remained wary of legislation, like employers' liability, that explicitly helped one group at another's expense. Roosevelt's rhetorical recognition of the conflict of interests was meaningful, but it by no means instantly inspired a policy process putting such recognition into practice.[52]

Canal improvement also gave Roosevelt the occasion to test new ways of handling economic differences. In 1900 a state canal commission, named by the governor the previous year, presented a plan for the construction of a water route from Lake Erie to the Hudson River, capable of accommodating thousand-ton barges and costing $62 million. Roosevelt endorsed the bold proposal, but, recognizing the opposition of "country Republicans," warned its supporters that, if the plan were to pass, "much missionary work [had] to be done." Roosevelt was right about country opposition. As one weekly newspaper in a town far from the canal put it, "We are confident that our Republican leaders will not favor . . . such a project. If they do they will soon find the remains of the party in the bottom of the deepest part of the present canal."[53]

With the Republican majority so divided, the barge-canal proposal could be carried without damage to the party coalition only if Republicans were encouraged to vote their economic interests on the matter, without regard to a party position. Five years before, the leaders had quietly allowed the party to divide on the $9-million canal improvement bill, but now, with a much larger project at stake, Roosevelt made the nonpartisan approach explicit. "I have been doing my best to devise some plan," he told one person, "by which we could get democrats and republicans together on that canal issue. . . . Our only chance is to have the canal improvement made a nonpartisan issue." Platt, who had risked his party's silent division on the issue in 1895, now shrank from Roosevelt's bolder approach. "The farmers . . . are so sensitive on the subject of taxation that we are in grave danger of wasting away our narrow margin of majority," he told the governor. "Perhaps it would be best to defer decided action on the Canal question until another year. By that time the Presidential question will be out of the way." Platt prevailed, and those who favored the canal had to settle for a $200,000 engineering survey of barge-canal routes. To get strong action on a controversial question, Roosevelt tried to separate it from party politics. Though he failed, this tactic would eventually secure a barge canal and become a common element of twentieth-century policymaking.[54]

The most important and most revealing economic act of Roosevelt's administration was the adoption of a tax on public service franchises. Passed in 1899, the measure addressed two problems which the Republicans until then had largely evaded: equitable taxation and fair compensation to the public for utility franchises. As usual, Roosevelt's main contribution lay in giving vitality to the issue, not in the final legislative achievement. At the outset of his governorship, Roosevelt recognized the ills of an inequitable tax structure and of uncompensated franchise grants, but he expressed uncertainty about how to deal with them.[55] While the governor hesitated, a popular bill redefining taxable real estate to include the valuable use of city streets by utility and transportation corporations made its way through the legislature. Only after the senate approved the measure in April did Roosevelt endorse it. Then, vigorously entering the fray, the governor awakened public opinion on the issue and compelled the assembly to pass it over the wishes of Platt.[56]

The franchise-tax bill that Roosevelt strongly, if belatedly, endorsed drew a sharp line between competing economic interests and disrupted the Republican party's usual relations with business. It found support among several groups that normally opposed Platt's organization, while it met opposition from the party's traditional business allies. Mercantile and manufacturing enterprises, whose real and personal property already bore a heavy tax load, naturally favored a measure spreading the burden. On the other side, utility and transportation companies, whose less tangible holdings commonly escaped full taxation, denounced the bill. While city interests disagreed on the franchise tax, rural voters heartily favored it. The resulting public debate on the measure, in the spring of 1899, brought the divisive tax issue fully before the people of New York for the first time since the Republicans came to power.[57]

Having encouraged the assembly to pass the franchise tax, Roosevelt faced immense pressure from within his own party to veto the measure or secure its amendment. Platt's own lengthy appeal to the governor, in expressing the boss's objections to the bill at hand, also revealed his fears about Roosevelt's entire approach to economic issues. Two things chiefly troubled Platt. First was that the franchise tax, in placing public service companies at the mercy of local Democratic assessors, would result in the drying up of the Republicans' corporate sources of campaign contributions. To Roosevelt, Platt expressed this point circumspectly by stressing that the Democrats would "bleed and blackmail" the taxed corporations. To an upstate ally, the boss was blunter: "the Republican party might as well go into bankruptcy" if the measure became law. Platt's second concern was subtler. He feared that the "agitation" of such issues carried the risk of drawing class lines in politics. This calamity Platt warned Roosevelt to avoid.[58]

The governor replied in detail to Platt's two criticisms. On the issue of campaign contributions, he defiantly answered that such a consideration would not affect him. But Roosevelt did appreciate the objection that the Democrats might use the franchise tax for corporate blackmail, and he agreed to an amendment transferring the control to state officials. The governor also responded to Platt's concern about class lines in politics. Acknowledging the risk of such a development, Roosevelt nonetheless declared it unsafe for the Republicans "to take refuge in mere negation and to say that there are no evils to be corrected."[59]

Roosevelt and Platt eventually compromised on an amended franchise-tax bill which the legislature passed in special session and the governor signed. That was not the end of the matter, however, for the taxed corporations challenged the measure in the courts and for a dozen years prevented the full collection of the levy.[60] Something of a failure in practice, the franchise tax nonetheless aroused a penetrating public discussion of the tax question that significantly shaped subsequent action. In both these respects—its failure and its farsightedness—it typified economic policy under Roosevelt. For his essential accomplishment was not the establishment of permanent policy landmarks, much less the creation of a new structure of economic policy, but the invigoration of public discourse on the state's material problems.

The key element here was Roosevelt's recognition and acceptance of interest-group conflicts and his search for ways to handle them. This was critical, for twentieth-century government would have to face, not bury, these conflicts. Roosevelt advanced part of the solution, the separation of divisive economic issues from party politics, but he did little to establish alternative means for making policy decisions. Indeed, the governor's own personal political virtuosity, by enabling him to attract diverse advisers and to compel the attention and support of antagonistic interests, may have diverted attention from the task of devising permanent governmental processes for managing economic conflict. The hard problems of which groups to recognize, how to identify their spokesmen, how to weigh and measure their competing demands, and how to represent the unorganized all remained to be faced and solved.

The recognition of diverse interests, by whatever means it was finally accomplished, meant that privileged business corporations would not continue to have exclusive access to government. Roosevelt saw this, and he took conspicuous, if inadequate, steps to sever the special politico-business ties that nineteenth-century distributive policies had long encouraged. In doing so, he outraged the Republican party's corporate allies and aroused expectations in other quarters for policies weakening big business. These expectations of course failed to be met. For Theodore Roosevelt's innovations pointed New York State not in an antibusiness direction but toward a political accommodation with the powerful, clashing interests of an industrial society.

In June 1900, Platt deftly maneuvered to have Roosevelt nominated for vice-president of the United States. Wanting another term at Albany, but also sensing dangers there, Roosevelt seems to have been divided in his own mind about whether he should take a place on the national ticket. In the end, Platt's desire to have the governor out of New York, in combination with Roosevelt's popularity at the national convention, led to his nomination as McKinley's running mate.[61]

It is not difficult to name the reasons why Platt wanted to be rid of Roosevelt: his independence from the party machine and his support for economic policies that divided the coalition and hurt its business allies. In 1898 the need for party unity had dictated Roosevelt's nomination, but by 1900 his administration had relieved the Republican organization of the immediate dangers it faced and made Platt long for a more pliable, predictable governor. Besides, with McKinley and

Bryan again running for president, New York was sure to go Republican whoever headed the state ticket. Roosevelt had brought to the governorship the very things that increasingly threatened the party organization: freedom from the machine's discipline and an urgent insistence upon new and divisive economic policies. Seeing the dangers to traditional politics that Roosevelt embodied, Platt wanted him out.[62]

Even as he challenged Platt's methods, Governor Roosevelt had offered at least partial solutions to the leading problems the party faced. Nominated in 1898 to bring the independents back into the coalition, Roosevelt had accomplished that and worked to maintain the accommodation between independency and partisanship. Though Platt had not expected Roosevelt to support innovative economic measures, he had done that, too, and marked out promising approaches to difficult policy problems. But despite the advantages the governor's innovations offered the party, his recognition of independency and of economic diversity created difficulties which the boss was anxious to try to be rid of when the opportunity offered.

Even though Republican victory was certain in the election of 1900, Platt's kind of politics and governance continued to be threatened by the very problems Roosevelt's administration had addressed. Indeed, independency and the demand for new economic policies were beginning to strengthen each other. Interest groups not satisfied by partisan policymaking increasingly experimented with nonpartisan politics, and the consequent weakening of support for the party in turn decreased the leaders' ability to shape economic policy. Many observers have noted the irony that Platt's plan to rid New York of Roosevelt backfired when McKinley died in 1901. Roosevelt's assumption of the presidency came as a blow to the boss, it is true, but the problems his organization faced at home posed even greater difficulties to Platt. In carrying out a new party strategy to solve those problems, the next governor weakened the boss far more than President Roosevelt did.

6

The Limitations of "Businesslike" Government, 1900–1904

The first four or five years of the twentieth century have often been pictured as a calm interlude between the assorted political crises of the 1890s and the era of reform that began around 1905. Amid relative prosperity, expressions of discontent slackened and innovation seemed less urgently needed. Neither presidential contest of these years compared in bitterness or fatefulness with that of 1896. In New York, apparent political calm also prevailed. Theodore Roosevelt, with his vigor and charisma, was gone from the state scene—replaced as chief executive by a dour, regular Republican who prided himself on applying "business" principles to government. City politics spawned no movement comparable to the independent "revolution of '97," while anguish over trusts and public service franchises abated.

Yet during these quiet years, the same forces—now maturing quickly—that had troubled the dominant Republicans in the 1890s continued to undermine traditional politics. In the cities, independence from party machines took new directions, while town and country voters learned to stray from pure and constant partisanship. Demands for new economic policies, helping some at others' expense, continued to be voiced, often softly now by organized groups learning to use their numbers and their knowledge. Thus, in the first years of the new century, as in the last years of the old one, those at the head of a party wishing to stay in power were forced to fashion political and governmental innovations to meet new conditions.

Thomas Collier Platt remained powerful in these years of deceptive quietude, but the Republicans' direction increasingly came from Benjamin B. Odell, Jr., who succeeded Roosevelt as governor and Platt as boss. From 1901 to 1904, Odell took impressive steps, which collectively may be labeled a party strategy, to strengthen the Republicans by addressing the conditions at hand. He embraced and extended the accommodations his party had made with the independents after the election of 1897 and won their praise by applying some of their methods to state government. His cooperation with Mayor Seth Low of New York City during 1902 and 1903 contrasted sharply with the treatment William L. Strong had received at Albany's hands from 1895 to 1897. In the economic area, Odell's innovations were even more considerable. He brought to completion a new tax system, heavily based on corporation levies; he introduced new methods and procedures of government that anticipated the more visible administrative reforms of later years; and he cooperated with some of the new, extra-governmental interests that were working, often successfully, to bring about policies they wanted. In actual achievements, Odell's record as governor surpassed Roosevelt's.

Yet the adjustments he fashioned failed to enable the traditional political system to accommodate to new conditions or to permit Republican leaders to keep control of political events. The spirit of independence from parties proved indomitable, despite the politicians' best efforts to encourage regularity. By 1904 Odell himself had become the chief target of growing antibossism and his behavior a potent stimulus for widespread ticket-splitting. The rise of demanding economic organizations also presented problems Odell could not solve, especially because his own statements obscured the need for permanent governmental means of resolving group differences. When his administration closed, difficult problems of managing an industrial economy could not be put off much longer. Seldom perceived as a crisis time, the calm years of Odell's governorship actually brought New York to the brink of a major transformation in politics and governance.

In August 1900 Platt candidly described to Roosevelt, then the nominee for vice-president, the kind of gubernatorial candidate he wanted that year: "some man who is a straight Republican and who has shown himself by his faith and his works . . . [that he] will carry out the wishes of the Organization." Benjamin B. Odell, Jr., gave every appearance of being such a person. A successful Newburgh business-man with interests in his family's ice concern as well as in transportation and utility companies, Odell had acquired political experience under the tutelage of his locally prominent father, sat in Congress for two terms, and in 1898 advanced to the chairmanship of the Republican state committee. By 1900, at the age of forty-six, Odell was indisputably his party's deputy leader. Skilled at organizing campaigns and predicting electoral outcomes with accuracy, Odell honed his reputation as one who applied "business" principles to party management.

Benjamin B. Odell, Jr. (Library of Congress)

His unanimous nomination for governor gratified Platt and unified the party organization, but it troubled those who had hoped for someone more independent. A few observers predicted that Odell, as a powerful member of the machine, might have the stature to defy Platt. But most probably believed that the Republicans had indeed found a man who would "carry out the wishes of the Organization."[1]

The 1900 campaign gave few indications that Odell would fail to do so, much less that he would put forward a party strategy of his own. As the gubernatorial candidate, Odell subordinated himself to the presidential ticket and emphasized national issues, as Platt believed he should. State questions played a secondary role in the campaign, and Odell straddled the most divisive of them. The nominee did, however, make several concessions to the public's rising concern about big-business corporations. He disposed of all his stock holdings, including his Newburgh utility interests, and he announced that, although still the party chairman, he would have nothing to do with the collection and expenditure of the campaign fund. These were unnecessary precautions. McKinley was sure to carry New York overwhelmingly against Bryan, and Odell's coattail victory was certain. Indeed, he won by 111,000 votes. When the governor-elect promised to lead as clean and honest an administration as Roosevelt, critics remained cautious. "Eschew Platt and lead a better life," the *New York Times* advised him, but not many people thought he would.[2]

In his first years as governor, Odell surprised almost everyone, not only by opposing Platt on a matter the old boss considered vital, but also by advancing an innovative policy program that temporarily transformed the agenda of state politics. Together these steps brought immense power and influence to Odell and gave him a real chance to solve some of the most difficult problems his party faced.

Economical government and a series of new tax levies formed the core of the program that Odell presented in his first annual message and supported for the rest of his administration. "Economy" had been a perennial Republican slogan, but it had been little practiced in recent years. Now, however, Odell offered detailed proposals for reducing the number of public employees, for consolidating some state boards and replacing others by single commissioners, and for curtailing the costs of printing, courts, municipal services, tax collection, and the most expensive state function, care of the insane. "No business man," he declared with authority, "would suffer such an enormous drain upon his resources for the small amount of work now performed."[3]

Taxation provided the other essential part of Odell's 1901 program. He announced his support for the abolition of direct state property taxes and called instead for new levies upon different classes of business corporations, particularly trust companies, savings banks, and insurance companies. Odell was not hostile to corporations; indeed, elsewhere in his first annual message he called for the liberalization of corporation laws to encourage companies to organize in New York State. Still, he explicitly noted that in return for the "protection and favors" they "receive from the State," corporations should "pay a tribute."[4]

Despite some resistance, Odell succeeded in having most of his recommendations enacted. "Economy" was not, of course, immediately popular among Republican leaders whose resources it threatened. Indeed, in earlier days, Odell himself had been adept at hiking up state expenditures that benefited the party. A year before he took office, in fact, he had criticized a draft of Roosevelt's 1900 message for some of the same proposals which he himself now made. Yet, if Odell's past suggested the suddenness of his drive for economy, it also had given him intimate knowledge of where state savings could be made. The sensibleness of his proposals, the acclaim with which they were popularly received, and the urgency with which the governor advanced them enabled him to win Platt's reluctant concurrence in the measures, and virtually all of them became law. After some initial opposition to his tax proposals by the affected interests, they, too, received approval in somewhat amended form. Newspapers across the state noted how effective Odell had been in putting his program across. Seldom if ever had "a governor's message served so thoroughly as a basis of legislative action," said an Ithaca daily. Odell's "is a splendid record," said the *Troy Daily Times*, as the legislative session neared its end. "Its lustre is reflected upon, as its glory is shared by, the entire Republican party of the state."[5]

The acceptance of Odell's proposals in 1901 gave the Republicans a coherent policy program and an appealing philosophy of state governance for the first time since they had entered office six years before. Despite its lack of drama, economical government possessed real strengths as a basis for a party strategy. If not a new issue, economy was at least a newly invigorated one that could be applied with visible benefits in dollars saved and taxes reduced. It had special advantages, as well, in light of the problems the Republicans faced at the beginning of the twentieth century. Odell's call for efficient, businesslike state government matched what many independents sought at the municipal level; so did his demand for the reduction of excessive patronage. Independents did not fail to notice the correspondence between the governor's program and their own. Economy also had the advantage of dampening divisive demands on the state. An accepted policy of decreasing government expenditures would discourage calls for new public undertakings and reduce conflicts between groups seeking state aid.[6]

Odell's tax proposals correspondingly gave the Republicans a good talking point in the rising public debate over big business. In muted language, for Odell had no use for "declamation against corporations," the governor established a policy of compelling large companies to pay a fair share of government expenses. His program offered a readily understandable position on a complex policy question and made "equitable taxation" a Republican slogan. By reorienting the legislative agenda, Odell's policies (the results of which will be considered below) gave his party a reasonable chance to defeat the threats it faced.[7]

The governor's program also provided the Republicans with a new package of state campaign issues. Under Platt, the party had always stressed national questions at election time; with Bryan to oppose, the Republicans needed little else. Now, however, facing new problems posed by independency and economic conflict, some party leaders in New York began to see the need for fresh state issues. These Odell formulated. In 1902 and again in 1904, the party based its campaigns on the issues he had created: economical government and equitable taxation. "The State [party] organization is coming to realize," observed the New York *Press,* "that to hold New York Republicans in State elections there must be reliance upon something besides Democratic depravity, national issues, Cuban laurels, and the 'God Almighty' who was 'the boss' in the . . . recent and happy-go-lucky successful campaigns."[8]

Odell's accomplishments won him public praise from Roosevelt, but privately the former governor—now shackled in the vice-presidency—ruefully recalled how differently Odell had behaved when he was Platt's henchman during Roosevelt's governorship. "When Paul was still Saul a year ago," Roosevelt told one correspondent in March 1901, he "was backing up Platt" on matters where he now departed from the old boss's line. Odell was making a good record "by carrying onward the policy which I put into operation," Roosevelt wrote to another. But Odell's program in his first year as governor was actually broader than his predecessor's. Where Roosevelt championed the franchise tax, Odell secured comprehensive tax reform. Where Roosevelt demanded isolated economies, Odell effected systematic ones.[9]

Several things help explain the difference. For one, Odell had the benefit of the considerable groundwork laid by the popular Roosevelt, particularly on the tax issue. For another, he had greater influence in the legislature, through his connection with the Republican organization, than did his predecessor, who was a party outsider. Where Roosevelt had agitated somewhat erratically for far-reaching changes that Republican leaders found threatening and had appealed directly to public opinion on occasion, Odell linked tax reform with the time-honored cry for economical government and worked steadily through the regular party channels. Odell's program was thus more successful than Roosevelt's, but it was also more traditional. Compared to Roosevelt, who had little interest in managing or changing the Republican party and its strategy, Odell found his chief interest in the party itself, its organization, its strategy, and its success. As Platt's assistant leader, he had seen at close range the things that threatened the kind of politics his mentor practiced. When he became governor, Odell accordingly adopted comprehensive tactics to address the challenges while maintaining the familiar patterns of party governance.

Although Odell does not seem to have sought a confrontation with Platt in the winter of 1901, a clash of some sort was inevitable. When it came, it was provoked by the old Republican problem of police legislation for New York City. Fearful that the Democratic-controlled police, under Chief William Devery, would prevent Republican votes from being counted in the 1901 municipal election, Platt advanced his familiar plan for a state constabulary. "If the country [legislators] will stand by me," the boss told one upstate senator soon after Odell's election, "we will put it through, home rule or no home rule. . . . One thing is certain, we never shall be able to do anything in this city until this action is taken, and now that we have the power, we want to exercise it." Platt's argument was direct and honest: the Republicans should use their state authority to get what they wanted in the largest Democratic city.[10]

While he had supported a state police plan in earlier years, Odell now opposed it on the grounds that its invasion of home rule would cost the Republicans more city votes than police control would win. Committed to cooperating with downstate independents, Odell believed that Republican success in New York City depended on acceding to the reformers' demand for replacement of the four-member, bipartisan police board with a single commissioner, to be named by the mayor. Odell persuaded Platt to abandon the constabulary scheme, and in February the governor's police measure became law.[11]

Almost immediately, however, Mayor Robert Van Wyck named a Tammany police commissioner who, in turn, appointed Devery as his first deputy. Republicans were furious and embarrassed, for under Devery their party's interests would have no protection. Platt now revived his plan for direct state control of the New York City police and predicted its enactment. But no legislator introduced the measure, and the governor remained silent. Platt and Odell met but resolved nothing. Several days later, the boss's son, Frank, visited the governor and demanded he agree to support the plan. Odell said he would never do so. The elder Platt then called a conference of Republican leaders but, upon assembling, they sided with the governor. Platt at this point gave in.[12]

After the police crisis, many agreed with the New York *Press* that "the end of Thomas C. Platt as a State boss has come. In his place, not as a boss, but as a leader, is Governor B. B. Odell."[13] But Platt's authority did not dissolve instantly in the winter of 1901. He remained the party's recognized head throughout his rival's gubernatorial administration and performed many of the same duties as before. Sent again to the U.S. Senate in 1903, Platt kept many of the symbols and some of the substance of his leadership.

He continued to carry out the tasks associated with financing the party, dispensing the campaign fund, and influencing legislation. As late as 1904, Platt raised money for personal distribution to legislative candidates, and, when the lawmakers convened, he protected the corporations which supplied the funds. Just as in the 1890s, the boss's power in the legislature depended upon the weakness of its individual members. Mainly middle-class men of undistinguished backgrounds, the legislators came to Albany in the hope of funding hometown projects and with a disposition to go along with the party's leadership on major bills. Platt remained a force to be reckoned with among these men, and each winter Odell took the precaution of consulting him.[14]

As a U.S. senator, Platt continued to direct the distribution of federal patronage in New York. He and President Roosevelt frequently corresponded on that subject, and as late as 1905, the president tried to satisfy the senator. Just as when he was governor, Roosevelt was content to leave party management in New York to the regular machine. But in raising questions about who really led the organization, the clash between Platt and Odell troubled Roosevelt, especially prior to his nomination for president in 1904. "My effort has been to keep Governor Odell and you together," the president told Platt in 1903. "I do not want a division in the party just now." Roosevelt grew annoyed at having to consider New York's factional strife with every appointment. "I do not quite understand the serious tone in which you speak of the possibility of my appointments returning to cause me trouble in the future," he wrote in reply to one of Odell's demands. "Do you mean as regards my nomination for President?" Persuaded by Elihu Root to send a milder version of the letter, Roosevelt muted his annoyance in the hope that Platt and Odell would settle their differences.[15]

They failed to do so, and Odell's power grew at Platt's expense. While some party leaders, like William Barnes, Jr., stayed neutral, and others, like the new state chairman, George Washington Dunn, stuck with Platt, Odell slowly obtained the support of most leading Republicans. A brusque and overbearing man, the governor did not win his authority through personal pleasantries. Platt had never particularly relied on sweetness either, but the old boss had a knack for harmonizing differences which Odell lacked. Without reliance on friendly touches, the governor grounded his leadership in his high office, his evident concern for the Republican party, and his identification with issues whose popularity exceeded his own.[16]

Odell proved his power in 1902, when the Republican state convention partly rejected Platt's slate of candidates. That was something it had never done before. Platt had supported Odell's inevitable renomination for governor that year and backed George R. Sheldon of New York City for the lieutenant governorship. When opposition to Sheldon surfaced among Brooklyn Republicans and rumor linked him to a so-called "Whisky Trust," Odell refused to have Sheldon on the ticket. After a bitter preconvention night of conferences, Platt's man withdrew. A conservative, economy-minded state senator, Frank W. Higgins, was named to run with Odell, and Platt accepted his most humiliating defeat since 1881.[17]

During Odell's second term, Platt slipped further from power. Though the governor refused to oppose Platt's reelection to the U.S. Senate in 1903, even the old boss's friends treated it simply as a final honor, which it would be ungracious to deny the declining Platt. In March 1904, the two men put in writing an agreement that gave Platt titular recognition as Republican leader but made Odell again the party's state chairman. Roosevelt accepted the leaders' arrangements and privately characterized the governor's power as "absolute." Although Odell never reached quite that height of authority, as governor-boss he made his party's strategic decisions and tried to solve its problems.[18]

The boldness and success with which Odell had advanced his programs in 1901 suggested that his governorship would mark a period of notable economic-policy achievements. This was true in several important areas: taxation, transportation, and, to a lesser extent, labor. Yet in an era of expanding expectations for government and rising interest-group conflict, Odell found how hard it was for a party leader to control economic policymaking. His heralded "economy" drive succeeded in reducing the costs of government itself, but elsewhere it succumbed to universal demands for increased state services. Almost every policy area was agitated by the clash of group interests. Their battles made

173

party policymaking both difficult and dangerous and encouraged the tacit relinquishment of governmental authority to the competing groups themselves. Civic reform organizations also gained added influence by skillfully wielding resources and expertise on the particular policy matters that concerned them. Together, these developments limited the ability of even an energetic party leader to shape economic decisions and reduced the policy process to confusion.

On state expenditures Odell was able to exercise control only within the limited sphere of the costs for the different branches of government. As a direct result of his economizing drive of 1901, executive, legislative, judicial, and administrative expenses declined over the next four years, or rose only slightly. Odell and his party proudly and deservedly claimed credit for the savings. Less noticed, but perhaps of more significance, were the governor's related efforts to summarize and explain New York's expenditures. There was no such thing as a state budget, so that only the recondite annual report of the comptroller systematically recorded the costs of government. To rectify the deficiency and create consciousness of overall state spending—as well as to publicize his own achievements—Odell began the practice of issuing messages each spring reviewing and summing up the annual appropriations. It was a small first step toward the systematic oversight of state costs.[19]

What these annual reports revealed, however, was that most expenditures were beyond Odell's, or anyone's, control. While the branches of government itself accounted for only about 11 percent of the state's spending, schools, hospitals, charities, roads, and canals used up about two-thirds of the total. During Odell's governorship, these major public undertakings grew steadily in cost. Each of them rose between 16 and 40 percent from 1900 to 1905, while the overall expenditures of state government went from $22.9 million to $27.6 million, a rise of 20 percent. Constitutional mandates, existing laws, and ongoing population growth dictated the increases, which were, by and large, popular. As Comptroller Otto Kelsey observed in his report of 1905: "The people have steadily approved the projects so undertaken, and an investigation of the legislative journals will show that every appropriation has been carried for every purpose named, except excise and canals, by practically a unanimous vote from all political parties."[20]

Compared to expenditures, tax policies owed more to Odell himself and were less consensual. The corporation levies of 1901, together with other measures passed in the subsequent years of Odell's administration, virtually completed a new state revenue system. Its essence was the replacement of the direct tax on property by expanded indirect levies on the earnings and privileges of certain classes of individuals and businesses. While the main components of the system, including liquor, corporation, and inheritance levies, had gone into effect before Odell's governorship, his administration almost totally abolished the direct state property tax, raised revenues from the indirect taxes, and shifted the relative burdens on different categories of business. By 1905 the three main indirect taxes provided over 80 percent of the state's revenue.[21]

Odell defended the new tax system with skill, and the Republican party echoed his advocacy. After each legislative session, the governor put out a special message lauding the virtual absence of direct state levies on property. Country weeklies picked up the theme and published charts detailing the extent of the relief which Odell's system gave to local farmers and small property owners. The governor also defended the new corporation taxes and made explicit the connection between privileges the companies received and the financial obligation they owed the state. While Odell seldom exploited the public's dislike for corporate wealth, his supporters sometimes did. As one upstate senator put it before the election of 1904, "These [new] taxes are levied and collected to a large extent upon the wealth of the millionaire who never in his lifetime has paid a tax." The repeated expression of that sentiment made Odell's tax policy popular.[22]

Businessmen who bore the new burdens did not share the general enthusiasm for the governor's tax program. Yet they reluctantly accepted their obligations. Odell's own reputation as a businessman, the swiftness and cogency with which he proposed the new corporation taxes in his first year as governor, and his linking of them with economy all contributed to the companies' toleration of the measures. Businessmen apparently considered the new corporation taxes to be inevitable and, by and large, they felt the ones Odell proposed were equitable. Some, no doubt, welcomed the uniformity and stability the new system offered and the relief it promised from anxiety that levies they considered unfair—like Roosevelt's franchise tax of 1899—would be sprung on them. Compared to some other states, such as Wisconsin and New Jersey, New York did not experience a political convulsion over the corporation-tax issue. The hated railroads, which elsewhere had largely escaped taxation, were already taxed in New York, and there was a widespread belief in the justice of spreading the burden to other classes of corporations too.[23]

Odell's tax program did, however, deepen the political cleavage between urban and rural citizens. As the Chamber of Commerce of New York City noted in 1901, the interests Odell proposed to tax "are only found in the cities, and not much elsewhere." Democratic spokesmen repeatedly made the same point. Though he frequently tried, the governor never dispelled the common belief among urban citizens that their taxes were inequitably high. His failure was all the greater because Odell seemed insensitive to urban-rural differences of interest. "New York City and the Empire State are in fact one and inseparable," he declared, "identical in interests and pursuits." City residents who felt that the new levies burdened them unfairly could not accept the governor's dictum. In western New York in 1903, the *Buffalo Evening News* and a small-town weekly, the *Fredonia Censor,* exchanged heated accusations over the issue. Fed up with criticism of country selfishness, the *Censor* called upon the *News* to stop "taunting rural counties with the false charge that they are dependents."[24]

Besides the geographic divisions it fostered, Odell's tax system was a spurious solution for the troubled relations between the people and the corporations. Like Roosevelt before him, Odell encouraged the illusion that if big business paid its share, the social and economic ills it brought would go away. But corporation taxes could easily be passed on to consumers; moreover, taxation had no effect on the companies' social practices or their internal management. While new corporation levies offered a logical and just way for the state to raise its revenues, New Yorkers discovered in time that taxation was no substitute for regulation.[25]

Except for the tax increases, however, the Odell years brought no major policy changes in the state's relationship to big-business corporations. With Platt still exercising influence in the legislature, his system of assisting companies in return for campaign contributions continued during 1901–4. The old boss's handling of the Pennsylvania Railroad tunnel bill of 1902, described in the previous chapter, was probably typical of his role on other matters. More secretly, some individual legislators sold their services to corporations in need of favors. There is no evidence that Odell participated in these arrangements, but, like Roosevelt, he wouldn't, or couldn't, stop them.[26]

Even as the old politico-business ties persisted, however, the favored companies found themselves threatened by hostile legislation. The problem was not simply that Platt's powers of assistance were lessening, but also that other groups, including rival economic interests and civic reform organizations, were now actively competing for legislative influence. Often the newer groups opposed the interests of corporations that had previously enjoyed untrammeled access to representation. The correspondence between the New York Central Railroad's general counsel and the company's Albany agents and legislative friends reveals their heightened concern about unfriendly legislation, often emanating from sources the railroad could not even identify. Phrases like "we are opposed to the bill," "delay it in every way possible," and "the bill is most mischievous" mark the correspondence. By 1903 and 1904, companies like the New York Central had real competitors for influence over legislation.[27]

While rival economic groups jockeyed to shape lawmaking, there was growing evidence of public discontent with policies that bestowed privileges on business, without significant regulation or restraint. Like Roosevelt before him, Odell scrutinized the granting of public favors to corporations and in several well-publicized instances squelched them. One case involved the Ramapo Water Company, a concern that had been chartered in 1895—at the behest of such leading Republicans as S. Fred Nixon and Benjamin F. Tracy—and given extraordinary rights to obtain water and sell it to the cities. In 1900 a controversy arose over a proposed contract calling for the Ramapo Company to supply water to New York City for forty years at a fixed price that many considered exorbitant. The deal was temporarily stopped by legislation that year, but the matter was not finally put to rest until the following winter when a measure strongly urged by Odell repealed the company's charter and extended New York City's authority to obtain and control its own water supply.[28]

The skepticism toward privileged grants that inspired the Ramapo outcry of 1900–1901 now became a fixed feature of New York politics. Each legislative session, especially those of 1903 and 1904, was marked by intense public and journalistic attention to alleged "grab" bills, said to have been introduced for the benefit of certain companies and to have the support of unscrupulous legislators. Civic groups lobbied and called mass meetings in opposition to such "grabs." By 1904 few New Yorkers could have been entirely unaware that the old distributive policy process was defective.[29]

The alternative to unrestrained distribution was stronger state regulation of the privileged corporations. For this there were rising demands during the Odell years. In 1901 the governor proposed giving the Board of Railroad Commissioners jurisdiction over gas and electric corporations, but his suggestion was not adopted, and he never renewed it. More persistent were the efforts of several downstate commercial organizations, especially the Merchants' Association and the New York Board of Trade and Transportation, to extend the regulation of steam and street railways. From 1902 on, they sought to have the railroad commission enlarged and given added powers, including rate-setting authority. In the same years, they attempted to get the legislature to penalize the railroads for poor service. Through petitions, publications, mass meetings, and legislative lobbying, the merchants pressed their proposals, but all were opposed by the railroads, and all were defeated.[30]

While they failed, these pressures provided one more indication that New York was nearing a watershed in business-government relations. Together with the intensification of competition for legislative influence and the spread of opposition to grants of privilege, the merchants' demands for regulation suggested deepening dissatisfaction with an economic-policy process mainly geared to unchecked distribution. But the energy and impetus to establish a new structure of policy were still missing.

While business regulation was stalled, several policy areas became more active, essentially through the devolution of governmental authority upon interested groups. This especially occurred on labor and canal matters, where functional economic associations and civic reform organizations devised policies they wanted and assumed responsibility for making them popular. When sufficient political support for the measures was demonstrated, the governing party ratified them. Even as they acceded to this method of policymaking, however, Republican leaders remained wary of it and took countervailing steps to dilute and disguise group conflict over government decisions.

Odell's own distinctive contribution to labor policy grew out of his economizing drive. In his first annual message, the governor proposed consolidating the Bureau of Labor Statistics, the office of Factory Inspector, and the Bureau of Mediation and Arbitration into a single Department of Labor. The legislators accepted Odell's plan. In a related move, the force of factory inspectors was reduced from fifty to thirty-seven.[31] But while Odell's economizing eroded the already feeble enforcement of existing labor laws, pressure from outside groups dictated an entirely different policy direction on two key subjects: employers' liability and child labor.

By the beginning of the 1900s, a law establishing employer accountability for industrial injuries had become the leading legislative goal of the Workingmen's Federation of New York. Under common-law doctrines, courts had usually exempted an employer from responsibility for a worker's injury if the victim himself had contributed to the accident, if a fellow employee was at fault, or if the worker had accepted a job knowing of its risks. Since these rules made it nearly impossible for a worker or his surviving family to compel an employer to pay compensation, organized labor sought their modification. Thwarted in 1900 and 1901, the Federation achieved this aim in 1902 when a measure meeting the specifications of labor leaders was passed with almost no dissent and became law. The statute left unchanged the injured worker's obligation to prove that he had not been negligent, but it at least partly closed the other two loopholes through which employers had evaded responsibility for injuries. While studies later showed that workingmen still found it extremely difficult to win injury compensation through court action, the measure's passage significantly marked the governing party's acquiescence in a law that labor had earned by its organized strength.[32]

A similar political reality stood behind the passage of four child-labor laws in 1903. Here, however, the group responsible was the New York Child Labor Committee, an energetic organization of settlement-house workers and their socially prominent sympathizers. Appalled by the conditions under which children then performed industrial work, the CLC gathered data, mobilized public opinion, and drafted legislation to curtail and regulate child labor. Endorsed by Odell, the measures easily became law. Enforcing them was more difficult than enacting them, however, since the statutes failed to provide for new administrative machinery. Yet the passage of these measures suggested how a civic group, willing to perform hard political labor, could compel the politicians to act.[33]

Even as he supported certain organized efforts to pass labor laws, Odell was reluctant to acknowledge—in the frank way that Roosevelt did—that workers and employers had legitimate differences with one another. "The two great elements which made for success, capital and labor, should never be antagonistic," Odell characteristically declared in his second inaugural address in 1903. "Their interests lie in the same direction. They should be in thorough accord." As governor, Odell made a rhetorical specialty of statements like this, as nineteenth-century Republican politicians often had. Thus, just at the moment when he and his party were accommodating to interest-group participation in policymaking, Odell's language—by proclaiming the prevalence of harmony—discouraged the search for lasting governmental means of adjusting group differences.[34]

A conventional politician, Odell was wary of the dangers that interest-group politics posed to partisanship, and nowhere were his fears more understandable than on the canal issue, which deeply divided the Republican coalition. From the moment that Governor Roosevelt's advisory committee had recommended a thousand-ton barge canal in 1900, mercantile organizations in New York City and Buffalo championed it avidly, while rural residents, railroad companies, and many upstate commercial interests strongly opposed the plan. In 1901 and 1902 Odell tried to compromise the issue by supporting lesser improvements on the existing Erie Canal, but in both years his proposals were defeated in the legislature by an unlikely alliance of anticanal interests and waterway advocates who would settle for nothing less than the barge canal. When the governor met with the waterway's supporters, he was noncommittal about his own position, but his advice to them was direct: "Get out and hustle." This they did. Through canal conventions, speaking tours, hundreds of boiler-plate editorials for the country weeklies, and persistent legislative lobbying, the organized big-city merchants educated skeptical New Yorkers about a barge canal and its benefits. By the time of the fall campaign of 1902, they were succeeding. As a candidate for reelection, Odell flatly endorsed the barge canal—though his party's platform was more vague—and thus entered his second term committed to the merchants' project.[35]

He did not make it a party question, however. When a barge-canal bond issue for $101 million came before the legislature in 1903, almost every Democrat supported it, while the Republicans divided along geographic lines, according to the interests of their constituents. That fall, when the proposition was presented to the voters as a referendum, Republican leaders and canal advocates continued to keep it out of party politics. "The question is . . . in no sense a partisan one," declared Francis V. Greene, author of the 1900 barge-canal report. Even Platt accepted the nonpartisan strategy. When the returns came in, it was clear that the electors had voted their economic interests as they saw them. In a relatively large off-year turnout, the referendum carried the state, because it received overwhelming support in the New York City and Buffalo areas. Most Republican counties opposed the measure, however, and the party's vote correlates with support for the canal at $-.42$.[36]

By permitting the canal to come before the voters as a nonpartisan question in 1903, Odell and the other Republican leaders had accepted their party's internal division. The risk paid off. At the same time that the referendum was winning approval, the Republicans were also carrying the elections for assembly. The party system could survive a divisive policy choice, but the experience made leading Republicans uncomfortable. Just to be safe, while they strove to keep the canal issue separate from party politics, they had also worked to persuade voters that there was actually no reason for disagreement on the question. Speaking at county fairs, Odell argued that a barge canal, in assisting New York City and Buffalo, would benefit the whole state and deserved to be supported by every voter. As the election results disclosed, he need not have been so disingenuous, for Republican voters were perfectly capable of distinguishing their material and partisan interests.

Still, as the leader of a heterogeneous party coalition, Odell was understandably skeptical of a policy process in which interested groups fashioned programs they wanted and then bore the responsibility for getting them adopted. What role was left for the party to play and what would become of it?[37]

That was one of the questions that economic-policy developments in early-twentieth century New York left unanswered. While Odell's administration produced several lasting accomplishments—especially on tax policy—the more notable products of these years were confusion and the dispersion of governing authority. The relentless rise of expectations for state services and the clash of interest-group demands together weakened the ability of a political party to shape government decisions. As yet, however, no alternative instrument for integrating governance had arisen.

The actual implications of the new expectations and demands differed from one policy area to the next. State expenditures grew steadily and, in a sense, uncontrollably. Promotional policies aiding business enterprises fell under deep suspicion, but there was not yet a consensus on an alternative structure of business-government relations. In other areas, interested groups virtually arrogated to themselves the right to dictate state policy. Everywhere, the tasks of government were growing, but there was no corresponding increase in the planning and coordination of them. The adoption of labor policies without adequate provisions for enforcement and the decision to spend $101 million on a barge canal that, as it turned out, came nowhere close to fulfilling its advocates' expectations were but two unfortunate results of a policy process that was still only incompletely adapted to industrial realities.

Odell himself, the "business" governor, provided a force for orderly policymaking, but he also contributed to the confusion. In scrutinizing and tabulating state appropriations, he anticipated the later adoption of budgeting techniques; by consolidating departments and replacing boards by single commissioners, he streamlined governance and centralized authority; by explicitly connecting the privileges that corporations received with the obligations they owed, he helped rationalize the state's promotional policies and its revenue system. Above all, his words about "businesslike" government suggested the unbiased, efficient process of decision making that reformers were beginning to call "administration."

But because he failed to couple his conception of "business" government with a recognition of interest-group conflict, Odell missed the opportunity to dispel confusion by developing permanent governmental methods of mitigating social differences. Indeed, he went to considerable lengths to insist, as Republican politicians traditionally had, that harmony prevailed—between labor and capital, between the cities and the country. "The citizen of the town, the mechanic and the farmer are inter-dependent," he declared in 1902 and often reasserted. "Whatever tends to the well-being of either is a benefit to all and should receive our cordial support."[38] Such declarations served to disguise the growing need for a government continuously involved in overseeing the clashing interests of an industrial society through regulation and planning. Those are truly "businesslike" functions, yet they are predicated on a recognition of the disharmony Odell—like most party leaders—denied. He managed to make certain existing governmental operations more efficient, but by neglecting the new purposes to which "businesslike" government might have been put, he helped sustain the confusion that industrialization was bringing to a nineteenth-century policy process.

While economic policymaking was becoming more difficult for Odell's party, the development and spread of independent political behavior were placing related pressures on the state Republican organization and on the party's local machines. No longer confined to electoral politics in the large cities, independency now had become a common inclination of the times, visible in different forms and potent for a diversity of purposes. If it had ceased to be as dynamic and coherent as the movement of 1897, it was because that movement had achieved its specific aims and had inspired new patterns of behavior challenging the dominance of traditional party politics.

As governor, Odell accepted the concessions the city independents had wrested from the Republican organization after 1897, and, indeed, he extended them, as his treatment of the New York City police question suggests. While Odell did not consult leading independents as frequently as had Roosevelt, his behavior and his language showed respect for their doctrines of efficiency in government and excellence in appointments. For their part, the urban independents were relatively satisfied with the gains they had won in the areas of election-law reform and municipal governance. The primary law of 1898 proved especially successful. Under the statute, one independent Republican from Buffalo informed Odell in 1901, "we have gotten back into the ranks of the party nearly all of the mugwumps, so-called, and have proselyted into the party a very large number of Cleveland Democrats." Accordingly, from 1901 to 1904, only minor revisions were made in the rules governing primaries. Other election-law reforms similarly languished in the Odell years, without ill effects on Republican-independent relations.[39]

The reformers also seemed much more content with the conduct of city politics than they had been in the 1890s. According to Albert Shaw, an expert on municipal reform and the editor of the nonpartisan *American Monthly Review of Reviews,* "New York [City] has now, in the main, secured honest elections; it has separated municipal from general elections; it has learned how to nominate candidates and conduct elections on real and vital issues." In a true sense, the particular independent concerns of the 1890s had been met, and with their settlement came a gradual abandonment of the nonpartisan electoral campaigns through which the urban reformers had achieved their goals. Out of their triumphs, however, had also emerged new independent purposes for which fresh methods were required; out of them, as well, had come a successful model for reform that other elements in the state now emulated.[40]

In the large upstate cities, regulars and independents continued the cooperation they had established late in the 1890s when the Republicans acceded to many of the reformers' demands and appropriated their rhetoric. Every two years, party leaders in Rochester, Albany, and Syracuse nominated mayoral candidates who appealed for independent support, won easy election victories on the basis of local issues, and led efficient, mildly progressive administrations. In Rochester, George Washington Aldridge allied with the Good Government forces to elect Adolph J. Rodenbeck in 1901 and James G. Cutler in 1903 and 1905. Helped by prosperity, both mayors satisfied demands for efficiency and for expanded city services, and they brought Rochester balanced budgets, as well as improved schools, streets, sewers, and parks. In Albany, under William Barnes, Jr., Charles H. Gaus attracted independent support as an efficient city executive and was elected three times. In Francis H. Hendricks's Syracuse, Mayor Alan C. Fobes served consecutive terms on the basis of policies and appeals that matched those of his counterparts in Albany and Rochester. These mayors abjured extreme partisanship, kept their attention on local issues, and applied impartial, "businesslike" methods. In their cities, where the problems of municipal governance were not overwhelming, Republican leaders thus found it possible to satisfy the independents while winning victories for the party.[41]

New York City's far more complex conditions presented graver difficulties to independent-Republican relations. Even in the great downstate metropolis, however, the first years of Odell's administration brought signs that cooperation was continuing on the same terms as in the late 1890s. In 1901, the state legislature approved a revised charter for the city that reformers considered "a decided improvement upon the charter of 1897." That year, Republicans and independents cooperated in the fusion campaign that elected Seth Low as mayor, and, during the following legislative session, Odell supported a series of measures at Low's request.[42]

Even as the governor did so, however, certain of his state policies worsened the independent mayor's political position. The very tax measures that shifted the burden from real estate to personal property and business corporations also shifted it heavily to the cities, particularly to New York City. Low tried gamely to defend Republican tax policies, and he even asked the governor for figures and arguments to use. But praising the new tax system was a losing proposition for the mayor; he found himself sharing the blame for taxes his constituents considered blatant jobbery by a "hayseed" administration.[43]

The state's policy of requiring saloons to close on Sunday provided an even greater liability for Low. In 1901 he had captured crucial German support by promising a "liberal enforcement" of the Sunday law; to close the bars in violation of that pledge would invite Tammany's return at the next election. Police connivance at infractions of the Sunday statute, on the other hand, would alienate moral reformers and deprive Low of the police-corruption issue he had used successfully against the Democrats. His administration's only escape from the dilemma lay in a relaxation of the legal restriction on Sunday closing, but this Odell refused to grant.[44]

Republican legislative leaders casually dismissed Low's liquor dilemma. Speaker Nixon avowed, "I know of no demands in my section of the state for Sunday opening of saloons." Senator John Raines, author of the 1896 liquor law, claimed that its maintenance was vital to Republican success. He may have been right. In 1902 the Prohibition party endorsed John Cunneen, the Democratic candidate for attorney general. When Cunneen won, while his Democratic running mates without Prohibition support all lost, the Republicans caught a glimpse of the results a lax liquor policy might have. New York City independents viewed the liquor issue's electoral impact precisely the other way. According to the *Times*, upstate opposition to a modification of the Sunday law constituted "in effect a recommendation that the government of this city be turned over to [Tammany boss] Richard Croker at the next Mayoralty election."[45]

The "recommendation" was realized. In the gubernatorial election of 1902, Odell was reduced to 37 percent of New York City's vote (compared with the 46 percent McKinley had won in 1900), and the following year Low was defeated for reelection by a Tammany Democrat, George B. McClellan, Jr. The 1902 contest produced the era's closest and most sectionally polarized electoral result. Despite his dismal downstate showing, Odell was able to carry the state by eight thousand votes because he won 56 percent of the ballots from above New York City. Contemporary observers noted how heavily the city had shifted against the Republicans and how polarized the electorate had become. A weekly paper from northern New York explained what had happened by acknowledging something Odell himself repeatedly denied: "It is impossible not to think that the city feels it has a grievance, and that its interests are not exactly those of the rural sections."[46]

With such a sectional division of interest in the state, it is not surprising that the party whose base lay upstate found it difficult to maintain an alliance with New York City independents whose predominant political concern was their city. Low's defeat for reelection in 1903 suggested just how difficult it was. To be sure, the mayor himself contributed to his own loss. Despite his considerable achievements in franchise regulation, fiscal reform, and city services, Low lacked personal magnetism or the ability to dramatize his accomplishments. Renominated without much enthusiasm by the Citizens' Union, the Republicans, and most of the independent organizations that had supported him two years before, Low faced a Tammany machine made vigorous and less corrupt by the Hall's new leader, Charles Francis Murphy.[47]

To these weaknesses of Low, the Republican party added others. Besides the damage done by taxation and Sunday closing, Odell's party bore the responsibility for a city-charter change, reducing the mayoral term from four years to two, that had been adopted despite Low's repeated warnings that the briefer period allowed insufficient time for citizens to feel the beneficial effects of a nonpartisan administration. Within the city, the Republican organization, still under Platt, bitterly felt shortchanged in the matter of patronage, and, by the time of the 1903 election, the fusion forces were barely cooperating, despite their joint ticket. Low himself observed afterward that "the amount of friction between the Republicans and the Citizens' Union, in different parts of the city, was much greater this year than two years ago."[48] What the defeated mayor did not realize, however, was that the failure of independent-Republican cooperation brought an end to an era in New York City politics. Never again would there be fusion campaigns quite like those of 1894, 1901, and 1903. For New York City's independents were coming to realize that other means besides electoral politics offered them a better chance to influence municipal government.

Civic group organizations of all sorts began to take permanent roles pressuring, advising, and cooperating with the different agencies of New York City government, no matter which party was in office. Such a function was not, of course, entirely new. For years, the City Club had performed it, as the Citizens' Union did during Low's term as mayor. Now, however, around 1903, many more reform groups and special-interest organizations assumed the tasks of regularly prodding and informing city officials. Low's administration had taught the reformers how difficult it was for even a well-intentioned mayor to solve the highly technical problems of municipal administration, and his defeat in 1903 suggested the limitations of a strategy of reform based on electing good men to office.[49]

While the City Club and the Citizens' Union were interested in every facet of municipal governance, many of the new groups focused their efforts on particular urban problems. Tenement-house reform, health and sanitation matters, schools, utility franchises, and mass transit all drew the attention of specialized reform organizations. Some occupational groups, especially merchants, lawyers, doctors, engineers, and other professionals, also began using their economic-interest associations to inform and pressure city officials about particular matters where they had demands to make and expertise to offer. Common to these efforts were certain methods of operation: the collection of information, the reliance on experts, the establishment of close working relations with the relevant city departments, and the acquisition of the influence that came with regularly having answers to difficult problems of municipal governance.[50]

In the years after 1903 the new civic groups made their weight felt in the mayoral administrations of Low's successors, most of whom were Tammany Democrats. Here were informed and aroused citizens who had found nonelectoral means of permanently participating in municipal administration and of modernizing it according to their own lights. Their successes gave a new meaning to the tradition of urban independency that was particularly ominous for the minority party in New York City. Reformers who regularly exercised influence in city government felt less need to participate in anti-Tammany coalitions of Republicans, independents, and disgruntled Democrats. For the Republican organization, the new state of affairs spelled less power in New York City government, the very eventuality Platt had devoted so much effort to preventing. For the reformers, now pioneering the extraparty means of influence which were destined to become a familiar element of twentieth-century politics, it meant the achievement of greater potency than they had ever had before.[51]

While new forms of independent political behavior were becoming common in downstate New York, upstate citizens were beginning to catch up with the older independency of the 1890s. Urban and rural independency should not, of course, be seen as one. Outside the large cities, where there were not complex problems of municipal government, voters found fewer reasons to reject party organizations and less need to devise nonpartisan political methods. When they did so, their actions were responses to their own problems, timed according to their own conditions. Yet it is impossible entirely to escape the conclusion that rural and small-town New Yorkers of the early twentieth century were influenced by the successful example set by urban independents, some of whose language and habits they cautiously copied.

Political editorials in the country weeklies provide one kind of evidence of growing independence. The criticism of bossism, the issuance of warnings to party leaders, and the observation of waning partisan enthusiasm all became increasingly common. The battle for Republican leadership between Platt and Odell particularly seems to have inspired disgust with party bossism. "A plague on both your houses," fulminated one Republican weekly paper in western New York. Election time now brought editorial remonstrances against bad behavior by the party's local leaders, while postelection commentaries pointed out the influence that independent voters had wielded. Especially in the off years, editorials frequently noted the dearth of political excitement and participation.[52]

Actually, off-year electoral turnout varied considerably from year to year and place to place in upstate New York. Having fallen to 63.5 percent in 1897, it rose in 1899, fell in 1901, and then jumped sharply in 1903 to 74.7 percent, a level characteristic of a gubernatorial-year election. Amid the variability, certain patterns stand out. Most of the overall decline in turnout was concentrated in the rural counties of northern and western New York. Here the Republican party was sure to carry every election, and in years when there were not state and national candidates on the ballot, many voters stayed home. In far northern St. Lawrence County, to take an extreme example, turnout was 89 percent in the presidential years of 1900 and 1904 but fell to 28 and 29 percent, respectively, in the succeeding off years.

The high turnout for the election of 1903 presents a revealing exception, both in St. Lawrence—where participation was double that of 1901 and 1905—and in upstate New York generally where the total vote for assembly slightly exceeded the previous year's vote for governor. Almost certainly the barge-canal referendum explains 1903's unusual turnout, especially in anticanal counties like St. Lawrence, where the referendum was defeated by 92 percent to 8 percent. Across the state, the increase in voter participation from 1901 to 1903 correlates at $-.40$ with support for the canal. What brought so many voters to the polls was evidently not partisanship, but the canal issue, and this was especially true for the waterway's opponents.[53]

Fearful that off-year electoral laxity might endanger the Republican vote at on-year elections, when much more was at stake, party leaders supported a number of legal measures designed to reverse the trend. Beginning in 1898, the legislature passed laws permitting the rescheduling of town elections from the spring to the fall of the odd years. In this way, it was hoped, local contests would encourage voting, much as mayoral elections brought urban citizens to the polls. Most rural communities preferred to keep their town elections separate from partisan assembly contests, however, and, despite subsequent laws encouraging them to shift, turnout in many rural areas continued to be low.[54]

The election results of 1902 suggest the validity of Republican concerns that the loss of the voting habit at off-year contests jeopardized even-year participation. That year, 73 percent of the state's eligible electors voted for governor, compared with 77 percent who had done so in the previous nonpresidential gubernatorial election, 1898. While they were modest, the turnout losses of 1902 were surprisingly pervasive: in fifty of fifty-nine counties participation fell. Yet of the ten counties where the losses were greatest, nine were in far northern and western New York where off-year turnout was falling the most. Nonparticipation was evidently spreading to even-year contests.[55]

Other features of the 1902 vote also suggest that upstate electors were beginning to become less partisan. That year, the average county-level change in the Republican percentage of the vote since the previous year (absolute values, weighted according to county size) was 3.9 percent. This was a modest level of change, to be sure, but it was larger than in the realignment year of 1894, or at any gubernatorial election since 1894. The upstate electorate's increased volatility was maintained at succeeding elections, particularly ones, like 1902, when a governor, but not a president, was chosen. Since every section of upstate New York included counties that gained in Republican strength, as well as ones that lost, no one factor seems able to explain the shifts of 1902. The Odell years were conspicuously charged with issues that affected rural and small-town voters, especially taxation and canal improvements. To judge from private correspondence and public statements, numerous political observers believed that these issues were potent enough to shake the traditional partisanship of many electors.[56]

It would be misleading all the same to overstate the independence of upstate New Yorkers during the first years of the twentieth century. Aggregate returns show that the great majority of voters remained firm partisans and habitual participants. Yet there were signs, in the political language they used and the electoral behavior they manifested, that the partisanship of upstaters was yielding ground to both issues and apathy. Together with indications from elsewhere in the state, these changes suggest that independency from party machines was a growing, if diffuse, phenomenon in New York. Odell's own conduct of the governorship and the behavior of Republican organizations in the large upstate cities show that the formal concessions made to nonpartisanship at the end of the 1890s were being continued. In New York City, independency had taken a new direction, based on new methods. By 1904 these related developments were subtly but crucially transforming the environment in which politics was practiced by the party that had come to state power a decade before.

The elections that year, while they kept the Republicans in power, forced into the open the party's long-standing struggle to deal with the political problems brought on by independency and industrialization. These were the very causes of difficulty Odell's strategy had been designed to deal with or disguise. Now, however, his own behavior accentuated and magnified his party's troubles over them.

First, there was his ill-advised decision to reassume the state party chairmanship in the spring of 1904. Considered improper by many independents, as well as regular Republicans, Odell's ascent to formal party leadership while he was still the governor cost him more in popular support than it won him in organizational leverage. Never personally well liked, Odell was now described in the press as a more despicable boss than Platt himself. Even his virtuosity at putting his programs through the legislature, which previously had won praise, brought forth harsh rebukes. "His orders issue, and his puppets in either House execute them," charged the mugwumpish *Nation*.[57]

That fall, Odell's "puppets" in the state convention nominated Lieutenant Governor Frank W. Higgins for governor. Actually, Odell seems to have preferred Elihu Root or Nicholas Murray Butler—either of whom would have appealed to the independents—but when both of them declined to be considered, Odell turned to Higgins, whom Roosevelt favored, in order to beat Platt's candidate, Timothy L. Woodruff. Odell's role in the nomination fed suspicions that the next governor would be the present governor's plaything.[58]

To the growing dislike of Odell's tactics as boss, new disclosures added the taint of financial corruption and big-business connections. Among the many charges made against Odell, the one that did him the most damage was the accusation that the canal board, with the governor's consent, had wrongly approved a claim of $18,618 upon the state by the Furnaceville Iron Company. A canal contractor in the 1890s, the firm allegedly had classified certain excavated material as rock rather than earth, and Republican officials were said to have approved an inflated claim for the work. Belief in the truth of the charges took hold, especially when it became known that Edward H. Harriman was the Furnaceville's president. A close friend of Odell, the railway magnate was rumored by some to have considerable influence with the governor. Others went further and declared Odell to be Harriman's "lackey." Whatever the precise relationship between Odell and Harriman, the Furnaceville incident blackened the governor's reputation for integrity in money matters and associated him in the public mind with an unpopular business giant.[59]

The Democrats focused their state campaign of 1904 largely on Odell's misdeeds. His assumption of the party chairmanship, their platform said, "constitutes a public scandal and amounts to the grossest contempt of duty in the history of the State." The Democratic gubernatorial candidate, D. Cady Herrick of Albany, appealed explicitly to independents to abandon the corrupt Republican organization and return to the Democracy. Herrick's party also accused the Republicans of favoritism to big corporations. The great issue in the campaign, said the *Buffalo Enquirer*, was "whether the partnership established between the Governor-Chairman and the [business] combines in this State . . . shall continue."[60]

The Democratic charges alarmed Republicans and forced them virtually to renounce their own state leader. President Roosevelt, himself a candidate in 1904, urged that Republican speakers "relegate . . . State matters to an entirely secondary place." If the Democrats "succeed in keeping Odellism the main issue," he warned, "we shall be beaten out of our boots." To dispel the aura of "Odellism," party speakers and editors proclaimed Higgins's independence. "You can vote for Mr. Higgins, and in voting for him you will not be voting for any machine or for anyone else," an upstate weekly declared. "He will tolerate no dictation." Speaking in Troy, former Governor Black denied Higgins would be controlled by Odell. "I have always found Higgins so independent that I told him I thought he was slightly mugwump."[61]

In making a virtue of independence, the Republicans were accommodating to what observers acknowledged was a changed political atmosphere in 1904. "The present political campaign seems different from any of its predecessors," observed one small-town weekly newspaper. "The day of monster parades, waving banners and blare of trumpets is gone by. . . . The people are reading and thinking and will

190

not be greatly influenced by noise or crowds. In fact, they seem to be pretty nearly indifferent to what the politicians say." Privately, Republican leaders worried that thousands of the party's voters would split their tickets against the state candidates. In New York City, the anti-Odell *Sun* was urging voters to do just that and day after day printing a marked sample ballot illustrating how. It was another indication that the political rules and rhetoric were changing—to what, the party politicians were not yet sure.[62]

When the votes were counted, the predictions of ticket-splitting proved accurate. Higgins won, but his majority was almost 100,000 less than Roosevelt's. The presidential candidate led all Republican nominees in fifty-one counties, while Higgins trailed the ticket in forty-four. To judge from the aggregate returns, most electors who voted for Roosevelt and rejected Higgins did not abstain in the gubernatorial contest but cast their ballots for Herrick, the Democratic nominee. While it was not uncommon for Republican presidential candidates to lead their tickets in New York, Roosevelt's margin over Higgins was unprecedentedly great and the phenomenon of split ballots surprisingly pervasive across the state. Observers did not fail to notice the high levels of ticket-splitting elsewhere in the country in 1904, but they agreed that the revolt against Odell explained the New York electorate's unusual departure from ordinary partisanship.[63]

The election presented another disturbing aspect to the Republicans. The Furnaceville scandal and Harriman's connection with it had given the voters a moment of insight into the secret cooperation of party leaders with men of wealth. That year's presidential campaign had raised the same issue when Alton B. Parker charged Roosevelt with receiving contributions from large corporations in return for promises of protection. The president denied the allegations and temporarily stilled the matter, but Parker had introduced an issue destined to become explosive. Events soon proved the validity of his concern and, in New York, showed the relationship between Odell and Harriman to reflect a larger pattern of corrupt alliances.[64]

For four years, Benjamin B. Odell, Jr., had struggled to contain problems the election now exposed. But in every vital area his strategy had weakened the Republicans' grasp on new conditions. His policies undercut the basis for independent-Republican cooperation in New York City and helped persuade many reformers to abandon electoral politics in favor of extraparty means of influence. Elsewhere in the state, his actions as party leader provoked the rise of antimachine feelings and the spread of independent voting. Where divisive economic issues were at stake, Odell was unwilling to recognize conflict or

191

to propose the means of adjusting it. His own behavior contributed to the distrust of corporations and their privileges, but he did little to bring about the vitally needed restructuring of business-government relations.

The problems Odell failed to solve were Republican problems because that party was in power. But they had implications for the entire conduct of traditional politics. Voter independence meant a weakening of the constant party loyalties upon which nineteenth-century American elections were based. Conflicts between competing groups, each learning to achieve what they wanted through nonpartisan means, lessened the party leaders' control of governance. Public skepticism about corporate behavior threatened the familiar distributive policy process and endangered the system of campaign contributions on which politicians depended. In the two years following Odell's administration, striking events intensified these perils to traditional politics. In response, some party leaders ventured "progressive" solutions, which, while scarcely revolutionary, addressed more fundamentally the problems Platt and Odell had treated without success.

7

Politics at the Crossroads: The Crisis of 1905–1906

By 1905 the varied forces of political change that had been gathering for a decade in New York State finally became unstoppable. Independent opposition to the party machines had already made its mark on elections, policies, and political rhetoric. Already, too, economic changes had created an urgent need for the adjustment of group differences and the restructuring of relations between business and government. In their behavior and their language, the leading party politicians in the state took account of these pressures on traditional politics and tried to alleviate them. But despite their efforts, the issues and results of the 1904 election suggested that an upheaval was imminent. In the next two years it took place. Striking events crystallized the forces for change and caused the adoption of concrete solutions for political and governmental problems.

Even in 1905 and 1906, however, much remained the same in New York politics. The new governor, Frank W. Higgins, provided a symbol of continuity. He entered office a supporter of most of Odell's programs and with a disposition to be friendly though not subservient to his predecessor, who was still the party's state chairman. In many respects, Higgins's administration represented a continuation of Odell's. A series of constitutional amendments brought to completion some of the party chairman's chief policies, including the total abolition of direct state taxes. Expenditure patterns changed little under the new governor, except that the barge canal's huge costs began to be felt during his term. Higgins proved reasonably able in defending the new tax system and the continued growth of state expenditures. He gave the impression of an honest man using familiar methods to govern the state.[1]

From the outset, however, Higgins's administration faced conditions for which the past provided no preparation. In 1905 two dramatic legislative investigations disclosed vast wrongdoing within several industries—including gas, electricity, and life insurance—that directly affected ordinary people. The misdeeds exposed were not only financial but also political, and of all the disclosures the most vivid and vital concerned the corrupt cooperation between businessmen and politicians, the details of which now became familiar elements of political rhetoric. By fusing the long-standing grievances against bosses and corporations, the discovery of such corruption brought together the previously distinct forces of independence from party machines and of economic-policy change. In consequence, the perceptions created by the legislative inquiries of 1905, especially the life insurance investigation, generated a transformation of New York State politics more basic than the upheaval of the 1890s. The events of 1905–6 destroyed some careers and launched others. They spread independency to the electorate at large. And they forced decisive responses to the era's most characteristic policy problem: the government's relationship to organized economic-interest groups.

These changes have often been identified with progressivism. Their details and their timing, however, owed as much—and probably more—to the efforts of Republican leaders trying to stay in power as to the work of "reformers." Interpreting the transformation of the state's politics is thus more complex than merely accounting for the motives of progressives. One problem is to explain why the peak of change came when it did, from about 1905 to 1908. Another difficulty involves distinguishing the rhetoric of reform from the intentions behind it and from the results it achieved. Still another problem lies in seeing the significance of the changes while recognizing their sharp limits. These problems of analysis occupy much of the rest of the present study.

The first crisis of 1905 originated in Manhattan where long-standing discontent over utility rates and services now exploded. Several years earlier, Mayor Seth Low had broken precedent by rejecting the Consolidated Gas Company's arbitrary bids for city lighting on the grounds that a privileged, quasi-public corporation ought to receive only a reasonable return based on its costs. The company defended its own right to set prices, and for two years the matter stood unresolved. Then late in 1904, with Tammany back in power, the city agreed to the Consolidated's controversial contract. Newspapers raised an outcry against the settlement, and civic groups demanded that the state intervene to prevent it. The Republicans at Albany had several avenues of action open: a legislative investigation of the Consolidated, a law reducing gas and electricity rates, or state approval for municipally owned utility plants. When Platt seemed to side with the hated power company, from which he presumably received campaign contributions, Odell called for a legislative inquiry that he hoped might help destroy the old boss's remaining power. Higgins agreed, and a joint committee, chaired by Senator Frederick C. Stevens, was named.[2]

The gas and electric investigation of April 1905 exhibited many of the same elements that later characterized the even more dramatic life insurance inquiry: the arousal of widespread public concern about the activities of a large corporation; the jockeying for position among Republican politicians having competing stakes in the issue; the appointment of a legislative committee—counseled by Charles Evans Hughes—that took its work more seriously than anticipated and generated significant new knowledge; and the adoption of effective regulatory measures that the supervised interests at first opposed but later accepted. These developments and their ironies tell us a good deal about the political changes New York State was undergoing.

Led by Hughes, who was acting in his first public role, the Stevens committee uncovered a wide range of corrupt practices by the Consolidated and its subsidiaries, including overcapitalization, fraudulent bookkeeping, tax evasion, and the illegal monopolization of the city's utilities. The investigation disclosed the huge profits reaped by the companies and the inflated prices that consumers paid for power. Testimony by Charles Murphy and other Tammany politicians left the impression that the Democratic party had acquiesced in the gas and electricity frauds. When the investigation concluded, Hughes holed up in the Fifth Avenue Hotel to draft the committee's report. With public interest high, considerable attention focused on what the lawmakers would recommend.[3]

Many observers hoped the legislature would propose municipal gas and electricity. In 1905 this was neither rare nor radical. Twenty-eight villages and three small cities in New York State already owned electric plants, and three villages had public gas facilities. Most of the municipally owned plants had been established before 1900, and they aroused little concern. In the large cities, public ownership remained more controversial, but in New York City it found support among businessmen who hoped to lower taxes by having the city meet its own lighting needs. Few were surprised, then, when Hughes recommended and the legislature approved a law permitting the city to use its own water supply to generate electricity. Originally suggested by the Democrats, such a plan provided an entering wedge for municipal electricity but did little to effect it. Despite the ideological acceptability of limited municipal ownership, Republican legislators probably felt it was not their issue. They needed a "Republican" solution to the volatile utility problem.[4]

Legislative determination of gas and electricity prices offered an approach the party had used before. On the basis of his own calculations, Hughes proposed reducing the maximum price of gas from one dollar per thousand cubic feet to seventy-five cents; electricity would go down from fifteen cents to ten cents per kilowatt-hour. With the support of Odell and Higgins, the rate bills passed the assembly almost unanimously, but in the senate a bipartisan majority defeated the gas-price proposal. While Higgins expressed regret that the Republicans had failed to respond to the clamor for cheaper gas, Hughes, the rate bills' author, was less concerned. For a more important recommendation that became law just as he wrote it obviated the need for legislative rate-setting: the creation of a state commission to regulate gas and electricity companies.[5]

In certain respects, the commission was as familiar a solution as the passage of intermittent rate laws. Republicans had frequently relied on state boards to handle problems that emanated from New York City; besides, the measure offered real patronage possibilities. But the three-member Commission of Gas and Electricity was not just another state agency, for it had wider regulatory powers than any similar board. In addition to the authority to supervise power companies, to investigate their property and books, and to require annual reports, the commissioners could allow or disallow the establishment of new companies, set quality standards for gas and electricity, and regulate the issuance of company stocks and bonds. Unlike the state's existing railroad, insurance, and banking departments, the new board was to be supported by public funds, not by the affected interests. Of most importance, the commission would have the power to regulate rates. While its decisions remained subject to court review, the board's powers were unprecedented for such a body. Its authority to deal permanently and continuously with complex utility matters foreshadowed the scope and nature of future regulation.[6]

Only a special combination of circumstances—including Hughes's presence as counsel, the level of public outrage, and the Republicans' need for party action on the utility issue—made possible such an innovation in regulatory policy in 1905. Senator Stevens had sought a counsel without ties to the utility interests or to party politics, and chance led him to Hughes, a successful, nominally Republican New York City lawyer. Hughes had no previous knowledge or experience in the fields of gas and electricity, and the details of his proposals could not have been foreseen. When the Stevens committee released Hughes's report, public pressure left the Republicans little choice but to support it. Odell moved behind the commission proposal, and

Higgins brought Platt into line. The utility board became a Republican party measure, and it passed both houses on party votes. Not a single assembly or senate Democrat supported it; only six Republicans, all in the senate, failed to do so.[7]

Utility companies opposed the gas and electricity measures of 1905, and lobbyists were said to have offered unprecedented sums for votes against them. Hughes's rate proposals worried the corporations more than did the regulatory board, and, in the end, they successfully concentrated their opposition on the gas-price bill. By the time of the commission's establishment, most utility companies had reportedly accepted the idea of such a board. But the companies went no further than grudging acquiescence in the commission's creation. They had not initiated it and would have preferred to remain under the old system. Probably only a few people understood the Citizens' Union's prediction that in time the board would "become a safeguard to the corporation rather than a protection to the public."[8]

Well hated for its arrogance and high rates, the Consolidated Gas Company had offered a likely target for an investigation. By comparison, the second, greater legislative inquiry of 1905 focused on an industry with a far better public image: life insurance. An aura of disinterested public service surrounded the large life insurance companies. Even in the midst of the investigation, the president of one company could call his work "a great movement for the benefit of humanity." In an age of monopoly, moreover, the life insurance industry had not entirely succumbed to combination. Smaller companies remained competitive and continued to be successful. Life insurance firms seemed willing to accept governmental supervision, and in New York they sometimes even asked the Insurance Department to investigate their business. The life insurance industry thus retained unusual prestige. As a result, the disclosures that finally destroyed its aura caused a more severe public shock than did the corresponding utility revelations. That was all the more true because political and financial abuses proved to have been so intertwined.[9]

The scandal originated early in 1905 in the giant Equitable Life Assurance Society where two leading executives captured headlines by struggling publicly for power. Rumors sprang up about the misuse of policyholders' funds and about the involvement in the Equitable crisis by several of the wealthiest men of the day, including J. P. Morgan and E. H. Harriman. The New York *World* stirred public concern by running more than one hundred editorials on the subject, and other newspapers picked up the topic. When street railway magnate Thomas Fortune Ryan purchased a majority interest in the troubled company for $2.5 million, editorials asked why shares of a business presumably conducted for the benefit of its policyholders should be worth so much.

Two announced investigations, one within the Equitable and one by the state's Insurance Department, as well as a reorganization of the controversial company, failed to quiet concern. Demands arose for a legislative inquiry, and Odell, confident he could control such an investigation, joined the clamor for one. Governor Higgins hesitated, but in July he relented and advised the legislature to name a joint committee for the investigation of the life insurance business. The lawmakers complied, and on September 6, the committee, with Senator William W. Armstrong as chairman and Charles Evans Hughes as counsel, began taking testimony. No one who had helped lead the Republican party during the previous decade could have been entirely unworried about what would follow.[10]

Those who originated and conducted the investigation were not out to ruin the life insurance business. Governor Higgins hoped that the inquiry would not harm the companies, and Odell plainly had the protection of E. H. Harriman's insurance interests in mind. Even Hughes, though not a servant of the companies, was concerned to preserve the industry. As he recalled years later, "It was my aim to disclose such abuses as there were in the insurance business and seek to provide for their correction, while at the same time maintaining the credit of the companies . . . and the public esteem and confidence in which the essential life insurance enterprise had been held."[11]

Despite the sympathies of those responsible for it, the investigation disclosed a mass of unflattering detail concerning the business methods of the life insurance companies, particularly the three giants of the industry, the Equitable, the Mutual, and the New York Life. Hughes forced the officers of the companies to reveal their large and sometimes unauthorized salaries, to admit the fraudulence of their firms' bookkeeping procedures, and to acknowledge that their relentless drive to sell new insurance did not always serve the interests of established policyholders. Of particular importance, Hughes brought forth testimony regarding the companies' investment practices. By deferring some dividends and arbitrarily determining others, the firms accumulated huge surpluses which they invested not in the conservative manner expected of life insurance companies but in a highly speculative fashion. Their large liquid assets made the companies key participants in the world of high finance. They took shares in syndicate operations arranged by the great investment banking houses and sometimes acquired control of small banks and trust companies through which they made and concealed questionable investments. Hughes worked hard to make these complex dealings intelligible to outsiders. He met regularly with newspaper reporters to make sure they understood each day's disclosures. As a result, New Yorkers acquired a larger mass of information on a single industry than they had ever had before, and most of it was unfavorable.[12]

Besides the companies' methods of business management, Hughes's questioning also exposed their political affairs, particularly their legislative activity and their campaign contributions. The Mutual's employment of Andrew C. Fields and his maintenance of the "House of Mirth" at Albany for the entertainment of legislators came to light. So did the New York Life's even more elaborate structure of influence. Questioned by Hughes, company president John McCall acknowledged that one Andrew Hamilton "was given charge of the entire United States of [sic] the matter of legislation and taxation." Dividing the nation into districts, Hamilton had organized lobbying efforts in every state. All the major life insurance companies helped support Hamilton, who worked closely with Fields in New York. Fields and Hamilton both avoided testifying before the insurance committee, and no public accounting of their expenditures, reported to exceed $1 million, was ever made. Yet the disclosure of the companies' systematic efforts to influence legislation, the huge sums involved, and the hints of moral turpitude devastated the insurance business's public image.[13]

Equally weighty evidence was heard concerning secret campaign contributions. Hughes got George W. Perkins of the New York Life to acknowledge that his company had concealed a payment of $48,000 to Theodore Roosevelt's 1904 presidential campaign. That revelation soon led to the disclosure that since 1896 all the largest life insurance companies had contributed sizably to the Republicans at every election. While most of the money went for national purposes, the state party shared in it, too. The secrecy of the gifts and the evidence of corrupt collusion with politicians severely discredited the companies. As the chief recipient of the funds, the Republican party also suffered from the revelations, especially when its leaders took the stand, one by one, and revealed the extent of their cooperation with the life insurance industry.[14]

Senator Chauncey M. Depew, an Equitable director, bared his complex relations with the company, including his service as a paid counsel on investment matters. While Depew portrayed his advisory duties as arduous and time-consuming, he failed to allay suspicions that his $20,000 annual retainer mainly purchased political influence. The disclosure that Depew's advice chiefly concerned railroad stocks and bonds, which were considered improper investments for life insurance companies, did not enhance confidence in the senator's account. His credibility suffered further when he could not adequately explain his connection with the Depew Improvement Company, a real estate operation in western New York, to which the Equitable had improperly lent money. Such dealings brought up old questions about Depew's continuing services to the New York Central Railroad and to its owners, the Vanderbilts. "A railroad lobbyist for a lifetime," one newspaper labeled Depew, who now came under concerted pressure to resign from the United States Senate.[15]

Midway through the insurance investigation, Odell also had his reputation scarred. One past officer of the Equitable charged that in 1904 Governor Odell had compelled settlement of a personal claim against the Mercantile Trust Company by supporting a bill repealing the company's charter. The facts showed that after the withdrawal of the bill, Odell and representatives of the Mercantile, which had close Equitable connections, agreed upon a payment of $75,000 to the governor, who then dropped his claim. On the stand, Odell admitted he had seen "no objections" to the repeal bill, but he strongly contested its interpretation as a blackmailing measure. Nonetheless, the former governor's testimony failed to eradicate the impression that he had wrongly used his public position. To abet Odell's disgrace, other disclosures during the investigation revived the old accusation that he was the hireling of E. H. Harriman.[16]

Unlike Depew and Odell, Platt stood under no suspicion of personally profiting at the hands of the life insurance companies. But Platt's brief testimony, clouded through it was with an old man's vagueness and repetition, provided the investigation's clearest portrait of the process through which the insurance companies bought influence in the state government of New York. Though he occasionally confused one company with another or one election with the next, the aged senator freely acknowledged that for years he had received large campaign contributions, in cash, from the life insurance companies. Asked whether the firms acquired power in the legislature or the Insurance Department as a result of their contributions, Platt at first maintained he knew of no such influence. Under skillful interrogation by Hughes, however, Platt laid bare what money bought. "What advantage really could they get?" the committee counsel asked. "They get it through me being connected with the State Committee," Platt admitted. The senator was at first vague about how his connection was of use to the companies, but Hughes brought Platt's testimony to a stunning, if understated, climax:

Charles Evans Hughes (Library of Congress)

Q. Is not that the way it really comes about, Senator, that the use of these contributions in the election of candidates to office puts the candidates under more or less of a moral obligation not to attack the interests supporting?

A. That is what would naturally be involved.

Q. That is really what is involved, is it not?

A. I should think so.

Q. And that is what you meant when you said that they would expect you, through your relations to the State Committee, to defend them?

A. Yes.[17]

To judge from the newspaper coverage it received and the editorial comment it provoked, the life insurance inquiry created a sensation across New York State in the fall of 1905. "The wrath of thousands of private citizens whose voices are never heard in public is at white heat over the disclosures," declared a Republican daily in Rochester. "Civic virtue and civic pride are passing through the greatest and most dangerous crisis in the history of the republic," warned a Democratic weekly in Cortland. At the year's end, one Buffalo editor judged the investigation a more significant occurrence than Roosevelt's bringing of peace between Russia and Japan. It is important to understand why the insurance inquiry aroused such passions and how they, in turn, gave new political understanding to middle-class New Yorkers.[18]

The public's lofty regard for life insurance measured the security it promised to the families of ordinary, hardworking people who filled middling jobs and owned small businesses. To this sort of citizen, the financial abuses Hughes uncovered were deeply and personally troubling. Company money squandered on railroad stocks would not be available for dividends and death benefits. Little wonder, then, that throughout the course of the investigation, editors, politicians, and company executives repeatedly took pains to assure the people that even the mismanaged firms were solvent and that it would be a mistake for policyholders to give up their insurance. The economic fears the investigation created guaranteed that its disclosures would be taken seriously. Indeed, by bringing financial anxiety to ordinary people, the life insurance inquiry crystallized their long-standing discontent about big business.[19]

The dishonoring of a "good" industry like life insurance shocked even those who already "knew" that oil companies and railroads were managed corruptly. Newspapers now dismissed the claims of philanthropy and benevolence the insurance companies put forward. Theirs was the sort of charity that "covers a multitude of sins," declared the New York *Evening Mail*. The revelations were "sickening," said a weekly in western New York, and they showed "the utter lack of conscience among men who have stood as magnates of finance." As nearly as can be determined, the life insurance investigation of 1905 had a climactic effect on public opinion. To the extent that a middle-class populace was capable of becoming aroused, of reconsidering long-held assumptions, and of supporting and sustaining reform, middle-class New Yorkers now did so.[20]

Of all the new knowledge and understanding they gained from the investigation, the most dynamic and instrumental perceptions concerned the relationship between business and politics. That privilege-seeking private enterprises corrupted the government was not, of course, a brand-new insight. It had a long history in republican thought and had been powerfully repeated by a succession of nineteenth-century voices. But especially among middle-class Americans and particularly in the Republican party, the fear of politico-business corruption had remained a secondary concern. Now, however, the insurance investigation forced it to the front, with vital effects on how people felt about politics and what they expected from government.[21]

As never before, citizens of New York learned about the systematic means through which the large business interests of an industrial society shaped politics and governance to their own ends. After the evidence given by McCall and the other company officers, it was no longer possible to consider businessmen the harmless victims of venal lawmakers, for what the officers' testimony had described was a deliberately organized structure of legislative influence which left nothing to chance where the companies' interests were at stake. After Platt's appearance on the stand, there could be no pretending that only a few isolated politicians were responsible for corruption, for what he had admitted to was the efficient delivery of the majority party's governing power in return for campaign contributions. Earlier scandals had disclosed aspects of the corrupt arrangement Hughes now uncovered, but never were the revelations so rich or so timely. For coming in 1905, as it did, the insurance investigation's portrait of a corrupt alliance between business and politics provided just the stimulation needed to move a polity already feeling the force of economic and social pressures toward fundamental change.

The public response to the discovery of the insurance companies' interference with legislation attested to the new understanding of political corruption. Just as businessmen had traditionally done when their lobbying efforts inadvertently came to light, insurance executives defended their firms' activities on the grounds of their need for protection against "strike" bills, introduced by corrupt legislators for the purpose of drawing bribes from the threatened corporations. According to McCall, "three-quarters of the insurance bills introduced in the United States are blackmailing bills." While such explanations had previously found sympathy and acceptance, this time they were not believed. The *New York Tribune*'s opinion was typical. "A company with a clean record need have no fear," the paper declared. "A [strike] bill interfering with sound business would only need to be openly denounced and explained, and it would almost surely fail." The Syracuse *Evening Herald* agreed. The companies' right course when faced with venal legislation was "to lay their cause and their arguments frankly before the people and depend upon public opinion for their protection." Not to do so, said the *Wall Street Journal*, was "unnecessary" and "criminal." Previously considered the victims of political corruption, businessmen now came to be regarded as equally guilty with the politicians for perpetrating it.[22]

Reaction to the revelations of company campaign-giving also furnished evidence of the people's new grasp of politico-business corruption. Here, too, the insurance officers defended their actions, now by pointing to the industry's interest in opposing Bryan and his threatening doctrine of free silver. But their excuses were not accepted. Many policyholders were Democrats and, besides, Bryan and silver could scarcely account for the gifts of 1904 when the Democratic party repudiated the Great Commoner. Editors across the state decried the grave dangers in corporation campaign contributions. They were "utterly repugnant to our democratic principle of government," declared a Syracuse paper. They posed "a danger to republicanism," said the *Tribune*. "If carried far enough," they might give the companies "control of the Government," cautioned the *Journal of Commerce*. These warnings, echoed in editorials, articles, and speeches throughout late 1905, suggest that New York citizens had come to a new understanding of "the close and vital connection between politics . . . [and] high finance."[23]

Newspaper stories often commented on the newness of the insights the investigation was creating. "A few months ago who would have believed that [these] charges against big corporations were true?" asked a small upstate weekly. They "have never before [been] fully understood by the public," declared a Rochester paper. Just at the time that national muckraking journalists were probing the relations between business and politics and describing them for their readers, local reporters and editors in New York were doing the same. The corruption they laid bare startled a people who had perhaps seen it at work in their home towns but had never understood how pervasive and systematic it was or known that it shaped the behavior of their party's legislators at Albany.[24]

The new perceptions of 1905 brought together two strands of discontent which had each been evolving for years in New York politics: dislike of party bosses and distrust of big-business corporations. Now the misdeeds of these two villains were seen to have been mutual and their corruptions to have been practiced jointly. The testimony by Depew, Odell, and Platt fixed the popular impression that the Republican party's state leaders had become thoroughly corrupt. Fittingly, in March 1906, the initial installment of David Graham Phillips's "Treason of the Senate" series in *Cosmopolitan Magazine* portrayed New York's senators, Depew and Platt, as immoral servants of the plutocracy. Republicans did not bear the infamy alone, however, for the earlier gas and electricity inquiry had implicated the Democrats. Considered together, the two investigations of 1905 pointed to a corrupt alliance between the corporations and all classes of party politicians. Once conjoined, the dual hatreds of bosses and businessmen became a more powerful political force than either hatred had been alone.

The working out of that force shaped much of New York State's politics in the years after 1905. Parties and party leadership were now severely stigmatized, and actions curtailing the power of bosses and restraining the sway of partisanship followed. The disgrace of a "good" business such as life insurance completed the discrediting of a policy process based on unchecked distribution, inspired increased regulation, and led overall to a significant readjustment of the government's relations with organized economic groups. These developments and their sequels mark 1905 as a decisive political and governmental turning point.

Crucial as that year was, however, its events are most properly viewed not as sui generis occurrences but as the energizers of long-standing forces for political change. Independence from party machines was not new; nor were the pressures to bring traditional patterns of governance into line with industrial realities. But a catalyst had been needed to quicken the long-term forces and to push New York's political system across a fundamental divide. The events of 1905 provided it.

Even before the insurance investigation ended late in December 1905, New York politics began to show the effects of the new perceptions the inquiry was creating. In November, the off-year elections took place. Especially in the large cities, mayoral and assembly candidates vied to meet the issues of business and political corruption raised by the year's scandals and discoveries. When the voting results were in, surprised observers agreed that the old parties had taken a battering. After the elections, Odell and Platt made their damaging appearances at the insurance investigation. Their mid-November testimony precipitated a major Republican crisis over both leadership and strategy and destroyed most of the remaining power of both men. By the beginning of 1906, traditional party politics was under an assault more damaging even than the one it had experienced in the "revolution of '97."

As usual in an off year, big-city mayoral elections, especially New York City's, received most of the attention. But 1905's downstate contest was far from usual. In place of the politics of fusion, which had shaped New York City elections since 1890, William Randolph Hearst's class appeals on behalf of his own mayoral candidacy now provided the moving force. Tammany, finding its working-class base threatened, flaunted a new respectability in an effort to win the support of middle- and upper-class voters whom Hearst frightened. The minority Republicans virtually abandoned the contest for mayor but allied with Hearst at the assembly level, while the Citizens' Union devoted all its energies to electing a district attorney who echoed the C.U.'s traditional antibossism. All four political elements tried to take advantage of the peculiar circumstances and sentiments of 1905. The result was something of a standoff.[25]

More than any other figure that year, Hearst, the flamboyant publisher of the *American* and the *Evening Journal*, grasped the political potency of antibusiness feelings. Hearst was elusive and contradictory. Best known for the sensationalism and demagoguery of his newspapers, he was also capable of impressing respectable reformers with his sincerity and farsightedness. In October, Hearst received the mayoral nomination of the Municipal Ownership League, an established nonpartisan group that advocated public ownership of the city's utilities essentially as a matter of efficiency and businesslike government. Through his two newspapers, as well as innumerable speeches and rallies, Hearst appealed to a mainly working-class constituency, already sympathetic to his pro-labor, anticorporation message. Not since Henry George's campaign of 1886 had a mayoral candidate used such explicit economic appeals or so threatened Tammany's base among the city's poor.[26]

In response, Tammany sought to offset the inevitable losses in its usual areas of strength by attracting the support of Republicans and independents through an appeal reminiscent of Seth Low's. Mayor George B. McClellan, Jr., the son of the Civil War general and a

Princeton graduate, had conducted an uncommonly respectable administration during 1904 and 1905, and he well suited the Hall's new image. For their part, the Republicans first offered their mayoral nomination to Charles Evans Hughes, the year's political hero, but when he declined on the grounds of the importance of completing the insurance investigation, the party named a little-known lawyer, William Mills Ivins, who had almost no chance to win. What chance Ivins had was lessened by a deal Odell made with Hearst to nominate joint assembly candidates in half of the city's sixty districts. The overwhelming success of the joint nominees, together with Ivins's inglorious failure, suggests that Odell, now in his final days as a political boss, agreed to trade mayoral votes for assembly ballots. Finally, the Citizens' Union named no mayoral candidate but backed William Travers Jerome for reelection as district attorney. Jerome, who had originally been elected on Low's fusion ticket in 1901, campaigned as the "people's candidate," independent of the parties, just as C.U. nominees traditionally had. Like the other aspirants that year, Jerome hoped he had found a way to exploit the unusual political conditions of 1905.[27]

A few days before the balloting, the *New York Herald* reported the results of a remarkable poll of ten thousand voters showing that the Hearst and Jerome candidacies had upset traditional partisanship, while Hearst had polarized the city along class lines. The *Herald* forecast several currents of drift within the electorate. Many voters in both parties would give up their usual allegiances to support Hearst; other Republicans would vote for the Democrat McClellan. Voters in both parties would split their tickets to support Jerome. According to the paper's summary, "Tammany Hall has been split wide open. The republican party has been knocked to pieces. . . . There is an uprising against bosses and machines, and it only remains to be seen whether the revolt will be far reaching enough to overthrow them both on election day." Behind the impending upheaval, the *Herald* saw a class alignment of voters. Of 2,104 businessmen polled, including members of the Stock Exchange, Produce Exchange, and Real Estate Exchange, only 241 (11 percent) favored Hearst, while the rest divided between McClellan and Ivins. Among 3,022 workingmen interviewed, including transit employees and factory workers, 2,182 (72 percent) chose Hearst.[28]

The results of the election confirmed much of the *Herald*'s analysis: independence from the major parties had nearly become a majority phenomenon. McClellan beat Hearst for mayor by the reported margin of 3,485 votes out of 600,000 cast, while the Republican Ivins ran a distant third. Hearst challenged the results, but Tammany had the strength to count its man in. The publisher ran well throughout the city and captured at least 22 percent of the vote in every assembly district. In addition to his working-class supporters, Hearst won many middle-class independents and Republicans who considered him the leading anti-Tammany candidate or who voted in fulfillment of Odell's bargain for assemblymen. Seven of the twenty-one assembly districts that had favored Seth Low in 1903 now went for Hearst; two of them gave the editor more than 50 percent of the vote. Conservative Republicans and independents whose chief aim was stopping the radical Hearst evidently voted for McClellan, who now carried nine of Low's 1903 districts. At the same time that the Democratic mayor won Republican support, he gave up to Hearst fifteen of his own thirty-nine districts from the previous election.[29]

Running solely as an independent, Jerome was reelected as district attorney. His victory was remarkable, since every vote he received reflected either a split ticket or an abstention from the mayoral contest. Ticket-splitting also played a role in other city contests. While Ivins carried only five of sixty districts, his party elected a majority of the aldermen and half the assemblymen. Odell's alliance with Hearst had actually enabled Republican assembly nominees to benefit from the year's scandals. Twenty-five of the thirty-one fusion candidates won election, giving the Republicans a net gain of ten seats. The election results are difficult to characterize as a whole, but several trends were visible: independence was on the rise, party lines were in disarray, and class politics was on the horizon.[30]

North of New York City, the year's events also made their mark on the campaign, but traditional electoral behavior was somewhat less disrupted. Charges of politico-business corruption, inspired by the insurance investigation, became the most familiar element of political rhetoric in the large upstate cities. In Albany, the opponents of William Barnes, Jr., denounced him for having "a secret compact with the corporations and monopolies of this city to protect and foster their interests at the expense of the public." Across the state, Buffalo Republicans similarly charged that "the Democratic party is in alliance with the corporate interests that now have the city by the throat." Down in Elmira, the leaders of both parties, sensitive to accusations that they had accumulated a corruption fund from the corporations to use in bribing voters, loftily publicized an agreement to limit their campaign expenditures and foreswear the purchase of votes. It was good political symbolism for 1905. When the returns came in, however, Republican mayors in Albany, Rochester, and Syracuse had surmounted any suspi-

cion of corruption and won reelection. Only in Buffalo, among the
largest cities, did the tide turn against the Republicans; there the Democrats swept the city and captured the mayoralty.[31]

In rural New York, the insurance investigation received wide coverage during the campaign, but any relevance it had to the election went
largely unnoticed by Republican papers. A few of them said their party
deserved support for its fearless inquiry; most kept silent. Outside the
large cities, the Republicans lost only two of the assembly seats they
had held before. Three Republican counties in western New York
swung strongly toward the Democrats, but in each one the party's
assembly candidates narrowly survived.[32]

After the election Republican editors throughout the upstate region
achieved a sort of vicarious independence—presumably shared by their
readers—by praising the voters of New York City. One far-northern
editor approvingly noted the "revolution" in downstate politics. "Men
of high reputation have been cast down, a powerful political machine
has been wrecked, new men, preaching the gospel of independence
have come to the front." Jerome's victory drew particularly favorable
attention in upstate New York. There "were fundamental principles on
which Mr. Jerome ran," one paper observed, "and the strength with
which he ran is a harbinger of the new era about to dawn." That new
era's main characteristic would be electoral independence. The returns
"show that party lines are no longer impassable corrals that herd voters
into fixed groups," said one editor. Others noted that machine bosses
"seem to have been slaughtered throughout the country" and that the
election brought an "extraordinary exhibition of independent voting
. . . where party regularity used to be a fetish." The upstate election
returns of 1905 make plain that the new era had not yet quite begun, but
its dawning was fervently awaited.[33]

While the Republicans had suffered little in the election, the year's
final weeks became a time of party trial. The revelations about Odell
followed the balloting by only a few days, and Platt's devastating
testimony came the next week. Real contention now began over the
party's future: its rules, its strategy, and, of course, its leadership.[34]

The disclosure that Odell had used his political influence for personal
profit immediately led to calls for his retirement as boss. President
Roosevelt told one ally that "these revelations about Mr. Odell's conduct render it impossible that he should continue to be leader of the
Republican party." In New York City, where many Republicans believed the state chairman had sacrificed their mayoral candidate by
bargaining with Hearst, the insurance testimony served to reinforce
existing dissatisfaction with the party leader. Up the state, Barnes's

Albany Evening Journal and the *Elmira Daily Advertiser*, under the influence of J. Sloat Fassett, led the drive for Odell's ouster. Fassett's organ noted "the evil genius of this man, his extraordinary selfishness, extreme avariciousness and almost brutal domination." According to the *Advertiser*, "In all these 11 years [since the Republicans came to power in 1894] there has been nothing that could alienate the support of the people or excite their distrust, except the policies of Governor Odell."[35]

Implausible though it may seem, the insurance investigation gave Platt thoughts of returning as leader. The few days between Odell's testimony and his own found Platt less discredited than his successor and gave him time to act. He wrote to Roosevelt of his determination to take a hand in reorganizing the Buffalo Republican party, and that same week Platt commenced a fight to regain control of the Republican machinery in New York City. But any chance he might have had of getting the president's support vanished with his admission of corruptibility before the insurance committee. Determined to purge both disgraced bosses from party authority in New York City, Roosevelt opposed Platt's choice for a new party chairman there—to replace the incumbent, an Odell man—and instead helped elect Congressman Herbert Parsons to the position. Parsons's selection marked a real turning point in downstate Republican affairs. For the next five years, the new chairman enjoyed remarkable success in extricating the New York City Republican organization from its usual close relations with both Tammany Hall and the public service corporations.[36]

At the next stage of the drive for new party leadership, Governor Higgins played a key role along with Roosevelt. S. Fred Nixon's recent death had created a vacancy in the assembly speakership, and Higgins sought to fill it with a man who would put an end to the corruption Odell evidently inspired. To the surprise of everyone, Higgins endorsed twenty-eight-year-old James W. Wadsworth, Jr., who had served only one year in the assembly. With the support of Roosevelt, Barnes, and most other important county leaders, Wadsworth defeated Odell's candidate and won election as speaker. Most Republican newspapers applauded the choice, for, as the Rochester *Democrat and Chronicle* put it, "The organization of the Republican party in this state had, to a large degree, been discredited by disclosures made in the insurance investigation and by methods of management which, it may be hoped, are rapidly becoming obsolete. The Republicanism of the state demanded that the party be placed upon higher and broader ground than [that occupied by] the leadership it has had recently."[37]

Roosevelt had not intended to get involved in New York's leadership struggle, for, as he explained it, "I was elected President and not boss." Indeed, his participation in reorganizing the party represented a step Roosevelt had never before taken. As both governor and president, he had relied on private persuasion, public appeals, and patronage to get what he wanted in New York, but he had always worked through the established Republican leadership. The political crisis of 1905 changed Roosevelt's relationship to his home state's politics, and for the next five years he frequently intervened with a view to controlling the Republican party there, not merely influencing it.[38]

Despite Roosevelt's intervention and the leadership changes he helped arrange, those now at the head of the Republican party by no means all agreed on the future course of their organization or on its strategy. Nor, even if they had agreed, could the party's leaders be sure of keeping control of political events. Many Republicans who concurred late in 1905 that Odell had to be deposed as state chairman nonetheless disagreed on why. Some felt the boss system he represented was outmoded, while others acted not against a system of leadership but against a particular man who had become a liability to the party. Barnes and Fassett, for instance, opposed Odell but also wrote or inspired editorials defending party machines that were strongly led. In similar fashion, leading Republicans disagreed on the most sensitive policy questions involving business-government relations. All would acknowledge that the worst abuses disclosed in the insurance investigation had to be halted, but what policies should replace them remained controversial.[39]

While they disagreed, Republican leaders also found that the power to decide these matters was slipping out of their hands. The political passions of 1905, the perception of politico-business corruption, the evident saliency of class issues that Hearst's campaign disclosed, and the drive of voters toward independent behavior all struck at the heart of traditional politics and at the power of party leaders to shape events. This became clear in the legislative session of 1906, when public opinion and interest-group pressures combined to bring about new economic policies, with little help from established Republican leaders.

In 1906, for the second consecutive year, the New York legislature adopted significant regulatory measures affecting a major industry. Just as they had done in regulating gas and electricity the year before, the lawmakers acted in response to public opinion and against the expressed wishes of the affected industry, in this case, life insurance. "If . . . [the legislature] does not reflect the sentiment of the people . . . if it permits mere machine dictation and a continuation of graft," one newspaper editor warned, "then the republican party will lose the next state election." Prominent party leaders agreed. "The public purpose is distinct to stop the kind of business that has been going on," Elihu Root told Governor Higgins, "and it rests with the Legislature . . . to take immediate action in response to the already clear and well understood public demand."[40]

Higgins's annual message on January 3, 1906, laid the issue before the legislators. Identifying reform of the life insurance industry as a problem of "overshadowing importance," the governor distinguished between the state's traditional policy of merely certifying the companies' solvency and the "thorough regulation" which the people now demanded. Not waiting for the investigating committee to present its report, Higgins recommended numerous measures governing the management and investment practices of life insurance companies. On the related subject of utility regulation, the governor took a hard line. "Such corporations should be tolerated," he said, "only so long as their rates are reasonable and their service prompt and efficient." Election-law reform also received Higgins's attention. He demanded that corporate campaign contributions be prohibited, and he advised the more careful supervision of election expenditures. The governor's message addressed the major issues raised by the previous year's investigations. By and large, the lawmakers took up these same topics.[41]

Rather than act immediately on Higgins's insurance recommendations, however, the legislature waited to receive the report of its own investigating committee. On February 22, it came. Written by committee counsel Hughes, the 440-page document summarized the inquiry's findings and advised remedial legislation in sixteen areas, covered in ten proposed bills. The measures, which eventually became law almost exactly as Hughes wrote them, changed the requirements for organizing life insurance companies, placed added authority in the hands of policyholders, and limited the powers of company officers. They prohibited the companies from owning stocks or from participating in syndicates and set standards concerning permissible investments. The laws fixed ceilings on the amount of new business that companies could write each year, provided in detail for annual reports and frequent company audits, and mandated standard forms to be used in policies. Other states soon copied many of the statutes which, in their entirety, broadly shaped the nation's life insurance industry in the twentieth century.[42]

Two measures addressed the corrupt relations between business and politics which the investigation had disclosed. One law, to be considered below, forbade campaign contributions by corporations, while the other provided for the regulation of legislative lobbying. Both applied beyond the insurance industry alone. In its discussion of legislative influence, Hughes's report rejected the argument that the threat of "improper and ill-advised measures" justified the companies' secretive operations. Since so many voters held life insurance policies, the report said, "It is easy for the company to apprise them of hostile legislative measures" and rely on open and public pressure rather than on "large sums . . . [and] clandestine methods." Accordingly, the new lobbying law obliged corporations to account for monies spent in connection with legislation, required the registration of all legislative agents, and forbade paying lobbyists contingently upon the success or failure of a bill.[43]

The insurance report shocked company executives who had not expected to have their management techniques so thoroughly revised or their political influence so sharply curtailed. According to the *New York Times,* insurance men found the recommendations "radical beyond all expectation." One lawyer for the Equitable, writing in a conciliatory vein to Hughes, acknowledged the report's basic fairness but noted that "some of the recommendations seem rather drastic" and that they "came as a rude shock to the men who have been brought up in the insurance business as heretofore conducted." To George W. Perkins of the New York Life, the measures "seemed to undermine the whole structure of the insurance business."[44]

To prevent the bills' enactment, or at least to secure their significant amendment, insurance officers undertook an intensive campaign, in public and in private. Hearings held in Albany during early March gave company executives an opportunity to make their case openly, but they placed more confidence in behind-the-scenes endeavors to stop the measures. Just as they had often done before, the largest companies worked together; the Equitable, the New York Life, and the Mutual each took responsibility for particular areas of proposed legislation. The New York Life's lobbyist, William Collins Beer, consulted privately with Speaker Wadsworth and afterward informed Perkins that "the Armstrong committee crowd has only one member on the House Committee [that is, the assembly insurance committee] whom they can rely on. The other 12 can be influenced our way." Beer was wrong. The companies' usually efficient legislative operations now failed before the glare of newspaper publicity and the lawmakers' concern to satisfy public opinion. Every one of Hughes's measures passed the legislature almost without opposition and received Higgins's signature.

213

Perkins reacted to the news with acerbity: "The Armstrong recommendations have now all become laws and a nice mess they are going to make of the New York State life insurance companies."[45]

As company officials predicted they would, the new laws deeply affected the life insurance industry. Incumbent executives departed, and new managers came to power. Stock-held companies became mutualized, while the officers of those already on a mutual basis faced challenges by aroused and organized policyholders. Executive salaries fell, and internal management techniques changed. The proportion of business controlled by the three largest life insurance companies dropped drastically after 1905, as did the amount of new insurance they wrote each year. The foreign business of the large companies fell off, and their investment practices became far more conservative. Finally, the companies withdrew from politics. They made no further campaign contributions and dismantled their systems of legislative influence. Chastened, even humbled, the great life insurance companies went through what one historian of the industry has called "a profound evolution of their corporate being."[46]

In the long run, however, the remedial legislation of 1906 benefited the life insurance business. While the new laws were far more rigorous than the old ones had been and continuously involved the government in the companies' operation, life insurance officers soon found that the Insurance Department meant to be cooperative in enforcing the regulations. Superintendent William H. Hotchkiss, appointed by Governor Hughes in 1909, took pride in assisting the companies to meet their new obligations and to restore their tarnished image. The legislature, too, proved helpful; in 1909 and 1910, the lawmakers actually revised some of the 1906 statutes along lines the companies wanted. All told, the new regulatory laws revived public trust in the life insurance companies and gave them—albeit against their will at first—a business structure better suited to twentieth-century conditions than the one they had evolved on their own. Many years later, the board chairman of the Metropolitan Life declared that Hughes and the Armstrong Committee were "'in considerable part' responsible for the prosperity of the life-insurance business."[47]

The insurance investigation and its legislative aftermath present several paradoxes. Begun and conducted by men committed to upholding the insurance business, the inquiry discredited that industry before the people and heightened popular antagonism to business and wealth generally. In the glare of a hostile press that reflected the views of an aroused public, the legislature enacted sweeping measures that the companies opposed but from which they ultimately benefited. This pattern was destined to become familiar, though the scenario varied from case to case. In 1905 gas and electricity companies had fought against new legislation but eventually acquiesced in the creation of a commission to regulate their industry. Besides the insurance laws, other measures enacted in 1906 provided variations on the same theme.

One vital area of legislative concern that year involved company campaign contributions and the party protection they bought. Money in elections was an old bugbear in New York politics, but with Alton B. Parker's charges about corporate donations in 1904 and the revelations of 1905, the issue changed. Historically, most interest had focused on how campaign funds were spent, rather than where they came from, and on their electoral impact, rather than their policy effects. But the disclosures of 1905, in rekindling public interest in the control of campaign money, now directed attention to its sources.[48]

Three proposals dealing with the problem came before the legislature. The simplest of the three, a prohibition on corporate campaign contributions, encountered the least debate. Governor Higgins's annual message had called for such a law, and the report of the insurance investigating committee echoed his appeal. Almost no one objected. A second proposal, which found its chief champion in Perry Belmont, a wealthy Democrat with experience as a party fund-raiser, relied on publicity to regulate campaign contributions and expenditures. Belmont's measure, for which he made a personal crusade at both the state and federal levels, required candidates and political committees to make public a careful accounting of all their receipts and expenditures. A third measure extended the familiar concept of corrupt practices by defining what campaign expenditures were permissible. All three proposals became law, virtually without legislative opposition.[49]

Although corporation leaders had not generally sought the new election laws, it is doubtful that they regretted them for long. The developments of 1905–6, in changing the basis of business-government relations, made it less necessary than before to buy influence in the legislature through the party boss. With the enlargement of the government's regulatory duties and the transfer of many such functions from partisan lawmakers to independent boards and departments, new methods of influence were needed. Businessmen had not, as a rule, been farsighted enough to initiate steps toward stopping the needless contributions, but when public opinion mandated the prohibition of such gifts for the purpose of curtailing corporation control of politics, businessmen soon discovered advantages in the new laws.[50] Their satisfaction with the changes merely suggests that "progressive" reforms often served purposes that were neither foreseen nor intended by those who advanced them.

New York's new election-fund laws became models for statutes elsewhere. Fifteen states prohibited corporate campaign contributions in 1907, and, prodded by President Roosevelt, Congress took similar action. Three years later, the federal government adopted a publicity measure similar to New York's. By all accounts, these laws and the public pressure behind them drastically reduced the secret election funds which had multiplied since the 1880s. In New York, an era of cooperation between politicians and businessmen based on campaign contributions now ended, though it remained to be seen exactly what policy difference that made.[51] Even in 1906, when anticorporation feelings were at a peak, the state government's response to developments involving New York's steam railway system suggested how tenacious business influence might be.

Following several years of complaints by freight shippers about high rates and shoddy railroad service, the winter of 1906 brought unusually severe delays in grain hauling. In response to dissatisfaction, the legislature approved a bill setting fines for unsatisfactory railway service, but Governor Higgins vetoed it. Several related measures reflecting shipper discontent met opposition from the railway lobbies and failed even to pass the legislature. A more important bill, considerably enlarging the authority of the Board of Railroad Commissioners and providing for state assumption of the board's costs, was opposed by the railways and died in the assembly. Despite these defeats, most observers recognized that New York's transportation system was soon headed for significantly greater government regulation than it had had in the past. Some thoughtful observers might also have predicted that the railroad companies would not necessarily suffer from the new measures when they came.[52]

While railroad supervision remained on the agenda, other regulatory proposals met approval in 1906. These included an eighty-cent gas bill for New York City (an amended version of the measure the companies had killed the year before), an employers' liability act for railroad workers, a law permitting the legislature to set the wages and hours of employees on municipal public works, and a measure strengthening New York City's regulation of rapid transit. Together with the life insurance laws and the election-fund acts, as well as the gas and electricity laws of 1905, these measures demonstrated an uncommon degree of legislative acquiescence in actions providing for the continuous state supervision of organized interest groups. Significantly, however, the most important of the new laws had been framed not by the legislators, or by the governor, but by an "expert," Charles Evans Hughes, who immersed himself in technical details and furnished the elected officials with complex bills they could not have written themselves. This fresh approach to economic policymaking, begun in 1905–6, marked a major departure in the governance of New York State.[53]

That new policy departure, together with the corresponding decay of traditional party politics, had been in preparation for many years, but the legislative investigations of 1905 were needed to catalyze the changes. The importance of the life insurance inquiry, in particular, as a turning point in New York State politics can scarcely be overstated. The public opinion it created forced the Republican party's leading men out of power and transformed opposition to bossed party machines into the conventional wisdom. It crystallized discontent with big-business corporations and propelled New York across the threshold from an economic-policy structure mainly grounded in distribution to one based on regulation, administration, and planning. These changes were not all completed in a single year, but the events of 1905 point persuasively to that year as the one in which nineteenth-century politics, as New Yorkers knew it, came effectively to a close.

Why was the life insurance investigation so potent a political catalyst? Amidst the mounting pressures to which traditional politics and governance were subjected by 1905, the insurance inquiry unified the existing antagonisms toward bosses and corporations and suggested concrete remedies for long-standing political ills. The discovery that party politicians and businessmen were in a corrupt alliance shocked middle-class people and led them to renounce party machines and to demand governmental restraints on the behavior of business corporations. Neither antibossism nor regulation was new in 1905, but that year's disclosures vitalized these old ideas, created the momentum needed to move the polity toward specific reforms, and so pointed to an escape from the mounting political and governmental crisis.

The developments of 1905–6 were later refined and revised, but the basic thrust of the changes made then persisted. Afterward, politics and governance in New York were crucially different from what they had been before. Parties, to judge from aggregate returns, never again enjoyed the constant loyalty of so high a proportion of the electorate as they had had in the nineteenth century, while party leaders no longer dominated political participation or guided government policymaking as thoroughly as they had in earlier times. Privileged business enterprises ceased to receive their benefits with so few strings attached, and organized economic groups of all sorts now continuously jockeyed to influence the "expert" government boards affecting their interests.

Decisive as the political changes of this moment were, they were also limited in key respects. The rejection of parties was manifested in lower levels of electoral turnout, in higher rates of ticket-splitting, and in a diminution of the role played by party machines. But such rejection also had something of a barren quality because, especially outside the large cities, alternative structures of political participation proved difficult to create and because party bosses rather quickly learned to break through many of the institutional restraints to which they were now subjected. Often antipartyism meant exchanging one roster of political leaders for another, or temporarily quashing bossism through new rules that soon were broken or overcome. These limitations do not mean that nineteenth-century practices were restored, but they do suggest the need to qualify carefully the extent of the political changes that occurred.

Correspondingly, the popular feelings forged by the insurance investigation were sufficient to force the adoption of new economic policies but not strong enough to prevent them from falling under the control of powerful, organized interests. This did not happen because the regulated businesses had originated the drive for government supervision; indeed, they opposed it vigorously—certainly in the cases of gas, electricity, life insurance, and railroads that came up in 1905–6—and only later discovered the advantages of continuous regulation. The satisfaction that businessmen ultimately found in the new policies may be attributed to their own abilities to shape the application of the rules; to the underlying sympathies for business held by those, like Hughes, who actually wrote the laws; and, above all, to the ultimate limitations of middle-class fervor. A people driven to protect their own security and to clean up a political system that businessmen and party politicians evidently dirtied not surprisingly failed to sustain their fury once the threats abated. Still, it was ironical that the "progressive" passions of 1905 later served business purposes, for it was not foreordained that they should.

8

Charles Evans Hughes and
the New Political Order,
1906–1910

After 1905 politics and governance in New York State differed in fundamental respects from what they had been throughout most of the nineteenth century. New forms of political participation and expression, especially interest-group organization and public opinion, became more important than they had ever been before, while purely partisan modes of influencing the polity declined in importance. Electoral turnout continued to fall and levels of ticket-splitting significantly rose. At the same time that patterns of participation were changing, so were the functions of government, especially in the economic area. State officials, operating through a diversity of administrative agencies and relying on the advice of experts, assumed responsibility for the continuous supervision of conflicting interests. These developments all had nineteenth-century precedents, but the events of 1905 caused them to reach fulfillment.

Charles Evans Hughes, the leading figure in the legislative investigations of 1905, dominated the state during the five following years and prominently shaped the political changes that took place. Elected governor in 1906 and again in 1908, he provided a reminder of the perceptions the inquiries of 1905 had created and fashioned responses to the new political conditions that prevailed after the investigations. Hughes was not an organization Republican, and his tactics were scarcely intended to shore up the machine as Platt's and Odell's had been. Yet he *was* a Republican and considered his methods necessary to restore his party's reputation. By appealing to public opinion, by applying anti-machine standards to state government, and by relying heavily on expert administrative decision making, Hughes pursued his own strategy for the Republican party. Even as he succeeded in having many of his programs and methods adopted, however, the aloof governor failed almost completely to persuade other top Republicans of the rightness and value of his tactics.

Hughes's singularity and his estrangement from the leaders of his own party suggest that the years 1906 to 1910 were exceptional. Indeed, these *were* unusual years, as the years of any important transition period must be, and the style of politics characteristic of them soon waned. Hughes's departure from the state scene in 1910—when he became an associate justice of the United States Supreme Court—together with his party's defeat in the state elections that year, restored party regulars to authority in the Republican organization and caused the repudiation of many things Hughes had done. Yet the basic political and governmental practices established during these years were maintained. There was no return to a system where party voting provided the people's only regular means of political participation and where the unplanned distribution of resources and privileges formed the government's most characteristic activity.

Hughes came to power in the midst of the continuing crisis of leadership into which the life insurance investigation had plunged the Republican party. In February 1906 President Roosevelt made known his feeling that Governor Higgins ought to force Odell from the party chairmanship. "Let the Governor start to work instantly," the president ordered. "I do not mean next week. . . . Let it be handled just as the [James W.] Wadsworth [speakership] campaign was." Despite the president's insistence, Higgins was reluctant to oppose Odell, and "after a little beating around the bush"—as Roosevelt later recalled—he asked the president to stay out of New York party affairs. Roosevelt complied—for the moment—and Odell, now his enemy, remained chairman throughout the spring and summer.[1]

During these same months, Roosevelt came to a final political parting from Platt. Until now their relations had continued, at least on patronage matters, and as late as October 1905 the president had even told a friend that "it would be most unfortunate to have anything like a break with Platt." Then in June, however, a United States judgeship became vacant, and the president and the senator strongly disagreed about filling it. "It ought to suffice for me to simply say that I prefer [James Addison] Young to [Charles Merrill] Hough, both men being admittedly qualified for the position," Platt told Roosevelt. "On a simple statement of this kind, it occurs to me you should hardly hesitate to appoint Mr. Young." Platt had become a caricature of the boss he used to be. His advanced age—he was seventy-three—and his relative powerlessness now caused him to act in such a way as to close off his relationship with Roosevelt, a man whose political fortunes had been so entwined with his own.[2]

Each wholly alienated from the president, Odell and Platt now undertook a curious and futile partnership. Odell denounced Higgins and calculatingly endorsed Hughes for the Republican gubernatorial nomination. Then, with Roosevelt looking on but still not interfering, Odell and Platt together captured control of the Republican state committee in mid-August. The old bosses' triumphant alliance created a sensation. "What is needed," Herbert Parsons warned Roosevelt, "is the absolute licking of Odell and his kind, if the party is to have public confidence."[3]

Though he had promised Higgins he would stay out, and despite the bosses' feigned support for Hughes, Roosevelt ultimately took a strong hand in the New York political situation and forced the insurance investigator's nomination for governor. "Odell and Platt want Hughes," the president told Elihu Root in August, "and upon my word I am not at all certain but that it would be well to nominate him." Party regulars who joined the president in opposing Platt and Odell understandably scorned Roosevelt's enthusiasm for the untested Hughes. "I never spoke to this man," complained William Barnes, Jr., of Albany. "I never saw him," echoed George Washington Aldridge of Rochester. But working carefully through Parsons, who beat the forces of Platt and Odell in the Manhattan primaries of early September, Roosevelt laid plans to have Hughes chosen, and at the state convention that month a telegram from the president clinched the nomination. Odell, who had abandoned Hughes when the president backed him, relinquished his chairmanship to Brooklyn boss Timothy Woodruff and departed from state power. The triumph was Roosevelt's. Under "the new conditions in the Republican party," he told his friend Henry Cabot Lodge, "I had to take the initiative myself even at the risk of being called a boss, dictator, and so forth." "If we had nominated an ordinary machine hack we should have been beaten out of sight."[4]

Hughes accepted the nomination with a pledge to administer the state without "taint of bossism or servitude to any private interest," a promise the Republicans echoed in the campaign that followed. Some observers noted the parallel between Hughes's nomination for governor in 1906 and Roosevelt's eight years earlier. In both cases, a discredited Republican machine, fearing defeat, reluctantly accepted a man from outside the regular organization. But now Roosevelt himself filled the role Platt had played in 1898. And now the party's need for a nominee who seemed free of bosses and businessmen far surpassed the burden of independence Roosevelt had borne.[5]

The new nominee's first campaign speech, on October 3, 1906, provided insight into Hughes's party strategy. Identifying himself as "a life-long Republican," he showed his talent for old-fashioned partisan rhetoric. "What do we find in opposition to us?" he asked. "A masquerade . . . a so-called but spurious Democratic party which has violated every principle of Democratic government." But Hughes proved equally adept at the rhetoric of independence: "What, then, is the supreme issue of this campaign? It is not an issue of the Republican record. It is not an issue of Republican principles or of Democratic principles. It is not a partisan issue at all. It is the vital issue of decent government." Hughes's speech also recalled both the gas and electricity and the life insurance inquiries. By reminding his listeners of those investigations, he implicitly reminded them of his own responsibility for uncovering the corrupt alliance between bosses and business interests. Much of what Hughes accomplished during the next four years stemmed from his unique brand of antipartisan partisanship and from his ability to sustain the perceptions the life insurance investigation had created.[6]

Hughes emerged as a better campaigner than anyone expected. He spoke forcefully, yet with a friendliness that his icy demeanor as committee counsel had not disclosed. Reporting to the president on an upstate speaking tour by Hughes, state chairman Woodruff said only Roosevelt himself was better on the stump. The Republican campaign needed all the talent Hughes had, for his Democratic opponent was William Randolph Hearst, the only other man in the state who personified the issues of 1905 as well as did Hughes.[7]

Hearst's nomination, like Hughes's, focused attention on a popular personality who stood apart from his party. Having first undertaken an independent campaign for the governorship, the publisher—fortified by public sympathy following Tammany's apparent theft of his mayoral victory the year before—forced the Democrats to terms in September and became their nominee. It was an uneasy marriage. Even as the party candidate, Hearst attacked Tammany. "[Boss Charles] Murphy may be for me," he said, "but I'm not for him and never have been." While they nominated Hearst, the Democrats' platform opposed the municipal ownership of public utilities, the publisher's most prominent issue. Hearst repudiated his party's stand. His unique talent for advertising himself, his evident independence from his party's bosses, and his identification with the issues raised by the investigations of 1905 made him a formidable nominee.[8]

The independence of Hughes and Hearst created anxiety among Republican leaders about whether traditional party lines would hold in 1906. Recalling how completely the previous year's mayoral election had scrambled the usual voting patterns in New York City, one Man-

Charles Evans Hughes campaigning (Library of Congress)

hattan Republican warned Roosevelt that Hearst's "inroad into our own vote last year should not be underestimated." What Hearst had done once he could do again. North of New York City Republican politicians also lacked confidence they could poll their party's usual strength. Roosevelt warned Hughes of the need for upstate leaders to be "zealous and thoroly [*sic*] on the alert and watchful about any . . . move by Hearst's people to cut down our vote in the Republican counties." Elihu Root predicted to Woodruff that "party lines are going to be badly broken. We will lose a great number of votes to Hearst, and we have got to get a great many from the Democratic side."[9]

To meet the expected rise in voter independence, the Republicans ran a campaign uncommonly free of traditional appeals to partisanship. One New York City Republican advised a state senate candidate not "to eulogize the virtues of the Republican party and the vices of the Democratic party too much. Make your campaign solely on Mr. Hughes's strength and Mr. Hearst's weakness." In Ithaca, a party paper reported after Hughes's visit there that the nominee generated the greatest enthusiasm when he "declared his independence of all parties and all partisanship." Even with Roosevelt's popular presence in the White House, New York Republicans steered clear of the usual national issues. Writing to Woodruff, Roosevelt himself explained the reason: "We want to get tens of thousands of people to vote for Hughes who do not approve of my administration or of the Republican Party from the national standpoint, and we should be scrupulously careful not to scare away these men."[10]

The election returns on November 6 confirmed the forecasts of voter independence. While party lines were not as disrupted as some leaders had feared they would be and while electoral turnout (74 percent) actually exceeded that of 1902, ticket-splitting reached unprecedented levels. Hughes beat Hearst by almost 58,000 votes (out of 1.5 million cast), but all his Republican running mates for lower state office lost. The somber governor-elect said the result gave him a feeling of "responsibility" rather than "elation." To regular Republican leaders it brought disappointment, for their ticket's only successful candidate was a man from outside the organization. For observers familiar with the state's usual electoral patterns, the returns must have occasioned surprise. Enough voters had split their tickets to produce a divided result.[11]

In New York City, Hughes ran ahead of his party by over 30,000 votes, while Hearst trailed his own ticket by a similar margin. (See Table 10.) The ticket-splitting in Hughes's favor was remarkably broad-based: he polled more votes than the Republican candidate for

Table 10. New York State vote for governor and lieutenant governor, by region, 1906

Party and candidate	New York City*	Upstate	Entire state
Republican candidates			
Hughes (governor)	268,979	480,023	749,002
Bruce (lieutenant governor)	234,969	478,099	713,068
Hughes's margin over Bruce	34,010	1,924	35,934
Net ticket-splitting†	12.6%	0.4%	4.8%
Democratic candidates			
Hearst (governor)	343,246	347,859	691,105
Chanler (lieutenant governor)	372,396	346,246	718,642
Hearst's margin over Chanler	−29,150	1,613	−27,537
Net ticket-splitting†	8.5%	0.5%	4.0%

*New York, Kings, Richmond, Queens/Nassau counties.
†The difference between the two votes as a percentage of the gubernatorial vote.
Source: Manual (1907), pp. 814–17.

lieutenant governor in all but one of the city's sixty-three assembly districts, and in fifty of them his running mate trailed Hughes's vote by 10 percent or more. At least three separate ticket-splitting trends were probably at work. Of most importance, the Democratic machines in Manhattan and, to an even larger degree, in Brooklyn persuaded their members to "knife" Hearst, whom they could not control. One Kings County politician estimated that between 22,000 and 25,000 Brooklyn Democrats supported Hughes for governor but otherwise voted their own party's ticket. While machine Democrats in lower Manhattan and Brooklyn cut Hearst in deference to the organization's wishes, many uptown Democrats apparently voted against him without prompting because they feared his radicalism. In Manhattan's "silk-stocking" twenty-ninth district, for example, all the Republican candidates won, but Hughes ran 12 percent ahead of his ticket. Finally, a smaller countertrend, favoring Hearst, was evident in some socialist-leaning areas. Manhattan's eighth district, the banner socialist enclave in the city, was the only one in which Hughes ran behind the Republican ticket. There many voters preferred Hearst for just the reasons others feared him and so split their tickets in his favor.[12]

To the north of New York City, there was far less ticket-splitting at the gubernatorial level but a great deal of it for assembly and Congress. In five counties to the south and west of Rochester, for instance, voters split their tickets against Congressman James W. Wadsworth, Sr., whose unpopular defense of the "beef trust" fueled a successful Democratic challenge. Each county in his district gave Wadsworth, the father of the assembly speaker, at least 16 percent fewer votes than it gave Hughes. One county gave him 44 percent fewer. In a number of upstate counties, Republican assembly candidates conspicuously trailed the party's other nominees. In several counties, both the assembly and congressional candidates ran well behind Hughes and the state ticket.[13]

A survey of the votes in every county suggests how widespread ticket-splitting had become in 1906. In almost half of the state's counties the least popular Republican candidate fell short of the vote of the most popular nominee by 5 percent or more. In seventeen counties, the gap exceeded 10 percent. Two years earlier, by contrast, the respective numbers of such counties were sixteen and two. (See Fig. 6.) Every region of the state included counties where ticket-splitting now measured above 10 percent. The tendency to vote selectively was by no means confined to downstate urban citizens.[14]

Ticket-splitting afterward remained an established feature of New York politics. Subsequent elections produced as much or more independence from straight party voting as had the 1906 contest. Leaders came to expect ticket-splitting and to try to persuade members of the rival party to practice it. One Republican in New York City later recalled receiving a pewter mug in 1907 for obtaining more split tickets in his election district than any other local leader! After the 1908

Figure 6. The rise of ticket-splitting, 1894–1910

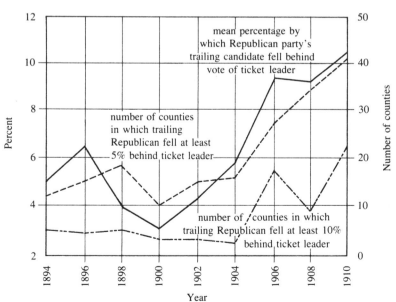

contest, politicians commented on how far William Howard Taft ran ahead of his party's gubernatorial nominees across the country. But few were surprised anymore.[15]

Many observers agreed with the *New York Times* that the 1906 election results "make it clear that the voters have very largely lost confidence in both old parties" and with the *Nation* that the voters were "tired of the corrupt alliance between corporations and machine politicians." Most newspapers carried the same messages, and many noted that no other Republican but Hughes, with his record in the life insurance investigation, could have beaten Hearst. It was now up to Hughes, the *Tribune* said, to bring about "the sober, orderly . . . correction of those abuses about which the vote for Hearst . . . shows the intensity of public feeling." From the Republican point of view, it was also up to Hughes to restore the party to favor.[16]

While the new chief executive keenly felt his duty to the party, his performance of that duty dismayed Republican politicians. Probably the best governor of his era, Charles Evans Hughes nonetheless aroused a degree of hatred among the party leaders that surpassed their annoyance with the independent Roosevelt or their dislike for the aloof and selfish Odell. Hughes, though he saw more clearly than his contemporaries how the Republicans could meet the changed political conditions after 1905, seemed to ignore the feelings of those who led the party organization. Thinking it most important to take his case to the people, he was less successful in persuading the leaders.

There were plenty of leaders to persuade. During Hughes's administration, for the first time since the 1880s, the Republican party had no real boss. With Platt too ill and discredited for restoration, Odell capable of only sporadic grabs for power, and Roosevelt hardly in a position to provide day-to-day direction, a group of county bosses and legislative leaders shared authority in the organization. Parsons in New York, Woodruff in Brooklyn, Aldridge and Hendricks in Rochester and Syracuse, respectively, Raines in the senate, and Wadsworth in the assembly were among the strongest. As time passed, William Barnes, Jr., of Albany became first among equals, though not until after 1910 did he briefly succeed to Platt's old role as state boss. Describing the contrast with times past, one upstate leader recalled, "In the old days I would go down to New York and see Senator Platt and find out what was going to happen. Then I would come back and get the boys in line. But now I go to New York and learn nothing."[17]

Hughes refused to fill the Republicans' leadership vacuum or to do the party things that politicians always did. "It is of great importance in my judgment," he told New York City Republicans in 1907, "that the discharge of the duties of the governorship should not be embarrassed by attempts at political management. . . . I do not aim to be a party boss. I want simply to be Governor during my term." Hughes often repeated that determination. In fulfillment of it, he invariably declined to mediate factional disputes, to help determine nominations, or to advise about assignments to legislative committees. Even when his own programs were at stake, Hughes refused to pressure legislators to support them. Even during his short-lived candidacy for the Republican presidential nomination in 1908, he turned away requests for advice about the makeup of his own state's delegation to the convention.[18]

On the critical matter of patronage, Hughes dumbfounded and angered the Republican leaders. Where they considered appointments a return for party work, Hughes seemed to consider such service a disqualification for office. When Job Hedges, who had worked hard to elect the governor, asked for a position on one of the new Public Service Commissions, Hughes turned him down to avoid the appearance of rewarding a man for his support. "I can't very well appoint you because you're a personal friend," Hughes is reported to have said. "By God, you need no longer consider that an obstacle," was Hedge's sarcastic reply. The governor's apparent obliviousness to the significance his appointments had for factional disputes within the party outraged the politicians. To the prized post of superintendent of public works, Hughes named Frederick C. Stevens, chairman of the gas and electricity investigating committee that Hughes had served as counsel in 1905. By his own later admission, the governor was unaware that Stevens had become a bitter enemy of the James W. Wadsworths.[19]

Such misunderstandings soon poisoned Hughes's relationship with the party organization. The governor was sometimes cold and tactless, and the leaders came to resent his aloofness from officeholding politicians. Speaker Wadsworth later described how the governor assailed the motives of those who disagreed with him. "If you didn't 'go along' you were a crook," Wadsworth recalled. Roosevelt, too, grew disenchanted with Hughes. To Elihu Root, the president complained in 1908 that the governor had "treated . . . [the party leaders] with such wanton and foolish insolence, and has shown such entire selfishness and disregard of anybody's interests but his own, that it is very difficult to get the organization people to support him."[20]

Hughes was actually behaving carefully and rationally. Believing that only an antimachine governor could rehabilitate his party's image, Hughes set out to be such an executive. Like the party strategies followed by Platt and Odell, Hughes's never became fully conscious or explicit. Moreover, like Platt and Odell, Hughes had personal motives that had nothing to do with the pursuit of Republican success. Nonetheless, during his governorship he took deliberate steps to restore his party's ability to stay in power amidst new political conditions. Those steps rightly deserve analysis as a party strategy.[21]

The evidence is strong that Hughes thought himself a good Republican. "I am a party man and I am a party Governor. . . . I believe in Party Organization. . . . I believe in Party Machinery," Hughes told the City Club of New York in 1908. He said it again and again while he was governor.[22] Hughes also made it plain he intended to help the Republican party win elections. "We are all interested in the success of the Republican party," the governor began a speech before Barnes's Albany County organization in February 1907. Writing privately to the leaders, Hughes said the same thing, less simply. To Barnes, he observed that "if the party rises to its opportunity it can obtain that hold upon the good-will of the people which will make it practically invincible."[23]

But Hughes's loyalty to the party did not blind him to its present weaknesses. In his speech to the Albany Republicans, he reminded them of the electoral pattern since 1894. While the state gave "remarkable pluralities" to the Republican presidential candidates in 1896, 1900, and 1904, the party's gubernatorial nominees ran far behind each time. Moreover, Hughes noted, at the intervening gubernatorial elections of 1898 and 1902, the Republicans had won but narrow victories. In 1906 all but one of the party's candidates had lost. "The Republican who fails to realize the significance of these figures," Hughes said, "is paying little attention to the demands of the people of the State and the relation of these demands to party success. Undoubtedly there were special circumstances in the case of each election. But it is clearly evident that on State issues the Republican party will be doomed to defeat unless it gives new assurances to the people of its capacity to govern in their interest."[24]

Hughes's advice seemed simple: the Republican party should restore itself to favor by giving good government. Frequently the governor observed that he could do most for the party by leading an honest, efficient administration, the credit for which would accrue to the Republicans at the next election. "As a party man . . . [the governor] will serve his party best in office," Hughes said, "by adhering strictly to his duties and maintaining the highest standards of impartial administration." Despite the simplicity of his formulation, Hughes had specific tactics in mind: the establishment of an administration that was independent of the party organization, the reliance on direct appeals to the people, and the delegation of divisive policy questions to impartial experts. Together, these things made up Hughes's strategy for restoring Republican strength.[25]

An heir of the tradition of independence that had flourished in New York City in the 1890s, Hughes would probably have established an antimachine administration even if such a course had not been of strategic value. But Hughes was thoroughly aware of the popular advantages his approach offered. "The people are tired of bossism," he told an audience in 1908. "Large numbers of voters hold their party ties very loosely and now vote with one party and now with another," he observed on a later occasion. In such a state of affairs, an aura of opposition to the machine had strong popular appeal. To Barnes, Hughes explained the tactic clearly: "There are measures the advancement of which will win support for the party from the very fact that at first blush they might seem to be against mere partisan interest."[26]

While Hughes's distance from the party organization angered the leaders, they could not deny that his independent stance won public approval. As Parsons privately acknowledged, "the Governor's strength is undoubtedly due in some measure to his apparent antagonism of the organization."[27]

Hughes's approach to government also involved frequent and direct appeals to the people. "The only strength that I or my Administration may have," he said early in his first term, "is the confidence of the people of this State, and, in any difficulty that may arise, to the people of this State I propose to appeal." While Governor Roosevelt had sometimes appealed over the politicians to the voters, Hughes did so often. Especially in the midst of legislative sessions, when measures he wanted seemed likely to fail, Hughes made speaking tours to explain his case to the citizens. They in turn pressured their assemblymen and senators to act. "The procedure was in the nature of a referendum," one astute reporter noted, "with the legislators acting as the special agents of the people to carry out their definite decrees."[28]

Besides compelling the legislature to pass his measures, Hughes's use of direct popular appeals had other advantages. For one, it strengthened his administration's appearance of independence from the party organization and its methods. Instead of putting "the screws on" the legislators (as Hughes's secretary, Robert H. Fuller, expressed it), the governor operated openly and without the usual means of political pressure. Of more importance, Hughes's appeals created a new kind of bond between the voters and their representatives. With electoral participation declining and party loyalty weakening, Hughes's speaking tours provided an antidote for the loss of popular interest in politics and government. From the narrower Republican point of view, the governor's appeals increased the likelihood that at the next election the voters, having been consulted, would find themselves in accord with what the party had done.[29]

The most important element of Hughes's strategy lay in his approach to government itself, especially his reliance on executive administration instead of partisan legislation. Hughes did not, of course, originate the distinction between the two forms of government. Woodrow Wilson and Frank J. Goodnow had done that, and city reformers had applied their theories. But Hughes successfully explained the benefits of impartial administration to a popular audience, defended the transfer of various legislative functions to the executive branch, and devised state policies to make the transition. What he failed to do, however, was bring his fellow Republican leaders to understand how administrative government could free the party from the debilitating task of resolving interest-group conflicts over policy.[30]

By good administration, Hughes meant efficiency, expertise, and accountability. Due to the inevitable "extension of governmental activity," he observed, "efficiency is no longer to be thought of as simply a theoretical obligation, defaults in which entail only negligible losses, but . . . is a practical matter of first consequence." The government's expanded functions, Hughes said, "involve so many considerations, and demand such patient, expert, and thorough inquiry," that only knowledgeable men, given continuous responsibility, could resolve the most complex issues. Yet those who made the decisions, he insisted, had to be held accountable to the people. "The true remedy . . . is to unify administration, to concentrate administrative power, and thus sharply define administrative responsibility."[31]

In a sensational case, begun in 1907 and renewed in 1908, Hughes illustrated his commitment to administrative government by seeking to remove Otto Kelsey, the superintendent of insurance whom Governor Higgins had appointed. Though he acknowledged Kelsey's honesty, Hughes exposed and assailed his inefficiency and lack of expertise. When Kelsey refused to resign, the governor asked the senate to remove him, but twice the legislators refused. While he lost in Kelsey's case, Hughes's drive for expert, accountable administrators elsewhere met success. The Moreland Act of 1907 gave the governor the right to initiate investigations into every department, bureau, and commission of the state government. And although Kelsey remained in office, other officials whom Hughes deemed to be inefficient or inexpert were removed.[32]

At the same time that he championed efficient administrative government, Hughes distinguished it from legislative party government. He drew the line without precision. Nowhere did he fully explain the two separate patterns of decision making. But from the very beginning of his governorship Hughes evidently had the difference between them in mind.

A partisan legislature was not the place to make decisions that properly belonged to administration, he held, for neither parties nor legislators were capable of performing many of the newer, exacting tasks of government. "As citizens you are all interested in having the government well administered," Hughes told one audience in 1907. "On this question there is no division along party lines." "In connection with the larger part of administrative work," the governor said on another occasion, "there is no room for the controversies of political platforms." Besides being irrelevant, partisanship lessened governmental efficiency. "Partisan incumbrances," the governor declared, "to a great extent account for administrative palsy." Behind all these observations lay Hughes's belief in a general diminution of the parties' role. "We may . . . accomplish much," he said, "by seeking to limit . . . [the parties'] activity to what properly belongs to them, and thus to narrow the range of appeals to party loyalty where party concerns are not involved."[33]

Lawmaking, like partisanship, was often valueless to good government. "Legislation is not a substitute for administration," Hughes observed, "and . . . it is a frequent mistake to suppose that law is needed instead of the enforcement of law." Indeed, legislation sometimes actually hindered the management of government. "There has . . . been a tendency to cripple administrative officers by laws that are too minute," Hughes noted. Even when the laws did no harm, they proved unequal to the enlarged tasks of government. Speaking in favor of regulation by commission, the governor argued that legislators "sit only a portion of the year and cannot deal with these matters satisfactorily." Regulatory questions were so complex "that they cannot be dealt with to advantage through sporadic legislative action."[34]

Hughes frequently and approvingly commented on the rise of executive administration. "In considering the trend of our democracy," he said in an address before the Phi Beta Kappa Society of Harvard University, "we cannot fail to note . . . the tendency to increase the relative importance and influence of the executive department." In the hands of impartial administrators, Hughes suggested, the old conflicts became less divisive. The "tasks [of administration] may be created and defined with reference to political policy," he said, "but once created and defined there is little room for disagreement as to the manner in which they should be performed." Administrators in the executive branch,

Hughes implied, could settle differences that partisans in the legislature could not. As he put it obliquely in his Harvard address, "Out of the conflicts between competing interests or districts the Executive emerges as the representative of the people as a whole."[35]

While he welcomed such a development, Hughes apparently never made clear the advantages it offered to the Republican organization. By limiting the legislature's responsibility for divisive policy tasks, the rise of administrative government allowed the party to avoid problems it could not solve anyway. If Hughes had explained that in simple, partisan terms, the leaders might have grasped his strategy's usefulness for accommodating the Republican party to changed political conditions.

Considered as a whole, Hughes's strategy offered solutions to the most difficult problems his party faced. He never put it quite that way; nor was Republican success always uppermost in his motivation. But it is not hard to see his program's capacity to surmount the party's gravest perils. The antimachine aura that Hughes created helped dispel the ill effects on the Republican image of a dozen years of bossism by Platt and Odell. His frequent appeals to the public offered a way to reconstitute the close relationship with the people that the weakening of party loyalties was destroying. Above all, his proposal to transfer the most difficult policy issues from the legislative halls to the administrative arena provided a way for the party to escape having to resolve group conflicts.

Republican leaders nonetheless rejected Hughes's tactics, especially his antagonism toward the party machine. According to them, just the opposite approach was needed. "The party spirit is falling off and the party faith is growing drowsy," lamented former Governor Frank S. Black. "We magnify ourselves and minimize our party. . . . No man who is not ashamed of his party should be ashamed of being an intense partisan in its cause." Antagonizing the machine, the leaders felt, would cost more electoral support than it would win. As Parsons told the governor, "It is true that the party organization does not amount to much if the people are opposed to it; but it does represent a certain percentage of the vote, and it is that percentage which has been winning elections." Hughes's cultivation of public opinion also outraged the regular leaders because his appeals seemed to circumvent and undermine the people's usual partisan behavior. As Barnes put it angrily, "We have suddenly developed a new rule regarding public opinion. I do not care anything about that sort of public opinion that comes to me on the street and says, so and so is the case, and so and so must be done. I say, come to the ballot box."[36]

Since they opposed his methods, Republican politicians were anguished by Hughes's announcement in July 1908 that he was available for a second term as governor. "His colossal conceit and unique selfishness" made him an unacceptable candidate, according to J. Sloat Fassett. His renomination would "put the Republican party in this state in the hands of the Mugwumps," said Barnes. Most Republican politicians agreed.[37]

While the machine opposed him, however, Hughes was popular among several segments of the electorate upon whom Republican success in state elections depended. Upstate Protestants loved him for fighting successfully to obtain a law against racetrack gambling in 1908. As Roosevelt told Root, a failure to renominate the governor would "offend the religious and moral sentiment of the men who make up the backbone of the Republican party." Hughes also had the active support of the growing mass of urban independents, many of whom hoped he would destroy the party organization. The governor's strength with each group had its cost, of course. His support among moral reformers made him unpopular with those who feared "a Puritanical policy" of opposition to liquor and recreation. Correspondingly, Hughes's appeal to the independents sharpened the machine's opposition to him. But upstate Protestants and urban independents had kept the Republicans in power since 1894, and Hughes's popularity with both was undeniable.[38]

Recognizing the governor's support and fearing the damage to the national ticket that the party's failure to renominate him might cause, Roosevelt reluctantly concluded that Hughes had to be named for a second term. While the president renounced "any intention of seeming to dictate" to the state convention, he made his decision known and put pressure on the leaders to go along. Unable to find a satisfactory alternative to the governor, the politicians unhappily accepted Hughes's renomination.[39]

Getting out the vote for the governor was something else again, however, and the election returns of 1908 suggest that many county leaders may have encouraged their constituents to cut him. In fifty-four counties, Hughes ran behind William Howard Taft, who had the luxury of opposing Bryan and who led the governor by 65,000 votes across the state. Yet the high ticket-splitting that year (see Fig. 6) by no means entirely came at the gubernatorial level. Of the thirty-three counties where the least popular Republican candidate fell 5 percent or more behind the ticket-leader's vote, fifteen counties saw the party's assembly nominee run furthest behind the leader, while in five the candidate for lieutenant governor trailed the ticket. In thirteen of the counties

234

where net ticket-splitting reached 5 percent, it was Hughes who got the fewest votes. There the party leaders who hated the governor evidently put to their own use what the *New York Times* now called "the general trend toward independence in voting."[40]

Some Republican politicians interpreted the results as proof that the party did not need Hughes and his strategy after all. "Any real Republican," Chauncey M. Depew bitterly observed after the election, ". . . would have won by at least 100,000 [votes]." With such machine hostility to Hughes—some of which the governor had plainly earned—it is surprising how much he was able to accomplish during his administration, especially on economic matters.[41]

Hughes brought almost to completion New York's transition to a structure of economic policy that recognized and dealt with the clashing interests of an industrial society. In 1905 Hughes had helped to create the understandings that lay behind the demand for regulation. Now, as governor, he supplied the method to put it into effect: expert, impartial administration. Believing that administrators could perform tasks and resolve conflicts that party legislators could not, the governor relied on them in a wide range of areas. His leading accomplishment was the creation in 1907 of two powerful Public Service Commissions charged with regulating every public service corporation in the state. Afterward, the governor frequently used boards of experts to investigate complex economic problems and recommend action. In 1908 one such commission proposed a revision of the state's banking laws; two years later another produced the nation's most advanced workmen's compensation measure. In the area of state expenditures, too, Hughes believed that impartial planning could replace the continual competiton for appropriations between diverse interests. His method provided a way of adjusting the economic conflicts that nineteenth-century governments had mostly avoided.

By the time Hughes became governor, the behavior of public service corporations already had been a controversial issue for several years. Now a pair of transportation crises added urgency to the growing demand for increased regulation. Steam railway freight service had become practically intolerable to shippers because of what they considered excessive and discriminatory rates, inadequate facilities, and inexcusable delays. In New York City, rush-hour transit had also reached a crisis point. Merchants who considered the Board of Railroad Commissioners worthless and downstate reformers who believed the Rapid Transit Commission incapable of improving commuter service alike demanded state action. A response of some sort was inevitable.

235

The Republican platform of 1906 had pledged the regulation of all public utility corporations, and Hughes, who had devised the successful Commission of Gas and Electricity in 1905, was known to favor such commissions. His public service proposal thus came as little surprise.[42]

The measure, outlined in the governor's first annual message and placed formally before the legislature in early March 1907, took two approaches to regulation. First it codified the basic responsibilities borne by all public utility corporations (except telephone and telegraph companies) to provide adequate service at fair and nondiscriminatory rates. Second it replaced the existing regulatory boards with two Public Service Commissions, one for New York City and one for the rest of the state. Among their powers, the new commissions were to have extensive authority to examine the corporations' property and books, to fix rates, and to order the improvement of facilities and service. In addition, the measure required companies to obtain commission approval to enlarge their operations, to issue stocks and bonds, or to merge with other corporations. Even by comparison with the powerful Gas and Electricity Commission (soon to be abolished), Hughes's proposed agencies were strong. One provision allowed them to initiate rate changes without waiting for complaints, a right the existing board lacked.[43]

The utility and transportation companies opposed the bill, and, led by the steam railroads, they worked together to defeat or amend it. Their objections were basic, not technical or superficial, and they would have preferred to kill the measure outright. As the Delaware and Hudson Company's general counsel William S. Opdyke told Congressman George R. Malby (who had agreed to help the companies fight the bill), "The steam railroad men believe the Bill to be pernicious in the extent to which it gives the power of regulating their business to any commissioners, and especially to [a] changing board of commissioners." Yet once they realized that utility regulation of some sort was almost sure to be enacted in 1907, the affected interests tried to have Hughes's measure amended. Two changes particularly interested the companies, one mandating judicial review of commission decisions and another prohibiting the governor from removing public service commissioners from office. This second amendment was considered vital since, as Opdyke warned privately, "Hearst may be the next Governor."[44]

Besides the usual behind-the-scenes efforts to persuade legislators to oppose or revise the utility bill, the interested companies undertook a massive public relations campaign against it. "It is of importance," wrote Albert H. Harris, vice-president of the New York Central, "that the leading men and newspapers throughout the State should be brought to realize the probable harmful effects, from the public standpoint, of trying to push the bill through." The D&H's counsel agreed: "The Program proposed is to convince the ordinary citizen that the passage of the Bill would cripple the railroads seriously." To that end, the companies encouraged opponents of the measure to organize in towns across the state, persuaded local commercial associations to adopt resolutions against the bill, and wrote editorials for publication in friendly newspapers.[45]

Only Hughes's own campaign of public appeals saved the commissions bill. Speaking throughout New York, he argued the case for stronger regulation and defended the unamended measure. Above all, Hughes discussed the meaning of impartial regulation by administrative experts and explained his confidence in it. "The remedy," he said at Buffalo, "is to provide such regulation of public service as will assure the people that provision has been made for the investigation of every question and that each matter will be decided according to its merits in the light of day." "You must have administration, and you must have administration by administrative officers," Hughes told listeners at Elmira. "You cannot afford to have it otherwise."[46]

Hughes was not entirely dispassionate in his defense of the regulatory bill. Sometimes he reminded listeners of the gas and electricity and life insurance investigations and of the corrupt alliance they had disclosed. In so doing, the governor rekindled the passions of 1905 and brought public feeling to his side. He exploited the intense politicization of the utilities issue, indeed, he contributed to it, for the ironic purpose of putting the question permanently out of politics.[47]

In response to Hughes's appeals, private citizens voiced their support for the utility bill. As the governor's biographer told it, "The Capitol was deluged with mail—entreaties, threats, and scathing denunciations from constituents. . . . Never within the memory of men had the machine been subjected to such a bombardment from so many sources." Republican leaders in the senate and assembly, who had declined to back the measure before, now swung behind it. Despite his annoyance with Hughes, President Roosevelt added his support. John Raines personally helped secure an endorsement from the senate party caucus. When the bill came to a final vote, amended in no significant way from its original form, every assemblyman favored it, as did all but six senators, all Democrats.[48]

Hughes filled the new commissionerships with generally nonpolitical figures, several of whom were utility and transportation experts. Most of them believed in administrative regulation but also sympathized with the corporations. So constituted, the utility boards proved adept at mitigating the state's transportation crises. Most of the downstate commission's work involved supervising the building of the New York City subway system, including the completion of a tunnel to Brooklyn and the extension of existing lines. The commission also undertook a full investigation of the city's surface railways and, in consequence, ordered a wide range of improvements in facilities, service, and safety. The members of the upstate board successfully encouraged the steam railroads to expand and improve their freight service. Under the commission's eye, moreover, the roads cooperated with the shippers and began a policy of cultivating friendlier relations with the public.[49]

Strenuous opponents of the utility bill in 1907, the regulated companies soon became supporters of the new system. While the commissioners kept up an aura of protecting the public against the corporations, the members of both boards actually proved conservative in their policies, especially in regard to rates. Most of them preferred to deal congenially and privately with company officials, rather than to encourage public confrontations. Such a turn of events probably surprised almost everyone but Hughes. Without much notice in 1907, he had predicted his proposal would benefit business and bring about "friendly cooperation" between corporations and the government. The work of the Public Service Commissions further strengthened a pattern begun in 1905 and 1906. Supported by an angry public and opposed by business corporations, the new program unexpectedly satisfied the regulated interests.[50]

Despite the moderation of the commissions, Hughes had trouble convincing his own party of their value. His repeated suggestions for adding telephone and telegraph companies to the jurisdiction of the Public Service Commissions met with no response. Only in the midst of a serious party crisis in 1910 did the legislators finally adopt the proposal. At least twice the lawmakers bypassed the commissions and approved bills reducing transportation rates; in each case, Hughes vetoed the measure on the grounds that expert commissioners were better qualified than legislators to make the decision. Despite the advantages of doing so, party lawmakers only reluctantly gave up the regulatory functions they had exercised without conspicuous success.[51]

Hughes relied on expert commissions in other policy areas, sometimes with greater legislative cooperation than he received on utility and transportation matters. When the financial panic of 1907 caused the collapse of one large trust company, the Knickerbocker, and threatened to ruin others, the governor named six bankers to propose changes in the state's statutes. In December Hughes received their recommendations, which formed the basis for a package of new banking laws passed in 1908. The measures strengthened the Banking Department, increased reserve requirements, and put new restrictions on bank investments and loans.[52]

Pleased with his success, Hughes called for additional committees of experts to study subjects that were complex and controversial. In a special message on April 9, 1908, the governor recommended the creation of four expert groups to investigate speculation in securities and commodities, the condition of aliens, the problem of unemployment, and, finally, the inferior court system. He repeated his request a month later, but the legislators approved only the commissions on aliens and the courts. Both groups recommended legislation that was enacted in 1910. The lawmakers' failure to name a body to study speculation caused Hughes to move independently late in 1908. He asked a special committee of nine to propose changes in the laws governing securities and commodities, although, he informed them, in the absence of legislative authorization, the state government could not even pay their expenses. They accepted nonetheless. When they presented their recommendations, the legislature took no action. Hughes's fourth proposed commission, to study unemployment, also failed to result in legislation.[53]

One final expert board, appointed by Hughes in 1909, under the chairmanship of Senator Jonathan M. Wainwright, studied the related problems of employers' liability and workmen's compensation. Composed of representatives from both labor and industry, as well as of social reformers and legislators, the commission held extensive hearings, examined European compensation plans, and issued its findings in 1910. The report recommended the closing of loopholes in the employers' liability law and the establishment of a system of mandatory compensation for injured workers in certain hazardous trades. With amendments proposed by labor groups and their supporters, the bills became law in 1910. Though the measure was struck down by the Court of Appeals in 1911, a constitutional amendment several years later allowed the adoption of an even stronger compensation law. Like several groups of experts established under Hughes, the Wainwright Commission proved able to propose policy on a controversial economic question that political parties had addressed only with difficulty.[54]

Hughes's commitment to impartial, expert administration was also reflected in his approach to government expenditures. Like his predecessors, the governor had only limited control over most classes of state costs. In accordance with policies adopted before Hughes's term began, highway and canal expenses rose by 450 percent between 1905 and 1910, and overall state expenditures grew by 105 percent to over $50 million a year. To be sure, some governmental expenditures did fall within the direct control of the Hughes administration. Regulative costs jumped sharply with the creation of the Public Service Commissions, just as agricultural expenses rose with the establishment of two new agricultural colleges and with the enlargement of the Agriculture Department's functions. Indeed, expenditures rose for almost every executive department of the state.[55]

While Hughes had little ability to affect the basic pattern of expenditures, which went up because of demographic and economic developments he could not change, he repeatedly called for the systematic planning of state costs. Applying the principle first to salaries and supplies, he asked the different state institutions to standardize their expenditures for such purposes. By 1909 Hughes was advising adoption of "some permanent method for comparative examination of departmental budgets." The next year, he proposed a full-scale budget-making plan under which each department would file an appropriation request in advance of the legislative session in order to facilitate the "examination, comparison and criticism" of the state's overall costs. Partly adopted in 1910, Hughes's proposal anticipated the budgeting process routinely used by most states and the nation itself in the later twentieth century.[56]

The governor also scrutinized the distribution of state aid to local projects. In place of "special appropriations for roads, river improvements and other purposes," he asked for "a general method which will permit these matters to be dealt with in justice to all interests." In an unusual plea, Hughes actually asked farmers to forswear their traditional demands for local improvements at state expense. "Don't! don't! bombard your representatives who go to Albany trying to do the square thing . . . by trying to have them get something for you which you know if they were trying to get for somebody over in Essex County you would say was not right," the governor told an audience in Washington County. To be sure, Hughes knew how to use local expenditures to build political support. In a speech at the State Fair in Syracuse in September 1910, he pointed with pride to numerous agricultural, educational, and highway projects for which his administration could take the credit. In the same speech, however, the governor explained his new budget plan and endorsed a systematic analysis of the very expenditures of which he boasted.[57]

Hughes's scrutiny of local improvements symbolized the basic change in economic policymaking New York had undergone. Leaving behind a system characterized by the partisan, legislative determination of relatively unplanned distribution, the state now had a fundamentally new structure of policy that was not merely broader and more complex than the older one had been, but was characterized above all by new methods, especially expert regulation and administration. There had been two vital steps in the state's transition to new policies. First was Governor Roosevelt's frank acknowledgment of economic diversity and his recognition that policies helping one group did not necessarily help others. Second was Hughes's tactic—adopted in the aftermath of the investigations of 1905—of taking complex and controversial decisions out of party politics and making them according to impartial standards. Hughes's methods provided continuous governmental means of regulating and mitigating the conflicts Roosevelt had recognized but done little to resolve. Together, their innovations had brought about a real departure from nineteenth-century patterns of governance.

Permanent and fundamental as the change was, its significance and results were not always easy to understand, much less to predict in advance. Repeatedly, as we have seen, the regulated interests opposed the new policies, only to discover later the advantages they offered. Hughes himself, it seems fair to speculate, probably considered it less surprising than did most of his contemporaries that the corporations ultimately found the new commissions satisfactory. For Hughes had seemed, all along, to desire the result he so substantially contributed to achieving: the establishment of new methods for using the government to harmonize the dominant, clashing interests of an industrial society.

While Hughes was bringing administrative government to its culmination, the concurrent drive for independent means of political expression also attained a qualified realization during his governorship. Straight-ticket voting for regular party candidates now became less pervasive than it had been throughout most of the previous century, while other means of participation became more common than ever before. Hughes bore little direct responsibility for these trends, which began prior to his governorship and which were simultaneously occurring all across the country. He was, moreover, conspicuously unable to enact the most important of his own proposals for changing the nature of political participation, the direct primary. Yet Hughes's own example of independence served to symbolize and encourage the partly successful efforts of various groups of New Yorkers to find fresh political methods for making their voices heard.

During his governorship, the outlines of what may be termed a new structure of political participation became visible. Voter turnout at

Table 11. New York State vote for president or governor, by party, 1896–1910

Year and office	Republican candidate	Democratic candidate	Other	Estimated turnout
1896				
President	57.6%	38.7%	3.7%	84.2%
1898				
Governor	49.0	47.8	3.3	76.8
1900				
President	53.1	43.8	3.1	84.6
1902				
Governor	48.1	47.5	4.4	73.5
1904				
President	53.1	42.3	4.6	83.4
1906				
Governor	50.5	46.6	2.8	74.2
1908				
President	53.1	40.7	6.2	79.6
1910				
Governor	43.3	48.0	8.7	67.9

Source: Trib. Alm. (1897–1911).

presidential and gubernatorial elections, which until now had held nearly firm at nineteenth-century levels, fell significantly. In 1908 it dropped to just below 80 percent (marking the lowest rate at any presidential election since 1848), while in the gubernatorial contest of 1910, turnout fell to 68 percent. (See Table 11.) In the coming years, these participation losses were not reversed but grew larger. And of those electors who still came to the polls, a higher proportion than ever before now split their tickets. (See Fig. 6 above.)[58]

While regular party voting declined, some citizens found alternative means of political expression. For a small but growing minority, third parties, especially of the socialist variety, offered one possibility, though for reasons that are well known to students of American politics, third parties were destined to lead an uncertain and precarious existence. Other New Yorkers found nonelectoral ways of being heard. Those who belonged to organized economic-interest groups put pressure directly on government officials, especially the ones who staffed the newer administrative agencies of government. For citizens in general, public opinion increasingly offered an indirect means of expressing political sentiment. Such opinion continued to play the pervasive role it had assumed in 1905, and the politicians grew used to gauging it and abiding by it. Together these developments marked the establishment of new ways of influencing the government, different from the ones nineteenth-century people had known. Their inherent limitations and the disappointments that attended them should not obscure the new condition of politics they marked.[59]

Though it failed, Hughes's campaign for direct primaries in 1909 and 1910 provided New Yorkers their best opportunity of the era to examine and debate the means and methods of political participation and the role that party machines ought to play in shaping it. Determined to curtail the power of the party bosses—though not, as we have seen, to weaken the Republican party itself—Hughes helped revive the old movement for electoral procedures that would facilitate voter independency. He championed a new ballot law removing the premium on straight-ticket voting by listing the nominees according to office, not party, and by requiring the voter to mark his preference for each candidate separately. The governor also supported a primary-election law placing nominations in the hands of party voters instead of conventions. While ballot reform was not even seriously considered by the legislature, Hughes's sophisticated proposal for direct nominations inspired a true debate over party government and provided the most important issue of his second term as governor. Yet the particular details of Hughes's proposal for primary-election reform and the fate it ultimately met suggest the limitations of the long-standing assault on party machines and bosses and of the drive for genuinely independent electoral behavior.[60]

Popular interest in nominating methods, which had flagged since the 1890s, was revived by the life insurance investigation. In disclosing how party leaders used the businessmen's money to keep control of primaries and elections, the inquiry led to demands for curtailing their corrupt alliance. Regulating the corporations was one way to do it; regulating the primaries was another. Just as in other states during these same years, those who advocated direct nominations in New York repeatedly urged them as a means of stopping the special interests from working through the bosses to dictate the choice of party candidates. "These interests," Hughes himself said, "are ever at work stealthily and persistently endeavoring to pervert the government to the service of their own ends. All that is worst in our public life finds its readiest means of access to power through the control of the nominating machinery of parties." In his annual messages of 1907 and 1908, Hughes called, unsuccessfully, for a voluntary plan of direct nominations, but not until the fall of 1908 did he take up the issue in earnest. Although the Republican state convention refused to endorse direct primaries, the governor made them his leading issue and suggested that if he won reelection, he would consider his victory a mandate for direct nominations.[61]

Just as he promised he would, Governor Hughes spent much of his second term working for a law abolishing delegate nominating conventions and replacing them with mandatory direct primaries. Introduced in March 1909 as the Hinman-Green bill, his plan called for the statewide enrollment of party members and their direct choice of both party committees and party candidates at state-supervised primary elections. This much of the plan was controversial, but it was not surprising in light of Hughes's promises and his avowed aim to prevent the corrupt alliance of bosses and business interests from controlling party nominations. What distinguished the governor's measure was its provision that the official party committees at each level should designate candidates who would then have first place on the nominating ballots. At the ensuing primary election, enrolled party members would choose between the designated nominee for each office and any others placed on the ballot by petition. Independents who wished to deprive the bosses of all control over the primaries were disappointed by the Hinman-Green bill. So were the party leaders who disliked any form of direct nominations. Since it engendered little enthusiasm but inspired considerable opposition, Hughes's bill repeatedly failed to win enactment.[62]

The governor's proposal for designated nominees presents a real puzzle. Some evidence suggests that he fashioned that feature of his direct-primary plan as a compromise with the party leaders to whom it gave the privilege of picking the candidates, subject to popular approval. If this was Hughes's aim, it backfired, for instead of commending the Hinman-Green bill to the Republican leaders, the designation provision gave the regulars—led by Barnes and Wadsworth—grounds for deriding the bill's establishment of "legalized bossism." Hughes may indeed have been hoping for a compromise (his speeches in early 1909 were unusually conciliatory), but it is nonetheless plain that he regarded the provision for designated candidates as a good thing in its own right. By requiring the leaders to choose their nominees openly and to submit them to the members for approval, the Hinman-Green bill provided for responsible party leadership.[63]

Hughes defended the measure in just those terms. "Party organization will continue," he told an audience in Brooklyn, "and the proper course is to give it a recognized place for discharging its legitimate function." Speaking in Buffalo, the governor proclaimed that "this plan provides for responsible party action, with all the important advantages of consultation and deliberation on the part of those chosen as the party representatives, while at the same time placing the party voters in absolute control of the nomination of candidates for elective office."

Hughes, along with other supporters of the Hinman-Green plan, expressed concern that it should be presented as a device to strengthen the parties. As William H. Wadhams, who took charge of organizing upstate support for the bill in 1909, told Hughes's secretary, Robert H. Fuller, "This is distinctly a party measure. . . . It is . . . in no sense a non-partisan movement and it appears to me to be important that it should . . . not [be] permitted to become an anti-party or non-partisan measure."[64]

Where Hughes saw the direct primary as strengthening the party, the regulars saw it as destroying the organization. The loss of party conventions—and with them the opportunity for consulting on party principles, framing a platform, and naming a balanced ticket—gave the leaders one strong reason to protest direct nominations. The complexities of Hughes's system, the incentive it gave to party factionalism and to minority nominations, and the likelihood that it would place Republican nominations in the hands of big-city voters offered regulars other reasons to oppose the plan. It is not difficult to imagine that the leaders were sincere. Hughes "has put forward a most cumbersome and ridiculous measure," one regular senator told a friendly newspaper editor. "Its attempts at reform are purely theoretical." But the regulars were also shrewd. That the existing system of nominations could twice bring forward Charles Evans Hughes for governor was alone evidence of its satisfactory nature, they were fond of arguing. Marshalling these points skillfully, the opponents of direct nominations matched the measure's proponents speech for speech and point for point.[65]

If the balance of public opinion eventually swung against Hughes's plan, as it seems to have done, the reason probably lies in the regulars' success in portraying direct nominations as subversive of representative government. "The real question involved," said Barnes's *Albany Evening Journal*, "is: Shall the state of New York set its face against representative and in favor of a democratic form of government? Shall this state follow the lead set by others less mature in judgment, and strike a blow at the principle of representative government established in the constitution of the United States and the constitution of the state of New York? In the train of the direct primary follow the initiative and referendum and election of United States senators by direct vote of the people." Opponents of the Hinman-Green bill, by repeating this argument again and again, successfully presented the debate over primary reform as an ideological battle of the first importance.[66]

Their argument about representative government left Hughes outmaneuvered in a double sense: first, because although he had *not* abandoned the representative principle in favor of direct democracy, his opponents succeeded in creating the impression that he had; and second, because with each thrust against "pure democracy," Barnes and the others made it more difficult for Hughes to ground his case in democratic principles, the very thing he would have had to do in order to win his battle for direct nominations. The governor's plan plainly mixed representation and democracy: chosen leaders would propose and party members would dispose. Hughes was cautious in advocating pure democratic methods. The people "seek opportunity for a freer and more direct expression of public opinion," he observed. But immediately he added that measures for this purpose were "in an experimental stage and much care and study are needed . . . to make representative government more truly representative."[67] Elsewhere, the governor took pains to distinguish his direct-primary proposal from the wide open, unguided type of primary, characteristic of the western states, where citizens of one party were free to help choose the candidates of the other. While Hughes thus showed no wish to fight the battle on the ideological terms the regulars set, doing so might have brought him success. By including the "representative" provision for designated candidates in his primary-election plan, Hughes confused his supporters, who expected a simpler, more direct system of nominations. Had Hughes offered such a plan and come out strongly for "democratic" government, he might have won. Instead, he was trapped by the spurious—but effective—loftiness of his opponents, who based their case on what they called "representative" government.

As a result, Hughes lost. In 1909 the Hinman-Green bill met a bad defeat in both legislative houses. After its loss, the lawmakers established a joint committee to study other states' primary-election methods. Composed almost entirely of opponents of direct nominations, the committee eventually reported a plan for the closer state regulation of the existing nominating system. For the next year, the debate over primaries continued. In 1910 the lawmakers again defeated the Hinman-Green bill, though by much closer margins than before. Hughes called a special legislative session and even agreed to support a compromise measure restricting the direct primary's application to certain offices. Although he gained the support of Theodore Roosevelt, who had recently returned from a triumphant year of world travels, Hughes once again lost. He ended his term without enacting the direct primary. It was his most severe and bitter defeat.[68]

The victorious party leaders who had accused Hughes of abandoning representative government may have intentionally misinterpreted his primary-election plan, but they correctly saw that the principle of independence for which he stood led logically to direct democracy. If Hughes was not willing to carry it there, others—like Theodore

Roosevelt in 1912—were. Perhaps Hughes's caution was sensible, given the basic conservatism of middle-class New Yorkers; perhaps, on the other hand, he could have succeeded in converting them. But since he withdrew to a modified form of representative party government, direct democracy had no prominent Republican advocate (save Roosevelt), and, as a result, what might have been independency's most far-reaching result was not achieved in New York while that party was in power. Even after 1910, the methods of direct democracy which Barnes most feared were not tried.[69] Thus the tradition of independence, while it served to undermine nineteenth-century methods of political participation, did not lead to alternative electoral means through which the people's awakened public opinion could be directly expressed.

In the same year that Hughes met final defeat on the direct primary, his party went out of power in New York State. Like their achievement of majority status seventeen years before, the Republicans' loss in 1910 directly reflected national conditions over which men in New York had little control. Taft's unpopularity as president and the fierce Republican factionalism that had developed in Congress weakened the party almost everywhere. So did the highly protective Payne-Aldrich tariff act of 1909, which Midwestern insurgents persuasively painted as a schedule of sops to bloated business interests and as a major cause of the sudden inflation of consumer prices. Nineteen hundred ten was a Democratic year, and even the passage of a direct-primary law in New York would not have made it a Republican one.[70]

Of course, New York's party leaders did not consider their state's affairs to be inexorably determined by national circumstances. To be sure, the Republicans' division over the direct primary paralleled, in certain respects, the factional split between "insurgents" and "standpatters" which had developed elsewhere, especially in the Midwest. But these phrases were not used to describe the party factions in New York; nor did the disagreement there over primary elections extend to the full range of social and economic questions at issue in the Midwest; nor did Hughes's style resemble that of the flamboyant Wisconsin senator, Robert M. La Follette, leader of the insurgents. Throughout the year, politicians in New York treated the Republicans' fate as a matter to be shaped by actions and decisions taken at home. But with their party split over the direct primary and with a new series of crises breaking, the leaders failed to keep control of events. Their electoral defeat in November thus seemed comprehensible without reference to circumstances outside the state.

In the winter of 1910 fresh scandals badly damaged New York's

Republicans. The first came after Jotham P. Allds was chosen as the new senate majority leader after John Raines died. An informer told an eyewitness tale of how Allds had received a bribe in return for killing a "strike" bill in 1901. The senate's investigation of the matter not only caused Allds to resign but also turned up further foul details of the Republicans' relations with business interests that recalled the life insurance testimony of five years before. That same winter, Superintendent of Insurance William H. Hotchkiss began uncovering evidence that fire insurance companies were paying graft to Republican lawmakers. Hotchkiss's report led to a complete investigation of legislative wrongdoing, undertaken during the fall of 1910. The inquiry disclosed yet more details of bribery by various groups of businessmen over the course of the previous decade. It showed that if the corrupt alliance had become somewhat less organized since Platt's demise, it had by no means ended. The new revelations further discredited the legislature, now no longer the dominant branch of state government, and the Republican party, soon to be forced out of power.[71]

Hughes played a vacillating and inscrutable role in this latest party crisis. Soon after the Allds scandal broke, the governor, by directly intervening in party affairs, did something he had never done before. He devised a multipronged plan for rehabilitating the Republicans and personally pressed it upon sympathetic leaders, including President Taft and Elihu Root, who now held Platt's old U.S. Senate seat. Among the steps that Hughes urged were the retirement of Chauncey M. Depew from the U.S. Senate and of Timothy L. Woodruff from the state party chairmanship; the election of Harvey D. Hinman, a Hughes supporter, as state senate majority leader; the passage of a direct-primary measure; and the expansion of the Public Service Commissions' jurisdiction to include telephone and telegraph companies. Broad as his program was, Hughes's commitment to it wavered. At times during 1910, he seemed to care only about the direct primary. In late April the impression of Hughes's virtual abandonment of politics was confirmed by his surprise announcement that he had accepted an appointment to the U.S. Supreme Court, effective in October. This stunning turn of events transformed the governor into a lame duck and killed his program for party reform. Of the various steps he had proposed, only the regulation of communications companies was accomplished.[72]

As Hughes became less of a factor in Republican affairs, Roosevelt reassumed an active role. Drawn to Hughes's side of the struggle in early summer, at the very time when the governor's own commitment was waning, Roosevelt established his leadership of Hughes's branch

of the party. Yet the national role Roosevelt was simultaneously playing in 1910 greatly complicated his efforts in New York. Perceived as
too radical by many in his home state, the former president's doctrine
of the New Nationalism, with its associated proposals for direct democracy, alienated men who might otherwise have stuck with the Republicans. When he gained control of the party's state convention in
September and shaped both its nominations and its platform, Roosevelt
added the burden of extremism to the discredit born of corruption that
already encumbered the party.[73]

Just as they had done in 1898 and 1906, the Republicans responded
to suspicions of scandal by naming a gubernatorial candidate from
outside the party organization. But despite the best efforts of Henry L.
Stimson, to whom the nomination now fell, the formula was too pat
and the party division was too deep for the tactic to work again. Stimson did what he could to heal the factional division; he muted appeals
based on traditional partisanship; and he denied he was beholden to
Roosevelt. Of most importance, perhaps, Stimson took account of the
political perceptions to which Hughes had tried to accommodate the
Republican party. The nominee attacked the "corrupt combination of
dishonest business and venal politics" and declared that "it is against
this evil that the system of direct nominations [which Stimson sup-
ported] is aimed." But amidst party scandal, Roosevelt's perceived
radicalism, and the adversity of national politics, Stimson's efforts
proved insufficient.[74]

The election recorded a defeat for his party such as it had not suffered since 1892 and confirmed the trend toward voter independence.
All the Republican candidates for state office lost, including Stimson,
who was beaten by John A. Dix, the first Democratic governor of New
York since Roswell P. Flower, who had served in the early 1890s. In
New York City, Stimson received only 35 percent of the total vote
(compared with Taft's 47 percent in 1908), while upstate he fell to 49
percent (compared with Taft's 57 percent). In every county the Republicans lost ground relative to 1908. Ticket-splitting continued to be
pronounced, especially (but not exclusively) between the governor and
the rest of the ticket, and voter turnout sharply declined, especially in
New York City. There only slightly more than six voters in ten cast
ballots. In the state as a whole, the turnout was 68 percent compared
with the 78 percent it had been sixteen years before when the Republicans captured the state government they now lost.[75]

By the time the votes were counted, Charles Evans Hughes had
already left the governorship to take up his new position on the Supreme Court. The departure from New York apparently caused little

regret either to Hughes or to the leaders of the Republican party. His second term had frustrated them both, and the fault was by no means all theirs. Yet Hughes in six years—from the investigations of 1905 to his resignation in October 1910—had done more than any other single figure to shape the details of the political and governmental transformation New York had undergone. To be sure, the essential forces for change were already in place by the time Hughes made his initial political appearance in 1905. Admittedly, as well, the five years that followed were unusual and, at least in the Republican party, soon partly repudiated. Yet Hughes placed a distinctive mark on the political conditions he faced and contributed to innovations that long outlasted his own years in New York politics. In some respect, the political changes that Hughes helped shape must be termed ambiguous, paradoxical, and incomplete. But for an American polity so relatively static that it has been called "Tudor," they were changes of the first importance.[76]

9

From Realignment to Reform in New York

Platt's final years were not happy. Although he remained a U.S. senator until 1909, he was virtually isolated from the course of public affairs after 1906. Ill health kept him from significant participation in the work of the Senate, while his breach with Theodore Roosevelt deprived him of influence over federal patronage. He despised Charles Evans Hughes the man and hated Hughes's antimachine style of politics. A convenient symbol of political corruption, the senator must have found his popular image painful to bear. "The sooner Mr. Platt retires from public position, the more charity will be left for him," said a once-loyal upstate weekly. On March 6, 1910, Thomas Collier Platt died, aged seventy-six.[1]

On the occasion of Platt's death, editorial writers dwelt approvingly on the political changes since his days of power. He "lived too late," said the New York *Press*. "A new era has begun since Platt went into his political tomb. The methods which he fixed so firmly on the politics of this State have not all been shaken off; but their desperate clutch is relaxing." Platt "represented a kind of politics which has fortunately passed out of fashion," echoed the New York *Morning World*. His career "remains, and will long remain, as a thing full of instruction and full of shame," declared the *Evening Post*. The paper expressed "a sense of relief at having forever escaped" Platt's kind of politics.[2]

There was truth in the observation that Platt's political methods had gone out of date. The collection of corporate campaign contributions was now illegal, as were some of the old activities that party election funds had once financed. The state government regulated the organization of the parties and their nominations, and many of the devices Platt and his lieutenants formerly used to control the Republican machine were proscribed. Strict rules governed appointments to public office, with the result that the party organization's patronage powers had declined. Many of the era's political innovations thus struck directly at the techniques Platt had used when he led the Republican party.

251

Whether the editorial writers who bade farewell to the boss recognized it or not, these changes in political methods were part of a larger transformation in the means of influencing New York State government and in the substance and process of governance itself. Between the mid-1890s and 1910, the relatively stable nineteenth-century political system had encountered social and economic developments that created new expectations and new demands. And to a greater degree than the authors of his obituaries cared to admit, Platt and his fellow Republican leaders had played a significant role in bringing about the political accommodation to the new conditions.

One vital category of change involved the forms and patterns of political participation. Regular party voting became less pervasive, while other means of political expression began to be relied upon more commonly than ever before. The most significant electoral change was the decline in voter turnout. Figure 7 shows the percentage of New York's adult males who cast ballots in presidential and gubernatorial

Figure 7. Turnout of adult males in presidential and gubernatorial elections, New York State, 1880–1916

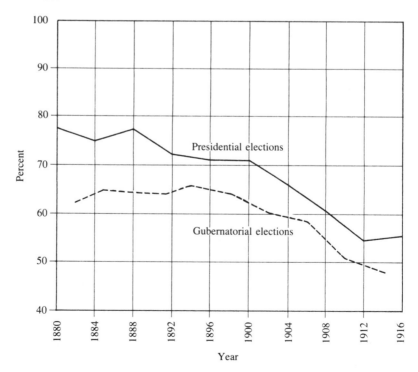

elections from 1880 to 1916. Where almost 80 percent had voted for president in the 1880s, only about 55 percent did so by 1912 and 1916. A comparable decline occurred in gubernatorial-election turnout. Most of the loss in voter participation occurred between 1904 and 1912. And as Figure 8 suggests, the turnout levels reached by 1912–16 were— except for the anomalous 1920s—approximately maintained thereafter. While relatively fewer electors went to the polls, an increasing propor-

Figure 8. Turnout of eligible voters in presidential elections, New York State and United States, 1876–1968

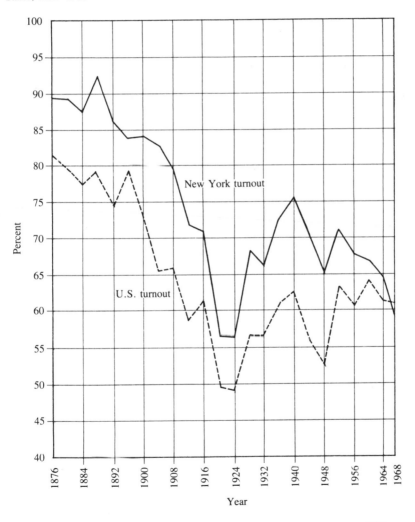

tion of those who did cast split tickets, instead of straight-party ballots. (Figure 6, in the previous chapter, shows the rise of ticket-splitting between 1894 and 1910.) Just as in the case of turnout decline, most of the change came during the years beginning in 1904, and thereafter ticket-splitting continued to be a common practice.[3]

Where once-a-year party voting had formed the people's most regular means of political expression during the nineteenth century, new and continuous methods of influencing New York State government became familiar early in the 1900s. Of most importance, specialized groups systematically organized and well informed by expert opinion put pressure on public officials not just at election time but throughout the year, whenever government decisions they cared about were being made. Many of these groups were formed to give voice to the particular demands of their members; others, acting with less apparent self-interest, took it upon themselves to seek the "reform" of social and economic conditions affecting weaker elements in the community. It was difficult for the unorganized to be heard, but there was at least one new avenue of political expression open to them too: public opinion. Politicians and poll-takers now regularly gauged it and took it seriously. However vague and susceptible to distortion it was, and however much it overrepresented the educated middle class, the new public opinion provided a kind of political expression not generally known in the nineteenth century, when opinion was commonly channeled by the parties or ignored.

By the time of Platt's death, governance, too, had become different from what it had been throughout most of the previous century. The state's most characteristic role, the relatively unplanned distribution of benefits to promote commerce and industry, was in disrepute, while new tasks of economic policymaking, especially regulation, had become firmly established. Just as the substance of governance had changed, so had the methods. Administrative agencies, staffed by experts, performed the most important new functions of the state and were coming to replace the legislature as the leading branch of government.

These policy innovations came about at almost exactly the same time as the transition to new means of political expression. Although the pressures behind the changes in governance had been building for a long time, most of them reached fruition during the half-decade after 1904. These years unmistakably mark a turning point, when the momentum shifted, the weight of opinion changed, and the forces of localism and opposition to governmental authority, which had sustained the promotion of commerce and industry but opposed regulation and administration, lost the upper hand to the forces of centralization, bureaucratization, and government actions to recognize and adjust group differences.

Such changes in politics and governance were not unique to New York. Figure 8 shows that electoral turnout in the United States declined sharply from 1900 to 1912 and that the levels reached by 1912–16 roughly persisted thereafter, except for 1920 and 1924. Across the country, ticket-splitting took an upward turn around 1904–6 and afterward continued to be characteristic of the nation's electoral behavior. While voting became less regular and partisan than before, interest-group organizations provided certain elements in the population with a new means of political influence. Numerous state and local political studies covering the early 1900s have established how widespread this development was. The rise of public opinion as a political force has received less explicit treatment from scholars, but several works at least implicitly direct attention to its new importance during these same years. A. Lawrence Lowell's seminal study, *Public Opinion and Popular Government*, written in 1909, testifies to the recognition that the phenomenon commanded from contemporaries.[4]

The economic policy changes that New York experienced were also paralleled across the country. Emerging contemporaneously with the electoral changes of the early 1900s, the new policy structure flowered during what Willard Hurst has called "the creative decade from about 1905 to 1915." These were the years when governments at every level began to take explicit account of clashing interests and to assume the responsibility for adjusting them through regulation, administration, and planning. In the states, fifteen new railroad commissions were created from 1905 to 1907 alone; most were "strong" ones, with rate-setting powers and a wide range of administrative authority to supervise safety, service, and finances. In the years to come, many of them extended their jurisdiction to other public utilities, including gas, electricity, telephones, and telegraphs. At the same time, the federal regulatory machinery was greatly strengthened, beginning with the railroad, meat inspection, and food and drug acts of 1906. In 1900 American governments did very little in the way of formally recognizing and adjusting group differences. Fifteen years later, innumerable policies committed officials to that formal purpose and provided the bureaucratic structures for achieving it.[5]

Besides their similarity in substance and timing to New York's governmental changes, many of the specific policy innovations that other states adopted also came after wrenching moments of discovery like the one New Yorkers experienced as a result of the life insurance investigation. Indeed, the majority of state and local political studies of this period identify a time—very often in 1905 or 1906—when through a scandal, an investigation, or a particularly divisive election campaign, the perception that privileged business interests corrupted politics was transmitted across the community with visible effects on party rhetoric, popular expectations, electoral behavior, and government policies.[6]

In the aftermath of scandal came "reform." Many states passed laws to curtail the corrupt cooperation between business and politics. These included measures regulating legislative lobbying, prohibiting corporate campaign contributions, and outlawing the acceptance of free transportation passes by public officials. In 1903 and 1904 there had been almost no legislation on these three subjects; in 1905–6 several states acted on each question; and in 1907–8 ten states passed lobbying laws, nineteen took steps to prevent corporate contributions, and fourteen acted on the question of passes. Closely associated with these measures were two more important categories of legislation, usually assumed to represent the essence of progressivism in the states: mandatory direct-primary laws and measures establishing or strengthening the regulation of transportation and utility corporations by commission. These types of legislation, too, reached a peak in the years just after 1905–6, when many states had experienced crises disclosing the extent of politico-business corruption. Like the laws concerning lobbying, contributions, and passes, primary and regulatory measures were brought forth amidst intense public concern with business influence in politics and were presented by their advocates as remedies for that problem. Both types of laws had been talked about for years, but it took the events occurring around 1905–6 to catalyze their enactment.[7]

Imitation partly explains these parallels between New York and other states. Hughes's life insurance exposures inspired similar inquiries elsewhere, and the laws passed in the investigation's aftermath were copied by other legislatures. But emulation was almost certainly less important than the widespread existence of the basic conditions for political and governmental change. To be sure, New York was not a typical state; it was too populous, too wealthy, and too imitated for that. But the dynamics of New York's transition to a new order of politics and governance early in the twentieth century were far from unique. It is useful, in light of these comparisons, to recapitulate what my findings show about the origins of New York's early-twentieth-century political order—especially the state's new patterns of participation and governance, the relationship these contemporaneous changes bore to one another, and their relevance for previous interpretations of politics in the 1890s and early 1900s.

Anyone who studies the political and governmental transformations of this period is heir to a rich scholarly literature. It is, however, a diverse literature, several branches of which have developed in virtual isolation from one another. Far too little effort has been devoted to a synthesis of our knowledge of American politics from the onset of "critical realignment" in 1893–94 until the peak of "progressivism" approximately two decades later. The very juxtaposition of those phrases suggests how varied the scholarship on late-nineteenth and early-twentieth-century politics has been. In reviewing New York's political transition, therefore, it is important to keep in mind how the record of that state's experience may assist in bringing coherence to our understanding of a political era that has been richly studied but eclectically interpreted.

The politics of no decade have received more attention in recent years than the 1890s. The economic depression beginning in 1893 and the electoral realignment that followed are now widely regarded as marking one of the most important turning points in American political history. To judge from the experience of New York, however, the significance of the years from 1893 to 1896 may have been exaggerated. Compared to the changes that occurred a decade later, the upheaval of the 1890s looks less momentous than it is sometimes described as being. To be sure, seeds of the political transformation New York underwent early in the twentieth century may be found in the crisis years of the mid-1890s, but neither the depression nor the partisan realignment of that decade directly led to the most important political changes of the era. In this respect, New York's experience differed from Wisconsin's as David P. Thelen has described it, and from the general pattern predicted by the theory of critical realignment that Walter Dean Burnham and others have advanced. In New York, most aspects of a nineteenth-century political culture survived both the depression and the subsequent electoral shift to the Republicans.

Just as in Thelen's Wisconsin, the economic collapse of 1893–96 created desperation among many urban New Yorkers, but it did not generate on a broad scale the questioning, the intergroup cooperation, or the powerful insurgency that he describes.[8] In most large cities of New York, the corrupt behavior of the Democratic machine inspired more outcry and stimulated more political response than did the depression. Throughout the state, both political parties felt safe in virtually ignoring the hard times, and neither party did anything to revise its agenda of economic policies. The constitutional convention of 1894 received numerous far-reaching, depression-inspired proposals, but its members buried them all and obtained overwhelming popular approval for a new constitution that left the economic role of state government unchanged. Only when prosperity returned in the late 1890s did discontent with the course of industrialism reach such proportions that the dominant parties were compelled to readjust their economic policies.

Even if it was not immediately productive of significant policy change, the depression did help shift New York from electoral equilibrium to Republican dominance. This has been shown beyond any question by Samuel T. McSeveney's careful analysis of the state's voting patterns from 1893 to 1896, and to his findings my study adds evidence that independent reform movements in the five largest Democratic cities contributed to determining the shape and timing of the change. Although a few scholars have questioned whether this shift to the Republicans, which occurred simultaneously across much of the country, was momentous enough to warrant being called a realignment, many of those who have actively studied the period accept the term and, with it, critical-election theory. Led by Burnham, they view the electoral upheaval of the 1890s as one of a series of periodic shifts separating successive eras in American politics and imparting to each era distinctive electoral characteristics and policy patterns.[9] That an important voting shift occurred in New York in the 1890s there can be no doubt. In addition to bringing the Republicans into state office, the change contributed to weakening traditional loyalties and placed innovative urban reformers in strategic positions of power. But whether the realignment was responsible for establishing New York's early-twentieth-century patterns of politics and governance is less certain.

Critical-election theory suggests at least two connections between the realignment of the 1890s and the subsequent political order. Both linkages were first suggested by E. E. Schattschneider in his conception of "the 1896 system," and they have been further developed by others, especially Burnham. First, the establishment of one-party dominance throughout much of the country after the realignment of 1893–96 deprived voters of the opportunity to register meaningful choices and so served to depress electoral turnout.[10] Second, in the aftermath of realignment, the dominant party (in this case, the Republicans) was obliged to take "effective policy action" to address the conditions that had precipitated the crisis; this brought about a "significant" transformation "in the general shape of policy."[11] In New York, however, the realignment of the 1890s does not appear to have been directly responsible for doing either of these things. When significant political and governmental changes finally occurred early in the twentieth century, they are largely explained by other reasons.

258

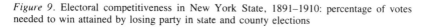

Figure 9. Electoral competitiveness in New York State, 1891–1910: percentage of votes needed to win attained by losing party in state and county elections

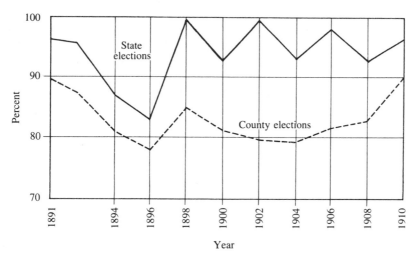

It is questionable, first of all, to what extent the realignment affected the competitiveness of New York elections. At the state level, they continued to be closely contested even after 1896, especially in gubernatorial years. In the individual counties, competitiveness did decrease somewhat from its levels in the early 1890s, but, as county leaders well knew, it was the statewide vote that mattered when a president or governor was up for election. (See Fig. 9.) Since New York's largest turnout losses came more than a decade after the realignment, it is doubtful that the declines were due to the "noncompetitiveness" of "the 1896 system." Indeed, the steepest single decline in gubernatorial turnout came in 1910, the very year the Democrats proved the state's electoral competitiveness by regaining power.[12]

It is doubtful, in the second place, that most Republicans placed in positions of authority by the realignment felt any obligation to readjust state policy in response to the electoral upheaval. Certainly, they showed few indications that they intended to do so. In the first several years of Republican rule, Platt had considerable success in imposing a traditional strategy on the party and in dampening demands for innovative economic policies. Except on questions involving the large cities or the liquor issue, the Republicans under Platt did not govern New York State very differently from the way the Democrats could have been expected to. Not until the end of the decade, under Governor

Theodore Roosevelt, did new economic issues achieve political importance in New York, and not until after 1905 was there a pronounced shift in the state's traditional patterns of policymaking.

For all the electoral turbulence of the 1890s, that decade did not see a fundamental transformation of politics and governance in New York State. In fact, compared to the years immediately following the life insurance investigation, 1893–96 marked the less decisive political turning point.[13] Origins of the changes that came later may, of course, be found in the 1890s, but the realignment alone scarcely explains them. Indeed, after 1896, it was not an enormous Republican majority but rather the party's narrow victory margins in New York that compelled Platt's party to begin to recognize urban independence and interest-group conflicts. These were the two developments that did more than anything else to prepare the way for the enduring political changes that occurred approximately a decade after the realignment of the 1890s.

City independents played the most innovative single role in beginning New York's transition to twentieth-century patterns of political participation. The revival of their movement in 1893–94, their tentative inclusion in the Republican coalition, and their ability to compel concessions from Platt's organization made independency from political parties both respectable and successful. In time, other elements in the population borrowed the independents' rhetoric and applied their methods. The eventual result was a considerable departure from nineteenth-century political ways.

Like the municipal reformers of Pittsburgh whom Samuel P. Hays has described, those in the large cities of New York were led by an upper-class elite of businessmen and professionals. Having a citywide view of municipal affairs, tending to place confidence in experts, and increasingly inclined to enlarge the scope of government, they fought what they considered to be the parochialism and the corruption of the dominant party machines, which often excluded men like themselves. Their movement was not, however, as rational, as unified, or as anti–lower class as the one Hays recounts. While the independents could usually agree on measures to curtail the authority and discipline of party organizations, they by no means always concurred on what he calls "desirable public policy." In their clubs and associations, the reformers constantly debated taxation, franchises, and city services and frequently showed themselves to be not at all of one mind in defining the city's functions and deciding how to carry them out. Nor did New York's independents as a whole consciously seek to reduce the power of lower-class elements in the city. Some did, to be sure, but many sought the support of lower-class citizens and increasingly favored the expanded city services and cultural toleration they wanted. Certainly most reformers sincerely believed that the changes they proposed would make their cities more democratic, not less.[14]

Another influential description of political independents also fails to fit New York's urban reformers of the 1890s: the portrait of the careless, uninformed citizen drawn from mid-twentieth-century survey research. Clearly, the Citizens' Union types who debated what municipal government ought to be, who put forward Seth Low for mayor of New York City, and who consciously spread their antimachine ideology were not abandoning their local party organizations out of apathy or ignorance. Quite the contrary. But in denouncing party organizations and in discouraging partisanship, the independents of the 1890s unquestionably contributed to creating the other sort of independent, the one whom the survey researchers have described: a person who distrusts parties but lacks other ways of making his voice heard. The prevalence of this second kind of independent in the twentieth century suggests that while the reformers of the 1890s succeeded in discrediting the party machines, they and their successors ultimately found it much more difficult to devise and maintain alternative means through which ordinary citizens could express their political opinions.[15]

In the short run, however, New York's urban independents not only achieved many of their municipal goals but also spread their innovative kind of politics to the state. Much of the credit for their success must be attributed to the volatility of the reformers' own electoral behavior. Having joined the Republican coalition in 1893–94, they deserted it in 1897; then, over the course of the next four years, they were slowly won back through the efforts of Platt and Theodore Roosevelt. By the time Low was finally elected mayor in 1901, the independents had placed their stamp securely on the state's politics. In particular, they had introduced three elements that would vitally help transform the nature of political participation by New Yorkers: a rhetoric and rationale for opposing the party machines, a series of election laws encouraging new kinds of voting behavior, and a successful example of how organized groups could win political influence outside the regular parties. None of these three elements directly caused other groups in the state to become independent of the parties, but all of them helped arouse the independence that others—for their own reasons—were also beginning to feel.

The new election laws that the city reformers inspired—including the Australian ballot, the separation of local from state and national elections, voter registration requirements, and the regulation of party nominations—contributed tangibly to spreading and encouraging a falling away from traditional party voting across the state. But while they facilitated independent electoral behavior, the laws themselves were only secondary to the attitudes of independence which formed the basic source of changed voting habits. The secret, blanket (Australian) ballot's relationship to ticket-splitting illustrates this conclusion. As city independents knew it would, an official ballot listing all the nominees for every office made ticket-splitting far easier than the old system of separate, party-printed tickets. Even with the party-column format and the straight-ticket circle, which regular Republicans had insisted upon, this was true. Yet for a decade after the new ballot's adoption in 1895, there was no significant decline of straight-party voting among New Yorkers. Only around 1906, when political events caused larger numbers of citizens than ever before to want to register discontent by dividing their tickets, did they do so—with the help of the Australian ballot. (See Fig. 6.)

Just as the new ballot law facilitated—but by no means solely caused—ticket-splitting, voter registration requirements played an ancillary role in depressing turnout among New Yorkers. Personal registration, which was mandated for all cities in 1890 and for villages with a population of over five thousand in 1895, discouraged participation simply by making voting more difficult. Similarly, the requirement of signature identification for voters in New York City, passed in 1908, undoubtedly helps account for Manhattan's decline in turnout from 80 percent in 1904 to only 70 percent at the next presidential election. Yet the state's actual pattern of turnout losses cannot be explained by registration laws alone. Some of the sharpest declines occurred in the rural counties of northern and western New York which were least affected by the new registration requirements. (See Table 12.) The heaviest losses, moreover, occurred more than a decade after the passage of the laws of 1890 and 1895. These measures only assisted a tendency away from voting that lay deeper than the laws themselves.[16]

New York's experience thus lends support to Walter Dean Burnham's contention that the shift away from high levels of regular party voting was "profound and system-wide," rather than narrowly attributable to the new election laws, as Jerrold G. Rusk and Philip E. Converse have suggested it was. The state's record also strengthens Burnham's denial that the changes in electoral behavior were what Converse has called "unintended consequences" of the new statutes. The men who advocated and adopted the laws—although they by no means all shared the same motives—knew perfectly well that the Australian ballot might encourage ticket-splitting and that personal registra-

Table 12. Ten New York counties registering greatest decline in voter turnout, 1894–1910

County	Turnout in 1894	Turnout in 1910	Percentage of decline, 1894–1910	Percentage of county's population covered by personal registration in 1910*
Chautauqua	84.0%	63.9%	20.1%	51.2%
St. Lawrence	84.8	67.0	17.8	18.0
Franklin	79.9	62.9	17.0	14.1
Erie	81.2	64.8	16.4	84.4
New York	73.2	59.4	13.8	100.0
Kings	77.6	64.2	13.4	100.0
Wyoming	80.0	67.0	13.0	0.0
Dutchess	85.4	73.1	12.3	39.5
Steuben	77.0	64.8	12.2	32.8
Cattaraugus	78.6	66.8	11.8	31.2

*Percentage of people living in cities or villages with populations over 5,000.
Source: The Appendix explains the estimation of voter turnout.

tion requirements could inhibit voter participation. To treat the measures as an "uncaused cause" of the voters' new behavior both exaggerates the laws' independent impact and understates the framers' foresight. The laws, in sum, cannot be understood apart from the larger, systemic forces causing discontent with traditional party politics.[17]

New York's record does not, however, support Burnham's far-reaching account of those larger forces. Although he has withdrawn from his earlier suggestion of the existence of a conspiracy, he basically contends that a Republican-corporate elite assumed domination of the political system after 1896 and instituted the new election laws as part of a general effort to weaken political participation for the purpose of insulating industrial capitalism from mass pressures.[18] The laws may have contributed to that result, but that was not the intention behind them. Indeed, supporters of the measures did not even usually agree on what they were supposed to do. Where city independents favored an Australian ballot to reduce bribery and facilitate ticket-splitting, regular Republicans supported the law as a kind of literacy test likely to discourage voting by immigrant Democrats. No group, moreover, failed to be somewhat surprised by the results of the laws. Independents were disappointed when their vaunted primary-election statute of 1898 left nominations generally in the regulars' hands, while the regulars for their part were appalled by the rural and town turnout losses that the separation-of-elections amendment encouraged. In New York State, no single group—Republican-corporate elite or otherwise—was sufficiently powerful and far-seeing to dictate the reforms and assure the wanted results.

By the late 1890s and early 1900s, in fact, discontent with traditional politics and governance transcended groups and sections. City independents had begun the disaffection, but it spread and, with it, efforts to compel those in authority to adopt new policies. Hindsight suggests that a diffuse urban-corporate-professional elite probably benefited most from the new political and governmental order that was coming into being. But during the years just prior to its inception, most of the impetus for change arose not from large business corporations but from other economic groups and from an unorganized middle class. Together they came to oppose an existing policy structure that was mainly designed to bestow benefits on industry and a party system that thrived on distributing the favors.

The organizational impulse that Samuel P. Hays and Robert H. Wiebe have described was certainly present in New York during this period: diverse producer groups, each becoming conscious of its own separate interests, organized intensely to press their demands upon the state.[19] Particularly following the depression of the 1890s, workers, farmers, merchants, and professionals joined with others like themselves in trade associations, educational campaigns, and sometimes independent political parties. Where certain classes of large industrial corporations had previously enjoyed a fairly clear field in the legislature, other groups now mounted effective lobbying efforts. What each wanted, above all, was government help in its own endeavors and restraints upon—instead of special favors for—its rivals. Such interest-group competition for influence over the government was not new, but it now became more pervasive and systematic. Inherent in this development was a challenge to the old system of allocating government benefits without taking significant account of whom the favors helped and hurt.

During the same years, from roughly 1897 to 1904, dissatisfaction with existing economic policies also spread among middle-class people generally, who remained unorganized. "Trusts" gave them a convenient symbol of discontent, but trusts were remote and little understood, and the tangible opposition to them did not amount to much. Closer to home, and of greater importance, were the franchise-holding transportation and utility corporations whose services and rates outraged people in large and small cities across New York. Without powerful lobbies or significant coordination of their efforts, discontented consumers did not form as potent a force for economic-policy change as did the organized producer groups. But over the course of time, through the efforts of independent parties and of local civic associations, their voices, too, were heard in state politics. The message those voices mainly carried was one of opposition to traditional government policies which granted generous favors, with little restraint, to public service corporations.

Effective regulation of the privileged interests presented an obvious alternative to unchecked distribution. Far from unknown to New Yorkers, economic regulation formed a historic component of state policy, but it had seldom involved the application of meaningful restraints. Now around the beginning of the twentieth century, demands increasingly arose for making regulation much more effective than it had traditionally been. These demands did not, however, originate with the interests to be supervised; they came rather from groups that wanted the government to restrain their rivals and, more diffusely, from unorganized consumers. In this respect, New York does not exemplify the pattern of regulatory policymaking that Gabriel Kolko has described.[20]

For while it is true that the regulated concerns had sometimes found benefits in mild state supervision (for instance, the life insurance companies that commonly asked the Insurance Department to certify their solvency), they feared and fought against strongly empowered administrative agencies with authority to intervene in management decisions and set rates. When proposals for such boards were heard, as they increasingly were in this period, the affected corporations opposed them—with great success until 1905. And when strong regulatory measures were finally adopted in New York—as they were in 1905 for gas and electricity companies, in 1906 for life insurance companies, and in 1907 for transportation and utility companies—the supervised interests tried to defeat them in every instance. The corporations' later discovery that effective government regulation had its benefits should not obscure the strong opposition they offered to its original implementation.[21]

In response to the demands for new and divisive economic policies, particularly regulation, the governing Republican party of New York acted cautiously and reluctantly before 1905. During the party's first few years in power, Platt maintained a fairly traditional distributive policy program based on close relations between public officials and the favored industries. As nineteenth-century parties commonly had, the Republicans did what they could to forestall divisive policies that threatened elements of their broad coalition and, when they could not avoid acting altogether, relied on symbolic measures and legislative inquiries. Throughout the depression, and indeed until the end of the 1890s, this approach sufficed.

Then in 1899 and 1900, Governor Theodore Roosevelt cautiously departed from the Republicans' traditional way of handling economic issues. Where his party had historically tended to deny that diverse producer groups had clashing interests, Roosevelt admitted the differences, consulted the warring groups, and accorded them each respect. This was important, for although nineteenth-century Democratic rhetoric had often recognized—indeed, had emphasized—conflicts of economic interest, such recognition had usually been accompanied by demands that the government scale down its activity in order to avoid helping one group at another's expense. Now Roosevelt innovatively coupled the acknowledgment of diversity with an acceptance of the active state. He did not, to be sure, take the next step toward the development of permanent and continuous governmental means of resolving economic differences; that would not come in New York until 1905 and afterward. But Roosevelt at least brought his party into open touch with interest-group leaders and with the growing reality of economic conflicts—whose resolution would pose the most pervasive task of twentieth-century American government.

Other leading Republicans, including Platt and Benjamin B. Odell, Jr., were wary of Roosevelt's approach. As governor from 1901 to 1904, Odell reverted to his party's traditional practice of affirming the harmony of interests. The result was a gradual loss of control over policymaking. Big-city merchants wanting a barge canal, organized workers wanting an employers' liability law, and reformers wanting to curb child labor each virtually took control of the policy area that concerned them. In the legislature, competing interest-group lobbies mounted pressures that a partisan body of lawmakers was ill prepared to handle. Outside the government, civic reform organizations increasingly railed against "grab" bills, alleged to be corruptly passed for the benefit of public service corporations. By 1904 New York's economic policy process was nearly in chaos. Conditions "demanded" public policies recognizing group conflict and regulating privileged interests, but the will, the energy, and the imagination to create them seemed missing. The next year's life insurance investigation pointed a way out of the crisis.

The crisis, in its largest sense, involved the nineteenth-century system of politics and governance. The growth of cities and industries had created needs for new and regular means of political participation other than party voting and had engendered demands for public policies beyond the accustomed realm of government. By 1905 Republican leaders had been trying for more than a decade to adjust New York's traditional ways to the new conditions and expectations. The accommodations they fashioned are not to be sneered at. New election laws had already changed important details of the voting process. A revised tax structure was in place. Innovative political language, proclaiming independence from parties and the value of economic-interest organizations, had become respectable. And fresh political heroes had come to the front. One of them sat in the White House. Another was in New York City, publicly baring the secrets of the venerable life insurance companies, as well as those of the not-so-venerable gas and electricity monopoly. Yet with all the adjustments the Republicans had fashioned, there was still the felt need for more sweeping changes. Charles Evans Hughes's revelations now set them in motion.

Vital to this moment of transition to a new political order was the perception, encouraged by both investigations of 1905, that big-business interests systematically corrupted politics. Not entirely unexpected, to be sure, the discovery of such corruption nonetheless contained enough that was new and came at such a propitious time that it provided just the impetus needed to push New York across a basic political divide.[22] By disclosing the corrupt alliance and jointly discrediting party machines and large corporations, Hughes's inquiries joined the long-standing drive for independence with the growing opposition to privileged business and inspired a series of concrete remedies for the bad behavior of the paired villains. The political changes these remedies brought about had been in progress for some time, but the events and perceptions of 1905 were needed to catalyze their completion. In consequence, New York now moved toward a political system different in fundamental respects from that of the nineteenth century.

What happened in 1905 is important in itself and should not be lost sight of in the effort to analyze the complex political adjustments that followed. For whatever meaning we assign to progressivism in New York must be based heavily on an understanding of that year's events. They are not well explained by the "organizational" interpretation of progressivism. As advanced by Robert H. Wiebe and others, that view of the era locates the progressive impulse in the drive of newly formed business and professional groups to achieve their goals through organization and expertise. This was the age, these historians have told us, when America became an organized society, whose model institution was the large corporation.[23] Yet, while their thesis explains a great deal about the era's overall modernizing significance, it is silent—for New York, at least—about the actual circumstances in which the most vital changes occurred.

Far from a time of accommodation to large corporations and their ways, New York's climactic "Progressive moment" of 1905 was characterized, above all, by intense popular anxiety about big business, its corrupt behavior, and its power over people's lives. Fear and outrage, not the drive for expertise, were the main movers. There was not, to be sure, a pronounced desire to tear down the industrial machine, but there certainly was a demand for restraining it, for weakening its political might, and for punishing its errant leaders. After the investigations, laws were passed for just these purposes, against the strongly voiced opposition of the affected corporations. The experts and organizers that Wiebe describes were not absent while all this was going on—indeed, one of them, Hughes, was at the center of it all. Yet it was not they, but ordinary people, who gave significance to the year's events. The organizers had helped prepare the ground for 1905, and they were to have an even larger role in fashioning the response to that year's experience. But the essence of New York's Progressive moment and the source of the state's subsequent political and governmental changes was popular outrage against the corporations and their political allies. Without that, the experts and organizers would not have had the opportunity they did to shape so many new policies in such a brief span of time.

Within just a few years after the investigations of 1905, New York's new political order assumed a distinctive shape. Strong regulation of the corrupt industries now seemed imperative, and both legislative inquiries led directly to laws, written by the expert Hughes, imposing effective restraints. The confidence in regulation extended beyond the industries investigated, and in 1907 it inspired the creation of two Public Service Commissions, filled and staffed by men who were knowledgeable about the utility business. Ironically, the legislature, whose committees had conducted the key inquiries of 1905, reduced its own relative importance in government by delegating most of the state's new functions to independent boards. These agencies, together with others that were subsequently modeled on them, formed a new and enduring branch of government. Their primary task was one that nineteenth-century public authorities had generally not assumed, that of continuously overseeing and adjusting the clashing interests of an industrial society. Far from sacrosanct, the new boards' behavior was often controversial (as, for instance, in 1914–15 when dissatisfaction led the legislature to investigate both Public Service Commissions), but there was never a movement to dismantle them, and their powers steadily grew.

The events of 1905 also affected patterns of political participation, although the causal connections are somewhat harder to establish and must be inferred from circumstances. While electoral turnout remained high in 1906—due, no doubt, to the campaign of personalities between Hughes and Hearst—ticket-splitting rose sharply that year in every section of the state. Some of the increase came in response to the orders of downstate Democratic bosses who told their followers to "cut"

Hearst, but much of it, especially upstate, reflected the people's new willingness to act independently of the parties. In subsequent years they continued to do so.

Voter participation afterward dropped, too, especially in 1908 and 1910. Some of the decline directly reflected one particular legal outgrowth of 1905: the prohibition of corporate campaign contributions. Getting voters to the polls had always required money—much of it spent legitimately—and, to judge from the politicians' complaints, there was now simply less of it available. That meant that preelection rallies were rarer, transportation to the polls was harder to come by, and bribes were probably fewer. More of the turnout decline seems to have been systemic, however. The events of 1905 had severely discredited the party organizations, and people showed their loss of faith by staying home. The process was cumulative, for as politicians came to recognize the voters' new independence, they toned down their old-fashioned appeals for party loyalty, which, in turn, inspired a further loss of interest. Independence thus bred apathy. The result was a far less active electorate.

These changes in participation and governance effectively reinforced one another. As loyal, partisan voting declined, the party leaders' power to shape policy was weakened, and they lost some of their old ability to promote distribution and forestall regulation and administration. During Hughes's governorship the Republican bosses were forced to accept reluctantly most of his various proposals for government by boards and commissions. The loss of the old loyalties also strengthened the new policy patterns in another way: by encouraging people to place the confidence they once had reserved for parties in interest-group associations that pressed continuously for new and divisive government actions.

The resulting policies, in turn, further weakened the old patterns of participation. People who became accustomed to regulation and administration saw the irrelevance of parties to these forms of governance and loosened further their partisan attachments. At the same time, the rise of new government agencies and bureaucracies encouraged forms of political participation that made voting less important. Ranging from formal hearings before regulatory agencies to routine communications with administrative officials, these new kinds of contact with government required money and special skills to carry on, just as electioneering did. Inevitably they reduced the resources and manpower available in the electoral arena. These entwined developments together forged a political order having a logic and coherence of its own, much as the nineteenth-century system did.

That old system's ways were not completely gone, however.

Weakened, they continued to be practiced alongside the new ones. For many citizens, partisan attachments were still strong and retained their association with ethnic and religious identifications. Despite new election laws prohibiting many of the parties' old methods, the structure of party organizations remained unchanged, and they yielded to no one in the performance of the nominating function.[24] Distributive decisions continued to be an element of twentieth-century policymaking, and parties maintained a strong voice in shaping them. But this traditional system no longer formed the entire political order; next to it now stood a parallel system, having its own distinctive types of political expression and government policy.

The new order, like the old one, was conservative. Its characteristic forms of participation inherently favored organized interest groups having the membership and the muscle to compel attention from government officials. Frequently these groups "captured" the boards and agencies that were authorized to supervise them and gained the power to shape whatever mix of distribution and regulation they found most conducive to their interests. Considered to be "nonpartisan," and "expert," moreover, the new administrative agencies were often free to serve their "clients" and make their decisions with little accountability to anyone. For the poor and unorganized, direct access to this kind of government was difficult to gain. Where the interest system bent to the will of organized elites, the new public opinion of the early twentieth century correspondingly tended to reflect the views of an articulate minority. Since New York did not adopt the measures of direct democracy, like the initiative and referendum, which would have given public opinion actual power, the influence of such opinion was inevitably diluted and its expression weighted toward the views of those with education and access to means of communication.

Whether the new system as a whole was less democratic than the old one is a problem lying beyond the scope of this book. Any effort to resolve it will have to take account of several contradictory trends. Compared to the nineteenth-century system, relatively fewer people voted, and among those who ceased doing so were many unquestionably legitimate electors, discouraged by an increasingly restrictive voting system. To judge from fragmentary evidence, a disproportionate share of the disfranchised may have come from the urban, immigrant sections of the community, though in New York, at least, the decline in turnout was statewide and heavily visible in the rural areas of native-born population, too. Whatever their exact social profile, many who had participated in nineteenth-century elections were now alienated from the voting process and failed to find alternative means of political expression. Their experience suggests that the new order was less democratic than the old one.

It is also true, however, that access to government probably became more widely dispersed at the beginning of the twentieth century. Where business elites alone had enjoyed regular cooperation with late-nineteenth-century political leaders, now other economic groups were also represented in government. The interest system may have excluded the poor and unorganized, but it at least assured a hearing for any group able to mobilize its membership—workers, farmers, and manufacturers alike. A great diversity of specialized interests thus gained a voice in government; many, indeed, institutionalized their access to power through the establishment of suitable administrative agencies whose clients they became. It will not be an easy job to sort out whether or not this diffusion of access to government outweighed the concentration of power caused by the curtailment of voting. Both the old system and the new one were most effective in representing elites, but both also had their characteristic ways of permitting others a voice too.[25]

The new order's conservatism was the product of a long political process, not the successful result of anyone's design. In New York, the origins of change lay in the widespread discontent with nineteenth-century ways, particularly with the existing partisan means of political expression and with the government's economic policies. The urban independents of the 1890s began the transformation, but other groups followed, each with its own dissatisfactions and demands. Party leaders, trying to stay in power by accommodating to the new conditions, originated many of the changes associated with the new order. Yet no group was able to get everything it wanted or even to be sure that the reforms it promoted would achieve the desired results. No one had imagined the finished product that eventually emerged.

Earlier scholars of these political changes commonly erred by heavily basing their interpretations of the era on its democratic, antibusiness rhetoric. They wrongly assumed that the "reformers" intended to do what they said they were doing and that their ideology sufficiently explained their achievements.[26] Many of the most provocative and thoughtful recent students of the period—including Burnham, Hays, Kolko, and Wiebe—have tended, either explicitly or implicitly, to make the opposite assumption, that the era's conservative results and the gains it brought to business and professional elements explain the intentions behind the changes. This teleological approach is equally as perilous as the earlier rhetorical one. In New York, conservative elites were eventually able to shape the new political system because they possessed the resources to adjust to new rules and practices and because the middle-class fervor of 1905 could not sustain the radical implications of that year's perceptions. The victors did not stage the transition to a new political order. It was the product of an industrializing economy, of circumstance, and, not least, of politics.

Appendix: Analysis of
New York State Voting Data

This book is not based on complex statistical analysis. The reader will find nothing more difficult to interpret than an occasional correlation coefficient. Several findings about New York State voting behavior are nonetheless central to the study, particularly the decline of electoral turnout and the rise of ticket-splitting. Since the estimation of these phenomena required the collection of considerable voting data and presented a number of problems, the following brief discussion may be useful to the reader who wonders where the numbers came from.

Sources

Two annual documents together provided nearly all the election results I needed: *Manual for the Use of the Legislature of the State of New York* (Albany, 1892–1911); and *The New York Red Book* (Albany, 1892–1911). In addition, *The* [New York] *Tribune Almanac and Political Register* (New York, 1892–1911) was useful for filling in occasional gaps and for verifying or correcting suspect data.

Counties, Offices, and Elections

The county is the basic unit of analysis here (except in several clearly noted instances where I have looked at the wards and assembly districts of the largest cities). All the data sources invariably combine Fulton and Hamilton counties (which shared an assembly district), so these two form a single county in the analysis. Nassau County was created from Queens in 1898, but I have treated Nassau-Queens as a single county for the entire period. The total number of countries is thus fifty-nine.

While often the highest office contested at an election is of particular interest and receives discussion in the text, in general I have relied on the analysis of the vote for multiple offices for each year. Where ticket-splitting is to be estimated, this is obviously essential. For every year from 1891 to 1910 in which state officers were chosen, the two highest such offices, as well as the lowest, were included in the data. (When the two major parties nominated the same person for the lowest statewide office, as they often did for Court of Appeals judgeships, I used the next lowest office instead.) The vote for president is included for every appropriate year, as is the vote for Congress in nonpresidential years. Every year the vote for state assembly forms part of the data. After 1895 only judges were elected at the state level in odd-numbered years, and, except in 1897, the parties did not contest such judicial offices. Hence in the odd years after 1899 only the vote for assembly was used. On the basis of the above criteria, the following elections formed my base of data:

1891	Governor		1897	Chief Judge
	Lieutenant Governor			Assembly
	State Engineer			
	Assembly		1898	Governor
				Lieutenant Governor
1892	President			State Engineer
	Assembly			Assembly
				Congress
1893	Secretary of State			
	Comptroller		1899	Assembly
	Associate Judge			
	Assembly		1900	President
				Governor
1894	Governor			Lieutenant Governor
	Lieutenant Governor			State Engineer
	Associate Judge			Assembly
	Assembly			
	Congress		1901	Assembly
1895	Secretary of State		1902	Governor
	Comptroller			Lieutenant Governor
	Associate Judge			Associate Judge
	Assembly			Assembly
				Congress
1896	President			
	Governor		1903	Assembly
	Lieutenant Governor			
	Associate Judge		1904	President
	Assembly			Governor

	Lieutenant Governor	1908	President
	State Engineer		Governor
	Assembly		Lieutenant Governor
			State Engineer
1905	Assembly		Assembly
1906	Governor	1909	Assembly
	Lieutenant Governor		
	State Engineer	1910	Governor
	Assembly		Lieutenant Governor
	Congress		State Engineer
			Assembly
1907	Assembly		Congress

Unless otherwise noted, party percentages refer to the mean vote for all offices used that year. The total vote always includes the minor as well as major parties, but it excludes votes reported as blank, defective, or scattered. Candidates nominated jointly by a major and a minor party presented a special problem. Whenever a candidate had the endorsement of one of the major parties, his votes were counted entirely for that party even though he received some of them on another column of the ballot. While this procedure inevitably distorts a small number of values for ticket-splitting, the data sources left me little choice since the votes for fusion candidates were usually not broken down by party. This situation was particularly true at the assembly level where most fusion candidacies occurred.

In about two dozen cases, one party (usually the Democrats) failed to name a candidate for assembly or Congress. Since the inclusion of such elections would have distorted both the party percentages and the estimates of ticket-splitting, I excluded uncontested elections from the analysis.

Turnout

Turnout refers to the percentage of potential voters who cast ballots. Usually, as noted in the text and tables, it has been computed on the basis of the total vote for the highest office; when no specific office is mentioned, turnout has been based on the largest total vote among all the offices in the analysis for that year.

The computation of turnout crucially depends on an estimation of the potential electorate, for which the decennial U.S. census figures on adult male citizens provide the closest obtainable approximation. For 1900 and 1910, the published census volumes conveniently furnish the number of adult male citizens in every county. For 1880 and 1890, however, they do not provide exact data on naturalized citizens, so certain assumptions had to be made. The 1890 census reports that 60.74 percent of New York's foreign-born males were naturalized, and this figure was assumed to be approximately correct for 1880, too. On the basis of it, a statewide estimate of adult male citizens in 1880 was calculated. (Table 1 relies on this figure; county-level turnout rates were not computed for the 1880s.) For 1890 the county-level naturalization percentages of 1900 were used, except for New York and Kings counties, for which the census gives the exact percentages of foreign-born males who were naturalized.[1]

Once census-year, adult-male citizenship figures were obtained, interpolation yielded estimates of the potential electorate for every county for every year from 1890 to 1910. Since no interpolation method can account for such vagaries in population growth as the year-to-year fluctuation in immigration, I have simply assumed a steady rate of growth in the potential electorate (that is, interpolation by a constant percentage of increase—or, in the case of some rural counties, decrease—from one year to the next).

Two graphs in Chapter 9 rely on different turnout estimates from the ones described here and so require a special word of explanation. Figure 7 bases turnout on the total adult male population, without eliminating unnaturalized immigrants. The sharp decline of turnout portrayed there thus includes the effect produced by the heavy influx of immigrants, many of whom were not eligible to vote. Figure 8, covering nearly a century and comparing New York to the United States, is based on turnout estimates by Walter Dean Burnham.[2]

Besides the problem of calculating reliable turnout figures, there is the further difficulty of knowing what they mean. To some extent, the estimates undoubtedly reflect fraud. Each party commonly charged the other with various acts of electoral dishonesty, and to judge from the testimony taken in several legislative investigations (such as those conducted in 1894 on New York City and Troy), at least some of the accusations were probably true. Among several scholars who have studied the problem of the extent of late-nineteenth-century voting fraud, however, the weight of opinion seems to be that its levels were probably not such as to affect our general understanding of the high rates of voter mobilization in that period.[3] Accordingly, I have not adjusted the turnout estimates for fraud. To do so would have involved making a series of assumptions and estimates for which I lacked reliable data. The problem is an important one, however, and deserves further attention. In studying it, several things should be kept in mind:

1. It cannot be assumed that fraud necessarily inflated the recorded turnout levels. Particularly in rural New York, Republican leaders often

charged the Democrats with paying Republican voters to stay home on election day and warned that any nonvoting Republican would be suspected of taking a Democratic bribe.[4] Urban fraud, too, sometimes involved preventing electors from casting their ballots through intimidation and violence. Not all fraud, in short, involved "stuffing" the ballot box.

2. Numerous sources suggest that many late-nineteenth-century voters were paid to go to the polls. It is not, however, altogether obvious that this ought to be treated as fraud. Most such voters probably considered themselves loyal members of the party that assisted their "transportation" to the polls, a perfectly legal practice.

3. The new registration laws of the 1890s and 1900s made certain kinds of electoral fraud more difficult and no doubt partly explain the decline in estimated levels of turnout after 1900. But, as noted in Chapter 9, New York's turnout losses were by no means confined to places where the registration laws applied, and much more was thus involved in the turnout declines of the early twentieth century than the elimination of fraud.

Ticket-Splitting

Levels of ticket-splitting must be estimated, not measured, and the estimates invariably understate the true amount of divided ballots. The basic index of ticket-splitting used throughout the book is the percentage by which a party's least successful candidate (among the offices analyzed) fell behind the ticket-leader's vote:

$$\text{T-S} = \frac{\text{High Vote} - \text{Low Vote}}{\text{High Vote}} \times 100$$

A statewide mean of county percentages (weighted according to size of the electorate) provides an estimate of overall ticket-splitting.

There are two obvious difficulties with this index. First is its inability to account for voters who split in opposite directions. Their divided ballots cancel each other and become invisible in the aggregate. This is unavoidable. It must simply be assumed that as genuine ticket-splitting rises it will be reflected, if only incompletely, in the aggregate votes for the different candidates.

Second is the contamination of the index by "roll-off"—the tendency for fewer total votes to be cast at the bottom (or, in some cases, the top) of the ticket. This problem is less troublesome because roll-off levels are known and, if they are high, the estimates of ticket-splitting will clearly be inflated. In fact, however, roll-off was a negligible factor in New York elections during the period studied here, except in 1894 and 1897. In 1894 (as noted in Chapter 2) there were significantly fewer total votes cast for assembly and Congress than for governor (3.7 percent fewer for assembly), and almost all the abstentions appear to have been on the Democratic side. Three years later, 47,000 fewer votes were cast for chief judge of the Court of Appeals than for assembly. This result occurred (as explained in Chapter 4) because supporters of the independent mayoral candidate, Seth Low, in New York City found no independent judicial candidate on their ballots and evidently abstained for that office. For these two cases, roll-off inflated the estimates of ticket-splitting, but otherwise it was not a significant factor in New York State elections from 1891 to 1910.

Bibliography

BIBLIOGRAPHICAL ESSAY

All the major primary sources and secondary works on which this book is based are cited in the Notes. A comprehensive bibliography thus seemed unnecessary, and I have accordingly chosen a briefer format, divided into two parts. First, a bibliographical essay discusses the major classes of primary sources and comments on the most important items in each category. At the end of the essay, I have added a few words about several indispensable secondary studies of New York State politics. (Since the first and last chapters of the book make clear the relationship of my work to the secondary literature in political history and political science, I have not provided a separate discussion of existing scholarship.) Second, following the bibliographical essay are complete lists of manuscript collections and newspapers used.

Manuscript Collections. Because the heart of this book represents an effort to explore political change in New York State by studying the behavior of the leaders of the majority party there, the manuscript papers of Republican politicians provided my most valuable sources. Their letters to one another, as well as to government officials, constituents, editors, businessmen, and interest-group representatives of all sorts, enabled me to understand how those formally at the head of the state's political system responded to changing conditions and expectations from 1893 to 1910. Nowhere can one learn as much about their responses—or "strategies" as I designate the coherent, crafted responses of the top leaders—as in their surviving manuscripts.

The Thomas Collier Platt Papers in the Yale University Library and in private hands formed the single most important group of letters I used. Since the Platt family apparently destroyed some of the senator's correspondence in the years after his death, the letters that remain cover his career in New York episodically rather than comprehensively. Several figures, including Theodore Roosevelt and William Barnes, Jr., are well represented in the letters, while others with whom Platt undoubtedly corresponded are not. By the same token, the papers extensively document some incidents in his career, including the decision to nominate Roosevelt for governor in 1898, but shed little light on others. The Platt Papers that are still in private hands include five letterbooks covering the 1880s and 1890s which proved especially valuable for examples of the routine communications the boss sent to Republican politicians throughout the state.

Compared to the numerous but incomplete Platt Papers, those of Theodore Roosevelt are voluminous and comprehensive. Used selectively—in conjunction with Elting E. Morison, ed., *The Letters of Theodore Roosevelt,* 8 vols. (Cambridge, Mass., 1951–54)—they reveal Roosevelt as perhaps the most articulate and insightful (if also self-serving) observer of New York affairs in this period. Indeed, his letters have a seductive quality of which historians must beware lest their own perspective become an extension of Roosevelt's.

Somewhat less useful were the manuscripts of this book's two other major figures, Benjamin B. Odell, Jr., and Charles Evans Hughes. The tiny collection of Odell Papers (NYPL) was of almost no help, and, while some of Odell's letters turned up in other manuscript collections, I had to construct my account of his party strategy largely from published sources. The Hughes Papers (LC and NYPL) include a moderate amount of correspondence, but relatively few letters proved very helpful. The NYPL collection, however, contains other valuable items, especially the governor's speeches, as well as materials relating to the direct-primary campaign and to the Republican party crisis of 1910.

Of the surviving manuscripts concerning the other three Republican governors (besides Roosevelt, Odell, and Hughes) who served between 1895 and 1910, the papers of Levi P. Morton were the most useful. The large Morton collection (NYPL) includes a letterbook, marked "confidential," that consists entirely of letters from the governor and his secretary, Ashley W. Cole, to Platt, while the boss's replies are preserved elsewhere in the Morton Papers. No collection of correspondence documents more completely than does this one Platt's strategy during his party's first years in power. A small collection of Frank W. Higgins Papers (GARL) and a number of scrapbooks of clippings pertaining to Frank S. Black (NYSL) rather poorly document the era's other two governors.

Fortunately, the papers of numerous top Republicans compensate for the dearth of letters by Higgins and Black. Perhaps the three most valuable such collections were those of Samuel Frederick Nixon, George Washington Aldridge, and Lemuel Ely Quigg. Nixon's papers extensively document his assembly leadership, especially during the Odell years, and, of equal importance, tell about his relations with constituents and politicians back home in Chautauqua County. The Aldridge collection covers patronage matters, canal affairs, and Rochester politics, especially for the period before 1900. Quigg was close to Platt and, for a time, to Roosevelt, and thus his letters disclose a good deal about the surprising partnership of the boss and the Rough Rider. Two other important manuscript collections of regular Republican leaders do for the Hughes years what the papers of Nixon, Aldridge, and Quigg do for the earlier period: the Horace White Papers and the Herbert Parsons Papers. Both heavily concern local party affairs (in the cities of Syracuse and New York, respectively), legislative matters, and, perhaps of most importance here, Hughes's stormy relations with the Republican organization.

A number of manuscript collections cover the independent Republicans. The best of the group are the Seth Low Papers which include voluminous correspondence on the "revolution of '97" and on independent-Republican relations generally from 1897 to 1903. The Elihu Root Papers (LC) are also valuable for the antimachine side of things, particularly for the Odell years and the life insurance investigation. A third collection of considerable value was the Whitelaw Reid Papers which extensively document the opposition to Platt in the years before 1900. Besides the many manuscript collections of other individual independents, I found helpful a number of collections gathered by their organizations and associations. Of most use in this group were the Citizens' Union Papers which include correspondence, minutes, and pamphlets reflecting the development of independent ideas and methods in New York City.

One final type of manuscript collection should be mentioned: those of the business corporations and commercial organizations. I found the New York Central Railroad Company Corporate Records especially useful, mainly for the correspondence between the company's officers and its lobbyists and legislative friends in Albany. The Delaware and Hudson Corporation Papers include similar letters which hold particular interest for the light they throw on the railroad companies' opposition to state regulation in 1907. On the other side of the issue of railroad regulation were the downstate merchants, whose opinions and behavior are recorded in the papers of the New York Board of Trade and Transportation.

Newspapers. For the nuts-and-bolts details of large and small political happenings, for the opinions and gossip of the politicians, and for remarkably astute (if biased) editorial commentary, newspapers are, of course, a necessary source for the political historian. The reader of this book will observe that I have used newspapers as a guide to the beliefs and strategies of the political leaders who owned and influenced the papers, but that I have also assumed that the newspapers expressed—sometimes loudly, sometimes not—the opinions of ordinary citizens and interest groups. Undoubtedly I have made some mistakes in dually interpreting the newspapers. Yet in studying an era of declining partisan domination of the press, it seemed important to try to work this "elite" source both for the light it throws on the leaders and for what it reflects of an emergent public opinion that was separate from traditional party opinion.

The well-indexed *New York Times* (independent-Democratic) and *New York Tribune* (Republican) were used for every year of the period. For selected spans of time covered by this book, I examined every issue of these papers. The New York *Sun* (which supported Platt beginning about 1896) and the New York *Press* (which also did so in the late 1890s) have both been checked for particular events and periods, especially legislative sessions and election campaigns. Other downstate newspapers used less often include the *Herald,* the *Evening Post,* the *Commercial Advertiser,* the *World,* and the *Brooklyn Daily Eagle.*

Among upstate city dailies, the following were most valuable for the regular Republican point of view: the *Albany Evening Journal,* the *Buffalo Evening News,* the *Elmira Daily Advertiser,* the *Ithaca Daily Journal,* the Rochester *Democrat and Chronicle,* the Syracuse *Post-Standard,* and the *Troy Daily Times.* For independent Republican opinion, the *Buffalo Commercial* and the Syracuse *Evening Herald* were useful. All these newspapers proved helpful in studying local election campaigns, legislative developments, and the response to major events like Roosevelt's nomination for governor and the life insurance investigation.

Small-town weekly newspapers provided a major source of information on the Republican appeal to upstate citizens and on the waning of their habitual partisanship early in the twentieth century. Two such papers, located in securely Republican counties at opposite ends of the state, were checked for every week of the period: the *Fredonia Censor* and the *St. Lawrence Plaindealer* (Canton). Others from around the state (listed below) were used mainly for the fall election campaigns, for the responses to major legislative enactments, and for the life insurance investigation.

Finally, scrapbooks of clippings enabled me to extend the scope of my newspaper research. The Platt, Morton, Nixon, Aldridge, and Black papers all contain numerous volumes of newspaper clippings, chronologically arranged and reliably labeled. Multiple volumes of New York *Sun* clippings (used for 1893–1906) are located at the NYPL.

Government Documents. The formal record, compiled by state authorities, of what the government of New York accomplished in the 1890s and 1900s provided an almost unlimited source of information for my analysis of how the substance and process of government changed over time. No single class of documents tells more about the regular functions of the state in this period than do the yearly volumes of the governor's *Public Papers.* Each January the governor issued an annual message giving a comprehensive—and in some cases astoundingly insightful—summary of the state's activities, as well as a clear statement of the Republican leadership position on the whole range of policy problems before the government. Besides the annual messages, the *Public Papers* contain special messages, veto memoranda, speeches, official correspondence, and miscellaneous materials. Their value to this study cannot be overstated.

Legislative documents also proved essential. The *New York Assembly Journal* and the *New York Senate Journal* do not contain legislative debates, but they provide the complete record of assembly and senate action, including roll-call votes. Used in conjunction with newspaper accounts, the journals make it possible to trace the work of the legislature. The *Assembly Documents* and *Senate Documents* contain miscellaneous materials. For my purposes, they were particularly useful for the testimony and reports of various special legislative inquiries—from the Lexow police investigation of 1894 to the Allds scandal inquiry of 1910. Two annual documents, properly grouped with legislative materials, provided handy sources of information on state government: the *Manual for the Use of the Legislature of the State of New York* and *The New York Red Book.* Especially for biographical data, election returns, and legislative membership information, they were indispensable.

Published annual reports by the various departments of the state yielded unexpectedly comprehensive information on the activities of the government, as well as on the private interests at least nominally overseen by each department. The typical report consists of a lengthy essay by the department head, followed by hundreds of pages of statistical material. Special note should be made of the comptroller's reports for 1898 and 1905, because of their astute analyses of state revenues and expenditures, but other reports by the departments of excise, agriculture, labor statistics, the state engineer, and the state tax commissioners also furnished needed data.

Two final groups of state documents deserve mention. First, are the various records of the constitutional convention of 1894, including the complete debates of the convention and a wealth of supporting materials. These formed an essential source for Chapter 2 of this book. Second, in a very different category, are the four volumes of testimony taken in a unique court case in 1915 in which William Barnes, Jr., sued Theodore Roosevelt for libel. The published record includes the extensive statements by Barnes and Roosevelt, as well as considerable correspondence introduced as evidence. Much of the case hinged on questions concerning the degree to which Platt controlled Governor Roosevelt and financial interests controlled Platt. Despite their coming years later, some of the witnesses' recollections on these topics had the ring of authenticity.

Contemporary Magazines and Journals. Ordinary citizens and trained scholars alike—from both within and beyond the state—found New York politics an absorbing subject of interest in the 1890s and 1900s. Magazines and journals of all types accordingly covered the state's affairs. Complete citations to the useful articles are given in the Notes, but it may be helpful to mention here the different kinds of periodical publications that rewarded study.

The independents had their journals of opinion, several of which were immensely prestigious and gave special attention to New York politics— whose redemption they sorely sought; these included the *Nation* and *Harper's Weekly,* as well as the *Century Magazine.* Educated citizens of the upper middle class found highbrow commentary in the *Forum* and the *North American Review,* while the *Outlook* was more accessible to a general audience. All had articles on New York politics. The muckraking journals of the early twentieth century covered the state, too, including *McClure's Magazine, Cosmopolitan, Everybody's,* and the *American Magazine.* Of considerable usefulness were the scholarly political science journals, which took New York's elections and public policies seriously and treated them analytically; especially helpful were *Political Science Quarterly,* the *American Political Science Review,* and the *Annals of the American Academy of Political and Social Science. Municipal Affairs* should be mentioned too: a serious journal published for only five years by the Reform Club of New York. And, finally, for quick insight into newspaper opinion, *Review of Reviews* and the *Literary Digest* proved excellent.

Political Pamphlets. No study of late-nineteenth and early-twentieth-century politics can ignore the voluminous literature of campaign tracts and pamphlets published by the parties, by dissident factions, and by special-interest groups of all sorts. Each gubernatorial-election year, the Republican State Committee issued a campaign handbook, often entitled *Facts and Figures Concerning the Government of the State of New York by Republican Officials.* The Democrats had theirs, as well, of course, as did the independent organizations. The Citizens' Union's book, issued in separate editions for each of Seth Low's mayoral campaigns, was called *The City for the People!* Not just elections but volatile policy issues, too, brought forth a considerable pamphlet literature. The Australian ballot, the direct primary, and the tax issue particularly inspired interested groups to place their pleas before the public in printed form.

Autobiographies and Memoirs. Just as they do today, politicians and political observers of the 1890s and early 1900s wrote accounts of their lives and times which cannot be ignored. Out of the many such autobiographies written by figures relevant to this book, three proved vital to it: Theodore Roosevelt, *An Autobiography* (New York, 1913); Louis J. Lang, ed., *The Autobiography of Thomas Collier Platt* (New York, 1910); and David J. Danelski and Joseph S. Tulchin, eds., *The Autobiographical Notes of Charles Evans Hughes* (Cambridge, Mass., 1973). None are particularly memorable in the annals of American letters, but all give insight into their authors. Roosevelt's chapter on his governorship, while not to be believed in its entirety, is extremely perceptive on such subjects as Platt's leadership, Roosevelt's own relations with the boss, and the passage of the franchise tax law in 1899. Platt's *Autobiography*, composed with assistance late in life, is replete with inaccuracies, but parts of it provide remarkably candid and revealing accounts of events from the boss's point of view. Hughes's brief *Autobiographical Notes* is less useful than the memoirs of Roosevelt and Platt, but it does illuminate aspects of his roles as investigator and governor.

Besides these three autobiographies, a number of others, cited in the Notes, proved useful. These include the memoirs of Matthew P. Breen, Charles H. Parkhurst, George B. McClellan, Jr., Perry Belmont, and Chauncey M. Depew. A special word is needed about *The Autobiography of Lincoln Steffens* (New York, 1931). Where most autobiographies are turgid and shallow, Steffens's is probably the single most brilliant book on United States politics in the period studied here. It offers much insight into New York affairs, and Theodore Roosevelt in particular, and it suggested a way of understanding the "discoveries" of 1905 that decisively shaped my interpretation of them.

Published Letters and Speeches. Several published letter collections aided this study, but none matched in usefulness the magnificent *Letters of Theodore Roosevelt,* noted above. Since the analysis of political rhetoric forms an important element of my effort to dissect party strategy, speeches provided essential sources. Many of them must be ferreted out of newspapers and manuscript collections, but many too are published. For the organization Republican point of view, I found the collected speeches of Frank S. Black, Chauncey M. Depew, and Timothy Woodruff most useful. A good number of Roosevelt's speeches during his campaign for the governorship and afterward may be found in *The Works of Theodore Roosevelt: Memorial Edition,* 24 vols. (New York, 1923–26). Several published volumes of Hughes's speeches supplement those located in the NYPL: Jacob Gould Schurman, ed., *Addresses and Papers of Charles*

Bibliography

Evans Hughes (New York, 1908); and Charles Evans Hughes, *Conditions of Progress in Democratic Government* (New Haven, 1910).

Studies of New York State Politics. The political history of New York State in the 1890s and early 1900s is scarcely unexplored territory, and I have relied heavily on previous work by scholars. All of the most useful studies are cited in the Notes.

There are four books, however, that require special mention, both because they are excellent and because I relied on them so frequently. Harold F. Gosnell's *Boss Platt and His New York Machine: A Study of the Political Leadership of Thomas C. Platt, Theodore Roosevelt, and Others* (Chicago, 1924) is rightly considered a classic in the literature of party bosses and machines. Despite my access to many manuscript materials that were unavailable to Gosnell, I found myself able to add little to his basic account of how Platt directed the Republican organization. Three more recent studies together cover most of the era this book treats: Samuel T. McSeveney, *The Politics of Depression: Political Behavior in the Northeast, 1893–1896* (New York, 1972); G. Wallace Chessman, *Governor Theodore Roosevelt: The Albany Apprenticeship, 1898–1900* (Cambridge, Mass., 1965); and Robert F. Wesser, *Charles Evans Hughes: Politics and Reform in New York, 1905–1910* (Ithaca, 1967). McSeveney's study, which, besides New York, also explores New Jersey and Connecticut, brilliantly analyzes voting patterns and campaign appeals during the years when the Republicans assembled their majority. Chessman's book excellently narrates Roosevelt's election to the governorship in 1898 and his subsequent administration of the office. Wesser's beautifully written work does the same thing, just as well, for the Hughes years. I began my research by following the footnotes in these three books, and I was not misled.

MANUSCRIPT COLLECTIONS

George B. Agnew, Manuscripts and Archives Division, The New York Public Library, Astor, Lenox and Tilden Foundations
George Washington Aldridge, Rochester Public Library
Willard Bartlett, Columbia University Libraries
Beer Family, Yale University Library
Frank S. Black, New York State Library
Charles Hazen Blood, Cornell University Libraries
Richard Rogers Bowker, Manuscripts and Archives Division, The New York Public Library, Astor, Lenox and Tilden Foundations
Buffalo Republican League, Buffalo and Erie County Historical Society, Buffalo, New York

George Lincoln Burr, Cornell University Libraries

Silas W. Burt, Manuscripts and Archives Division, The New York Public Library, Astor, Lenox and Tilden Foundations; New York Historical Society

Nicholas Murray Butler, Columbia University Libraries

Chautauqua County Republican Committee Minute Book, Chautauqua County Historical Society, Westfield, New York (microfilm copy at Cornell University Libraries)

Joseph H. Choate, Library of Congress

Citizens' Union, Columbia University Libraries

City Club of New York, Manuscripts and Archives Division, The New York Public Library, Astor, Lenox and Tilden Foundations; New-York Historical Society

City Reform Club Minutes, Manuscripts and Archives Division, The New York Public Library, Astor, Lenox and Tilden Foundations

Grover Cleveland, Library of Congress

Ashley W. Cole, Manuscripts and Archives Division, The New York Public Library, Astor, Lenox and Tilden Foundations; George Arents Research Library for Special Collections at Syracuse University

Columbia Oral History Collection, Columbia University Libraries, "Reminiscences" of William Stiles Bennet, Frederick M. Davenport, Murray T. Quigg, Frederick C. Tanner, James W. Wadsworth; copyright © 1972, 1975, 1980, 1972, 1975 respectively, by The Trustees of Columbia University in the City of New York

George B. Cortelyou, Library of Congress

John C. Davies, Cornell University Libraries

Gherardi Davis, Manuscripts and Archives Division, The New York Public Library, Astor, Lenox and Tilden Foundations

Delaware and Hudson Railroad Corporation, New York State Library

Chauncey M. Depew, Yale University Library; Library of Congress

Equitable Life Assurance Society Collection, Baker Library, Harvard University Graduate School of Business Administration

Hamilton Fish, private

Richard Watson Gilder, Manuscripts and Archives Division, The New York Public Library, Astor, Lenox and Tilden Foundations

Harold F. Gosnell, Interviews relating to the career of Thomas C. Platt, Columbia University Libraries

Andrew H. Green, Manuscripts and Archives Division, The New York Public Library, Astor, Lenox and Tilden Foundations

Francis Vinton Greene, Manuscripts and Archives Division, The New York Public Library, Astor, Lenox and Tilden Foundations

John R. Hazel, Buffalo and Erie County Historical Society

Frank Wayland Higgins, George Arents Research Library for Special Collections at Syracuse University

David B. Hill, Manuscripts and Archives Division, The New York Public Library, Astor, Lenox and Tilden Foundations; New York State Library; George Arents Research Library for Special Collections at Syracuse University

Charles D. Hilles, Yale University Library

Bibliography

Frederick W. Holls, Columbia University Libraries

Charles Evans Hughes, Library of Congress; Manuscripts and Archives Division, The New York Public Library, Astor, Lenox and Tilden Foundations

Seth Low, Columbia University Libraries

William McKinley, Library of Congress

John E. Milholland, New York State Historical Association, Hancock House, Ticonderoga, New York

Levi P. Morton, Manuscripts and Archives Division, The New York Public Library, Astor, Lenox and Tilden Foundations

New York Board of Trade and Transportation, New-York Historical Society

New York Central Railroad Company Corporate Records, George Arents Research Library for Special Collections at Syracuse University

New York State Civil Service Reform Association, Cornell University Libraries

Samuel Frederick Nixon, Chautauqua County Historical Society (microfilm copy at Cornell University Libraries)

Benjamin Barker Odell, Jr., Manuscripts and Archives Division, The New York Public Library, Astor, Lenox and Tilden Foundations

Herbert Parsons, Columbia University Libraries

George W. Perkins, Columbia University Libraries

Thomas Collier Platt, Yale University Library; private; New York State Library

Lemuel Ely Quigg, Manuscripts and Archives Division, The New York Public Library, Astor, Lenox and Tilden Foundations; New-York Historical Society

Whitelaw Reid, Library of Congress

James A. Roberts and Frank S. Sidway, Buffalo and Erie County Historical Society

Theodore Roosevelt, Harvard College Library; Library of Congress

Elihu Root, Library of Congress; George Arents Research Library for Special Collections at Syracuse University

Gustav Scholer, Manuscripts and Archives Division, The New York Public Library, Astor, Lenox and Tilden Foundations

Jacob Gould Schurman, Cornell University Libraries

James Rockwell Sheffield, Yale University Library

Edward Morse Shepard, Columbia University Libraries

James S. Sherman, Manuscripts and Archives Division, The New York Public Library, Astor, Lenox and Tilden Foundations

Edwin Crowell Stewart, Cornell University Libraries

Henry Lewis Stimson, Yale University Library

William Sulzer, Cornell University Libraries

Benjamin F. Tracy, Library of Congress

University Settlement Society of New York City, State Historical Society of Wisconsin, Madison, Wisconsin

James W. Wadsworth, Jr., Library of Congress

Jonathan M. Wainwright, New-York Historical Society

Richard Ward Greene Welling, Manuscripts and Archives Division, The New York Public Library, Astor, Lenox and Tilden Foundations

Everett P. Wheeler, Manuscripts and Archives Division, The New York Public Library, Astor, Lenox and Tilden Foundations

Andrew D. White, Cornell University Libraries
Horace N. White, George Arents Research Library for Special Collections at Syracuse University
Timothy Shaler Williams, Manuscripts and Archives Division, The New York Public Library, Astor, Lenox and Tilden Foundations

NEWSPAPERS

Dailies

Albany Evening Journal, 1894–1905
Albany *Times-Union,* 1905
Auburn Daily Advertiser, 1897–98, 1905
Brooklyn Daily Eagle, 1893–94
Buffalo Commercial, 1893–1905
Buffalo Courier, 1893–94
Buffalo Daily Times, 1897, 1902
Buffalo Enquirer, 1904
Buffalo Evening News, 1895–1905
Buffalo Morning Express, 1893, 1895, 1901
Elmira Daily Advertiser, 1905
Ithaca Daily Journal, 1893–1910
New York *Commercial Advertiser,* 1894
New York *Evening Post,* 1894, 1898
New York Herald, 1894, 1897–98, 1905–6
New York *Press,* 1894–95, 1901
New York *Sun,* 1893–1906
New York Times, 1890–1910
New York Tribune, 1893–1910
New York *World,* 1894
Norwich Sun, 1905–6
Owego Daily Record, 1897–1902
Rochester *Democrat and Chronicle,* 1901, 1905–6
Syracuse *Evening Herald,* 1894–1905
Syracuse *Post-Standard,* 1901–5
Troy Daily Times, 1894–1904
Watertown Daily Times, 1898, 1905

Weeklies

Adirondack News (St. Regis Falls), 1905
Boonville Herald, 1894–1908
Canton *Commercial Advertiser,* 1894, 1905–6
Cayuga Chief (Weedsport), 1893–1904
Cobleskill Index, 1894

Bibliography

Cortland Democrat, 1893–94, 1902, 1905
Essex County Republican (Port Henry and Keesville), 1894–1900
Fredonia Censor, 1894–1910
Hammond Advertiser, 1908, 1910
Jamestown Sun, 1889–90
Jefferson Courier, 1894
Lowville *Journal and Republican,* 1905–6
Malone Paladium, 1897–1908
Massena Observer, 1905–6
Orange County Times (Middletown, semiweekly), 1905
St. Lawrence Plaindealer (Canton), 1893–1910
Schoharie Republican, 1894
Steuben Courier (Bath), 1905–6
Waverly Free Press, 1902–5, 1909
Yates County Chronicle (Penn Yan), 1897–1910

Notes

1. Nineteenth-Century Politics in Decline

1. On the nondevelopmental qualities of American politics, see Samuel P. Huntington, *Political Order in Changing Societies* (New Haven, 1968), pp. 93–139; and Walter Dean Burnham, *Critical Elections and the Mainsprings of American Politics* (New York, 1970), pp. 175–93.

2. Richard P. McCormick, "New Perspectives on Jacksonian Politics," *AHR* 65 (Jan. 1960): 288–301; Walter Dean Burnham, "The Changing Shape of the American Political Universe," *APSR* 59 (March 1965): 7–28. Richard L. McCormick, "The Party Period and Public Policy: An Exploratory Hypothesis," *JAH* 66 (Sept. 1979): 279–98, presents in more detail the interpretation of nineteenth-century politics set forth here.

3. Lee Benson, *The Concept of Jacksonian Democracy: New York as a Test Case* (Princeton, 1961); Paul Kleppner, *The Cross of Culture: A Social Analysis of Midwestern Politics, 1850–1900* (New York, 1970); Richard Jensen, *The Winning of the Midwest: Social and Political Conflict, 1888–1896* (Chicago, 1971); Ronald P. Formisano, *The Birth of Mass Political Parties: Michigan, 1827–1861* (Princeton, 1971); Michael F. Holt, *Forging a Majority: The Formation of the Republican Party in Pittsburgh, 1848–1860* (New Haven, 1969); Samuel T. McSeveney, *The Politics of Depression: Political Behavior in the Northeast, 1893–1896* (New York, 1972).

4. On the responsiveness of the nineteenth-century political system, see Morton Keller, "The Politicos Reconsidered," *Perspectives in American History* 1 (1967): 401–8.

5. Michael F. Holt, *The Political Crisis of the 1850s* (New York, 1978), pp. 39–66; Ballard C. Campbell, "Did Democracy Work? Prohibition in Late Nineteenth-Century Iowa: A Test Case," *Journal of Interdisciplinary History* 8 (Summer 1977): 87–116; Jensen, *Winning of the Midwest*, pp. 89–121.

6. The concept of distributive policies employed here is based on Theodore J. Lowi's seminal typology of policy outputs presented in his article "American Business, Public Policy, Case-Studies, and Political Theory," *World Politics* 16 (July 1965): 677–715. See also: James Willard Hurst, *Law and the Conditions of Freedom in the Nineteenth-Century United States* (Madison, 1956); Carter Goodrich, *Government Promotion of American Canals and Railroads, 1800–1890* (New York, 1960); Louis Hartz, *Economic Policy and Democratic Thought: Pennsylvania, 1766–1860* (Cambridge, Mass., 1948); Oscar and Mary Flug Handlin, *Commonwealth: A Study of the Role of Government in the American Economy: Massachusetts, 1774–1861* (New York, 1947); and Harry N. Scheiber, *Ohio Canal*

Era: A Case Study of Government and the Economy, 1820–1861 (Athens, Ohio, 1969).

7. Several recent studies of nineteenth-century politics point to the centrality of the urge to secure liberty against governmental authority: J. Mills Thornton III, *Politics and Power in a Slave Society: Alabama, 1800–1860* (Baton Rouge, 1978); Holt, *Political Crisis*; and Lloyd Ray Gunn, "The Decline of Authority: Public Policy in New York, 1837–1860," Ph.D. diss., Rutgers University, 1975.

8. Harry N. Scheiber, "Federalism and the American Economic Order, 1789–1910," *Law and Society Review* 10 (Fall 1975): 89; Lowi, "American Business," pp. 690–95.

9. Robert A. Lively, "The American System: A Review Article," *Business History Review* 29 (1955): 94; Carter Goodrich, "The Revulsion against Internal Improvements," *Journal of Economic History* 10 (Nov. 1950): 169; Michael H. Frisch, *Town into City: Springfield, Massachusetts, and the Meaning of Community, 1840–1880* (Cambridge, Mass., 1972).

10. Wallace D. Farnham, "'The Weakened Spring of Government': A Study in Nineteenth-Century American History," *AHR* 68 (April 1963): 662–80; Morton Keller, *Affairs of State: Public Life in Late Nineteenth Century America* (Cambridge, Mass., 1977), pp. 171–81, 409–38; Leonard D. White, *The Jacksonians: A Study in Administrative History, 1829–1861* (New York, 1954); Leonard D. White, *The Republican Era: A Study in Administrative History, 1869–1901* (New York, 1958); Gerald D. Nash, *State Government and Economic Development: A History of Administrative Policies in California, 1849–1933* (Berkeley, 1964); James Willard Hurst, "Legal Elements in United States History," *Perspectives in American History* 5 (1971): 63.

11. Hurst, *Law and the Conditions of Freedom*, p. 73.

12. Lee Benson, "Research Problems in American Political Historiography," in Mirra Komarovsky, ed., *Common Frontiers of the Social Sciences* (Glencoe, Ill., 1957), pp. 123–46; McSeveney, *Politics of Depression*, pp. 3–31; Lee Benson, Joel H. Silbey, and Phyllis F. Field, "Toward a Theory of Stability and Change in American Voting Patterns: New York State, 1792–1970," in Joel H. Silbey, Allan G. Bogue, and William H. Flanigan, eds., *The History of American Electoral Behavior* (Princeton, 1978), pp. 91–94; Albert C. E. Parker, "Empire Stalemate: Voting Behavior in New York State, 1860–1892," Ph.D. diss., Washington University, 1975.

13. Harold F. Gosnell, *Boss Platt and His New York Machine: A Study of the Political Leadership of Thomas C. Platt, Theodore Roosevelt, and Others* (Chicago, 1924), pp. 12–38; Herbert J. Bass, *"I Am a Democrat": The Political Career of David Bennett Hill* (Syracuse, 1961); DeAlva Stanwood Alexander, *Four Famous New Yorkers: The Political Careers of Cleveland, Platt, Hill and Roosevelt* (New York, 1923); McSeveney, *Politics of Depression*, pp. 3–31.

14. Noble E. Whitford, *History of the Canal System of the State of New York*, 2 vols. (Albany, 1906); Jeremy P. Felt, *Hostages of Fortune: Child Labor Reform in New York State* (Syracuse, 1965), pp. 17–37; Morton Keller, *The Life Insurance Enterprise, 1885–1910: A Study in the Limits of Corporate Power* (Cambridge, Mass., 1963), pp. 194–226; Lee Benson, *Merchants, Farmers & Railroads: Railroad Regulation and New York Politics, 1850–1887* (Cambridge, Mass., 1955), pp. 172–73.

15. D. W. Meinig, "Elaboration and Change, 1850's–1960's," in John H. Thompson, ed., *Geography of New York State* (Syracuse, 1966), pp. 179–81, 184.

16. Meinig, "Elaboration and Change," pp. 179–81, 184; U.S. Department of Commerce, Bureau of the Census, *Fourteenth Census of the United States: Population* (Washington, D.C., 1922), vol. 2, p. 36.

17. This paragraph is based on chapters 2 and 3 of David C. Hammack, *Power and Society in Greater New York, 1886–1903* (New York, to be published in 1981).

18. Meinig, "Elaboration and Change," pp. 178–79, 183–84.

19. U.S. Department of Commerce, Bureau of the Census, *Fourteenth Census of the United States: Agriculture* (Washington, D.C., 1922), vol. 4, pt. 1, p. 201; Ann Ratner Miller, "Labor Force Trends and Differentials," in Simon Kuznets and Dorothy Swaine Thomas, eds., *Population Redistribution and Economic Growth: United States, 1870–1950,* 3 vols. (Philadelphia, 1957–64), 2: 82; Eric Brunger, "Dairying and Urban Development in New York State, 1850–1900," *Agricultural History* 29 (Oct. 1955): 169–74; Meinig, "Elaboration and Change," pp. 177–78, 183.

20. The large Greenback vote in 1878, however, suggests that under the right circumstances farmers would express their economic grievances by deserting the major parties. That year the Greenback candidate for Court of Appeals judge received 9 percent of the statewide vote and did considerably better than that in some agricultural areas; Benson, *Merchants, Farmers & Railroads,* pp. 102–4; *Trib. Alm.* (1879), p. 87.

21. Martin J. Schiesl, *The Politics of Efficiency: Municipal Administration and Reform in America, 1880–1920* (Berkeley, 1977), pp. 6–67; Harold Coffin Syrett, *The City of Brooklyn, 1865–1898: A Political History* (New York, 1944), pp. 87–179; Gerald Kurland, *Seth Low: The Reformer in an Urban and Industrial Age* (New York, 1971), pp. 25–49; Robert Muccigrosso, "The City Reform Club: A Study in Late Nineteenth-Century Reform," *New-York Historical Society Quarterly* 52 (July 1968): 235–54; Martin Shefter, "The Electoral Foundations of the Political Machine: New York City, 1884–1897," in Silbey, Bogue, and Flanigan, eds., *History of American Electoral Behavior,* pp. 263–98.

22. Gustavus Myers, "History of Public Franchises in New York City," *Municipal Affairs* 4 (1900): 99–101; Blake McKelvey, *Rochester: The Quest for Quality, 1890–1925* (Cambridge, Mass., 1956), pp. 250–56; Helen G. Ebersole, *Electricity and Politics in Jamestown, New York, 1891–1931* (Jamestown, 1973), pp. 3–11; *Jamestown Sun,* Oct. 1889–Oct. 1890.

23. *Ninth Annual Report of the Bureau of Statistics of Labor* (Albany, 1892), pt. 2, p. 1080; Howard Lawrence Hurwitz, *Theodore Roosevelt and Labor in New York State, 1880–1900* (New York, 1943), pp. 25–30, 36–49, 114–45; Irwin Yellowitz, *Labor and the Progressive Movement in New York State, 1897–1916* (Ithaca, 1965), pp. 22–23; Thomas J. Condon, "Politics, Reform and the New York City Election of 1886," *New-York Historical Society Quarterly* 44 (Oct. 1960): 363–93; Louis F. Post and Fred C. Leubuscher, eds., *Henry George's 1886 Campaign* (New York, 1887); Samuel Gompers, *Seventy Years of Life and Labor: An Autobiography,* 2 vols. (New York, 1925), 1: 311–26; Shefter, "Electoral Foundations," pp. 289–90; *Trib. Alm.* (1887, 1888).

24. Benson, *Merchants, Farmers & Railroads.*

25. Bass, *"I Am a Democrat,"* pp. 61–65, 94–96, 115–19, 130–31, 135–37; McSeveney, *Politics of Depression,* p. 24; John Joseph Coffey, "A Political History of the Temperance Movement in New York State, 1808–1912," Ph.D. diss., Pennsylvania State University, 1976, pp. 177–202; *Trib. Alm.* (1889), p. 98.

26. McSeveney, *Politics of Depression,* pp. 3–31. Other recent treatments of late-nineteenth-century politics have also emphasized the ideological differences between the parties; see R. Hal Williams, " 'Dry Bones and Dead Language': The Democratic Party," in H. Wayne Morgan, ed., *The Gilded Age* (Syracuse, 1970), pp. 129–48; Lewis L. Gould, "The Republican Search for a National Majority," in *ibid.,* pp. 171–98; Kleppner, *Cross of Culture*; and Jensen, *Winning of the Midwest.*

27. The annual messages of New York's Democratic governors, Grover Cleveland (1883–84) and David B. Hill (1885–91), included frequent endorsements of state aid to a variety of industries, such as banking and agriculture, and regular pleas for government assistance in providing the transportation facilities needed by the state's producing interests; Charles Z. Lincoln, ed., *Messages from the Governors,* 11 vols. (Albany, 1909), 7: 945; 8: 7, 164, 923–26, 1068–69.

28. McCormick, "Party Period and Public Policy."

29. For similar accounts of the limitations of "reform" in the 1880s, see Robert H. Wiebe, *The Search for Order, 1877–1920* (New York, 1967), pp. 44–75; Samuel P. Hays, *The Response to Industrialism, 1885–1914* (Chicago, 1957), pp. 24–47; and David P. Thelen, *The New Citizenship: Origins of Progressivism in Wisconsin, 1885–1900* (Columbia, Mo., 1972), pp. 5–54.

30. Carl N. Degler, "American Political Parties and the Rise of the City: An Interpretation," *JAH* 51 (June 1964): 41–59; Gould, "Republican Search for a National Majority"; Jensen, *Winning of the Midwest,* pp. 269–308; Kleppner, *Cross of Culture*; McSeveney, *Politics of Depression.*

31. On symbolic politics see David Easton, *A Systems Analysis of Political Life* (New York, 1965); Murray Edelman, *The Symbolic Uses of Politics* (Urbana, Ill., 1964); and John C. Wahlke, "Policy Demands and System Support: The Role of the Represented," *British Journal of Political Science* 1 (July 1971): 271–90.

2. Democratic Crisis and Republican Ascendancy

1. Several of the most excellent and imaginative works on the electoral realignment of the 1890s have suggested that it marked a fundamental turning point, not simply in the partisan balance of power, but also in the nature and structure of politics and governance: Walter Dean Burnham, *Critical Elections and the Mainsprings of American Politics* (New York, 1970); Paul Kleppner, *The Cross of Culture: A Social Analysis of Midwestern Politics, 1850–1900* (New York, 1970); Richard Jensen, *The Winning of the Midwest: Social and Political Conflict, 1888–1896* (Chicago, 1971); and Samuel T. McSeveney, *The Politics of Depression: Political Behavior in the Northeast, 1893–1896* (New York, 1972).

2. McSeveney, *Politics of Depression,* provides the definitive study of these elections in New York State.

3. V. O. Key's seminal article, "A Theory of Critical Elections," *Journal of Politics* 17 (Feb. 1955): 3–18, took brief note of some shifting in 1894 but devoted most attention to 1896 itself. The more recent studies have traced the seeds of the upheaval back to the late 1880s: Kleppner, *Cross of Culture*; Jensen, *Winning of the Midwest*; McSeveney, *Politics of Depression*; Robert D. Marcus, *Grand Old Party: Political Structure in the Gilded Age, 1880–1896* (New York, 1971), pp. 151–94; and J. Rogers Hollingsworth, *The Whirligig of Politics: The Democracy of Cleveland and Bryan* (Chicago, 1963), pp. 1–9.

4. Herbert J. Bass, *"I Am a Democrat": The Political Career of David Bennett*

Hill (Syracuse, 1961), pp. 191–239; DeAlva Stanwood Alexander, *Four Famous New Yorkers: The Political Careers of Cleveland, Platt, Hill and Roosevelt* (New York, 1923), pp. 158–92; McSeveney, *Politics of Depression*, p. 44; Timothy Shaler Williams to Robert L. Miller, Oct. 17, 1892, Williams Papers; *NYT*, Nov. 9, 1892.

5. Bass, *"I Am a Democrat"*; McSeveney, *Politics of Depression*, pp. 11–12, 16–17; William C. Hudson, *Random Recollections of an Old Political Reporter* (New York, 1911), pp. 252–71.

6. *NYT*, March 20, 1893; Frank P. Demarest to Hill, Feb. 8, 1893; H. A. Reeves to Hill, Sept. 18, 1893; Francis A. Willard to Hill, Sept. 27, 1893, Hill Papers, NYSL; Grover Cleveland to Edward M. Shepard, April 4, 1894, in Allan Nevins, ed., *Letters of Grover Cleveland, 1850–1908* (New York, 1933), p. 349; Hill to Isaac H. Maynard, Oct. 4, 1893, Hill Papers, NYPL; Timothy Shaler Williams to George Cary Eggleston, Nov. 18, 1892; Williams to G. S. Fanning, Sept. 18, 1893; Williams to William F. Sheehan, Oct. 18, 1893; Williams to Maynard, Nov. 2, 1893; Maynard to Williams, Nov. 5, 1893, Williams Papers; Frederick W. Holls to Andrew D. White, Feb. 27, 1893, Holls Papers; Alexander, *Four Famous New Yorkers*, pp. 193–99; McSeveney, *Politics of Depression*, pp. 42–45.

7. Martin Shefter, "The Electoral Foundations of the Political Machine: New York City, 1884–1897," in Joel H. Silbey, Allan G. Bogue, and William H. Flanigan, eds., *The History of American Electoral Behavior* (Princeton, 1978), pp. 263–98; Richard Croker, "Tammany Hall and the Democracy," *North American Review* 154 (Feb. 1892): 225–30; Matthew P. Breen, *Thirty Years of New York Politics Up-to-Date* (New York, 1899), pp. 765–70; *NYT*, Nov. 7, 1888, Nov. 4, 1891.

8. *NYT*, April 17, 18, 19, 20, 21, 22, May 3, 5, 12, June 20, Oct. 9 (quote), 18, 19, 30, Nov. 3, 5, 7, 1893; *Buffalo Commercial*, Oct. 17, 21, 23, 25, 27, 31, Nov. 7, 1893; *Trib.*, Nov. 3, 1893; Brenda K. Shelton, *Reformers in Search of Yesterday: Buffalo in the 1890s* (Albany, 1976), pp. 55–56; McSeveney, *Politics of Depression*, p. 43.

9. *Brooklyn Daily Eagle*, Oct. 16–30 (quote Oct. 19), Nov. 1–7, 1893; *Trib.*, Nov. 3, 6, 9, 1893; Edward M. Shepard, "The Brooklyn Idea in City Government," *Forum* 16 (Sept. 1893): 38–47; Harold Coffin Syrett, *The City of Brooklyn, 1865–1898: A Political History* (New York, 1944), pp. 219–24.

10. *NYT*, Nov. 8, 9, 10, 1893; *Trib.*, Nov. 11, Dec. 4, 1893; *Brooklyn Daily Eagle*, Nov. 8, 9, 1893; *Buffalo Commercial*, Nov. 8, 9, 11, 1893; *Buffalo Morning Express*, Nov. 11, 1893; *Buffalo Courier*, Nov. 8, 10, 1893; *Ithaca Daily Journal*, Nov. 8, 1893; *Cortland Democrat*, Nov. 10, 17, 1893; *SLP*, Nov. 15, 1893; *Review of Reviews* 8 (Dec. 1893): 630; Alexander, *Four Famous New Yorkers*, pp. 199–203; McSeveney, *Politics of Depression*, pp. 49–55.

11. *NYT*, Nov. 19, 1893, March 21, April 7, 11, 1894; *AEJ*, April 7, 11, 1894; William Barnes, Jr., to Thomas Collier Platt, March 22, 1894, March 23, 1894, Platt Papers, Yale; Robert Emmett O'Connor, "William Barnes, Jr.: A Conservative Encounters the Progressive Era," Ph.D. diss., SUNY at Albany, 1971, pp. 24–25; National Municipal League, *Proceedings of the National Conference for Good City Government* (Philadelphia, 1894), pp. 323–24; William Howe Tolman, *Municipal Reform Movements in the United States* (New York, 1895), pp. 81–82.

12. *TDT*, Feb. 14, 15, 19, 20, 28, March 1, 3, 6, 7, 8, 9 (headline), 13 (quote), 14, Oct. 30, Nov. 8, 1894; *NYT*, March 6, 7, 8, 9, 16, July 11, 12, 1894; *Trib.*, April 2, May 24, 1894; Tolman, *Municipal Reform Movements*, pp. 71–72.

13. Three of the most useful accounts of late-nineteenth-century reform from the Tweed era to 1894 are: Seymour J. Mandelbaum, *Boss Tweed's New York* (New York, 1965); Allan Nevins, *Abram S. Hewitt With Some Account of Peter Cooper* (New York, 1935); and Richard Stephen Skolnik, "The Crystallization of Reform in New York City, 1890–1917," Ph.D. diss., Yale University, 1964.

14. Skolnik, "Crystallization of Reform," pp. 148–49; John D. Townsend, *New York in Bondage* (New York, 1901), pp. 196–207; *Nation* 58 (March 3, 1894): 170–71; John W. Goff, "Juggling with the Ballot," *North American Review* 158 (Feb. 1894): 203–10.

15. Charles H. Parkhurst, *Our Fight With Tammany* (New York, 1895), p. 5; Lincoln Steffens, *The Autobiography of Lincoln Steffens* (New York, 1931), pp. 215–20, 247–54; Tolman, *Municipal Reform Movements,* pp. 15–23, 183–219; "Report of the Special Committee Appointed to Investigate the Police Department of the City of New York," *Senate Documents,* No. 25 (Albany, 1895); *Auto. TCP,* pp. 231–39; James F. Richardson, *The New York Police: Colonial Times to 1901* (New York, 1970), pp. 232–40; Skolnik, "Crystallization of Reform," pp. 149–59.

16. *NYT,* June 12, 13, 21, July 1, 15, 23, 24, 27, 30, Aug. 2, Sept. 5, 16, 17, 18, 20, 29, Oct. 5, 6, 7, 10, 11, 12, 15, Nov. 3, 5, 1894; *Trib.,* June 15, 18, 22, 28, 29, 30, July 23, Oct. 10, 13, 1894; New York *Sun,* Oct. 7, 1894; *Auto. TCP,* pp. 268–85; *Trib. Alm.* (1895), pp. 324–25; McSeveney, *Politics of Depression,* pp. 100-103; Skolnik, "Crystallization of Reform," pp. 159–69.

17. City Reform Club Minutes, 1890–93, NYPL; William G. Low, "Municipal Government of Brooklyn," NML, *Proceedings* (1894), pp. 72–79; Edmond Kelly, "Municipal Government of New York," *ibid.,* pp. 103–10; W. Harris Roome, "The Separation of Municipal from Other Elections," *ibid.,* pp. 144–51. New York *Evening Post,* June 1, 12, 18, July 28, Sept. 21, Nov. 2, 1894; *NYT,* June 4, 8, Aug. 4, Nov. 5, 1894; *Buffalo Commercial,* Oct. 31, Nov. 11, 1893, Nov. 7, 9, 1894; *Buffalo Courier,* Nov. 1, 7, 10, 1893, Nov. 8, 1894; *Brooklyn Daily Eagle,* Nov. 20, 1893; *AEJ,* April 7, 11, 1894; *TDT,* Feb. 20, March 1, 3, 8, Nov. 7, 8, 1894. Nonpartisan municipal government also commanded scholarly attention in these years: Abram C. Bernheim, "The Relations of the City and the State of New York," *PSQ* 9 (Sept. 1894): 377–402; and Frank J. Goodnow, *Municipal Home Rule: A Study in Administration* (New York, 1895).

18. Record of Activities of the City Club of New York, 1892–1922, compiled by William F. Howes, typescript, City Club Papers, NYPL; *The Purpose of the Good Government Clubs* (New York, June 1, 1894), a flyer, Richard Ward Greene Welling Papers. Both Tolman, *Municipal Reform Movements* (quote 100), and NML, *Proceedings* (1894), contain brief sketches of the different cities' municipal associations.

19. A number of recent studies document both the upper-class origins of municipal reform in the 1890s and the divisions among the leaders on social and economic questions: David Conrad Hammack, "Participation in Major Decisions in New York City, 1890–1900: The Creation of Greater New York and the Centralization of the Public School System," Ph.D. diss., Columbia University, 1973; Shelton, *Reformers in Search of Yesterday*; Skolnik, "Crystallization of Reform"; and Martin J. Schiesl, *The Politics of Efficiency: Municipal Administration and Reform in America, 1880–1920* (Berkeley, 1977).

20. Kelly, "Municipal Government of New York," pp. 108–10; "Committee of Seventy's Platform," New York State Civil Service Reform Association Papers; Tolman, *Municipal Reform Movements,* pp. 43, 137–38; *Brooklyn Daily Eagle,*

Nov. 9, 1893; McSeveney, *Politics of Depression*, pp. 101–2; Shelton, *Reformers in Search of Yesterday*, p. 61.

21. Hill to Timothy Shaler Williams, March 17, 1894, Williams Papers.

22. Charles Manfred Thompson, "Attitude of the Western Whigs Toward the Convention System," *Proceedings of the Mississippi Valley Historical Association* 5 (1911–12): 167–89; Ronald P. Formisano, "Political Character, Antipartyism and the Second American Party System," *American Quarterly* 21 (Winter 1969): 683–709; Michael F. Holt, "The Politics of Impatience: The Origins of Know Nothingism," *JAH* 60 (Sept. 1973): 309–31; John G. Sproat, *"The Best Men": Liberal Reformers in the Gilded Age* (New York, 1968); Gerald W. McFarland, *Mugwumps, Morals and Politics, 1884–1920* (Amherst, Mass., 1975). For some representative independent opinions of the 1880s and early 1890s, see F. W. Whitridge, "A Brake on the Machine," *International Review* 8 (March 1880): 242–52; Dorman B. Eaton, "Parties and Independents," *North American Review* 144 (June 1887): 549–64; "Regularity and Independence," *Century Magazine* 44 (May 1892): 156; and "The 'Mugwump,'" *Harper's Weekly* 38 (April 14, 1894): 337–38. Seth Low to Edward M. Shepard, Feb. 22, 1893, Shepard Papers.

23. Platt to Howard Conkling, June 12, 1893 (quote); Platt to William Smyth, April 14, 1893, Platt Papers, private; Harold F. Gosnell, *Boss Platt and His New York Machine: A Study of the Political Leadership of Thomas C. Platt, Theodore Roosevelt, and Others* (Chicago, 1924), pp. 39–54; *Trib.*, Nov. 7, 1893; *Buffalo Commercial*, Oct. 17, 19, 21, 23, 25, 27, Nov. 4, 6, 1893; *Buffalo Morning Express*, Oct. 28, Nov. 4 (quote), 7, 11, 1893; *Trib. Alm.* (1894), p. 65 (quote).

24. "Report of the Special Committee of the Senate in the Investigation of the Election Methods in the Various Cities and Villages of the State," *Senate Documents*, No. 34 (Albany, 1895), p. 4; *Harper's Weekly* 38 (June 16, 1894): 555; *Review of Reviews* 10 (July 1894): 11; *NYT*, June 16 (quote), July 11, 12, 1894.

25. The three most recent studies of the 1894 constitutional convention are: McSeveney, *Politics of Depression*, pp. 63–86; Robert Crosby Eager, "Governing New York State: Republicans and Reform, 1894–1900," Ph.D. diss., Stanford University, 1977, pp. 2–55; and Richard L. McCormick, "Shaping Republican Strategy: Political Change in New York State, 1893–1910," Ph.D. diss., Yale University, 1976, pp. 44–86. The *Revised Record of the Constitutional Convention of the State of New York, May 8, 1894, to September 29, 1894*, 5 vols. (Albany, 1900) is the indispensable source for studying the convention and its debates [hereafter cited as *R.R.C.C.*].

26. *Harper's Weekly* 38 (May 26, 1894): 484, (June 2, 1894): 507; New York *Evening Post*, May 8, 1894; Canton *Commercial Advertiser*, May 16, 1894; *Trib.*, May 10, Sept. 3, 1894; *NYT*, Nov. 11, 1893; Rochester *Post-Express*, Sept. 5, 1894. The *Convention Manual of Procedure, Forms and Rules for the Regulation of Business in the Sixth New York State Constitutional Convention, 1894*, pt. 1, vol. 2: *Delegates' Manual and Introduction* (Albany, 1894), contains biographical sketches of all the delegates; comparative data on the legislators of 1894 may be found in *Red Book* (1894). Eaton to George McAneny, April 11, 1896, New York State Civil Service Reform Association Papers.

27. State of New York, *In Convention. Proposed Constitutional Amendments*, 3 vols. (n.p., 1894), gives the texts of all the amendments (numbering about four hundred) that the convention received for consideration; *R.R.C.C.*, 5: 1007–76, summarizes the disposition of the amendments.

28. Holls to John I. Gilbert, Jan. 29, 1894; Holls to Andrew D. White, June 25,

1894 (quote), Oct. 27, 1894, Holls Papers; Charles E. Fitch, "New York's Constitutional Convention," *Harper's Weekly* 38 (April 14, 1894): 347.

29. All three amendments were adopted by heavily partisan votes:

	Ayes		Noes	
	Republican	Democratic	Republican	Democratic
secrecy in voting	76	12	19	38
citizenship and voting	98	4	0	54
registration	97	6	0	45

R.R.C.C., 4: 447–48, 478, 724–25. Detailed accounts of these amendments may be found in Charles Z. Lincoln, *The Constitutional History of New York,* 5 vols. (Rochester, 1906), 3: 74–81, 91–106, 108–14. New York *Evening Post,* May 28, June 25 (quote), 1894.

30. *NYT,* March 3, May 8, 18, July 27, 28, 1894; New York *Evening Post,* June 1, 18, July 19, 28, 1894; *Harper's Weekly* 38 (May 26, 1894): 484; *Nation* 58 (June 7, 1894): 422–23, (June 14, 1894): 438; H. L. Nelson to Edward M. Shepard, April 6, 1894; R. W. G. Welling to Shepard, May 24, 1894, Shepard Papers.

31. New York *Sun,* April 6, 1894; *NYT,* June 13, 1894. A series of letters by Lemuel E. Quigg, a Republican congressman from New York City, shows plainly that leading Republicans were aware of the different meanings attached to the separation-of-elections amendment. Writing to independent-leaning delegates, Quigg stressed that separating elections would promote municipal nonpartisanship; to party regulars he emphasized the advantages to the Republicans; Quigg to W. Harris Roome, Aug. 21, 1894, Aug. 24, 1894; Quigg to Commodore P. Vedder; to Thomas G. Alvord; to Joseph H. Choate; and to Elihu Root, all Aug. 24, 1894, Quigg Papers, NYPL. In the final vote on the amendment, Republican delegates favored it by 85 to 7, while Democrats opposed it by 22 to 33; *R.R.C.C.*, 4: 739–40. McSeveney, *Politics of Depression,* pp. 68–69.

32. *R.R.C.C.*, 2: 239, 244–45, 250, 252–56, 372; 3: 303–4, 309–10, 326–28, 376–82; 4: 985 (quote), 992 (quote). In the final vote the Republicans favored the measure by 87 to 1, while the Democrats opposed it by 6 to 41; *R.R.C.C.*, 4: 1005. *NYT,* Aug. 24, 28, 31, 1894; *Trib.,* Aug. 6, 18, Sept. 3, 1894; New York *Sun,* April 3, 1895. Lincoln, *Constitutional History,* 3: 626–52; Eager, "Governing New York State," pp. 20–32.

33. Jesse Johnson to Edward M. Shepard, Sept. 6, 1894; Shepard to Johnson, Sept. 8, 1894, Shepard Papers; *NYT,* June 8, July 28, Aug. 4 (quote), 8, Nov. 5 (quote), 1894; Rochester *Post-Express,* Sept. 22, 1894; New York *Evening Post,* July 28, Aug. 4, 9, Sept. 21, 1894; *Harper's Weekly* 38 (Aug. 25, 1894): 794; *Nation* 59 (Sept. 27, 1894): 226–27, (Oct. 4, 1894): 241.

34. Richard Watson Gilder to Joseph H. Choate, Nov. 12, 1894; Choate to Gilder, Nov. 14, 1894, Gilder Papers; Andrew D. White to Frederick W. Holls, Oct. 15, 1894, Holls Papers. *Nation* 59 (Oct. 18, 1894): 280–81, (Nov. 15, 1894): 352; *Review of Reviews* 10 (Nov. 1894): 478; *Harper's Weekly* 38 (Sept. 8, 1894): 842–43, (Oct. 6, 1894): 939, (Nov. 3, 1894): 1034; *Century Magazine* 49 (Jan. 1895): 473–74; New York *Evening Post,* Oct. 1, Nov. 2, 5, 1895.

35. A sequence of complicated events took place within the Republican organization of New York City during 1894. After the previous year's election, two groups came forward with party reorganization plans: the Bliss-Root-Choate

"Committee of Thirty" and the self-styled "Anti-Machine Republicans," led by John E. Milholland, a protégé of *Tribune* editor Whitelaw Reid. Each conducted party enrollments, held primary elections, and claimed to be the regular organization. Platt succeeded in playing the two groups off against one another, so that while the supposedly anti-Platt Committee of Thirty was eventually recognized as "regular," matters actually stayed well within Platt's control. The beaten *Tribune* conceded that "the part he [Platt] took in the Republican reorganization which began after the election of 1893 was never surpassed in cleverness—it might indeed be called grand strategy." (Dec. 17, 1894.) All the newspapers in New York City reported on these events throughout the year; scrapbooks in the John E. Milholland Papers include boundless clippings documenting day-to-day developments. Platt's own account in *Auto. TCP,* pp. 253–58, is revealing but incorrect in certain details.

36. William M. Armstrong, ed., *The Gilded Age Letters of E. L. Godkin* (Albany, 1974), pp. 403, 427; New York *Evening Post,* Nov. 2, 5 (quote), 1894; *Public Opinion* 17 (Oct. 11, 1894): 666–67.

37. On the condition of the unemployed and the relief efforts made on their behalf, see Charles D. Kellogg, "The Situation in New York City During the Winter of 1893–1894," *Proceedings of the National Conference of Charities and Correction* (Boston, 1894), pp. 21–30; Carlos C. Closson, Jr., "The Unemployed in American Cities," *Quarterly Journal of Economics* 8 (Jan. and July 1894): 168–217, 257–60, 453–77, 499–502; Albert Shaw, "Relief for the Unemployed in American Cities," *Review of Reviews* 9 (Jan. 1894): 29–37; Albert Shaw, "Relief Measures in American Cities," *Review of Reviews* 9 (Feb. 1894): 179–91; Shelton, *Reformers in Search of Yesterday,* pp. 148–58; Paul T. Ringenbach, *Tramps and Reformers, 1873–1916: The Discovery of Unemployment in New York* (Westport, Conn., 1973), pp. 92–103.

38. Timothy Shaler Williams to Gompers, Sept. 2, 1893; Flower to Williams, Sept. 12, 1893, Williams Papers; *P.P., 1893,* pp. 345–54 (quote 351); Samuel Gompers, *Seventy Years of Life and Labor: An Autobiography,* 2 vols. (New York, 1925), 2: 4; Samuel Rezneck, "Unemployment, Unrest, and Relief in the United States during the Depression of 1893–97," *Journal of Political Economy* 61 (Aug. 1953): 332.

39. *P.P., 1894,* p. 37; *NYT,* Feb. 3, 9, 14, 20, 25, 28, March 6, 14, June 1, 7, 14, 15, Aug. 2, 13, 23, 24, Oct. 15, Nov. 5, 1894; *P.P., 1893,* pp. 351–52 (quote).

40. *Ithaca Daily Journal,* Nov. 4, 1893, Oct. 22, 1894; *SLP,* Oct. 11, 25, Nov. 1, 1893, Oct. 10, 1894; *Trib.,* Sept. 19, Oct. 11, 16, 1894; *NYT,* Sept. 21, 1894. McSeveney, *Politics of Depression,* pp. 87–94.

41. Altogether the convention received about one hundred proposed amendments dealing with social and economic questions. Convention President Joseph H. Choate warned the delegates at the outset that they would receive "a vast number of crude and undigested schemes, projects, [and] ideas, indicating every method of modern thought." He advised them not to debate at length proposals that were "utterly impracticable." *R.R.C.C.,* 1: 6–7.

42. *Labor's Demands of the Constitutional Convention* (New York, Feb. 1, 1894), printed circular; circular letter from Sam Kaufman, secretary of the Trades and Labor Conference, to members of the constitutional convention (n.d.), both in the Andrew H. Green Papers; *NYT,* May 31, June 28, 1894; *R.R.C.C.,* 3: 187–90, 199, 218–19, 230; 4: 518–19, 521, 527, 531–32; Gompers, *Seventy Years,* 2: 83–84.

43. *Buffalo Courier,* Sept. 26 (quote), Oct. 17, Nov. 3, 1894; Canton *Commercial Advertiser,* Oct. 24, 1894 (quote); *FC,* Sept. 26, 1894; *New York Herald,* Oct. 19, 1894; Noble E. Whitford, *History of the Barge Canal of New York State* (Albany, 1922), pp. 24–25; Lincoln, *Constitutional History,* 3: 375–90.

44. *R.R.C.C.,* 3: 118, 124, 126, 129; 4: 487–88 (quote 488), 493, 503–10. One loophole in the amendment allowed the wives of legislators to receive passes for their husbands' use; see, for example, a New York Central and Hudson River Railroad pass for Mrs. E. C. Stewart, good for use until April 30, 1897, in the Edwin Crowell Stewart Papers.

45. H. J. Cookinham et al., *Address to the People of the State of New York* (Albany, Sept. 28, 1894), p. 3; F. T. Hamlin, "The New York Constitutional Convention," *Yale Law Journal* 4 (June 1895): 222.

46. Some evidence of new thinking about social and economic questions may be found in: Washington Gladden, "Relief Work, Its Principles and Methods," *Review of Reviews* 9 (Jan. 1894): 38–40; the James B. Reynolds correspondence in the USS Papers; Ringenbach, *Tramps and Reformers,* pp. 92–103; and James B. Lane, *Jacob A. Riis and the American City* (Port Washington, N.Y., 1974), pp. 87–91.

47. *Trib.,* Sept. 27, 1894 (quote); Timothy Shaler Williams to Charles R. De Freest, Oct. 12, 1894; Williams to William Purcell and Purcell to Williams, both Oct. 13, 1894; Williams to John Boyd Thacher, Oct. 13, 1894, Williams Papers; Rochester *Democrat and Chronicle,* Oct. 24, 1894 (quote). McSeveney, *Politics of Depression,* pp. 94–108, treats the cultural and religious issues of 1894 in detail.

48. Robert McElroy, *Levi Parsons Morton: Banker, Diplomat and Statesman* (New York, 1930), pp. 207–16; Morton to Platt, July 18, 1894, Platt Papers, Yale; Platt to Morton, July 29, 1894, in McElroy, p. 212; *NYT,* Aug. 28, Sept. 1, 5, 6, 9, 18, 19, 1894; *Trib.,* Sept. 13, 19, 1894; Alexander, *Four Famous New Yorkers,* pp. 210–13.

49. Benjamin B. Odell, Jr., to Lemuel E. Quigg, Sept. 28, 1894, Odell Papers; Edward B. Harper to Henry B. Hyde, Oct. 22, 1894, Oct. 31, 1894 (multicopy letters), Equitable Life Assurance Society Collection; *NYT,* Sept. 21, 1894; *Trib.,* Sept. 19, Oct. 11 (quote), 1894; W. W. Dudley to H. O. Armour, Oct. 12, 1894; Platt to C. W. Hackett, Oct. 17, 1894; Patrick Ford to Morton, Nov. 22, 1894, Morton Papers. On the constitutional convention's handling of the sectarian aid question, see McSeveney, *Politics of Depression,* pp. 69–79.

50. *Trib.,* Sept. 19 (quote), 27, Oct. 10, 24, Nov. 4, 5, 6, 1894; *New York Herald,* Nov. 5, 1894; *Essex County Republican,* Oct. 25, 1894; *SLP,* Oct. 17, 1894; New York *Commercial Advertiser,* Nov. 5, 1894.

51. *Trib.,* Oct. 25, 1894; *Trib. Alm.* (1895), pp. 322–33; McSeveney, *Politics of Depression,* pp. 108–18.

52. *Trib. Alm.* (1894, 1895); *Manual* (1894, 1895); Carl N. Degler, "American Political Parties and the Rise of the City: An Interpretation," *JAH* 51 (June 1964): 41–59.

53. *Trib. Alm.* (1893, 1895) gives the city votes by ward and assembly district; McSeveney, *Politics of Depression,* p. 113.

54. Shepard to Henry A. Richmond, Nov. 12, 1894, Shepard Papers; Armstrong, ed., *Letters of E. L. Godkin,* pp. 458–60; *Trib.,* Nov. 7, 20, Dec. 22, 26, 1894; *NYT,* Nov. 7, 1894; New York *Evening Post,* Nov. 10, 1894; *Brooklyn Daily Eagle,* Nov. 7, 1894; *TDT,* Nov. 7, 8, 9, 1894; *Buffalo Commercial,* Nov. 7, 8, 9, 1894; New York *Sun,* Nov. 26, 1894; *Nation* 60 (Feb. 28, 1895): 159; Steffens to Joseph Steffens, Dec. 15, 1894, in Ella Winter and Granville Hicks, eds., *The Letters of Lincoln Steffens,* 2 vols. (New York, 1938), 1: 108.

55. McSeveney, *Politics of Depression*, p. 228; Lee Benson, Joel H. Silbey, and Phyllis F. Field, "Toward a Theory of Stability and Change in American Voting Patterns: New York State, 1792–1970," in Silbey, Bogue, and Flanigan, eds., *History of American Electoral Behavior*, p. 96.

56. *Nation* 59 (Nov. 15, 1894): 352; McSeveney, *Politics of Depression*, pp. 111–12.

3. *Thomas Collier Platt's Party Strategy*

1. Editorials appearing during January and February 1895, in the New York *Press*, which spoke for Platt, expressed most of the elements of his party strategy. See also *Auto. TCP* for the boss's point of view as he recorded it (with some assistance) late in life.

2. Parts of the following sketch of Platt are drawn from my articles "The Thomas Collier Platt Papers," *The Yale University Library Gazette* 50 (July 1975): 46–58; and "Prelude to Progressivism: The Transformation of New York State Politics, 1890–1910," *New York History* 59 (July 1978): 253–76. The most valuable study of Platt's political methods is Harold F. Gosnell, *Boss Platt and His New York Machine: A Study of the Political Leadership of Thomas C. Platt, Theodore Roosevelt, and Others* (Chicago, 1924); Robert D. Marcus, *Grand Old Party: Political Structure in the Gilded Age, 1880–1896* (New York, 1971) gives the best account of Platt's national role. A number of articles suggest how Platt's contemporaries viewed him: Lemuel Ely Quigg, "Thomas Platt," *North American Review* 191 (May 1910): 668–77; Joseph M. Rogers, "Thomas Collier Platt: A Study of the Easy Boss," *Booklovers Magazine* 4 (1904): 331–49; Edward G. Riggs, "Thomas C. Platt," in O. O. Stealey, *Twenty Years in the Press Gallery* (New York, 1906), pp. 392–98; Alfred Henry Lewis, "The Lesson of Platt," *Cosmopolitan Magazine* 40 (April 1906): 639–45; William Allen White, "Platt," *McClure's Magazine* 18 (Dec. 1901): 145–53; "Platt of New York," in Charles Willis Thompson, *Party Leaders of the Time* (New York, 1906), pp. 94–108.

3. Gosnell, *Boss Platt and His New York Machine*, pp. 14–30; *Auto. TCP*, pp. 124–66; Marcus, *Grand Old Party*, pp. 74–75; H. Wayne Morgan, *From Hayes to McKinley: National Party Politics, 1877–1896* (Syracuse, 1969), pp. 129–37.

4. Riggs, "Thomas C. Platt," p. 396; Marcus, *Grand Old Party*, pp. 76–77, 145–46; Gosnell, *Boss Platt and His New York Machine*, pp. 30–38; Quigg, "Thomas Platt," pp. 671–72; *Auto. TCP*, pp. 167–224; DeAlva Stanwood Alexander, *Four Famous New Yorkers: The Political Careers of Cleveland, Platt, Hill and Roosevelt* (New York, 1923), p. 143.

5. *Auto. TCP*, pp. xx, 357.

6. Gosnell, *Boss Platt and His New York Machine*.

7. *Ibid.*, pp. 55–72.

8. Except for Platt, these men have not received much attention from historians; only three have been the subjects of biographies: Clement G. Lanni, *George W. Aldridge: Big Boss, Small City* (Rochester, 1939); Robert Emmett O'Connor, "William Barnes, Jr.: A Conservative Encounters the Progressive Era," Ph.D. diss., SUNY at Albany, 1971; and Benjamin Franklin Cooling, *Benjamin Franklin Tracy: Father of the Modern American Fighting Navy* (Hamden, Conn., 1973). The biographical data in Table 8 has been drawn from the following reference works: *Encyclopedia of American Biography*, vol. 37 (New York, 1929); Charles Elliot Fitch, *Encyclopedia of Biography of New York*, 8 vols. (New York, 1916–25); *National Cyclopaedia of American Biography* (New York, 1893–); *Red Book*

(1899, 1901); *Republicans of New York* (New York, [1906]); *Who's Who in America,* vol. 1, 1899–1900 (Chicago, 1899); *Who's Who in New York City and State,* 1st ed. (New York, 1904); *Who's Who in New York City and State,* 3d ed. (New York, 1907); *Who Was Who in America,* vol. 1, 1897–1942 (Chicago, 1942).

9. Gosnell, *Boss Platt and His New York Machine,* pp. 59–72; Albert W. Atwood, "The Great Express Monopoly," *American Magazine* 71 (April 1911): 758–70.

10. Platt to Charles E. Fitch, Aug. 4, 1890 (quote); Platt to J. Sloat Fassett, June 7, 1890; Platt to J. C. Barry, June 26, 1890; Platt to Frank Hiscock, Aug. 4, 1890, Platt Papers, private; Barnes to Platt, Oct. 31, 1892, Platt Papers, Yale.

11. *New York Herald,* Dec. 31, 1894; Gosnell, *Boss Platt and His New York Machine,* pp. 154–58.

12. Platt to Fish, April 3, 1895, Jan. 29, 1896, April 23, 1896 (quote), Fish Papers; Platt to Nixon, May 5, 1899, April 9, 1901, Nixon Papers; New York *Press,* Jan. 16, 1895; *NYT,* Jan. 16, 21, 1895; *Trib.,* May 16, 1895, Feb. 28, 1898; *FC,* July 10, 1895; Gosnell, *Boss Platt and His New York Machine,* pp. 158–61.

13. This paragraph is based on occupational data on all assemblymen for 1895, 1897, and 1899; *Red Book* (1895, 1897, 1899); *Manual* (1895, 1897, 1899). Except for the near absence of farmers on the Democratic side, Republican and Democratic assemblymen were little different occupationally.

14. New York *Evening Post,* Jan. 10, 1895; New York *Sun,* Jan. 6, 1895 (Morton Papers); William L. Riordan, *Plunkitt of Tammany Hall* (New York, 1963), pp. 21–24; Brooklyn *Daily Times,* July 16, 1897 (Nixon Papers); *FC,* April 6, 1898 (quote), Jan. 18, 1899, Jan. 17, 1900.

15. *Red Book* (1899), pp. 716–17.

16. The concept of institutionalization in this context is Nelson W. Polsby's: "The Institutionalization of the U.S. House of Representatives," *APSR* 62 (March 1968): 144–68. *Red Book* (1899), pp. 716–17, 724.

17. *Red Book* (1899), pp. 126–246, 702, 724. *FC,* Feb. 20, 1895, May 6, 1896, July 14, 1897; *SLP,* May 6, 1896; Scrapbook 1, p. 69, Edwin Crowell Stewart Papers.

18. Edwin L. Godkin, *Unforseen Tendencies of Democracy* (Boston, 1898), pp. 120–25, 138–44; Paul S. Reinsch, *American Legislatures and Legislative Methods* (New York, 1907), pp. 126–58; Report of the Executive Committee, May 8, 1901, NYBTT Papers; *Report of the Commission to Recommend Changes in Methods of Legislation* (New York, 1895); Levi P. Morton to Jacob Cantor, June 25, 1895, Morton Papers; *P.P., 1897–98,* pp. 22–23, 244–46; Theodore Roosevelt, *An Autobiography* (New York, 1913), pp. 303–6; G. Wallace Chessman, *Governor Theodore Roosevelt: The Albany Apprenticeship, 1898–1900* (Cambridge, Mass., 1965), pp. 77–78.

19. Platt to Quigg, Dec. 21, 1896, Quigg Papers, N-YHS; Platt to Edwin Crowell Stewart, Jan. 19, 1897, Stewart Papers; Platt to Ashley Cole, Jan. 21, 1897, Cole Papers, GARL. A large scrapbook of letters Platt received after his election to the Senate is included among the Platt Papers in private hands; the letter quoted is from Morton Cromwell to Platt, Jan. 21, 1897. Gosnell, *Boss Platt and His New York Machine,* pp. 170–72; Alexander, *Four Famous New Yorkers,* pp. 283–85.

20. Gosnell, *Boss Platt and His New York Machine,* pp. 182–218; John A. Fairlie, "State Administration in New York," *PSQ* 15 (March 1900): 70.

21. Platt to Morton, Nov. 15, 1895, April 23, 1896, April 28, 1896, Morton

Papers; Platt to Morton, Jan. 3, 1896, in *Auto. TCP,* pp. 307–10. Morton to Platt, May 28, 1896 (quote), Platt Papers, Yale; Morton to Platt, March 27, 1895, May 3, 1895, Jan. 4, 1896, March 30, 1896, April 27, 1896, May 5, 1896, May 11, 1896, Morton Papers; Robert McElroy, *Levi Parsons Morton: Banker, Diplomat and Statesman* (New York, 1930), pp. 290–91.

22. Black to Platt, Feb. 10, 1897, Platt Papers, Yale; scrapbooks in the George Washington Aldridge Papers provide newspaper coverage of Black's efforts to build up a state patronage machine, in collaboration with Aldridge: Rochester *Herald,* Feb. 1, 9, March 17, 25, 26, 1897; Rochester *Post-Express,* Feb. 9, 1897; Rochester *Union and Advertiser,* March 16, 1897; *Buffalo Courier,* March 22, 1897. See also *Trib.,* April 12, May 18, June 2, 30, 1897.

23. Chessman, *Governor Theodore Roosevelt,* pp. 71–92; Roosevelt, *Autobiography,* pp. 297–334; *Auto. TCP,* pp. 374–75; Corinne Roosevelt Robinson, *My Brother Theodore Roosevelt* (New York, 1921), pp. 185–86, 191–92; *Barnes v. Roosevelt,* pp. 685–87.

24. "New York Legislation: Classification of Acts 1894–1900," *Assembly Documents,* No. 50 (Albany, 1901).

25. *The Annual Report of the Comptroller of the State of New York* is the essential document for studying state expenditures; in addition, Don C. Sowers, *The Financial History of New York State: From 1789 to 1912* (New York, 1914), includes useful tables summarizing the expenditures for every year; pp. 320–23.

26. The categories of expenditure used here and in the following three paragraphs are those defined in Sowers, *Financial History,* pp. 295–301, and the *Annual Report of the Comptroller* (Albany, 1910), p. xii. One exception to the generalization about the slow, steady growth of the costs of government itself was printing, the expenditures for which nearly doubled from 1894 to 1900.

27. On the state's policy of purchasing parkland in the Adirondack region, see *P.P., 1897–98,* pp. 19–21, 227–32; on the state capitol, see *ibid.,* pp. 14–15, 218; on canal improvements see Chapter 5 below.

28. On the increase in agricultural expenditures, see *P.P., 1900,* pp. 55–56; and the *Annual Report of the Comptroller* for 1900 and 1901. Not all regulative costs rose slowly; those for factory inspection doubled during the period, while those for the Quarantine Commission were cut in half. On expenditures for state care of the insane see *P.P., 1895,* pp. 36–38; *P.P., 1896,* pp. 11–16; *P.P., 1897–98,* pp. 15–16, 222–24.

29. Fairlie, "State Administration."

30. John A. Fairlie, *The Centralization of Administration in New York State* (New York, 1898), pp. 86–97, 106–10, 118–23; *P.P., 1895,* pp. 19, 39; *P.P., 1897–98,* pp. 221–22; *P.P., 1899,* p. 32; *P.P., 1900,* pp. 47, 52–53; Finlia G. Crawford, "Constitutional Developments, 1867–1915," in Alexander C. Flick, ed., *History of the State of New York,* 10 vols. (New York, 1933–37), 7: 220–22.

31. Fairlie, "State Administration," pp. 67–68.

32. James C. Mohr, *The Radical Republicans and Reform in New York during Reconstruction* (Ithaca, 1973), pp. 21–114.

33. The figures in this paragraph are derived from data presented in A. Lawrence Lowell, "The Influence of Party Upon Legislation in England and America," *Annual Report of the American Historical Association, 1901* (Washington, D.C., 1902), pp. 321–542, esp. 481–96.

34. Robert Mazet to Platt, April 19, 1899; Platt to Frank W. Higgins, April 20, 1899; Platt to Mazet, Oct. 13, 1899; Mazet to Platt, Oct. 13, 1899; Frank Moss to

Platt, Nov. 1, 1899, Dec. 5, 1899, Platt Papers, Yale; "Report of the Special Committee of the Assembly Appointed to Investigate the Public Offices and Departments of the City of New York and of the Counties Therein Included," *Assembly Documents*, No. 78 (Albany, 1901).

35. James W. Wadsworth, "Reminiscences," p. 56, COHC; Ashley W. Cole to Platt, April 23, 1895, May 28, 1895, July 17, 1895; Morton to Platt, May 1, 1895, May 3, 1895, May 8, 1895, May 28, 1896; Henry C. Bowen to Morton, May 2, 1895, Morton Papers; *P.P., 1895*, pp. 103–9.

36. *Outlook* 59 (July 16, 1898): 658, (July 23, 1898): 704–5; Laws of 1899, chap. 302.

37. On the history of bipartisan boards in New York State, see Delos F. Wilcox, "Party Government in the Cities of New York State," *PSQ* 15 (Dec. 1899): 681–98. Raymond B. Fosdick, *American Police Systems* (New York, 1920), pp. 103–6; James F. Richardson, *The New York Police: Colonial Times to 1901* (New York, 1970), pp. 214–19; *NYT*, Feb. 27, 1895; Platt to Fish, March 25, 1895, Fish Papers.

38. *A.J.* (1895), pp. 377–78; *S.J.* (1895), p. 434; *P.P., 1895*, pp. 60–64; *NYT*, Feb. 27, March 1, 2, 3, 1895; *Trib.*, March 2, 1895; *A.J.* (1896), pp. 877–78; *S.J.* (1896), p. 452; *NYT*, Feb. 6, 8, 20, 25, 27, March 19, 20, 1896; *Trib.*, Jan. 28, Feb. 19, 27, March 29, May 2, 1896; New York *Evening Post*, March 20, 1896.

39. "Report of the Special Committee Appointed to Investigate the Police Department of the City of New York," *Senate Documents*, No. 25 (Albany, 1895); the New York *Press*, speaking for Platt, called repeatedly for a bipartisan police board during January 1895; *Auto. TCP*, pp. 236–39; *NYT*, Jan. 17–26, 29, Feb. 4, 5, 15, March 14, April 17, 24, May 2, 5, 9, 1895; *A.J.* (1895), p. 3046; *S.J.* (1895), p. 1176; Gosnell, *Boss Platt and His New York Machine*, pp. 229–31; Richardson, *New York Police*, pp. 219, 241–44.

40. Platt to Theodore Roosevelt, April 6, 1899, Nov. 13, 1899, Dec. 1, 1899, Platt Papers, Yale; Frank Moss, "State Oversight of Police," *Municipal Affairs* 3 (1899): 264–68; Chessman, *Governor Theodore Roosevelt*, pp. 81–89.

41. Four useful accounts of consolidation are Harold Coffin Syrett, *The City of Brooklyn, 1865–1898: A Political History* (New York, 1944), pp. 245–74; David Conrad Hammack, "Participation in Major Decisions in New York City, 1890–1900: The Creation of Greater New York and the Centralization of the Public School System," Ph.D. diss., Columbia University, 1973, pp. 113–312; Barry Jerome Kaplan, "A Study in the Politics of Metropolitanization: The Greater New York City Charter of 1897," Ph.D. diss., SUNY at Buffalo, 1975; and Robert Crosby Eager, "Governing New York State: Republicans and Reform, 1894–1900," Ph.D. diss., Stanford University, 1977, pp. 115–49.

42. *P.P., 1895*, pp. 21–22; Syrett, *City of Brooklyn*, pp. 250–61; Kaplan, "Politics of Metropolitanization," pp. 180–201; McElroy, *Levi Parsons Morton*, pp. 253–54; *Trib.*, Jan. 5, 6, April 22, May 14, 15, 17, 1895; *NYT*, Jan. 3, 5, 31, April 10, 11, 16, 18, 20, May 10, 11, 16, 17, 1895; Ashley W. Cole to Platt, May 15, 1895 (quote); Platt to Morton, May 15, 1895, Morton Papers.

43. Robert D. Benedict, "Objection to Consolidation," *Independent* 48 (April 16, 1896): 510; William C. Redfield to Morton, Jan. 7, 1896 (quote); Wurster to Morton, Jan. 10, 1896 (quote), Feb. 5, 1896, Feb. 7, 1896, Morton Papers; Syrett, *City of Brooklyn*, pp. 256–65; Hammack, "Participation in Major Decisions," pp. 237–49.

44. *P.P., 1896,* p. 41; Morton to Tracy, Dec. 31, 1895; Morton to Platt, Jan. 4, 1896, Jan. 13, 1896, May 1, 1896; Morton to Edward Lauterbach, March 14, 1896, Morton Papers; McElroy, *Levi Parsons Morton,* pp. 253–79.

45. Platt to Morton, Jan. 3, 1896, in *Auto. TCP,* pp. 307–10.

46. *Brooklyn Citizen,* Feb. 13, 1896 (Morton Papers); New York *Sun,* March 15, 1897.

47. *NYT,* Jan. 1, 15, 24, 29, April 21, 22, 24, 27, 1896; *Trib.,* March 11, April 13, 16, 23, 1896; Edward Lauterbach to Morton, March 16, 1896, Morton Papers. Syrett, *City of Brooklyn,* p. 266; Kaplan, "Politics of Metropolitanization," pp. 190–91, 217–19, 232–34, 239–40; Hammack, "Participation in Major Decisions," pp. 261–67, 275–78.

48. Kaplan, "Politics of Metropolitanization," pp. 216–17, 238–39; Hammack, "Participation in Major Decisions," pp. 252–53, 280–81.

49. *A.J.* (1896), pp. 1733–34; *S.J.* (1896), p. 640; *NYT,* March 12, 27, 1896.

50. Statement by F. W. Wurster, April 9, 1896; Francis M. Scott to Morton, May 4, 1896; R. W. G. Welling et al. to Morton, May 8, 1896, Morton Papers; *A.J.* (1896), pp. 3280–81; *S.J.* (1896), pp. 1372–73; *NYT,* March 1, 3, 10, 27, April 8–23, May 13, 1896; *Trib.,* March 9, 11, April 13, 16, 23, May 12, 13, 1896; Platt to Morton, April 23, 1896 (quote), April 28, 1896; Morton to Platt, May 1, 1896, May 5, 1896, Morton Papers.

51. *NYT,* Feb. 19, 23, March 12, 24 (quote), 1897; Seth Low to H. L. Nelson, Feb. 23, 1897; Low to Mrs. F. P. Kinnicutt, March 23, 1897; Low to Alfred T. White, April 8, 1897, Low Papers; "Notes on Municipal Government," *AAAPSS* 9 (1897): 289–91, 466–67; Gherardi Davis, "The Story of My Life," Davis Papers; Albert Shaw, "The Municipal Problem and Greater New York," *Atlantic Monthly* 79 (June 1897): 733–48; Kaplan, "Politics of Metropolitanization," pp. 262–320; Hammack, "Participation in Major Decisions," pp. 282–97.

52. Syrett, *City of Brooklyn,* pp. 270–72 (quote 270); *NYT,* Feb. 26, March 23, 24, 26, April 10, 13, 14, 15, 20, May 6, 1897; *Trib.,* Feb. 24, 1897; Platt to Aldridge, March 9, 1897, Aldridge Papers; *A.J.* (1897), p. 1793; *S.J.* (1897), pp. 802–3; Gosnell, *Boss Platt and His New York Machine,* p. 165.

53. Previous accounts of the Raines law include Gosnell, *Boss Platt and His New York Machine,* pp. 162–65; Eager, "Governing New York State," pp. 56–113; John Joseph Coffey, "A Political History of the Temperance Movement in New York State, 1808–1912," Ph.D. diss., Pennsylvania State University, 1972, pp. 262–73; and William John Jackson, "Prohibition as an Issue in New York State Politics, 1836–1933," Ed.D., Teachers College, Columbia University, 1974, pp. 43–48.

54. Samuel T. McSeveney, *The Politics of Depression: Political Behavior in the Northeast, 1893–1896* (New York, 1972), pp. 20–24; Herbert J. Bass, *"I Am a Democrat": The Political Career of David Bennett Hill* (Syracuse, 1961), pp. 17–18, 62–65, 94–96, 112–13, 130–31, 135–37; Coffey, "Political History of the Temperance Movement," pp. 117–260; *Trib. Alm.* (1890–96).

55. Theodore Roosevelt, "Enforcement of Law," *Forum* 20 (Sept. 1895): 1–10; Warner Miller, "What Shall We Do with the Excise Question?" *North American Review* 162 (March 1896): 287–91; Frederick W. Holls, "The 'German Vote' and the Republican Party," *Forum* 20 (Jan. 1896): 588–604; Warner Miller to Whitelaw Reid, Oct. 8, 1895, Reid Papers; Frederick W. Holls to Andrew D. White, Oct. 11, 1895; Holls to John E. Milholland, Nov. 6, 1895, Holls Papers;

New York *Sun,* Oct. 18, Nov. 8, 1895; Richardson, *New York Police,* pp. 251–52; Alexander, *Four Famous New Yorkers,* pp. 237–38; McSeveney, *Politics of Depression,* pp. 143–47, 151–55.

56. *P.P., 1896,* pp. 31–32; Morton to Warner Miller, Jan. 3, 1896, Morton Papers.

57. Laws of 1896, chap. 112; except for the division of receipts, the measure became law almost exactly as Raines introduced it.

58. New York *Sun,* Jan. 25, 29, Feb. 3, 19, 1896; *Buffalo Daily Times,* March 19, 1896. Frederick W. Holls to Charles Z. Lincoln, Feb. 21, 1896, March 16, 1896; Holls to William Cary Sanger, March 11, 1896; Holls to Andrew D. White, Feb. 1, 1896, Holls Papers.

59. Platt to Lemuel E. Quigg, March 2, 1896, March 7, 1896, Quigg Papers, N-YHS; Platt to Hamilton Fish, Feb. 27, 1896, Fish Papers; *NYT,* Feb. 23, 1896; *A.J.* (1896), p. 1405; *S.J.* (1896), p. 610; Ashley Cole to Platt, March 9, 1896, March 23, 1896; Morton to Platt, March 20, 1896, Morton Papers; *P.P., 1896,* pp. 84–93; McElroy, *Levi Parsons Morton,* pp. 266–70.

60. Morton to T. E. Hancock, March 23, 1896, Morton Papers; Dorman B. Eaton to George McAneny, April 11, 1896; Everett P. Wheeler to Carl Schurz, April 15, 1896; Edward M. Shepard to McAneny, May 19, 1896, New York State Civil Service Reform Association Papers; Platt to Morton, May 25, 1896, Morton Papers; *Trib.,* March 26, April 4, 9 (headline), May 23, 1896; New York *Evening Post,* May 23, 1896.

61. Henry H. Lyman to James A. Roberts, May 26, 1896; Roberts to Lyman, May 26, 1896; Lyman to the Civil Service Commission, May 28, 1896, June 9, 1896, New York State Civil Service Reform Association Papers; Ellsworth to Platt, June 2, 1896; Platt to Ellsworth, June 4, 1896, Morton Papers; *Trib.,* May 25, 29, June 2, 10, July 25, 29, 1896.

62. New York *Sun,* May 23, 1897; *Buffalo Daily Times,* Oct. 21, 24, 1897; *Buffalo Commercial,* Nov. 9, 1898; Frederick W. Holls to Andrew D. White, Nov. 27, 1897, Holls Papers; E. H. Makk to George Washington Aldridge, Nov. 9, 1897; John R. Hazel to Aldridge, Nov. 21, 1898, Aldridge Papers; John De Witt Warner, "The Raines Liquor Tax Law: State Promotion of Vice," *Municipal Affairs* 5 (Dec. 1901): 842–51; John G. Agar, "The Saloon Problem in New York," *ibid.,* pp. 829–41 (quote 837); The Committee of Fifteen, *The Social Evil: With Special Reference to Conditions Existing in the City of New York* (New York, 1902), pp. 159–68.

63. John Raines, "The Raines Liquor-Tax Law," *North American Review* 162 (May 1896): 481–85; "Report of the Special Committee of the Senate Appointed to Investigate the Working of the Liquor Tax Law," *Senate Documents,* Nos. 31 and 41 (Albany, 1897).

64. New York *Sun,* March 12 (quote), 18, 1899, Aug. 8, 1900, June 23, 1902, Jan. 5, 1903, July 6, 1905, July 3, 1906; *Annual Report of the State Commissioner of Excise* (Albany, 1902), p. 696; *Annual Report . . . Excise* (1910), p. 620. Coffey, "Political History of the Temperance Movement," pp. 274–302; *Trib. Alm.* (1897–1911).

65. Quigg, "Thomas Platt," p. 675; *Auto. TCP,* pp. 468–78; C. A. O'Rourke to James B. Reynolds, Oct. 9, 1897, Low Papers; Eager, "Governing New York State," pp. 111–12.

66. The Republican platforms analyzed here may be found in *Trib.,* Aug. 26, 1896, Sept. 28, 1898, Sept. 5, 1900. See also: John Denison Champlin, ed.,

Orations, Addresses and Speeches of Chauncey M. Depew, 8 vols. (New York, 1910), 6; Chauncey M. Depew, *Autumnal Speeches in 1898* (n.p., n.d.); Timothy L. Woodruff, *Speeches Delivered by Timothy L. Woodruff During and Since the Campaign of 1896* (Albany, 1899); Frank S. Black, *Addresses by Frank S. Black* (n.p., n.d.); New York *Sun,* Aug. 15, Oct. 8, 1898; *Boonville Herald,* Oct. 14, 28, 1896, Nov. 3, 1898, Oct. 25, 1900; *SLP,* Sept. 30, Oct. 7, 14, 21, 28, Nov. 11, 1896, Sept. 7, 14, 28, Oct. 26, 1898, Oct. 3, 10, 1900; *Essex County Republican,* Oct. 8, 15, 1896, Oct. 13, 27, 1898, Oct. 5, 12, Nov. 2, 9, 1900; *Ithaca Daily Journal,* Oct. 15, 17, 21, 24, 31, 1896, Oct. 31, Nov. 7, 1898, Oct. 17, 24, 25, Nov. 3, 1900. McSeveney, *Politics of Depression,* pp. 176–88.

67. *Trib.,* Sept. 5 (quote), Nov. 1–5, 1900; *NYT,* Sept. 6, 1900 (quote); New York *Sun,* Nov. 3, 6, 1900; William Barnes, Jr., to S. Fred Nixon, Aug. 6, 1900, Nixon Papers.

68. *Trib.,* Aug. 26, 1896, Sept. 28, 1898, Sept. 5, 1900.

69. *Boonville Herald,* Oct. 14, 1896, Nov. 3, 1898, Oct. 25, 1900; *SLP,* Oct. 14, 1896, Oct. 26, Nov. 2, 1898, Oct. 24, 1900; *Ithaca Daily Journal,* Oct. 21, 1896, Oct. 29, 1898; *Yates County Chronicle,* Oct. 26, 1898; *Malone Paladium,* Nov. 3, 1898; *Auburn Daily Advertiser,* Oct. 29, 1898.

70. John Ireland to Platt, Oct. 2, 1895; Platt to Charles R. Skinner, Oct. 10, 1895, Platt Papers, private; Barnes to Platt, Feb. 21, 1890, June 8, 1895, Feb. 1, 1900, March 24, 1900, Platt Papers, Yale; Benjamin B. Odell, Jr., to Levi P. Morton, Nov. 16, 1894; T. A. Hendrick to Aldridge, Jan. 17, 1898, Aldridge Papers; Odell to Lemuel E. Quigg, Sept. 2, 1896, Oct. 12, 1898, Odell Papers; Eager, "Governing New York State," pp. 44–47; O'Connor, "William Barnes, Jr.," p. 15.

71. Coote to Platt, Oct. 8, 1898 (quote), Oct. 17, 1898, Oct. 31, 1898; Nov. 7, 1900; Platt to Coote, Oct. 17, 1898, Oct. 22, 1898, Nov. 8, 1900, Platt Papers, Yale.

72. *Trib.,* Sept. 28, 1898.

73. *Trib.,* Sept. 5, 1900. The New York *Sun,* which spoke for Platt, believed that national issues should continue to receive the heaviest emphasis in 1900; April 11, 1900.

74. The Democratic platforms may be found in *Trib.,* Sept. 18, 1896, Sept. 30, 1898, and Sept. 13, 1900.

4. *Independence from the Party Machine*

1. Rochester *Post-Express,* Sept. 5, 1894 (George Washington Aldridge Papers).

2. On minority parties as vehicles of political innovation, see Theodore J. Lowi, *At the Pleasure of the Mayor: Patronage and Power in New York City, 1898–1958* (New York, 1964).

3. DeAlva Stanwood Alexander, *Four Famous New Yorkers: The Political Careers of Cleveland, Platt, Hill, and Roosevelt* (New York, 1923), pp. 239–42, 261–81, 310–17, 339–57; Samuel T. McSeveney, *The Politics of Depression: Political Behavior in the Northeast, 1893–1896* (New York, 1972), pp. 133, 148, 169–75, 210–11.

4. Gerald Kurland, "The Amateur in Politics: The Citizens' Union and the Greater New York Mayoral Campaign of 1897," *New-York Historical Society Quarterly* 53 (Oct. 1969): 356n; Richard Stephen Skolnik, "The Crystallization of

Reform in New York City, 1890–1917," Ph.D. diss., Yale University, 1964, pp. 223–28; Rochester *Democrat and Chronicle,* Sept. 19, 1895; *Rochester Directory, 1895* (Rochester, 1895); Blake McKelvey, *Rochester: The Quest for Quality, 1890–1925* (Cambridge, Mass., 1956), pp. 73–79.

5. Numerous studies of urban reform have influenced this discussion: Samuel P. Hays, "The Politics of Reform in Municipal Government in the Progressive Era," *Pacific Northwest Quarterly* 55 (Oct. 1964): 157–69; Melvin G. Holli, *Reform in Detroit: Hazen S. Pingree and Urban Politics* (New York, 1969); Martin J. Schiesl, *The Politics of Efficiency: Municipal Administration and Reform in America, 1880–1920* (Berkeley, 1977); Augustus Cerillo, Jr., "Reform in New York City: A Study of Urban Progressivism," Ph.D. diss., Northwestern University, 1969; Augustus Cerillo, Jr., "The Impact of Reform Ideology: Early Twentieth-Century Municipal Government in New York City," in Michael H. Ebner and Eugene M. Tobin, eds., *The Age of Urban Reform: New Perspectives on the Progressive Era* (Port Washington, N.Y., 1977), pp. 68–85; Skolnik, "Crystallization of Reform"; Richard Skolnik, "Civic Group Progressivism in New York City," *New York History* 51 (July 1970): 411–39; Brenda K. Shelton, *Reformers in Search of Yesterday: Buffalo in the 1890s* (Albany, 1976); and Gerald Kurland, *Seth Low: The Reformer in an Urban and Industrial Age* (New York, 1971).

6. These generalizations are based on the manuscript collections cited throughout this chapter; on independents and the liquor issue, see the articles in *Municipal Affairs* 5 (Dec. 1901).

7. Robert Fulton Cutting, "City Government and the People," *Municipal Affairs* 5 (Dec. 1901): 881–85; and John De Witt Warner, "Municipal Betterment in the New York City Election," *ibid.* (Sept. 1901), pp. 625–40. Several studies of reform in the cities of New York demonstrate the cleavages among elites on economic and social issues: Cerillo, "Reform in New York City"; Skolnik, "Crystallization of Reform"; Shelton, *Reformers in Search of Yesterday;* and David Conrad Hammack, "Participation in Major Decisions in New York City, 1890–1900: The Creation of Greater New York and the Centralization of the Public School System," Ph.D. diss., Columbia University, 1973.

8. On the transition from electoral to pressure-group reform, see Skolnik, "Civic Group Progressivism"; and Augustus Cerillo, Jr., "The Reform of Municipal Government in New York City: From Seth Low to John Purroy Mitchel," *New-York Historical Society Quarterly* 57 (Jan. 1973): 51–71. William L. Riordan, *Plunkitt of Tammany Hall* (New York, 1963), pp. 17–20.

9. Citizens' Union, *The City for the People! Campaign Book of the Citizens' Union* (New York, 1897); Council of Confederated Good Government Clubs, *An Address to the Citizens of New York* (New York, 1897); Seth Low, "The Problem of City Government in the United States," *Outlook* 53 (April 4, 1896): 624–25; New York *Evening Post,* Jan. 9, 1895; *NYT,* Feb. 15, 1895; Schiesl, *Politics of Efficiency.*

10. Citizens' Union, *City for the People!,* pp. 7–8; John W. Keller, "Municipal Reformers in Party Politics," *Municipal Affairs* 4 (June 1900): 343–46; Bird S. Coler, *Municipal Government* (New York, 1900), pp. 186–200; Milo R. Maltbie, "Municipal Political Parties," National Municipal League, *Proceedings* (Philadelphia, 1900), pp. 226–37.

11. *Trib.,* Nov. 7, 8, 9, 13, 19, 20 (quote), 26, Dec. 12, 22, 26, 1894, Jan. 1, 1895 (quote); *Buffalo Commercial,* Nov. 12, 13, 19, 26, Dec. 6, 8, 12, 19, 27, 31,

1894, Jan. 2, 4, 5, 15, 16, 17 (quote), Feb. 1, 1895; *Buffalo Morning Express,* Jan. 22, 1895; *Buffalo Evening News,* Jan. 8, 1895; Syracuse *Evening Herald,* Jan. 3, 21, 22, 31, 1895; *TDT,* Nov. 9, 1894.

12. New York *Press,* Jan. 1, 2, 6 (quote), 8, 22 (quote), Feb. 5, 1895; *AEJ,* Jan. 1, 2, 7, 8, 9, 11, 21, 1895; Platt to Quigg, March 1, 1895, March 11, 1895, June 17, 1895, Nov. 15, 1895, Quigg Papers, N-YHS.

13. For the sources of the biographical data in Table 9, see Chapter 3, n. 8.

14. The sentence on Theodore Roosevelt paraphrases John Morton Blum, *The Republican Roosevelt* (Cambridge, Mass., 1954), p. 7. After 1900 still more of the antimachine leaders advanced to federal offices, including Roosevelt, who became president, and Whitelaw Reid, who became ambassador to England, a position from which Platt had blocked him for years.

15. On the long-standing feud between Platt and Reid, see Harold F. Gosnell, *Boss Platt and His New York Machine: A Study of the Political Leadership of Thomas C. Platt, Theodore Roosevelt, and Others* (Chicago, 1924), pp. 131–33; Harry W. Baehr, Jr., *The New York Tribune Since the Civil War* (New York, 1936), pp. 248–52, 261–64; and Platt to William McKinley, Aug. 14, 1898, Platt Papers, Yale.

16. *Social Register, New York, 1898* (New York, Nov. 1897).

17. William Mills Ivins, *Electoral Reform: The History of the Yates-Saxton Bill* (New York, 1888); John H. Wigmore, *The Australian Ballot System as Embodied in the Legislation of Various Countries* (Boston, 1889); Herbert J. Bass, *"I Am a Democrat": The Political Career of David Bennett Hill* (Syracuse, 1961), pp. 96–101, 128–35, 147–54; L. E. Fredman, *The Australian Ballot: The Story of an American Reform* (East Lansing, Mich., 1968).

18. William Mills Ivins, *Machine Politics and Money in Elections in New York City* (New York, 1887); Joseph B. Bishop, *Money in City Elections: Its Effects and the Remedies* (New York, 1887); Abram C. Bernheim, "The Ballot in New York," *PSQ* 4 (March 1889): 130–52; Charles Z. Lincoln, ed., *Messages from the Governors,* 11 vols. (Albany, 1909), 8: 566–80, 762–89, 949–67, 1012; Timothy Shaler Williams to Nathan Matthews, Jr., Dec. 2, 1889, Dec. 14, 1889; Matthews to Williams, March 14, 1890, Williams Papers; Charles T. Saxton, "The New Method of Voting," *North American Review* 149 (Dec. 1889): 750–52; *NYT,* April 19, 20, May 1, 3, 1890; *Century Magazine* 40 (July 1890): 474–76; *Nation* 50 (May 8, 1890): 368.

19. *Century Magazine* 38 (Sept. 1889): 794; 42 (Sept. 1891): 789; *Nation* 48 (June 6, 1889): 460; 50 (May 8, 1890): 368; 52 (June 18, 1891): 493.

20. *P.P., 1895,* pp. 22–24; *Buffalo Commercial,* Nov. 13, 1894; New York *Press,* Jan. 3, 1895; *NYT,* April 17, May 3, 30, 1895; *Century Magazine* 49 (Jan. 1895): 473–74; *Nation* 60 (Jan. 10, 1895): 24; printed letter from Preble Tucker, March 18, 1895 (quote), Richard Ward Greene Welling Papers; Ashley W. Cole to Tucker, May 29, 1895, Cole Papers, NYPL; Laws of 1895, chap. 810.

21. Laws of 1896, chap. 909; *P.P., 1896,* pp. 30–31; City Club of New York, *The Party Column Ballot and the Massachusetts Ballot* (New York, 1896); City Club of New York, *Supplement to the Pamphlet Entitled "The Party Column Ballot and the Massachusetts Ballot"* (New York, 1896), p. 6; Edward M. Shepard to Daniel Van Pelt, Oct. 23, 1896, Shepard Papers; New York *Sun,* Nov. 19, 1895, March 23, May 29, 1896; *NYT,* Feb. 13, 21, March 28, April 17, 1896; *Gloversville Leader,* May 29, 1896 (Morton Papers).

22. *SLP,* Oct. 23, 1895, Oct. 21, 28, 1896; *Ithaca Daily Journal,* Nov. 2, 1896; *Essex County Republican,* Oct. 3, 24, 31, 1895; *Boonville Herald,* Oct. 23, 1895; *FC,* Oct. 9, 1895; James B. Reynolds to Thomas R. Slicer, Nov. 24, 1899; Reynolds to Theodore Roosevelt, Dec. 1, 1899, Dec. 8, 1899, Dec. 9, 1899; Roosevelt to Reynolds, Dec. 2, 1899; James W. Pryor to Reynolds, Feb. 8, 1900, USS Papers; *Nation* 81 (Nov. 16, 1905): 395.

23. The Appendix discusses the estimation of ticket-splitting; for the view that the ballot law was more or less directly responsible for the rise of ticket-splitting, see Jerrold G. Rusk, "The Effect of the Australian Ballot Reform on Split Ticket Voting, 1876–1908," *APSR* 64 (Dec. 1970): 1220–38.

24. Frank D. Pavey, "State Control of Political Parties," *Forum* 25 (March 1898): 101; *National Conference on Practical Reform of Primary Elections* (Chicago, 1898), p. 131; City Club of New York, *Memorandum in Support of the Massachusetts-Ballot Bill* (New York, 1900), p. 3; R. Fulton Cutting to Everett P. Wheeler, June 25, 1902, Wheeler Papers; Wheeler to Seth Sprague Terry, Jan. 7, 1903, Citizens' Union Papers; John E. Milholland, "The Danger Point in American Politics," *North American Review* 164 (Jan. 1897): 92–105.

25. Robert McElroy, *Levi Parsons Morton: Banker, Diplomat and Statesman* (New York, 1930), pp. 227–29, 233–35, 243–44, 250–51; Platt to Ashley W. Cole, Jan. 21, 1895 (quote); Carl Schurz and George McAneny to Morton, June 8, 1896; Morton to Schurz, June 10, 1896; Silas W. Burt to Morton, June 13, 1896, July 20, 1896, July 29, 1896, Dec. 7, 1896, Dec. 8, 1896; Morton to the Civil Service Commission, Aug. 4, 1896; Platt to Morton, Nov. 29, 1896 (quote); William Brookfield to Morton, Dec. 14, 1896, Morton Papers; *P.P., 1896,* pp. 263–313; *Trib.,* Aug. 5, Dec. 10, 1896; *NYT,* Dec. 26, 1896.

26. *P.P., 1897–98,* pp. 18–19 (quote 18), 136–79, 232–40; New York *Evening Post,* Jan. 6, 1897; *Trib.,* Jan. 7, 1897; *Buffalo Commercial,* Jan. 7, 1897; *Buffalo Evening News,* Jan. 7, 8, 1897; *Nation* 64 (April 29, 1897): 215–16.

27. Robert D. Marcus, *Grand Old Party: Political Structure in the Gilded Age, 1880–1896* (New York, 1971), pp. 209–14, 239–42; Alexander, *Four Famous New Yorkers,* pp. 247–60; Gosnell, *Boss Platt and His New York Machine,* pp. 112–17; *Auto. TCP,* pp. 310–29.

28. Morton to George E. Green, Oct. 6, 1896, Morton Papers; *Essex County Republican,* Oct. 8, 1896; Robert Crosby Eager, "Governing New York State: Republicans and Reform, 1894–1900," Ph.D. diss., Stanford University, 1977, pp. 150–76.

29. New York *Sun,* June 1, July 10, 1895, April 19, 1896; Platt to Hamilton Fish, Feb. 27, 1896, Fish Papers; Milholland, "Danger Point in American Politics"; Buffalo Republican League, *Report of the Special Committee of the Buffalo Republican League on Primary Election Laws* (Buffalo, 1897), p. 13.

30. Albert Shaw to Frederick W. Holls, Aug. 4, 1895; Holls to Andrew D. White, Nov. 27, 1897, Holls Papers; Charles H. Parkhurst to Charles Stewart Smith, April 30, 1897; John Frankenheimer to James B. Reynolds, May 1, 1897; Reynolds to Seth Low, Sept. 8, 1897, USS Papers; Delos F. Wilcox, "Party Government in the Cities of New York State," *PSQ* 14 (Dec. 1899): 696–98.

31. Robert Emmett O'Connor, "William Barnes, Jr.: A Conservative Encounters the Progressive Era," Ph.D. diss., SUNY at Albany, 1971, pp. 24–33; *AEJ,* Nov. 1, 2, 4, 6, 7, 1895, Oct. 4, 7, 20, 21, 26, 28, 29, 30, Nov. 1, 3, 4, 5, 6, 1897; *Trib.,* Oct. 14, 20, Dec. 1, 1897.

32. McKelvey, *Rochester: The Quest for Quality,* pp. 73–79; Rochester *Democrat and Chronicle,* Sept. 19, 1895, Nov. 3, 1897; James G. Cutler to George Washington Aldridge, March 17, 1897; Ernest R. Willard to Aldridge, April 14, 1897; Joseph T. Alling to Aldridge, April 13, 1897; Clarence A. Barbour to Aldridge, April 16, 1897, Aldridge Papers; Joseph T. Alling, "Municipal Reforms in Rochester," National Municipal League, *Proceedings* (Philadelphia, 1897), pp. 175–83.

33. *Syracuse Post,* June 9, July 8, 14, 21, 23, Sept. 10, 1896; Syracuse *Evening Herald,* July 1, Sept. 26, Nov. 2, 1896, all in the Platt Papers, private; Syracuse *Evening Herald,* Sept. 10, Oct. 19, 20, 22, 23, 27, 28, 29, 30, Nov. 1, 3, 1897; *Trib.,* Oct. 13, Dec. 1, 1897; *AEJ,* Nov. 3, 1897; *The Citizens' Union of Syracuse,* Circular No. 3 [Syracuse, 1897], USS Papers.

34. Skolnik, "Crystallization of Reform," pp. 175–76, 182–83.

35. Morton to Strong, Feb. 14, 1895; Ashley W. Cole to Platt, March 25, 1895; Morton to Platt, March 27, 1895; Platt to Morton, Dec. 12, 1895; Edward Lauterbach to Morton, Dec. 14, 1895, March 16, 1896, Morton Papers; Platt to Lemuel E. Quigg, March 11, 1895, Quigg Papers, N-YHS; Platt to Cole, March 26, 1895, Platt Papers, private; New York *Sun,* Feb. 15, 18, April 24, 1895; *NYT,* Jan. 20, 22, 23, 24, 26, 29, Feb. 4, 5, 6, 7, 15, 19, 20, 21, March 3, 12, 14, April 17, 21, 24, 25, 26, 30, May 2, 5, 9, 11, 1895; Frank D. Pavey, "Mayor Strong's Experiment in New York City," *Forum* 23 (July 1897): 539–53; *Auto. TCP,* pp. 286–95; Alexander, *Four Famous New Yorkers,* pp. 230–36.

36. Morton to John Sabine Smith, Jan. 27, 1896; Morton to Edward Lauterbach, Jan. 27, 1896; Lauterbach to Morton, Jan. 28, 1896, Morton Papers; Henry L. Stimson to Lucas L. Van Allen, Aug. 21, 1896; Stimson to Henry M. Brookfield, Oct. 26, 1897, Stimson Papers; Committee of Twenty-Five, *Report of the Committee of Twenty-Five* (New York, 1896).

37. Kurland, *Seth Low,* pp. 82–106; Skolnik, "Crystallization of Reform," pp. 223–45; James Bryce, "The Mayoralty Election in New York," *Contemporary Review* 72 (Nov. 1897): 751–60.

38. *Auto. TCP,* p. 359; Andrew D. White to Platt, Oct. 13, 1897, White Papers; Levi P. Morton to Platt, Oct. 15, 1897, Platt Papers, Yale; Timothy L. Woodruff, *Speeches Delivered by Timothy L. Woodruff During and Since the Campaign of 1896* (Albany, 1899), speech of Sept. 28, 1897; Frank S. Black, *Addresses by Frank S. Black* (n.p., n.d.), pp. 101–2, 223; for a Democratic version of the responsible party argument, see Roswell P. Flower, "Is Non-Partisanship in Municipal Government Feasible?" *Forum* 23 (July 1897): 531–38; and for the independent reply, see Citizens' Union, *The City for the People!,* pp. 8–10. Republican newspapers throughout the state exhibited an intense interest in the New York City election and echoed the doctrines expressed by Woodruff and Black: New York *Sun,* Aug. 24, 29, 1897; New York *Press,* Oct. 22, 1897; *TDT,* Nov. 1, 1897; *Ithaca Daily Journal,* Oct. 1897 (throughout); *Auburn Daily Advertiser,* Oct. 1897 (throughout); *SLP,* Oct. 13, 1897; *Essex County Republican,* Oct. 14, 21, 28, 1897; *Cayuga Chief,* Oct. 23, 1897; *FC,* Sept. 8, 22, Oct. 20, 27, 1897.

39. *Trib. Alm.* (1898), pp. 324–25. The characterizations of the different groups of Manhattan assembly districts are only general and should not be interpreted to mean that any parts of the city were homogeneous in population; see McSeveney, *Politics of Depression,* pp. 50–52, 110–13, 151–53, 198–200, for descriptions of the voting population of Manhattan. The three areas of the city analyzed here

include the following assembly districts: (1) A.D.s 5, 19, 21, 25, 27, 29, and 31; (2) A.D.s 4, 8, 10, 12, 14, and 16; (3) A.D.s 1, 2, 3, 6, 7, 9, 11, and 13. See also Eager, "Governing New York State," pp. 257–79.

40. *Manual* (1898), p. 793; *Trib.*, Nov. 3, 11, 1897; New York *Sun*, Nov. 27, 1897.

41. *Trib. Alm.* (1897, 1898); Eager, "Governing New York State," p. 265; all the percentages in this paragraph refer to the two-party vote.

42. In eleven counties, the Republicans actually gained somewhat in strength since 1896; only a few nonurban counties matched the shifts recorded in the large cities. *FC*, Nov. 3, 1897 (quote); *Essex County Republican*, Nov. 4, 1897; *SLP*, Nov. 1, 8, 1899.

43. Theodore Roosevelt to Francis Cabot Lowell, March 16, 1900; Roosevelt to Seth Low, Aug. 3, 1900, *LTR*, II. *SLP*, Oct. 27 (quote), Nov. 10, 1897; *Essex County Republican*, Nov. 4, 11, 1897, Nov. 2, 1899; *Owego Daily Record*, Nov. 3, 1897, New York *Sun*, Sept. 5, 25, 1899; *Trib.*, March 3, 1898; *NYT*, March 21, 1898; Eager, "Governing New York State," pp. 345–47.

44. *AEJ*, Nov. 4, 6, 13, 1897; New York *Sun*, Dec. 28, 1897, Jan. 28, 1898; *Trib.*, Nov. 3, 4, 5, 8, 17, Dec. 17, 1897; Kurland, *Seth Low*, pp. 107–12; Carl Schurz, "The Task of the Citizens' Union," *Harper's Weekly* 41 (Dec. 11, 1897): 1215.

45. G. Wallace Chessman, *Governor Theodore Roosevelt: The Albany Apprenticeship, 1898–1900* (Cambridge, Mass., 1965), pp. 13, 78; *Trib.*, April 7, 1898; "Report of the Commissioners Appointed to Propose Legislation for Cities of the Second Class," *Assembly Documents*, No. 44 (Albany, 1896); White to Aldridge, May 10, 1897, May 18, 1897; Joseph T. Alling to Aldridge, May 12, 1897, Aldridge Papers; Alling, "Municipal Reforms in Rochester," pp. 180–81; E. Dana Durand, "Political and Municipal Legislation," *AAAPSS* 13 (March 1899): 221–23; Eager, "Governing New York State," pp. 315–20.

46. Henry L. Stimson et al. to Lemuel E. Quigg, Dec. 3, 1897, Stimson Papers; Committee of Fifty-Three, *Constitution of the Republicans of the County of New York* (New York, 1898); Buffalo Republican League, *Report of the Special Committee*, p. 3; Milholland, "Danger Point in American Politics"; *Trib.*, Nov. 25, Dec. 23, 1897; *Buffalo Evening News*, Nov. 8, 9, 10, 15, 1897, Jan. 8, 10, 17, 1898; *National Conference on . . . Primary Elections*, p. 128 (quote).

47. Black to Quigg, Feb. 15, 1898 (quote), Feb. 23, 1898, March 9, 1898, March 17, 1898, Quigg Papers, N-YHS; Root to Seth Low, Feb. 23, 1898, Low Papers; Whitelaw Reid to Root, Feb. 2, 1898, March 5, 1898 (draft); Root to Reid, Feb. 28, 1898; Reid to Paul D. Cravath, March 8, 1898; Reid to Frank D. Pavey, March 10, 1898, March 25, 1898, Reid Papers; Buffalo Republican League, *Open Letter to Hon. Henry W. Hill, Member of Assembly; From the Special Committee of the Buffalo Republican League on Primary Election Laws* (Buffalo, 1898); *NYT*, Jan. 19, 30, Feb. 3, 11, 19 (Raines quote), 20, 24, 25, 26, 28, March 2, 4, 9, 11, 24, 1898; Louis Sturcke, *Primary Election Legislation in the State of New York* (New York, 1898), pp. 3–4.

48. Laws of 1898, chap. 179; Sturcke, *Primary Election Legislation*; General Committee of the Republicans of the County of New York, *Synopsis of the Primary Law as It Affects Republicans in the County of New York* (New York, 1898), and *The New Primary Election Law* (New York, 1898); William H. Hotchkiss, "The Movement for Better Primaries," *Review of Reviews* 17 (May 1898): 583–89.

49. Low to Black, April 11, 1898; Low to Arthur von Briesen, March 30, 1898,

Low Papers; Woodruff, *Speeches,* speech of June 16, 1898; *Nation* 66 (March 3, 1898): 161–62; New York *Sun,* March 23, April 17, Dec. 8, 1898; *FC,* March 30, 1898.

50. Woodruff, *Speeches,* speech of June 16, 1898; E. H. Slocum to Aldridge, May 1, 1898, May 12, 1898; Charlie W. to Aldridge, May 12, 1898 (quote), Aldridge Papers; New York *Sun,* June 7, 1898; *Trib.,* March 31 (quote), June 30, 1898; *Outlook* 59 (June 18, 1898): 411; Gherardi Davis, "The Story of My Life," Davis Papers.

51. Chessman, *Governor Theodore Roosevelt,* pp. 7–24; Alexander, *Four Famous New Yorkers,* pp. 299–302; Frank D. Pavey to William McKinley, Aug. 24, 1898, McKinley Papers; *AEJ,* March 24, 1898; *Trib.,* Aug. 30, 1898; Eager, "Governing New York State," pp. 348–52.

52. Mark Sullivan, *Our Times, 1900–1925,* 6 vols. (New York, 1926), 1: 78; Chessman, *Governor Theodore Roosevelt,* pp. 20–21; Blum, *Republican Roosevelt,* pp. 7–23, emphasizes Roosevelt's proclivity for sticking with the party despite his misgivings about the organization.

53. Thomas Humphrey to Platt, Aug. 22, 1898; Leroy H. Van Kirk to Platt, Sept. 17, 1898; J. T. Williams to Platt, Sept. 20, 1898, Platt Papers, Yale.

54. Murray T. Quigg, "Reminiscences," COHC; John R. Hazel to Platt, Sept. 3, 1898; Platt to Hazel, Sept. 6, 1898; Platt to C. P. Vedder, Sept. 22, 1898 (quote), Platt Papers, Yale; Roosevelt to Quigg, Aug. 17, 1898, Aug. 27, 1898, Aug. 30, 1898, Sept. 11, 1898, Sept. 12, 1898, *LTR,* II; Quigg to Roosevelt, Sept. 10, 1898, March 19, 1913, April 23, 1913, Roosevelt Papers, Harvard; Quigg to Roosevelt, Sept. 14, 1898, Roosevelt Papers, LC; Theodore Roosevelt, *An Auto-biography* (New York, 1913), pp. 269–72; Chessman, *Governor Theodore Roosevelt,* pp. 28–42; Alexander, *Four Famous New Yorkers,* pp. 303–10.

55. *Buffalo Commercial,* Sept. 28, 1898, Nov. 7, 1898; *Nation* 67 (Sept. 8, 1898): 176; *Auburn Daily Advertiser,* Oct. 31, 1898; *Watertown Daily Times,* Sept. 27, 1898; *Trib.,* Sept. 28, 1898; "The Moral of Two Careers," *Harper's Weekly* 42 (Dec. 17, 1898): 1219; J. Lincoln Steffens, "Theodore Roosevelt: Governor," *McClure's Magazine* 13 (May 1899): 57–64; Roosevelt to Quigg, Sept. 30, 1898 (quote), Oct. 16, 1898, Oct. 21, 1898, *LTR,* II; Low to Choate, Sept. 30, 1898, Low Papers; Quigg to Reynolds, Oct. 18, 1898, USS Papers.

56. *Trib. Alm.* (1899); New York *Evening Post,* Nov. 9, 1898; *Trib.,* Nov. 13, 1898; *Nation* 67 (Nov. 10, 1898): 341; Paul Nichols to David B. Hill, Nov. 12, 1898, Hill Papers, NYSL; Quigg to Roosevelt, June 30, 1899, Roosevelt Papers, Harvard; Chessman, *Governor Theodore Roosevelt,* pp. 50–70; Eager, "Governing New York State," pp. 355–60.

57. Roosevelt to Francis Ellington Leupp, Sept. 3, 1898; Roosevelt to George Hinckley Lyman, Jan. 25, 1900; Roosevelt to Anna Roosevelt Cowles, April 30, 1900 (quote), *LTR,* II; *P.P., 1899,* pp. 248–49 (quote).

58. Roosevelt to Platt, Jan. 12, 1899, Feb. 8, 1899, Feb. 10, 1899; Roosevelt to Low, Aug. 3, 1900; Roosevelt to Maria Longworth Storer, Feb. 18, 1899 (quote), Dec. 2, 1899, *LTR,* II; William Allen White, "Theodore Roosevelt," *McClure's Magazine* 18 (Nov. 1901): 42; Frederick W. Holls to Andrew D. White, May 8, 1900, White Papers; James B. Reynolds to Hazen S. Pingree, June 15, 1899, USS Papers; Roosevelt, *Autobiography,* pp. 279–90.

59. *P.P., 1899,* p. 21; Chessman, *Governor Theodore Roosevelt,* pp. 78–81, 89–91 (quote 79); see the extensive correspondence during the winter of 1899 among Roosevelt, George McAneny, and Horace White in the New York State

Civil Service Reform Association Papers. Platt to Quigg, April 28, 1900, Platt Papers, Yale; Roosevelt to Platt, May 1, 1900 (quote), *LTR*, II.

60. Platt to Roosevelt, May 6, 1899, Platt Papers, Yale.

61. Quigg to Roosevelt, June 30, 1899 (quote), Sept. 20, 1899, Oct. 12, 1899, Roosevelt Papers, Harvard; Roosevelt to Benjamin B. Odell, Jr., June 7, 1899; Roosevelt to James B. Reynolds, July 15, 1899; Roosevelt to Henry Cabot Lodge, Aug. 10, 1899; Roosevelt to Quigg, Sept. 19, 1899; Roosevelt to Philemon Tecumseh Sherman, Oct. 28, 1899, *LTR*, II; Reynolds to R. Fulton Cutting, June 26, 1899; Reynolds to John W. Weed, Sept. 11, 1899; Reynolds to William T. O'Brien, Oct. 9, 1899; Reynolds to Wheeler H. Peckham, Sept. 20, 1899; Reynolds to Seth Low, Oct. 5, 1899, USS Papers.

62. New York *Sun*, Oct. 19, 1899; *AEJ*, Oct. 9, 14, 16, 18, 20, 26, Nov. 3, 4, 6, 8, 1899; *TDT*, Oct. 9, 10, 11, 20, 27, 28, Nov. 1, 8, 1899; Rochester *Democrat and Chronicle*, Nov. 8, 1899; *Buffalo Commercial*, Oct. 21, 23, 27, Nov. 2, 4, 8, 1899; Syracuse *Evening Herald*, Oct. 11, 12, 18, 26, 30, Nov. 1, 8, 1899; McKelvey, Rochester: *The Quest for Quality*, pp. 81–84.

63. McKelvey, *Rochester: The Quest for Quality*, p. 88; *TDT*, Nov. 1, 2, 6, 1901; *AEJ*, Oct. 10, 23, 29, Nov. 6, 7, 1901; Syracuse *Evening Herald*, Oct. 18, 19, 31, Nov. 2, 6, 1901; Syracuse *Post-Standard*, Oct. 13, 18, 21, 23, 24, Nov. 2, 5, 1901; *Buffalo Commercial*, Oct. 16, 21, 29, Nov. 6, 7, 1901; *Buffalo Morning Express*, Oct. 22, 23, 25, 30, 1901; *Buffalo Evening News*, Nov. 4, 6, 1901.

64. Citizens' Union, *The City for the People! Campaign Book of the Citizens' Union* (New York, 1901); Republican County Committee, *Honest Government for New York. Campaign Book of the Republican Party* (New York, 1901), p. 7 (quote); Black, *Addresses*, pp. 182–83; New York *Sun*, Nov. 6, 9, 1900, Nov. 1, 2, 1901; *NYT*, May 31, Aug. 5, 24, Sept. 24, 25, 29, Oct. 2, Nov. 1, 1901; Quigg to Low, Aug. 13, 1901, Aug. 27, 1901, Low Papers; R. Fulton Cutting, "Anti-Tammany Union," National Municipal League, *Proceedings* (Philadelphia, 1901), pp. 78–80; Kurland, *Seth Low*, pp. 113–39.

65. Roosevelt to Platt, Nov. 16, 1901, Nov. 19, 1901; Platt to Roosevelt, Nov. 18, 1901, Nov. 22, 1901; Seth Low to Platt, Nov. 18, 1901, Platt Papers, Yale; *Barnes v. Roosevelt*, p. 756; typescript of the speeches made at a City Club dinner in honor of Seth Low, Nov. 14, 1901, City Club Papers, NYPL; New York *Sun*, Nov. 8, 24, 1901.

66. Cutting, "City Government and the People," p. 881.

67. Wilcox, "Party Government in the Cities," p. 698.

5. *Republicans and Economic Policies*

1. Richard L. McCormick, "The Party Period and Public Policy: An Exploratory Hypothesis," *JAH* 66 (Sept. 1979): 279–98.

2. Davies to George E. Dunham, Feb. 15, 1901; Davies to Samuel A. Beardsley, May 9, 1901, Davies Papers.

3. Barnes to Platt, Nov. 15, 1894, Nov. 21, 1894, Nov. 27, 1894, Dec. 22, 1894, July 29, 1899, Platt Papers, Yale; Green to Aldridge, June 11, 1898, June 17, 1898, Aldridge Papers; Harold F. Gosnell, *Boss Platt and His New York Machine: A Study of the Political Leadership of Thomas C. Platt, Theodore Roosevelt and Others* (Chicago, 1924), pp. 59–69, 269–74.

4. William Collins Beer to Charles G. Dawes, March 25, 1897, Beer Family

Papers; Laws of 1895, chap. 178; Ashley W. Cole to Platt, March 25, 1895 (quote), Levi P. Morton Papers; an undated, unsigned typescript in the Platt Papers, Yale, presents the Platt family side of the Fidelity and Deposit Company matter; it appears to have been written by Henry B. Platt in 1896 or 1897. See also: Frank H. Platt to Thomas Collier Platt, April 6, 1895; Thomas Collier Platt to Levi P. Morton, April 8, 1895, Morton Papers; "Report of the Special Committee of the Assembly Appointed to Investigate the Public Offices and Departments of the City of New York and of the Counties Therein Included," *Assembly Documents*, No. 78 (Albany, 1901), pp. 2873–79; and Gosnell, *Boss Platt and His New York Machine*, pp. 246–48.

5. Gosnell, *Boss Platt and His New York Machine*, pp. 262–90.

6. The most important sources are the following: *Testimony Taken before the Joint Committee of the Senate and Assembly of the State of New York to Investigate and Examine into the Business and Affairs of Life Insurance Companies Doing Business in the State of New York*, 7 vols. (Albany, 1905) [hereafter cited as *Test.*]; "Report of the Joint Committee of the Senate and Assembly of the State of New York, Appointed to Investigate Corrupt Practices in Connection with Legislation, and the Affairs of Insurance Companies, Other than Those Doing Life Insurance Business," *Assembly Documents*, No. 30 (Albany, 1911); "Proceedings of the Senate in the Matter of the Investigation Demanded by Senator Jotham P. Allds," *Senate Documents*, No. 28 (Albany, 1910); United States Senate, *Campaign Contributions*, Testimony before a Subcommittee of the Committee on Privileges and Elections, 62nd Congress, 3rd Session, 2 vols. (Washington, D.C., 1913); *Barnes v. Roosevelt*; and Harold F. Gosnell, Interviews relating to the career of Thomas Collier Platt, Columbia University Library.

7. Gosnell interview with Benjamin B. Odell, Jr., Sept. 22, 1922; *Barnes v. Roosevelt*, p. 707 (quote); Theodore Roosevelt, *An Autobiography* (New York, 1913), pp. 298–99; *Test.*, p. 3397 (quote); U.S. Senate, *Campaign Contributions*, p. 625; Gosnell interview with Nicholas Murray Butler, Sept. 26, 1922; Gosnell, *Boss Platt and His New York Machine*, pp. 288–89.

8. James K. Pollock, Jr., *Party Campaign Funds* (New York, 1926), pp. 63–65; Earl R. Sikes, *State and Federal Corrupt-Practices Legislation* (Durham, N.C., 1928), pp. 105–7, 180–83; Robert C. Brooks, *Corruption in American Politics and Life* (New York, 1910), pp. 219–20; Louise Overacker, *Money in Elections* (New York, 1932), pp. 101–13, 180–81; Robert D. Marcus, *Grand Old Party: Political Structure in the Gilded Age, 1880–1896* (New York, 1971), p. 247; *Barnes v. Roosevelt*, p. 1317; U.S. Senate, *Campaign Contributions*, p. 628 (quote).

9. Gosnell interview with W. T. Arndt, Sept. 22, 1922 (quote); William Allen White, "Platt," *McClure's Magazine* 18 (Dec. 1901): 145–53; Burton J. Hendrick, "Governor Hughes and the Albany Gang: A Study of the Degradation of the Republican Party in New York State," *McClure's Magazine* 35 (Sept. 1910): 495–512; Joseph B. Bishop, "The Price of Peace," *Century Magazine* 48 (Sept. 1894): 667–72; Roosevelt, *Autobiography*, pp. 297–99; *Test.*, pp. 3385–97.

10. Platt to Fish, April 3, 1895 (quote), April 23, 1896, Fish Papers; Platt to Nixon, May 5, 1899, April 9, 1901 (quote), Nixon Papers; Platt to Robert Mazet, Oct. 13, 1899; Mazet to Platt, Oct. 13, 1899, Platt Papers, Yale; Henry B. Hyde to Platt, Feb. 23, 1898; Hyde to Chauncey M. Depew, Feb. 24, 1898, Equitable Life Assurance Society Collection; Platt to Morton, May 25, 1896, Platt Papers, private; James W. Wadsworth, "Reminiscences," p. 56 (quote), COHC.

11. Platt to J. P. Allds (quote); to S. Fred Nixon; to T. E. Ellsworth; to B. B.

Odell, Jr., all Jan. 20, 1902; A. J. Cassatt to Platt, Jan. 23, 1902, Jan. 24, 1902, Jan. 29, 1902; Platt to Cassatt; to Odell; to Nixon; to Ellsworth; to Timothy L. Woodruff, all Jan. 28, 1902; Platt to Cassatt; to Odell; to Nixon; to Ellsworth; to Woodruff, all Jan. 30, 1902; Nixon to Platt, Jan. 21, 1902, Jan. 29, 1902, Feb. 1, 1902; Ellsworth to Platt, Jan. 29, 1902; Woodruff to Platt, Feb. 4, 1902; Platt to Cassatt, Feb. 6, 1902, Feb. 14, 1902 (letter and telegram); Cassatt to Platt, Feb. 8, 1902, Feb. 14, 1902, Feb. 27, 1902 (quote); Platt to Nixon, Feb. 26, 1902 (quote); Platt to Allds, March 1, 1902, Platt Papers, Yale. *NYT,* Jan. 30, Feb. 19, 26, 27, March 13, 19, 21, 22, 23, 25, 26, 27, April 12, 13, 16, 1902.

12. Morton Keller, *The Life Insurance Enterprise, 1885–1910: A Study in the Limits of Corporate Power* (Cambridge, Mass., 1963), pp. 214–26; Ira A. Place to Joseph Mullin, April 10, 1895, April 13, 1895, Corporate Records of the New York Central Railroad Company; David Willcox to Lewis E. Carr, Jan. 3, 1899, Jan. 6, 1899, Jan. 21, 1899, Feb. 7, 1899, March 11, 1899, March 16, 1899, March 18, 1899; Willcox to Horace G. Young, Jan. 3, 1899, March 6, 1899, Delaware and Hudson Railroad Corporation Papers.

13. On transportation passes see Ira A. Place to Joseph Mullin, April 24, 1895, New York Central Railroad Papers; John C. Davies to Van R. Weaver, Sept. 14, 1900, Davies Papers; and Jonathan M. Wainwright to Thomas D. Dinwoodie, May 23, 1903, Wainwright Papers. All three legislative investigations cited in note 6 above occasioned charges concerning strike bills but also provided evidence that the companies sought and paid for positive actions in their interest. See also: Wadsworth, "Reminiscences," pp. 55–56; Bruce William Dearstyne, "Railroads and Railroad Regulation in New York State, 1900–1913," Ph.D. diss., Syracuse University, 1974, pp. 35–46; and Gosnell, *Boss Platt and His New York Machine,* pp. 266–71.

14. "Report of the Joint Committee . . . Appointed to Investigate Corrupt Practices," pp. 168–97, 552–627, 806–16.

15. *Barnes v. Roosevelt,* pp. 1833–37; Gosnell, *Boss Platt and His New York Machine,* pp. 264–84; Frederic C. Howe, *The City: The Hope of Democracy* (New York, 1905), pp. 61–91.

16. The Papers of the NYBTT voluminously document the activities of New York City's mercantile interests on behalf of regulation and canal imrpovement, as well as their discontent with regular party politics; see the Minutes of the Annual Meetings, Jan. 9, 1895, Jan. 12, 1898; Minutes of the Monthly Meetings, Oct. 9, 1895, Nov. 13, 1895, March 10, 1897, Dec. 14, 1898, Feb. 8, 1899, March 8, 1899; Report of the Special Committee on Telephone Legislation, April 8, 1896; Report of the Executive Committee, May 8, 1901.

17. *Buffalo Daily Times,* Oct. 19, 1897; Bishop, "The Price of Peace"; Joseph B. Bishop, "A New Form of Government," *Forum* 23 (June 1897): 396–408; Roosevelt, *Autobiography,* p. 298. A few New Yorkers clearly understood the alliance of business and politics; one was John Jay Chapman, a committed nonpartisan and the author of the brilliant *Causes and Consequences* (New York, 1898).

18. Howard Lawrence Hurwitz, *Theodore Roosevelt and Labor in New York State, 1880–1900* (New York, 1943), pp. 25–30, 37–38.

19. Laws of 1895, chap. 791; Laws of 1896, chaps. 384, 789, 991; Laws of 1897, chap. 415; Elizabeth Brandeis, "Labor Legislation," in John R. Commons et al., *History of Labor in the United States,* 4 vols. (New York, 1926–35), 3: 467–69, 541–42; Hurwitz, *Theodore Roosevelt and Labor,* pp. 45–47; Fred Rogers Fairchild, *The Factory Legislation of the State of New York* (New York, 1906), pp.

28–67; G. Wallace Chessman, *Governor Theodore Roosevelt: The Albany Apprenticeship, 1898–1900* (Cambridge, Mass., 1965), p. 202.

20. Jeremy P. Felt, *Hostages of Fortune: Child Labor Reform in New York State* (Syracuse, 1965), pp. 17–37; the data concerning factory inspection under O'Leary are derived from the table in Felt, p. 31; Claire Brandler Walker, "A History of Factory Legislation and Inspection in New York State, 1886–1911," Ph.D. diss., Columbia University, 1969, pp. 99–104, 174.

21. Clifford D. Gregory et al. to Hamilton Fish, March 15, 1895, Fish Papers; Noble E. Whitford, *History of the Canal System of the State of New York,* 2 vols. (Albany, 1906), 1: 368; Michael Kelly to Aldridge, March 3, 1897; Martin Reeb to Aldridge, June 26, 1897; Charles McKinnon et al. to Aldridge, Oct. 14, 1897; L. H. King to Aldridge, Feb. 7, 1898; Dominick A. Walsh to Aldridge, April 2, 1898; Thomas J. Rowe to Aldridge, Oct. 8, 1898, Aldridge Papers.

22. *P.P., 1897–98,* p. 10; Herbert Parsons to Charles Dewey Hilles, July 24, 1907, Parsons Papers (Woodruff quoted).

23. *Annual Report of the Comptroller* (Albany, 1898), pp. v–xx; Edwin R. A. Seligman, "Recent Discussion of Tax Reform," *PSQ* 15 (Sept. 1900): 629–46; *P.P., 1897–1898,* pp. 5–6, 242; C. K. Yearley, *The Money Machines: The Breakdown and Reform of Governmental and Party Finance in the North, 1860–1920* (Albany, 1970), pp. 3–134.

24. *P.P., 1895,* p. 7; *P.P., 1896,* pp. 8–9; Don C. Sowers, *The Financial History of New York State: From 1789 to 1912* (New York, 1914), pp. 152–68, 330–31, 340–41; Merlin Harold Hunter, *The Development of Corporation Taxation in the State of New York* (Urbana, Ill., 1917), pp. 68–69, 130; *Annual Report of the Comptroller* (Albany, 1899), p. xix.

25. *Annual Report of the Comptroller* (Albany, 1897), pp. xviii–xxvi (quote xxii); Roberts to Frank A. Dudley, May 5, 1897, James A. Roberts and Frank S. Sidway Papers; *FC,* Jan. 27, April 28 (quote), May 5, 26, 1897; *A.J.* (1897), pp. 2247–48; *S.J.* (1897), p. 1865; Platt to Henry B. Hyde, April 24, 1897 (quote), Equitable Collection; *P.P., 1897–1898,* pp. 55–57 (quote 55); Sowers, *Financial History,* pp. 175–76; Yearley, *Money Machines,* pp. 176–79.

26. *P.P., 1895,* pp. 7, 11; *FC,* Feb. 2, 1898, April 11, 1900; *SLP,* Oct. 14, 1896; *Annual Report of the Comptroller* (Albany, 1898), pp. v–xx; Yearley, *Money Machines,* pp. 137–65.

27. John A. Fairlie, "State Administration in New York," *PSQ* 15 (March 1900): 67–68; see also: Governor Black's comments on railroad, banking, and insurance regulation, *P.P., 1897–1898,* pp. 8–9, 12, 211–12; and Augustus Cerillo, Jr., "Reform in New York City: A Study of Urban Progressivism," Ph.D. diss., Northwestern University, 1969, pp. 60–96.

28. Dearstyne, "Railroad Regulation," pp. 46–55; Black to Platt, Feb. 10, 1897, Platt Papers, Yale; but see *P.P., 1897–1898,* pp. 49–50.

29. Hyde to James W. Alexander, Dec. 17, 1894; Hyde to B. K. Durfee, Oct. 15, 1896, Nov. 24, 1896; Hyde to William A. Fricke, March 18, 1897; Hyde to Louis F. Payn, Dec. 24, 1897; Payn to Hyde, Jan. 2, 1898; James F. Pierce to Theodore E. Hancock, June 15, 1894, Equitable Collection; John C. Davies to Platt, Oct. 23, 1900, Davies Papers; Keller, *Life Insurance Enterprise,* pp. 196–202.

30. Gustavus Myers, "History of Public Franchises in New York City," *Municipal Affairs* 4 (March 1900): 99–105; Max West, "Municipal Franchises in New York," in Edward W. Bemis, ed., *Municipal Monopolies* (New York, 1899), pp.

411–13; E. Dana Durand, "Political and Municipal Legislation in 1897," *AAAPSS* 11 (March 1898): 188; Laws of 1897, chap. 385.

31. Noble E. Whitford, *History of the Barge Canal of New York State* (Albany, 1922), pp. 6–21; Whitford, *History of the Canal System,* 1: 911; 2: 1062–63; *P.P., 1895,* pp. 25–28; Frank S. Gardner, "The Canal Improvement Union," *Buffalo Historical Society Publications* 13 (Buffalo, 1909): 1–11; Gustav Schwab, "New York City's Part in the Reconstruction of the State's Waterways," *ibid.,* pp. 35–75; Henry B. Hebert, "Action of the New York Produce Exchange," *ibid.,* pp. 77–108; John D. Kernen, "The Function of New York's Barge Canals in Controlling Freight Rates," *ibid.,* pp. 135–56; Minutes of Monthly Meetings, Oct. 9, 1895, Nov. 13, 1895; Darwin R. James to Theodore E. Hancock, Oct. 3, 1896, NYBTT Papers; George Clinton et al. to Levi P. Morton, Dec. 26, 1894, Morton Papers.

32. *P.P., 1895,* pp. 25–28; *P.P., 1896,* pp. 24–26; *P.P., 1897–1898,* pp. 15, 212–13; Rochester *Union and Advertiser,* Jan. 8, 1895 (Morton Papers).

33. *A.J.* (1895), p. 625; *S.J.* (1895), pp. 370–71; Whitford, *History of the Canal System,* 1: 354–62; *SLP,* Sept. 18, Oct. 2, 16, 1895; *Manual* (1896), pp. 969–70; Samuel T. McSeveney, *The Politics of Depression: Political Behavior in the Northeast, 1893–1896* (New York, 1972), pp. 83–86.

34. James A. Roberts to George Washington Aldridge, Jan. 5, 1898, Aldridge Papers; *P.P., 1897–1898,* pp. 250–52, 370–73; *FC,* Dec. 15, 29, 1897, Jan. 12, March 30, Aug. 17, 1898; *SLP,* Jan. 26, Feb. 2, 1898; Henry Wayland Hill, "An Historical Review of Waterways and Canal Construction in New York State," *Buffalo Historical Society Publications* 12 (Buffalo, 1908): 229–32, 240–44.

35. *Annual Report of the Bureau of Labor Statistics* (Albany, 1901), pp. 435, 442–43; for data on the continued growth of union membership after 1900, see Department of Labor, *Bulletin* 13 (Albany, 1911): 214. *NYT,* Jan. 10, 1898; Gosnell, *Boss Platt and His New York Machine,* pp. 8–9; Hurwitz, *Roosevelt and Labor,* pp. 22–32, 47–49, 190, 226; Irwin Yellowitz's *Labor and the Progressive Movement in New York State, 1897–1916* (Ithaca, 1965), significantly begins its coverage in 1897.

36. Hill, "An Historical Review," pp. 246–48; Gardner, "Canal Improvement Union," pp. 4–11; Schwab, "New York City's Part," pp. 35–48; *Annual Report of the Buffalo Merchants' Exchange . . . 1900* (Buffalo, 1901), pp. 34–36, 43–47; *ibid. 1901* (Buffalo, 1902), pp. 8–9, 20–21, 36–39; *ibid. 1902* (Buffalo, 1903), pp. 9–10, 29–31; "Official Call for the Second Annual State Commerce Convention," printed flyer, May 1, 1900; "The Improvement of Our State Canals," printed flyer, April 11, 1900, NYBTT Papers.

37. *P.P., 1899,* p. 33 (quote); *Annual Report of the Commissioner of Agriculture* (Albany, 1911), pp. 3e–7e; Western New York Horticultural Society, *Proceedings of the Forty-Third Annual Meeting* (Rochester, 1898), pp. 18–21; James Mickel Williams, *The Expansion of Rural Life: The Social Psychology of Rural Development* (New York, 1931), pp. 116 (quote), 192 (quote); Ulysses Prentiss Hedrick, *A History of Agriculture in the State of New York* ([Albany], 1933), p. 436; Gosnell, *Boss Platt and His New York Machine,* pp. 8–11, 265–67, 354–55.

38. Report of the Executive Committee, May 8, 1901, NYBTT Papers; *NYT,* July 24, 1899 (quote); Samuel P. Hays, "Political Parties and the Community-Society Continuum," in William Nisbet Chambers and Walter Dean Burnham, eds., *The American Party System: Stages of Political Development* (New York, 1967), pp. 152–81.

39. Henry White to James B. Reynolds, March 4, 1897, March 27, 1897; John

B. Pine to Reynolds, April 14, 1897; Arthur von Briesen to Reynolds, April 1, 1898, USS Papers; *NYT,* July 22, 24, Oct. 9, 23, 1899; Citizens' Union, *The City for the People! Campaign Book of the Citizens' Union* (New York, 1901), pp. 8–9; Robert Fulton Cutting, "City Government and the People," *Municipal Affairs* 5 (Dec. 1901): 881–85; John De Witt Warner, "Municipal Betterment in the New York City Elections," *ibid.* (Sept. 1901), pp. 625–40.

40. Hans B. Thorelli, *The Federal Antitrust Policy: Origination of an American Tradition* (Baltimore, 1955), pp. 329–43, 572–87.

41. *NYT,* Feb. 7, 18, 20, 25, March 4, 19, 20, 26, April 1, 2, 3, 24, 25, May 30, 1896; *FC,* Oct. 6, 1897; Morton to Chauncey M. Depew, April 15, 1896, Depew Papers, LC; Chessman, *Governor Theodore Roosevelt,* pp. 158–60; Robert Crosby Eager, "Governing New York State: Republicans and Reform, 1894–1900," Ph.D. diss., Stanford University, 1977, pp. 186–90.

42. L. H. Humphrey to Platt, Jan. 20, 1897, Platt Papers, private; Syracuse *Evening Herald,* Jan. 16, 21, 1897; David Willcox to Lewis E. Carr, May 14, 1897, May 17, 1897, June 16, 1897, July 13, 1897, Sept. 21, 1897, April 4, 1898, Delaware and Hudson Papers; Minutes of the Monthly Meeting, April 14, 1897, NYBTT Papers; *NYT,* July 13, Nov. 11, 1897; "Report of the Joint Committee of the Senate and Assembly Appointed to Investigate Trusts," *Senate Documents,* No. 40 (Albany, 1897); Laws of 1897, chaps. 383, 384.

43. Milo Roy Maltbie, "A Century of Franchise History," *Municipal Affairs* 4 (March 1900): 194–206; Myers, "History of Public Franchises," pp. 71–193; West, "Municipal Franchises," p. 420 (quote); Delos F. Wilcox, *Municipal Franchises,* 2 vols. (New York, 1910–11), 2: 127–28; U.S. Bureau of the Census, *Street and Electric Railways 1902* (Washington, D.C., 1905), pp. 143–44.

44. West, "Municipal Franchises," p. 399; James H. Hamilton, "Syracuse Water Supply," *Municipal Affairs* 4 (March 1900): 60–70; Myers, "History of Public Franchises," pp. 85–88; M. N. Baker, "Water-Works," in Bemis, ed., *Municipal Monopolies,* p. 22; New York *Sun,* Aug. 30, 1899; U.S. Bureau of the Census, *Central Electric Light and Power Stations 1902* (Washington, D.C., 1905), p. 127; *Annual Report of the Commission of Gas and Electricity* (Albany, 1906), pp. 18, 138–43.

45. David C. Hammack, "The Planning of New York City's First Subway," paper presented at the Eastern Historical Geography Association, April 5, 1974; Myers, "History of Public Franchises," pp. 102, 153–54; "Report of the Committee Appointed by the Assembly to Investigate the Question of Municipal Ownership of the Street and Elevated Railroads of the Various Cities of the State," *Assembly Documents,* No. 98 (Albany, 1896), p. 18 (quote); Cerillo, "Reform in New York City," pp. 60–84.

46. Roosevelt to Chauncey M. Depew, Jan. 23, 1899; Roosevelt to the Commissioners of the Land Office, Dec. 12, 1899; Roosevelt to Joseph Bucklin Bishop, March 22, 1900, April 11, 1900 (quote); Roosevelt to George Hinckley Lyman, March 22, 1900, *LTR,* II; *P.P., 1900,* p. 18; Chessman, *Governor Theodore Roosevelt,* pp. 156–57; Eager, "Governing New York State," pp. 407–15.

47. *P.P., 1900,* p. 15; Chessman, *Governor Theodore Roosevelt,* pp. 158–76; Roosevelt to Hermann Henry Kohlsatt, Aug. 7, 1899; Roosevelt to Henry Lincoln, March 15, 1900, *LTR,* II; Jeremiah W. Jenks, "Publicity: A Remedy for the Evils of Trusts," *Review of Reviews* 21 (April 1900): 445–49.

48. *P.P., 1900,* p. 20 (my italics); Elihu Root to Roosevelt, Dec. 13, 1899, Root Papers, LC; Roosevelt to Root, Dec. 15, 1899, *LTR,* II; Philip C. Jessup, *Elihu Root,* 2 vols. (New York, 1938), 1: 208–9.

49. *The Works of Theodore Roosevelt: Memorial Edition,* 24 vols. (New York, 1923–26), 16: 460, 512; Hurwitz, *Roosevelt and Labor,* pp. 277–78; John R. Commons, "Economists and Class Partnership," in Commons, *Labor and Administration* (New York, 1913), p. 67.

50. Theodore Roosevelt, "Fellow-Feeling as a Political Factor," *Century Magazine* 59 (Jan. 1900): 468–69.

51. Roosevelt to Odell, March 31, 1899; Roosevelt to Riis, May 11, 1899 (quote), May 13, 1899; Roosevelt to Thomas Roberts Slicer, April 22, 1899, *LTR,* II; Chessman, *Governor Theodore Roosevelt,* pp. 204–5; Hurwitz, *Roosevelt and Labor,* pp. 230–33; James B. Lane, *Jacob Riis and the American City* (Port Washington, N.Y., 1974), pp. 129–49.

52. *NYT,* Nov. 23, 1898; *P.P., 1899,* p. 10 (quote); *P.P., 1900,* pp. 28–31; *Works of Theodore Roosevelt,* 16: 509–21; Roosevelt to Josephine Shaw Lowell, Feb. 20, 1900, *LTR,* II; James B. Reynolds to Roosevelt, Nov. 14, 1898, Dec. 9, 1899; Reynolds to Jane Adams [*sic*], Feb. 14, 1899; Reynolds to John Gallagher, Oct. 19, 1899, USS Papers. Both Hurwitz, *Roosevelt and Labor,* pp. 188–259, and Chessman, *Governor Theodore Roosevelt,* pp. 200–225, provide thorough accounts of Roosevelt's labor policies, with Chessman the more sympathetic of the two.

53. Francis Vinton Greene, "The Inception of the Barge Canal Project," *Buffalo Historical Society Publications* 13 (Buffalo, 1909): 109–20; *P.P., 1899,* pp. 7–9, 47–48; *P.P., 1900,* 73–82; Roosevelt to Greene, Jan. 31, 1900, March 5, 1900 (quote); Roosevelt to Joseph Bucklin Bishop, Feb. 16, 1900; Roosevelt to Henry Cabot Lodge, April 9, 1900, *LTR,* II; *FC,* Jan. 31, 1900 (quote); Chessman, *Governor Theodore Roosevelt,* pp. 177–99; Whitford, *History of the Canal System,* 1: 381–84; Whitford, *History of the Barge Canal,* pp. 42–51.

54. Roosevelt to Charles Ransom Miller, Feb. 5, 1900 (quote); Roosevelt to Francis V. Greene, Feb. 10, 1900, Feb. 26, 1900; Roosevelt to Platt, Jan. 31, 1900, *LTR,* II; Platt to Roosevelt, Feb. 3, 1900, Platt Papers, Yale; Roosevelt to Frank S. Gardner, April 6, 1900, Roosevelt Papers, LC.

55. *P.P., 1899,* pp. 7, 54–57; *P.P., 1900,* pp. 13–16; Roosevelt to Elihu Root, March 14, 1899; Roosevelt to Benjamin B. Odell, Jr., March 15, 1899; Roosevelt to Nevada N. Stranahan, March 15, 1899; Roosevelt to Platt, March 15, 1899, March 17, 1899, *LTR,* II; Edwin R. A. Seligman, "The Franchise Tax Law in New York," *Quarterly Journal of Economics* 13 (July 1899): 445–52; Chessman, *Governor Theodore Roosevelt,* pp. 120–57; Eager, "Governing New York State," pp. 375–405.

56. Roosevelt to Paul Dana, April 7, 1899; Roosevelt to Edwin R. A. Seligman, April 17, 1899; Roosevelt to S. Fred Nixon, April 25, 1899, *LTR,* II; Roosevelt to Platt, April 14, 1899, May 8, 1899, Platt Papers, Yale; John Ford, "Taxation of Public Franchises," *North American Review* 168 (June 1899): 730–38; John De Witt Warner, "The Ford Act: Taxation of Local Franchises," *Municipal Affairs* 3 (July 1899): 269–98; *P.P., 1899,* pp. 88–89; Roosevelt, *Autobiography,* pp. 321–28.

57. Minutes of Monthly Meetings, March 8, 1899, April 12, 1899, NYBTT Papers; Chauncey M. Depew, *My Memories of Eighty Years* (New York, 1922), p. 163; Harold F. Gosnell interview with Chauncey M. Depew, Sept. 25, 1922; multicopy letter from G. Tracy Rogers, May 20, 1899; G. Tracy Rogers to Platt, May 31, 1899; Platt to Harry M. Glen, May 6, 1899; Glen to Platt, May 7, 1899; George R. Malby to Platt, May 29, 1899, Platt Papers, Yale; *FC,* Feb. 22, May 17,

1899; *SLP,* May 3, 24, 31, 1899; Syracuse *Evening Herald,* May 12, 16, 23, 1899; *NYT,* May 2, 1899.

58. Roosevelt to Anna Roosevelt Cowles, May 1, 1899; Roosevelt to Henry Cabot Lodge, May 27, 1899, *LTR,* II; Nixon to Platt, May 12, 1899, May 16, 1899; T. E. Ellsworth to Platt, May 15, 1899; Platt to Roosevelt, May 6, 1899 (quote); Platt to Harry M. Glen, May 6, 1899 (quote); Platt to Charles H. T. Collis, May 24, 1899, Platt Papers, Yale; *Barnes v. Roosevelt,* pp. 10, 170, 215–16, 707, 1901.

59. Roosevelt to Platt, May 8, 1899, May 12, 1899, *LTR,* II.

60. Roosevelt to James R. Garfield, May 13, 1899; Roosevelt to Frank W. Higgins, May 17, 1899; Roosevelt to John Raines, May 18, 1899; Roosevelt to Benjamin B. Odell, Jr., May 18, 1899, *LTR,* II; John C. Davies to Frederick S. Gibbs, July 6, 1900, Davies Papers; *P.P., 1899,* pp. 102–10; *P.P., 1900,* pp. 16–18; Hunter, *Development of Corporation Taxation,* pp. 153–65.

61. The standard accounts of Roosevelt's nomination to the vice-presidency are: G. Wallace Chessman, "Theodore Roosevelt's Campaign Against the Vice-Presidency," *Historian* 14 (Spring 1952): 173–90; Roosevelt, *Autobiography,* pp. 331–33; *Auto. TCP,* pp. 383–97; and Herbert Croly, *Marcus Alonzo Hanna, His Life and Work* (New York, 1912), pp. 308–18.

62. Roosevelt to Henry Cabot Lodge, Feb. 3, 1900, April 9, 1900; Roosevelt to Joseph Bucklin Bishop, April 11, 1900; Roosevelt to Anna Roosevelt Cowles, June 25, 1900; Roosevelt to Silas W. Burt, July 14, 1900; Roosevelt to Seth Low, Aug. 3, 1900, *LTR,* II; Frederick W. Holls to Andrew D. White, May 8, 1900, June 12, 1900; Benjamin I. Wheeler to White, July 23, 1900, White Papers; J. Lincoln Steffens, "Governor Roosevelt—As an Experiment," *McClure's Magazine* 15 (June 1900): 112.

6. *The Limitations of "Businesslike" Government*

1. Platt to Roosevelt, Aug. 9, 1900, Aug. 16, 1900 (quote), Platt Papers, Yale; Roosevelt to Platt, Aug. 9, 1900, Aug. 13, 1900, Aug. 15, 1900, Aug. 20, 1900; Roosevelt to Seth Low, Aug. 3, 1900; Roosevelt to Benjamin B. Odell, Jr., Aug. 10, 1900, *LTR,* II; Low to Francis V. Greene, July 26, 1900; Low to Roosevelt, July 31, 1900, Low Papers; *Red Book* (1901), pp. 31–35; Lyman Abbott, "Governor-Elect Odell, of New York," *Review of Reviews* 22 (Dec. 1900): 687–88; Harold F. Gosnell, *Boss Platt and His New York Machine: A Study of the Political Leadership of Thomas C. Platt, Theodore Roosevelt, and Others* (Chicago, 1924), pp. 165–66; DeAlva Stanwood Alexander, *Four Famous New Yorkers: The Political Careers of Cleveland, Platt, Hill and Roosevelt* (New York, 1923), pp. 336–38; G. Wallace Chessman, *Governor Theodore Roosevelt: The Albany Apprenticeship, 1898–1900* (Cambridge, Mass., 1965), pp. 283–86.

2. New York *Sun,* April 11, Nov. 1–6, 1900; *NYT,* July 27, Sept. 6, 9, 17, Oct. 6, 10, Nov. 3, 6, 7, 8, 9, 16, 17, Dec. 11, 1900 (quote); *Trib.,* Sept. 9, Nov. 7, 16, 1900; *AEJ,* Jan. 1, 1901; *Red Book* (1901), pp. 590–91; Theodore Roosevelt to Seth Low, Aug. 25, 1900, *LTR,* II; J. Sloat Fassett to Platt, Nov. 7, 1900, Platt Papers, Yale.

3. *P.P., 1901,* pp. 9–58 (quote 12); *Trib.,* Jan. 2, 4, 1901; *AEJ,* Jan. 1, 1901; Alexander, *Four Famous New Yorkers,* pp. 373–75.

4. *P.P., 1901,* pp. 26–29 (quote 27).

5. *Trib.,* Dec. 28, 1900, Jan. 2, 3, 5, April 22, 24, 1901; *NYT,* Dec. 10, 1900,

Jan. 3, 4, 6, 22, 27, Feb. 1, 2, 3, 13, 28, March 1, 13, April 1, 3, 11, 16, 18, 22, May 12, 1901; New York *Press,* Jan. 3, 4, 1901; Rochester *Democrat and Chronicle,* Jan. 4, 1901; Syracuse *Evening Herald,* Jan. 2, 3, 4, April 23, 24, 1901; *Buffalo Commercial,* Jan. 2, 3, April 23, 24, 1901; *SLP,* Jan. 9, May 1, 1901; *Ithaca Daily Journal,* April 24, 1901; *TDT,* March 21, 1901; Odell to Roosevelt, Dec. 26, 1899, Roosevelt Papers, LC. C. K. Yearley, *The Money Machines: The Breakdown and Reform of Governmental and Party Finance in the North, 1860–1920* (Albany, 1970), discusses the connections between state revenues and party finances.

6. *Trib.,* Jan. 2, 1901; *NYT,* Jan. 4, 1901; Rochester *Democrat and Chronicle,* Jan. 5, 1901; Syracuse *Evening Herald,* Jan. 4, 1901; *Nation* 72 (Jan. 10, 1901): 23–24; Theodore Roosevelt to Henry Loomis Nelson, April 8, 1901; Roosevelt to William Howard Taft, July 15, 1901, *LTR,* III.

7. *P.P., 1901,* p. 16; *NYT,* Feb. 7, April 24, 1901; *FC,* Jan. 23, May 1, 1901.

8. *Trib.,* Sept. 25, 1902, Sept. 16, 1904; *FC,* Oct. 29, 1902; John Denison Champlin, ed., *Orations, Addresses and Speeches of Chauncey M. Depew,* 8 vols. (New York, 1910), 6: 175–84, 217–27. For interesting comments on the tariff issue's inability to unify the Republican party any more, see William Barnes, Jr., to Platt, Nov. 19, 1902, Platt Papers, Yale. New York *Press,* Jan. 4, 1901.

9. Roosevelt to Lucius Nathan Littauer, March 25, 1901 (quote); Roosevelt to Charles Joseph Bonaparte, March 30, 1901; Roosevelt to Henry Loomis Nelson, April 8, 1901 (quote); Roosevelt to C. E. S. Wood, Aug. 27, 1901, *LTR,* III; Syracuse *Evening Herald,* Jan. 3, 1901; *Nation* 72 (Jan. 10, 1901): 23–24.

10. James F. Richardson, *The New York Police: Colonial Times to 1901* (New York, 1970), pp. 275–82; Platt to T. E. Ellsworth, Nov. 12, 1900 (quote); Platt to J. F. Parkhurst, Nov. 12, 1900; Platt to John R. Hazel, Nov. 12, 1900; Platt to Cornelius N. Bliss, Nov. 15, 1900, Platt Papers, Yale; *NYT,* Nov. 16, 17, 1900; New York *Sun,* Nov. 9, 15, 1900; *FC,* Nov. 14, 21, 1900.

11. *NYT,* Dec. 8, 9, 1900, Jan. 10, 24, 30, Feb. 6, 12, 18, 21, 23, March 23, 1901; *Outlook* 66 (Dec. 8, 1900): 872–74; *P.P., 1901,* pp. 37–40, 42; Seth Low to Odell, Jan. 25, 1901, Low Papers; Odell to Lemuel E. Quigg, Feb. 6, 1901, Odell Papers; for independent praise of Odell's police measure, see the speech by Everett P. Wheeler, Oct. 21, 1901, Wheeler Papers.

12. *NYT,* Jan. 2, Feb. 3, 4, 23, 24, 26, March 1, 10, 14, 17–25, 1901; *Trib.,* Feb. 26, March 17–25, 1901; New York *Sun,* March 19–24, 1901; New York *Press,* March 21–24, 1901; *FC,* March 27, 1901; upstate party newspapers tended to play down the clash: *AEJ,* March 21, 22, 24, 1901; Rochester *Democrat and Chronicle,* March 24, 1901. Platt's own side of the story may be found in *Auto. TCP,* pp. 424–29.

13. New York *Press,* March 21, 1901.

14. United States Senate, *Campaign Contributions,* Testimony Before a Subcommittee of the Committee on Privileges and Elections, 62nd Congress, 3rd Session, 2 vols. (Washington, D.C., 1913), p. 625; Platt to Frank W. Higgins, Feb. 20, 1902, Higgins Papers; Odell to Whitelaw Reid, March 3, 1903, Reid Papers; Platt to George B. Cortelyou, Sept. 26, 1904; Cortelyou to Platt, Sept. 28, 1904, Cortelyou Papers. Biographical data on the legislators and data on the partisan composition of the assembly and senate may be found in *Red Book* (1901–4); and *Manual* (1901–4).

15. Platt to Roosevelt, March 27, 1902, March 5, 1903, March 28, 1903, July 3, 1903, Aug. 18, 1903, Jan. 5, 1905, Platt Papers, Yale; Platt to Roosevelt, Feb. 25,

1903, Roosevelt Papers, LC; Roosevelt to Platt, March 28, 1902, March 27, 1903 (quote), Aug. 19, 1903, Platt Papers, Yale; Roosevelt to Platt, Aug. 9, 1902, Feb. 25, 1903; Roosevelt to Odell, March 23, 1903 (2 letters), August 26, 1903, *LTR*, III; Odell to Roosevelt, Feb. 20, 1903, March 19, 1903, May 21, 1904, Roosevelt Papers, LC; Roosevelt to Elihu Root, March 24, 1903, Root Papers, LC; Edgar T. Brackett to Platt, Oct. 3, 1901; Platt to Brackett, Oct. 4, 1901, Platt Papers, Yale; Platt to John R. Hazel, April 24, 1903, Hazel Papers.

16. Richard Duffy, "'Ben' Odell: A Study," *Van Norden Magazine* 1 (Dec. 1906): 41–47; Harold F. Gosnell interview with Charles H. Betts, Sept. 27, 1921; New York *Press*, March 2, 4, 1902; *Malone Paladium*, Oct. 2, 1902.

17. Alexander, *Four Famous New Yorkers*, pp. 378–82; Gosnell, *Boss Platt and His New York Machine*, pp. 294–95; *Auto. TCP*, pp. 429–40; *NYT*, March 5, 30, April 13, May 24, 25, June 29, 1902; *Trib.*, Sept. 9, 24, 25, 1902.

18. Odell to Platt, Jan. 22, 1902, Jan. 13, 1903, Jan. 23, 1903; Platt to Odell, Jan. 24, 1902, Jan. 21, 1903, Platt Papers, Yale; William Barnes, Jr., to Roosevelt, March 2, 1904; Platt to Nevada N. Stranahan, March 16, 1904; Platt to Roosevelt, March 20, 1904, Roosevelt Papers, LC; Roosevelt to Nicholas Murray Butler, March 8, 1904 (quote); Roosevelt to Odell, March 21, 1904; Roosevelt to Platt, March 21, 1904, *LTR*, IV; *Trib.*, Jan. 10, 11, 20, 21, Nov. 26, 1903, March 20, 21, 1904; Alexander, *Four Famous New Yorkers*, pp. 415–18.

19. From 1894 to 1900, by contrast, executive, administrative, legislative, and judicial costs all had grown by at least 40 percent; Don C. Sowers, *The Financial History of New York State: From 1789 to 1912* (New York, 1914), pp. 320–21. *P.P.*, *1902*, pp. 212–19; *P.P.*, *1903*, pp. 134–37; *P.P.*, *1904*, pp. 113–15; *Nation* 75 (April 14, 1902): 125–26.

20. Sowers, *Financial History*, pp. 321–22; the expenditure totals given in the text exclude trust fund payments and the repayment of temporary loans; *Annual Report of the Comptroller* (Albany, 1905), p. xvi.

21. Sowers, *Financial History*, pp. 145–83; *Annual Report of the Comptroller* (Albany, 1901), pp. vii–ix; *Annual Report of the Comptroller* (Albany, 1905), pp. xxv–xxix; Carl C. Plehn, "Revenue Systems of the State and Local Governments," U.S. Bureau of the Census, *Wealth, Debt, and Taxation* (Washington, D.C., 1907), pp. 756–60; Merlin Harold Hunter, *The Development of Corporation Taxation in the State of New York* (Urbana, Ill., 1917); Yearley, *Money Machines*, pp. 193–250.

22. *P.P.*, *1902*, pp. 212–19; *P.P.*, *1903*, pp. 134–37; *P.P.*, *1904*, pp. 113–15; *NYT*, Feb. 7, 1901, March 26, 1902; *Ithaca Daily Journal*, Oct. 14, 23, 24, 27, 29, 1902, Oct. 18–24, 1904; *TDT*, Oct. 19, 25, 28, 1904; *SLP*, Oct. 29, 1902, Nov. 2, 1904 (quote); *FC*, April 9, 1902, Oct. 19, 1904; *Yates County Chronicle*, Oct. 8, 22, 1902, Oct. 26, 1904; *Waverly Free Press*, Oct. 24, 1902.

23. *Annual Report of the Comptroller* (Albany, 1902), pp. xvi–xviii; Report of the Executive Committee, Feb. 13, 1901, NYBTT Papers; Robert S. Maxwell, *La Follette and the Rise of the Progressives in Wisconsin* (Madison, 1956), pp. 35–39, 51–55; Ransom E. Noble, Jr., *New Jersey Progressivism Before Wilson* (Princeton, 1946), pp. 7–9, 21–31, 113–18.

24. Chamber of Commerce of the State of New York, *Report of the Committee on State and Municipal Taxation* (New York, March, 1901), p. 12; Seth Low to Odell, March 13, 1903; Low to James G. Graham, July 15, 1903; Low to Henry Fuehrer, March 23, 1903, Low Papers. For evidence that the complaints by those in New York City had real justification, see the figures on the city's share of the

liquor and inheritance taxes in the *Annual Report of the Comptroller* for any year of the period; for data on the city's share of the assessed valuation of various classes of taxed corporations, see the *Annual Report of the State Board of Tax Commissioners* for any year of the period. *P.P., 1902*, pp. 357–64; *P.P., 1903*, pp. 9–10, 186, 202 (quote), 229; *P.P., 1904*, pp. 190–97; *Trib.*, July 14, 1902; *FC*, Sept. 2, 1903.

25. Hunter, *Development of Corporation Taxation*, p. 167.

26. The several legislative inquiries into politico-business relations, cited in n. 6 of the previous chapter, concerned the Odell years as well as the 1890s.

27. Samuel E. Williamson to William P. Rudd, March 7, 1901; Charles C. Paulding to Rudd, Jan. 27, 1903 (quote), Feb. 9, 1903; Ira A. Place to Rudd, Jan. 27, 1903 (quote), March 1, 1904 (quote); Paulding to James K. Apgar, Jan. 25, 1904, Feb. 3, 1904; Place to Louis Bedell, March 8, 1904, March 29, 1904; Place to John Raines, May 5, 1904; Place to George R. Malby, May 5, 1904, Corporate Records of the New York Central Railroad Company; William S. Opdyke to A. I. Culver, March 30, 1904, Delaware and Hudson Railroad Corporation Papers; Bruce William Dearstyne, "Railroads and Railroad Regulation in New York State, 1900–1913," Ph.D. diss., Syracuse University, 1974, pp. 31–46.

28. Chessman, *Governor Theodore Roosevelt*, pp. 244–49; Robert Crosby Eager, "Governing New York State: Republicans and Reform, 1894–1900," Ph.D. diss., Stanford University, 1977, pp. 370–75; *P.P., 1901*, p. 41; *P.P., 1904*, pp. 103–9.

29. *NYT*, March 6, 17, 20, April 2, 3, 9, 10, 24, May 8, 9, 1903; Committee on Railway Transportation, flyer entitled "All Citizens Are Interested In This Report," March 9, 1902; Minutes of a Monthly Meeting, March 12, 1902, NYBTT Papers.

30. *P.P., 1901*, pp. 48–50; Committee on Railway Transportation, flyer entitled "To Prevent Discrimination Against New York By Railways," Feb. 12, 1902, NYBTT Papers; *NYT*, March 19, 22, 1903, April 6, 7, 16, 1904; Ira A. Place to William P. Rudd, Jan. 26, 1904, Feb. 10, 1904, Feb. 16, 1904, March 23, 1904, March 24, 1904, New York Central Railroad Papers; Augustus Cerillo, Jr., "Reform in New York City: A Study of Urban Progressivism," Ph.D. diss., Northwestern University, 1969, pp. 139–42.

31. *P.P., 1901*, pp. 17–18; *P.P., 1902*, p. 44; *NYT*, Dec. 7, 1900; Claire Brandler Walker, "A History of Factory Legislation and Inspection in New York State, 1886–1911," Ph.D. diss., Columbia University, 1969, pp. 110–11.

32. *P.P., 1901*, pp. 19–20; *P.P., 1902*, p. 43; *NYT*, Jan. 9, March 19, 26, 27, 1902; Walker, "History of Factory Legislation," pp. 111–12; Irwin Yellowitz, *Labor and the Progressive Movement in New York State, 1897–1916* (Ithaca, 1965), pp. 107–10.

33. *P.P., 1903*, pp. 37–38; Jeremy P. Felt, *Hostages of Fortune: Child Labor Reform in New York State* (Syracuse, 1965), pp. 38–62; Yellowitz, *Labor and the Progressive Movement*, pp. 88–97; Fred Rogers Fairchild, *The Factory Legislation of the State of New York* (New York, 1906), pp. 70–88. A parallel measure, in many respects, was the tenement house law of 1901, which has been brilliantly analyzed by Roy Lubove in *The Progressives and the Slums: Tenement House Reform in New York City, 1890–1917* (Pittsburgh, 1962), pp. 117–84.

34. *P.P., 1902*, p. 44; *P.P., 1903*, pp. 4 (quote), 33–34.

35. Noble E. Whitford, *History of the Barge Canal of New York State* (Albany, 1922), pp. 54–136; Henry Wayland Hill, "An Historical Review of Waterways and Canal Construction in New York State," *Buffalo Historical Society Publications* 12 (Buffalo, 1908): 251–393; George H. Raymond, "New York State Canals From 1895 to 1903: A Chronicle of Achievement," *Buffalo Historical Society Publica-*

tions 13 (Buffalo, 1909), pp. 157–80; *P.P., 1901,* pp. 303–5; *P.P., 1902,* pp. 37–42; *NYT,* Dec. 8, 9, 1900, March 13, 28, 31, April 1, 3, 11, 16, 18, Oct. 11, 1901, March 18, 1902 (quote); G. H. Raymond to S. Fred Nixon, March 22, 1902, April 21, 1902, Aug. 21, 1902; Fred L. McMullen to Nixon, March 22, 1902; John Laughlin to Nixon, March 22, 1902, Nixon Papers. For the anticanal point of view see the protest on behalf of farmers and taxpayers, April 8, 1901, *S.J.* (1901), pp. 1382–84; *FC,* March 13, 20, April 24, Sept. 4, 1901, April 2, Sept. 24, Oct. 1, 1902; and *SLP,* Feb. 13, April 24, 1901, Jan. 29, 1902.

36. *P.P., 1903,* pp. 17–21, 238–45; *S.J.* (1903), p. 634; *A.J.* (1903), p. 1461; Francis V. Greene, "The Commercial Supremacy of New York," a speech before the Buffalo Chamber of Commerce, April 1903, Greene Papers; Platt to George H. Raymond, May 14, 1903, miscellaneous letter collection, NYSL; *Nation* 76 (Jan. 15, 1903): 45; *Trib.,* Jan. 28, 31, May 26, July 22, Nov. 5, 1903; *NYT,* March 26, 1903; Syracuse *Evening Herald,* Oct. 26, 1903; *FC,* Jan. 14, April 1, 29, July 15, 29, Aug. 5, Sept. 16, 23, Oct. 7, Nov. 11, 18, Dec. 19, 1903; *SLP,* March 18, April 1, Oct. 7, 28, Nov. 11, 1903; *Manual* (1904), pp. 766–67.

37. Hill, "An Historical Review," pp. 365–66; *P.P., 1903,* pp. 223, 239; *FC,* Jan. 14, April 1, 1903.

38. *P.P., 1902,* pp. 339–40, 367 (quote), 371; *P.P., 1903,* pp. 222, 250; *P.P., 1904,* p. 202.

39. Seth Low to Odell, Jan. 9, 1901, May 7, 1901; Odell to Low, May 10, 1901, Low Papers; *Nation* 74 (Jan. 9, 1902): 24–25, (April 3, 1902): 262–63; William H. Hotchkiss to Odell, March 9, 1901 (quote), Roosevelt Papers, LC; Root to Odell, March 11, 1901, Root Papers, LC.

40. Albert Shaw, "The New York Situation," National Municipal League, *Proceedings* (Philadelphia, 1902), p. 144; Richard Stephen Skolnik, "The Crystallization of Reform in New York City, 1890–1917," Ph.D. diss., Yale University, 1964; Cerillo, "Reform in New York City."

41. Blake McKelvey, *Rochester: The Quest for Quality, 1890–1925* (Cambridge, Mass., 1956), pp. 88–99; *AEJ,* Oct. 3, Nov. 3, 8, 1905; Robert Emmett O'Connor, "William Barnes, Jr.: A Conservative Encounters the Progressive Era," Ph.D. diss., SUNY at Albany, 1971, pp. 37–45; Syracuse *Post-Standard,* Oct. 13, 17, 21, 27, 29, 30, 31, Nov. 2, 4, 1903, Oct. 19, 27, 28, Nov. 4, 6, 1905; Syracuse *Evening Herald,* Oct. 21, 22, 24, 27, 30, 31, Nov. 2, 3, 4, 1903, Oct. 12, 19, 23, Nov. 5, 1905.

42. New York *Sun,* March 24, 1901; Low to Odell, Nov. 5, 1901; Odell to Low, Oct. 4, 1902, Low Papers; *NYT,* March 28, 1902; *TDT,* Oct. 21, 1902; *Nation* 74 (April 3, 1902): 262–63; *Trib.,* Sept. 25, 1902; Shaw, "New York Situation," p. 139; James W. Pryor, "The Revision of the New York Charter," National Municipal League, *Proceedings* (Philadelphia, 1901), p. 132 (quote).

43. Low to Odell, March 13, 1903; Low to James G. Graham, July 15, 1903, Low Papers; William L. Riordan, *Plunkitt of Tammany Hall* (New York, 1963), pp. 21–24.

44. Gerald Kurland, *Seth Low: The Reformer in an Urban and Industrial Age* (New York, 1971), pp. 149–57. The December 1900 issue of *Municipal Affairs* included a series of articles exploring all sides of the New York City liquor issue. William Travers Jerome to Richard Watson Gilder, Dec. 8, 1901, Gilder Papers; speech by Low, Aug. 7, 1902; Low to J. T. Newcomb, Jan. 18, 1904, Low Papers; William Barnes, Jr., to Platt, Feb. 19, 1904; Platt to Barnes, Feb. 22, 1904, Platt Papers, Yale; *P.P., 1902,* pp. 31–34; *P.P., 1904,* pp. 38–40, 209.

45. *Albany Press,* Dec. 22, 1901 (quote; clipping in Nixon Papers); Raines to

Nixon, Nov. 27, 1903, Nixon Papers; New York *Sun,* Nov. 9, 12, 1901; *FC,* Feb. 4, March 4, 1903; *NYT,* Jan. 2 (quote), 3, 6, 14, 20, 22, 1902.

46. *Manual* (1903), pp. 748–49; *Trib.,* Nov. 5, 6, 14, 15, 30, 1902; *NYT,* Nov. 5, 6, 1902; *Malone Paladium,* Nov. 6, 1902 (quote); *Owego Daily Record,* Nov. 5, 1902; *Waverly Free Press,* Nov. 7, 1902; *FC,* Nov. 5, 12, 1902; *Cayuga Chief,* Nov. 1, 1902; *SLP,* Nov. 12, 1902; *Nation* 75 (Nov. 13, 1902): 374–75; Low to Odell, Nov. 5, 1902, Low Papers.

47. Ervin Wardman, "Men and Issues of the New York City Campaign," *Review of Reviews* 28 (Nov. 1903): 545–55; Citizens' Union, *The City for the People! The Best Administration New York Ever Had* (New York, 1903); *Nation* 77 (July 23, 1903): 66, (Nov. 5, 1903): 351; *Outlook* 75 (Oct. 10, 1903): 343–46, (Nov. 14, 1903): 619–20; *NYT,* Nov. 4, 5, 1903; Kurland, *Seth Low,* pp. 143–214; Skolnik, "Crystallization of Reform," pp. 262–99.

48. Low to Nevada N. Stranahan, March 27, 1901; Low to Odell, Nov. 27, 1903, Dec. 14, 1903; Elihu Root to Low, Nov. 10, 1903; Low to Root, Dec. 8, 1903; Low to Roosevelt, Nov. 5, 1903; A. S. Haight to Low, Dec. 5, 1903; Low to Haight, Dec. 14, 1903 (quote), Low Papers; G. H. Putnam to Richard Ward Greene Welling, Oct. 23, 1903, Welling Papers; Roosevelt to Low, Nov. 3, 1903; Roosevelt to Nicholas Murray Butler, Nov. 4, 1903, *LTR,* III.

49. This paragraph and the two that follow are based heavily on the work of Richard Stephen Skolnik and Augustus Cerillo, Jr.: Skolnik, "Crystallization of Reform"; Skolnik, "Civic Group Progressivism in New York City," *New York History* 51 (July 1970): 411–39; Cerillo, "Reform in New York City"; Cerillo, "The Reform of Municipal Government in New York City: From Seth Low to John Purroy Mitchel," *New-York Historical Society Quarterly* 57 (Jan. 1973): 51–71; and Cerillo, "The Impact of Reform Ideology: Early Twentieth-Century Municipal Government in New York City," in Michael H. Ebner and Eugene M. Tobin, eds., *The Age of Urban Reform: New Perspectives on the Progressive Era* (Port Washington, N.Y., 1977), pp. 68–85. See also Martin J. Schiesl, *The Politics of Efficiency: Municipal Administration and Reform in America, 1880–1920* (Berkeley, 1977).

50. Frederick S. Hall, "New York," in "The Activities of Civic Organizations for Municipal Improvement in the United States," *AAAPSS* 25 (1905): 374–82. Several historians have described the work of New York City's civic associations: David Conrad Hammack, "Participation in Major Decisions in New York City, 1890–1900: The Creation of Greater New York and the Centralization of the Public School System," Ph.D. diss., Columbia University, 1973; Sol Cohen, *Progressives and Urban School Reform: The Public Education Association of New York City, 1895–1954* (New York, 1964); Felt, *Hostages of Fortune;* and Lubove, *Progressives and the Slums.*

51. Shaw, "The New York Situation," pp. 143–44; Theodore J. Lowi has described the slow growth of expertise, rather than partisanship, as the chief criterion for appointment to high city office in New York: *At the Pleasure of the Mayor: Patronage and Power in New York City, 1898–1958* (New York, 1964).

52. *SLP,* Oct. 30, Nov. 6, 1901; *Malone Paladium,* Oct. 24, Nov. 7, 1901; *Waverly Free Press,* Sept. 19, 1902; *Boonville Herald,* Nov. 4, 1902, Nov. 5, 1903; *FC,* April 22, 1903 (quote); *Adirondack News,* Nov. 4, 11, 1905; Lowville *Journal and Republican,* Oct. 19, 1905.

53. *Trib. Alm.* (1904), pp. 325–26.

54. Laws of 1898, chap. 363; Laws of 1899, chaps. 30, 145; Laws of 1900,

chap. 375; Laws of 1901, chap. 32; *FC,* Feb. 17, 1897, Nov. 23, Dec. 7, 1898, Jan. 25, Nov. 1, 1899, Feb. 27, Oct. 23, Nov. 27, 1901, Oct. 29, 1903; *SLP,* Feb. 2, 1898; *TDT,* Oct. 31, 1901.

55. The ten counties with the highest turnout losses in 1902 were: Allegany, Clinton, Essex, Orleans, Steuben, Ulster, Warren, Washington, Wayne, and Wyoming.

56. James K. McGuire to David B. Hill, Sept. 17, 1902, Hill Papers, NYSL; William Barnes, Jr., to Platt, Nov. 19, 1902, Platt Papers, Yale.

57. *Trib.,* July 14, 1902, March 29, April 15, Sept. 23, 1904; Alexander, *Four Famous New Yorkers,* pp. 417–18; *Nation* 74 (April 3, 1902): 262–63; 78 (April 21, 1904): 305 (quote).

58. *Trib.,* May 6, June 2, July 9, 22, 29, Aug. 23, Sept. 3, 14, 16, 1904; *Buffalo Enquirer,* Oct. 29, 1904; Root to Higgins, July 26, 1904, Higgins Papers; Root to J. Sloat Fassett, June 10, 1904; Root to Odell, July 23, 1904; Root to Platt, Aug. 18, 1904; Roosevelt to Root, Aug. 2, 1904, Root Papers, LC; Alexander, *Four Famous New Yorkers,* pp. 425–29.

59. *Trib.,* Oct. 23, Nov. 1, 1902, Oct. 30, 1904; New York *Sun,* Nov. 1, 1904; *NYT,* Sept. 30, Oct. 10, 11, 14, 1904; *AEJ,* Nov. 3, 1904; *View of Governor Odell's 'Business Methods' at Albany* (n.p., n.d.), a Democratic campaign pamphlet for 1904 consisting of a speech by Attorney General John Cunneen on the Furnaceville incident; Alexander, *Four Famous New Yorkers,* p. 461.

60. *Trib.,* Sept. 22, 1904; *Odell's Administration Unmasked* (n.p., n.d.), a Democratic campaign pamphlet consisting of a speech by the party's gubernatorial candidate, Herrick; *Buffalo Enquirer,* Oct. 20 (quote), 25, 29, 31, Nov. 4, 8, 1904.

61. Roosevelt to George B. Cortelyou, Sept. 29, 1904 (quote), *LTR,* IV; Roosevelt to Root, Oct. 3, 1904 (quote), Root Papers, LC; Roosevelt to Platt, Oct. 1, 1904; Platt to Roosevelt, Oct. 3, 1904, Platt Papers, Yale; Charles S. Francis to Higgins, Oct. 1, 1904; E. H. Butler to Higgins, Sept. 24, 1904, Higgins Papers; Platt to Fred Herbert Johnson, Oct. 17, 1904, miscellaneous letter collection, NYSL; *SLP,* Nov. 2, 1904 (quote); *TDT,* Oct. 19, 1904 (Black quote); *Ithaca Daily Journal,* Oct. 26, 1904; *FC,* Sept. 21, Oct. 5, 19, 1904; *Malone Paladium,* Oct. 13, 20, 27, 1904; *Yates County Chronicle,* Sept. 28, Oct. 2, 5, 1904.

62. *Cayuga Chief,* Oct. 15, 1904 (quote); *FC,* Oct. 5, 12, Nov. 2, 1904; *Waverly Free Press,* Nov. 4, 1904; *Ithaca Daily Journal,* Nov. 8, 1904; New York *Sun,* Nov. 3–8, 1904; Platt to Roosevelt, Oct. 3, 1904, Platt Papers, Yale.

63. *Trib.,* Nov. 9, 1904; *Ithaca Daily Journal,* Nov. 9, 1904; New York *Sun,* Nov. 9, 1904; *Cayuga Chief,* Nov. 12, 1904; *Waverly Free Press,* Nov. 11, 18, 1904.

64. *Literary Digest* 29 (Sept. 17, 1904): 339–40, (Nov. 19, 1904): 674; *AEJ,* Oct. 24, Nov. 7, 1904; *Trib.,* Oct. 21, 23, Nov. 5, 1904; *Ithaca Daily Journal,* Nov. 5, 1904; John L. Heaton, *The Story of a Page* (New York, 1913), pp. 206–11; Don C. Seitz, *Joseph Pulitzer: His Life and Letters* (New York, 1924), pp. 263–64.

7. Politics at the Crossroads

1. *Red Book* (1905), pp. 31–39; *P.P., 1905,* pp. 4–30, 118–21, 241–43; *P.P., 1906,* pp. 13–44, 89–91, 101–4; *Manual* (1906), pp. 197–98, 904–17; Don C. Sowers, *The Financial History of New York State: From 1789 to 1912* (New York,

1914), pp. 105–7, 321–22; Horace White to Jacob Gould Schurman, March 18, 1907, White Papers.

2. Robert F. Wesser, *Charles Evans Hughes: Politics and Reform in New York, 1905–1910* (Ithaca, 1967), pp. 21–33; Merlo J. Pusey, *Charles Evans Hughes*, 2 vols. (New York, 1951), 1: 132–39; Augustus Cerillo, Jr., "Reform in New York City: A Study of Urban Progressivism," Ph.D. diss., Northwestern University, 1969, pp. 90–96; David J. Danelski and Joseph S. Tulchin, eds., *The Autobiographical Notes of Charles Evans Hughes* (Cambridge, Mass., 1973), pp. 119–21; Robert Grier Monroe, "The Gas, Electric Light, Water and Street Railway Services in New York City," *AAAPSS* 27 (1906): 111–19; Merchants' Association of New York, *Memorial to the Legislature of the State of New York for an Investigation of the Conditions Surrounding Gas and Electric Lighting in the City of New York* (New York, Jan. 11, 1905).

3. Pusey, *Charles Evans Hughes*, 1: 132–39; Wesser, *Charles Evans Hughes*, pp. 29–32; "Testimony Taken before the Joint Committee of the Senate and Assembly of the State of New York to Investigate the Gas and Electric Situation in the City of New York," *Senate Documents*, No. 30 (Albany, 1905).

4. *First Annual Report of the Commission of Gas and Electricity* (Albany, 1906), pp. 18, 138–43, 162; for evidence of a pragmatic attitude toward municipal ownership in small-town New York, see *FC*, March 8, 1905; *Waverly Free Press*, Sept. 8, 1905; and *Malone Paladium*, Oct. 12, 1905. Monroe, "Gas, Electric Light, Water and Street Railway Services"; *NYT*, April 21, 29, 1905; *Trib.*, May 1, 2, 5, 1905; Wesser, *Charles Evans Hughes*, p. 32.

5. Laws of 1897, chap. 385; Wesser, *Charles Evans Hughes*, p. 32; Pusey, *Charles Evans Hughes*, 1: 138; *NYT*, May 1, 4, 5, 6, 1905; *Trib.*, May 1, 5, 1905.

6. Laws of 1905, chap. 737; *NYT*, May 6, 1905; Cerillo, "Reform in New York City," pp. 142–49.

7. Wesser, *Charles Evans Hughes*, pp. 24–25; Danelski and Tulchin, eds., *Autobiographical Notes*, p. 120; Pusey, *Charles Evans Hughes*, 1: 132–34; *P.P.*, *1905*, p. 81; *S.J.* (1905), pp. 1860–61; *A.J.* (1905), p. 3277. Both the senate and assembly passed the commission measure after futile efforts by the Democrats to assure minority representation on the new board; see *S.J.*, p. 1860, and *A.J.*, pp. 3274–75. *NYT*, April 29, 30, May 1, 2, 4, 5, 1905; *Trib.*, May 2, 4, 5, 1905.

8. *NYT*, April 30, 1905; *Trib.*, May 3, 4, 5, 1905; Frederic C. Howe, *The City: The Hope of Democracy* (New York, 1905), p. 115 (quote). On the work of the commission from 1905 through 1907 see William E. Mosher, "Public Utilities and Their Recent Regulation," in Alexander C. Flick, ed., *History of the State of New York*, 10 vols. (New York, 1933–37), 8: 238–39.

9. Much of this paragraph is based upon Morton Keller's superb study of the life insurance industry: *The Life Insurance Enterprise, 1885–1910: A Study in the Limits of Corporate Power* (Cambridge, Mass., 1963), pp. 26–33, 200–206; also useful were John A. Garraty, *Right-Hand Man: The Life of George W. Perkins* (New York, 1960), p. 194; and Neil Viny, "Abusing the Public's Trust: America's Insurance Elite and the Armstrong Investigation of 1905," senior essay, Yale College, 1977. *Literary Digest* 31 (Oct. 21, 1905): 567 (quote).

10. Wesser, *Charles Evans Hughes*, pp. 33–40; Keller, *Life Insurance Enterprise*, pp. 48–50, 246–51; Pusey, *Charles Evans Hughes*, 1: 140–41; Garraty, *Right-Hand Man*, pp. 161–63; Philip C. Jessup, *Elihu Root*, 2 vols. (New York, 1938), 1: 437–40; Don C. Seitz, *Joseph Pulitzer: His Life and Letters* (New York, 1924), pp. 268–79; John L. Heaton, *The Story of a Page* (New York, 1913), pp.

212–27; *Literary Digest* 31 (July 1, 1905): 2, (July 22, 1905): 106–7; *P.P., 1905,* pp. 176–80; Elihu Root to Higgins, March 24, 1905; Higgins to Root, March 27, 1905; Paul D. Cravath to Root, no date but clearly spring 1905, Root Papers, LC.

11. Danelski and Tulchin, eds., *Autobiographical Notes*, p. 126 (quote). Hughes had briefly served as a lawyer for one of the figures in the Equitable fight, and other members of the committee staff also had industry connections; Keller, *Life Insurance Enterprise*, p. 251; Danelski and Tulchin, eds., *Autobiographical Notes*, pp. 121–22; Pusey, *Charles Evans Hughes*, 1: 142.

12. "Report of the Joint Committee of the Senate and Assembly of the State of New York Appointed to Investigate the Affairs of Life Insurance Companies," *Assembly Documents*, No. 41 (Albany, 1906), pp. 9–155, summarizes the disclosures concerning the three largest companies. Keller, *Life Insurance Enterprise*, pp. 52–77, 128–84; Garraty, *Right-Hand Man*, pp. 165–83; Pusey, *Charles Evans Hughes*, 1: 151.

13. *Testimony Taken before the Joint Committee of the Senate and Assembly of the State of New York to Investigate and Examine into the Business and Affairs of Life Insurance Companies Doing Business in the State of New York,* 7 vols. (Albany, 1905), pp. 789–825 (quote 789), 1477–95, 3860–75 [hereafter cited as *Test.*]; "Report of the Joint Committee," pp. 17–24, 49–62; Keller, *Life Insurance Enterprise*, pp. 214–26; Pusey, *Charles Evans Hughes*, 1: 153–57.

14. *Test.*, pp. 751–62, 825–28, 839–41, 1471–77, 2915–17; "Report of the Joint Committee," pp. 24–25, 62–64, 110; Pusey, *Charles Evans Hughes*, 1: 146–47, 154, 156; Keller, *Life Insurance Enterprise*, pp. 228–35.

15. *Test.*, pp. 3167–205; Wesser, *Charles Evans Hughes*, p. 46; *Literary Digest* 31 (July 22, 1905): 106–7, (Dec. 30, 1905): 981 (quote); Harold F. Gosnell interview with Depew, Sept. 25, 1922; Timothy L. Woodruff to Depew, Dec. 12, 1905; Charles H. Clark to Depew, Feb. 6, 1906; J. R. Mansion to Depew, Feb. 19, 1906, Depew Papers, Yale; David Graham Phillips, "The Treason of the Senate," *Cosmopolitan Magazine* 40 (March 1906): 487–502.

16. *Test.*, pp. 3005–11, 3091–98, 3108–9, 3120–22, 3143–60 (quote 3144); "Report of the Joint Committee," pp. 135–38; Harold F. Gosnell interview with Odell, Sept. 22, 1922; Pusey, *Charles Evans Hughes*, 1: 163; Wesser, *Charles Evans Hughes*, p. 47; Syracuse *Evening Herald*, Dec. 16, 1905.

17. *Test.*, pp. 3385–97 (quotes 3396–97).

18. Rochester *Democrat and Chronicle*, Oct. 18, 1905; *Cortland Democrat*, Oct. 27, 1905; *Buffalo Commercial*, Nov. 25, Dec. 30, 1905; *Elmira Daily Advertiser*, Dec. 30, 1905; Syracuse *Post-Standard*, Oct. 30, 1905; Syracuse *Evening Herald*, Nov. 24, 1905; Pusey, *Charles Evans Hughes*, 1: 164–65.

19. *AEJ*, Oct. 11, 1905; *Elmira Daily Advertiser*, Oct. 11, 1905; *Norwich Sun*, Nov. 8, 1905.

20. *Literary Digest* 31 (Oct. 21, 1905): 567, (Oct. 28, 1905): 606 (*Evening Mail* quote); *Elmira Daily Advertiser*, Sept. 30, Oct. 20, 1905; *FC*, Sept. 20 (quote), Oct. 11, 1905 (quote), June 13, 1906; *Waverly Free Press*, Oct. 20, 1905; Keller, *Life Insurance Enterprise*, p. 254.

21. I have developed this argument at greater length in "The Discovery That Business Corrupts Politics: A Reappraisal of the Origins of Progressivism," *AHR* 86 (April 1981).

22. *Test.*, p. 1415; *Literary Digest* 31 (Oct. 11, 1905): 525–26 (quotes); *Buffalo Commercial*, Oct. 9, 1905; Syracuse *Evening Herald*, Oct. 9, 1905; *Yates County Chronicle*, Oct. 4, 1905; but see Albany *Times-Union*, Dec. 19, 1905. Elihu Root

to Paul Morton, Nov. 3, 1905; Morton to Root, Nov. 8, 1905, Root Papers, LC.

23. *Literary Digest* 31 (Sept. 30, 1905): 442 (quote); 32 (March 31, 1906): 468 (quote); Syracuse *Evening Herald,* Nov. 15 (quote), 23, Dec. 16 (quote), 1905.

24. Canton *Commercial Advertiser,* Dec. 19, 1905, June 12, 1906 (quote); Rochester *Democrat and Chronicle,* Jan. 9, 1906. The national muckraking magazines covered the life insurance investigation in detail during 1905 and 1906. For perceptive later comments on the insurance investigation's "enormous influence," see Burton J. Hendrick, "Governor Hughes and the Albany Gang: A Study of the Degradation of the Republican Party in New York State," *McClure's Magazine* 35 (Sept. 1910): 500. Harold F. Gosnell, *Boss Platt and His New York Machine: A Study of the Political Leadership of Thomas C. Platt, Theodore Roosevelt, and Others* (Chicago, 1924), pp. 356–57.

25. *NYT,* Sept. 13, 15, 16, 23, 26, 28, 1905; New York *Sun,* Aug. 28, 30, 1905; *Literary Digest* 31 (Oct. 7, 1905): 473–74; Irwin Yellowitz, *Labor and the Progressive Movement in New York State, 1897–1916* (Ithaca, 1965), pp. 191–92; Alan Astrow, "Beyond Good and Bad: 1905 and the Disruption of Traditional Electoral Politics in New York City," senior essay, Yale College, 1976.

26. Yellowitz, *Labor and the Progressive Movement,* pp. 188–97; W. A. Swanberg, *Citizen Hearst: A Biography of William Randolph Hearst* (New York, 1961), pp. 230–38; Wesser, *Charles Evans Hughes,* pp. 75–78; Herbert Mitgang, *The Man Who Rode the Tiger: The Life and Times of Judge Samuel Seabury* (Philadelphia, 1963), pp. 78–89; Samuel Seabury, *Municipal Ownership and Operation of Public Utilities in New York City* (New York, 1905); Charles Willis Thompson, *Party Leaders of the Time* (New York, 1906), pp. 232–47; *NYT,* Oct. 1, 13, 1905.

27. Harold C. Syrett, ed., *The Gentleman and the Tiger: The Autobiography of George B. McClellan, Jr.* (Philadelphia, 1956); Herbert Hillel Rosenthal, "The Progressive Movement in New York State, 1906–1914," Ph.D. diss., Harvard University, 1955, pp. 45–46; Danelski and Tulchin, eds., *Autobiographical Notes,* pp. 128–31; Pusey, *Charles Evans Hughes,* 1: 148–50; Herbert Parsons to Elihu Root, Oct. 7, 1905; J. Van Vechten Olcott to Root, Oct. 7, 1905; Olcott to Theodore Roosevelt, Oct. 7, 1905; Roosevelt to Root, Oct. 8, 1905, Root Papers, LC; Herbert Parsons to Root, Oct. 3, 1905; Roosevelt to Parsons, Oct. 9, 1905, Parsons Papers; *AEJ,* Oct. 7, 1905; *NYT,* Oct. 1, 3, 13, 14, 16, 20, 27, 28, Nov. 3, 6, 7, 1905; *New York Herald,* Nov. 5, 1905; *Literary Digest* 31 (Aug. 12, 1905): 199–200, (Oct. 28, 1905): 601–2.

28. *New York Herald,* Nov. 5, 1905; *NYT,* Nov. 6, 1905; Yellowitz, *Labor and the Progressive Movement,* pp. 193–97.

29. *NYT,* Nov. 9, 1905; *Trib. Alm.* (1904), p. 368; Yellowitz, *Labor and the Progressive Movement,* pp. 197–202.

30. *NYT,* Nov. 3, 6, 9, 1905; *Trib.,* Nov. 8, 9, 11, 1905; New York *Sun,* Aug. 28, 30, Sept. 12, Dec. 25, 1905, Jan. 4, April 16, 23, 30, 1906; *Watertown Daily Times,* Nov. 9, 1905; George B. Agnew, memorandum, Dec. 18, 1905, Agnew Papers; *Red Book* (1906), pp. 615–23.

31. Albany *Times-Union,* Oct. 27, Nov. 4, 6 (quote), 11, 1905; *AEJ,* Nov. 8, 1905; *Buffalo Evening News,* Nov. 3, 1905; *Elmira Daily Advertiser,* Oct. 23, 25, Nov. 3, 4, 6, 1905; Syracuse *Evening Herald,* Sept. 26, 27, 29, 30, Oct. 10, 16, 21, 23, 24, 27, 1905; *Trib.,* Nov. 8, 9, 1905; Blake McKelvey, *Rochester: The Quest for Quality, 1890–1925* (Cambridge, Mass., 1956), p. 98.

32. *SLP,* Oct. 4, 11, 1905; *Orange County Times,* Oct. 31, Nov. 10, 1905;

Cortland Democrat, Nov. 3, 1905; *Norwich Sun,* Nov. 18, 1905; *Steuben Courier,* Nov. 24, 1905; *Red Book* (1906), pp. 615–23. In Westchester and Niagara, the Republicans lost assembly seats; in Chautauqua, Wyoming, and Yates, the party's candidates prevailed despite a Democratic surge.

33. *AEJ,* Nov. 8, 1905; Albany *Times-Union,* Nov. 14, 1905 (quote); *Buffalo Commercial,* Nov. 8, 1905 (quote); *Buffalo Evening News,* Nov. 8, 1905; *Watertown Daily Times,* Nov. 10, 1905 (quote); *SLP,* Nov. 15, 1905; *Massena Observer,* Nov. 16, 1905; Lowville *Journal and Republican,* Nov. 9 (quote), 16, 1905; *FC,* Nov. 8, 1905; *Norwich Sun,* Nov. 18, 1905 (quote); Rochester *Democrat and Chronicle,* Nov. 27, 1905; *Literary Digest* 31 (Nov. 18, 1905): 729–30.

34. Odell took the stand on Nov. 16; five days later Platt testified.

35. Roosevelt to Nevada Northrop Stranahan, Nov. 17, 1905 (quote), *LTR,* V; Roosevelt to Frank W. Higgins, Jan. 3, 1906, Higgins Papers; Theodore Broadhead to Elihu Root, Dec. 28, 1905; John A. Sleicher to Root, Nov. 22, 1905; Root Papers, LC. A fragment of a lengthy handwritten memorandum, dated Dec. 20, 1905, gives an account of a meeting of Republican leaders in New York City, George B. Agnew Papers. *Literary Digest* 31 (Dec. 2, 1905): 813–14; *NYT,* Dec. 27, 1905; *AEJ,* Nov. 15, 17, 1905; Robert Emmett O'Connor, "William Barnes, Jr.: A Conservative Encounters the Progressive Era," Ph.D. diss., SUNY at Albany, 1971, p. 57; *Elmira Daily Advertiser,* Nov. 28 (quote), Dec. 20 (quote), 21, 30, 1905; Rochester *Democrat and Chronicle,* Nov. 16, 1905; Syracuse *Evening Herald,* Nov. 17, 20, Dec. 2, 1905; Lowville *Journal and Republican,* Nov. 23, 1905; *Orange County Times,* Nov. 24, 1905; *FC,* Dec. 27, 1905; Wesser, *Charles Evans Hughes,* pp. 50–51.

36. Platt to Roosevelt, Nov. 20, 1905, Roosevelt Papers, LC; Platt to John S. Shea, Nov. 22, 1905; Platt to Herbert Parsons, Nov. 22, 1905; Platt to James W. Wadsworth, Nov. 23, 1905; Parsons to Platt, Nov. 23, 1905; Roosevelt to Platt, Nov. 23, 1905, Nov. 25, 1905; Platt to Roosevelt, Nov. 24, 1905, Platt Papers, Yale; Roosevelt to Nevada Northrop Stranahan, Nov. 21, 1905, Nov. 23, 1905, *LTR,* V; William Barnes, Jr., to Elihu Root, no date, but clearly Nov. 1905; Roosevelt to Root, Nov. 30, 1905, Root Papers, LC; Roosevelt to Parsons, Nov. 27, 1905, Nov. 29, 1905; Parsons to Roosevelt, Nov. 28, 1905, Parsons Papers; Rochester *Democrat and Chronicle,* Nov. 16, 24, 1905; *Elmira Daily Advertiser,* Nov. 17, 1905; *Trib.,* Nov. 24, 1905; *AEJ,* Nov. 27, 1905; *Literary Digest* 31 (Dec. 30, 1905): 981; O'Connor, "William Barnes, Jr.," pp. 57–58; Wesser, *Charles Evans Hughes,* pp. 51–53.

37. George B. Agnew, memorandum, Dec. 20, 1905, Agnew Papers; Roosevelt to Herbert Parsons, Dec. 20, 1905, Parsons Papers; Higgins to Roosevelt, Dec. 21, 1905, Dec. 22, 1905, Jan. 4, 1906; Timothy L. Woodruff to Roosevelt, Dec. 23, 1905, Dec. 29, 1905, Roosevelt Papers, LC; Alford W. Cooley to Jonathan M. Wainwright, Dec. 20, 1905, Dec. 22, 1905, Dec. 26, 1905; Wainwright to Cooley, Dec. 21, 1905, Dec. 23, 1905, Wainwright Papers; James W. Wadsworth, "Reminiscences," pp. 57–64, COHC; Rochester *Democrat and Chronicle,* Dec. 22, 1905, Jan. 4, 1906 (quote); *Elmira Daily Advertiser,* Dec. 19, 1905; *NYT,* Dec. 22, 23, 1905; Lowville *Journal and Republican,* Dec. 28, 1905; *SLP,* Dec. 27, 1905; *Literary Digest* 31 (Dec. 30, 1905): 975; Wesser, *Charles Evans Hughes,* pp. 53–54; Martin L. Fausold, *James W. Wadsworth, Jr.: The Gentleman from New York* (Syracuse, 1975), pp. 29–38.

38. Roosevelt to Nevada Northrop Stranahan, Nov. 17, 1905, *LTR,* V; James R. Sheffield to Roosevelt, Dec. 23, 1905, Sheffield Papers; *Barnes v. Roosevelt,* pp.

1726, 1910, 2099; John M. Blum, *The Republican Roosevelt* (Cambridge, Mass., 1954), pp. 47–49, probably has overstated Roosevelt's dominance in the New York State Republican organization prior to 1905. Rochester *Democrat and Chronicle,* Nov. 25, 1905; *AEJ,* Nov. 22, 1905; *Elmira Daily Advertiser,* Dec. 2, 1905; *NYT,* Dec. 24, 25, 1905; *Literary Digest* 31 (Dec. 30, 1905): 975.

39. *AEJ,* Oct. 25, Nov. 10, 1905; *Elmira Daily Advertiser,* Dec. 30, 1905; Rochester *Democrat and Chronicle,* Dec. 11, 1905, Jan. 22, 1906.

40. *Watertown Daily Times,* Nov. 10, 1905 (quote); Rochester *Democrat and Chronicle,* Nov. 27, Dec. 16, 1905; *Steuben Courier,* Dec. 29, 1905, Jan. 5, 1906; Canton *Commercial Advertiser,* Jan. 9, 1906; Root to Higgins, Jan. 7, 1906, Root Papers, LC.

41. *P.P., 1906,* pp. 18–23 (quotes 19, 21), 27–28, 33–34 (quote 34); *NYT,* Jan. 4, 1906.

42. "Report of the Joint Committee," pp. 361–466, gives the committee's recommendations; the report also includes the texts of the proposed bills. *Literary Digest* 32 (March 3, 1906): 307–8; *NYT,* Feb. 23, 24, April 13, 28, 1906; Keller, *Life Insurance Enterprise,* pp. 257–59; Pusey, *Charles Evans Hughes,* 1: 167–69.

43. "Report of the Joint Committee," pp. 398–402 (quotes 399, 400).

44. *NYT,* Feb. 23 (quote), March 10, 1906; Paul D. Cravath to Hughes, Feb. 28, 1906, in Robert T. Swaine, *The Cravath Firm and Its Predecessors, 1819–1947,* 2 vols. (New York, 1946), 1: 760–61; Garraty, *Right-Hand Man,* pp. 186–89 (quote 186); Keller, *Life Insurance Enterprise,* pp. 261–62.

45. George W. Perkins to William Collins Beer, March 15, 1906; Beer to Perkins, March 17, 1906, Perkins Papers; Timothy L. Woodruff to Horace White, Feb. 27, 1906; White to Woodruff, March 5, 1906; White to Andrew D. White, April 26, 1906, Horace White Papers; Keller, *Life Insurance Enterprise,* p. 262 (Perkins quoted); *Literary Digest* 32 (March 17, 1906): 391; *Massena Observer,* May 13, 1906.

46. This paragraph is based on Keller's excellent account; *Life Insurance Enterprise,* pp. 262–92 (quote 292).

47. Keller, *Life Insurance Enterprise,* pp. 259–60; Pusey, *Charles Evans Hughes,* 1: 167–68 (quote 168).

48. Jeremiah W. Jenks, "Money in Practical Politics," *Century Magazine* 44 (Oct. 1892): 940–52; Joseph B. Bishop, "Insufficient Restriction of Campaign Expenditures," *Forum* 15 (April 1893): 148–53; Earl R. Sikes, *State and Federal Corrupt-Practices Legislation* (Durham, N.C., 1928), pp. 108–10; James K. Pollock, Jr., *Party Campaign Funds* (New York, 1926), pp. 7–11; Louise Overacker, *Money in Elections* (New York, 1932), pp. 234–35; *Buffalo Commercial,* Nov. 22, 1905; Rochester *Democrat and Chronicle,* Dec. 5, 1905, Jan. 9, 1906.

49. *P.P., 1906,* pp. 27–28; "Report of the Joint Committee," p. 397; Pollock, *Party Campaign Funds,* p. 10; Overacker, *Money in Elections,* p. 235; *Trib.,* Jan. 2, 11, 22, 31, Feb. 14, April 16, 18, May 1, 22, 1906; *NYT,* Jan. 4, April 3, 18, 1906; Perry Belmont, "Publicity of Election Expenditures," *North American Review* 180 (Feb. 1905): 166–85; Perry Belmont, *An American Democrat: The Recollections of Perry Belmont* (New York, 1940), pp. 472–98; Elihu Root to Higgins, Jan. 7, 1906, Root Papers, LC; Belmont to Horace White, March 3, 1906, White Papers; Seth Low to Herbert Parsons, July 30, 1906; Parsons to Low, Aug. 2, 1906, Parsons Papers; Laws of 1906, chaps. 239, 502, 503.

50. Belmont, *An American Democrat,* p. 481; Belmont, "Publicity of Election Expenditures," pp. 166–67; *Test.,* pp. 761, 841, 3168, 3885–86.

51. Overacker, *Money in Elections,* pp. 72–73, 234–38; Sikes, *State and Federal Corrupt-Practices Legislation,* pp. 188–201; Robert C. Brooks, *Corruption in American Politics and Life* (New York, 1910), pp. 234–35, 245–46; Pollock, *Party Campaign Funds,* p. 37.

52. Bruce William Dearstyne, "Railroads and Railroad Regulation in New York State, 1900–1913," Ph.D. diss., Syracuse University, 1974, pp. 6–29, 37–39, 68–74; Horace White to Ira A. Place, Feb. 28, 1906, White Papers; William S. Opdyke to Abel I. Culver, March 2, 1906, Delaware and Hudson Railroad Corporation Papers; *Trib.,* Feb. 22, 1906; *SLP,* March 14, 1906.

53. *P.P., 1906,* pp. 58–61, 78–81, 93–95, 102–4; James Blaine Walker, *Fifty Years of Rapid Transit, 1864–1917* (New York, 1918), pp. 162–99; Yellowitz, *Labor and the Progressive Movement,* p. 109; *NYT,* Dec. 23, 24, 27, 28, 29, 1905, Jan. 17, 26, 27, 31, Feb. 1, 3, 7, 8, 11, 15, 18, 27, 28, March 2, 14, 22, 29, April 6, 8, 12, 13, 21, 27, 1906; *Trib.,* March 7, 22, 29, April 11, 27, May 17, 30, 1906.

8. *Charles Evans Hughes and the New Political Order*

1. Roosevelt to Nevada N. Stranahan, Feb. 14, 1906 (quote), *LTR,* V; Roosevelt to Higgins, Jan. 3, 1906, Higgins Papers; Roosevelt to Herbert Parsons, July 18, 1906, Parsons Papers; Roosevelt to Elihu Root, Aug. 18, 1906 (quote), Root Papers, LC; Robert F. Wesser, *Charles Evans Hughes: Politics and Reform in New York, 1905–1910* (Ithaca, 1967), pp. 54–56.

2. Roosevelt to James Rockwell Sheffield, Oct. 7, 1905, Sheffield Papers; Roosevelt to Platt, June 2, 1906, June 6, 1906, June 8, 1906, June 17, 1906, June 18, 1906; Platt to Roosevelt, June 5, 1906, June 7, 1906, June 11, 1906, June 15, 1906 (quote), June 18, 1906, Platt Papers, Yale. Harold F. Gosnell, *Boss Platt and His New York Machine: A Study of the Political Leadership of Thomas C. Platt, Theodore Roosevelt, and Others* (Chicago, 1924), pp. 297–98, 308.

3. Wesser, *Charles Evans Hughes,* pp. 57–59; Gosnell, *Boss Platt and His New York Machine,* p. 303; Charles N. Anderson to Higgins, July 19, 1906, Higgins Papers; Parsons to Roosevelt, July 17, 1906, July 24, 1906, Aug. 17, 1906 (quote); Roosevelt to Parsons, July 18, 1906, Parsons Papers; Roosevelt to Root, Aug. 18, 1906, Root Papers, LC; *Literary Digest* 33 (July 28, 1906): 103–4; *FC,* Aug. 22, Sept. 26, 1906; *Steuben Courier,* Aug. 24, 1906.

4. Roosevelt to Root, Aug. 18, 1906, Sept. 4, 1906, Root Papers, LC; Roosevelt to Jacob Gould Schurman, Sept. 1, 1906, Schurman Papers; Barnes and Aldridge quoted in Merlo J. Pusey, *Charles Evans Hughes,* 2 vols. (New York, 1951), 1: 172; Parsons to Roosevelt, Sept. 19, 1906; Roosevelt to Parsons, Sept. 27, 1906; Hughes to Parsons, Sept. 27, 1906, Parsons Papers; Roosevelt to Lodge, Sept. 27, 1906 (quote), Oct. 1, 1906, Oct. 2, 1906 (quote), *LTR,* V. For Roosevelt's continuing role in the 1906 campaign, see Roosevelt to Hughes, Oct. 2, 1906, Oct. 4, 1906, Oct. 5, 1906, Hughes Papers, LC; Roosevelt to Timothy L. Woodruff, Oct. 3, 1906, Roosevelt Papers, LC; Roosevelt to Woodruff, Oct. 11, 1906, *LTR,* V. Wesser, *Charles Evans Hughes,* pp. 59–67.

5. Pusey, *Charles Evans Hughes,* 1: 172–73; Wesser, *Charles Evans Hughes,* p. 68; David J. Danelski and Joseph S. Tulchin, eds., *The Autobiographical Notes of Charles Evans Hughes* (Cambridge, Mass., 1973), p. 133 (quote); *Ithaca Daily Journal,* Sept. 27, 1906; *SLP,* Oct. 2, 1906; *Steuben Courier,* Nov. 2, 1906; *FC,* Oct. 24, 1906; *Literary Digest* 33 (July 28, 1906): 103.

6. Jacob Gould Schurman, ed., *Addresses and Papers of Charles Evans Hughes* (New York, 1908), pp. 9–18 (quotes 9, 13, 14); Danelski and Tulchin, eds., *Autobiographical Notes,* pp. 132–33.

7. Pusey, *Charles Evans Hughes,* 1: 175; Woodruff to Roosevelt, Oct. 8, 1906, Roosevelt Papers, LC; Roosevelt to Hughes, Oct. 17, 1906, Hughes Papers, LC.

8. Wesser, *Charles Evans Hughes,* pp. 70–87; W. A. Swanberg, *Citizen Hearst: A Biography of William Randolph Hearst* (New York, 1961), pp. 241–45 (quote 244); *Literary Digest* 33 (Oct. 6, 1906): 449–50; *Trib.,* Sept. 27, 1906; Gherardi Davis to Roosevelt, Oct. 27, 1906, Davis Papers.

9. Gherardi Davis to Roosevelt, July 26, 1906 (quote), Davis Papers; Roosevelt to Hughes, Oct. 2, 1906; Hughes to Roosevelt, Oct. 4, 1906, Hughes Papers, LC; Woodruff to Roosevelt, Oct. 4, 1906, Oct. 8, 1906, Roosevelt Papers, LC; *Nation* 83 (Oct. 4, 1906): 276; *Literary Digest* 33 (Oct. 13, 1906): 491, (Oct. 27, 1906): 573; *Malone Paladium,* Oct. 8, 25, 1906; Root to Woodruff, Oct. 4, 1906, Root Papers, LC.

10. B. Aymar Sands to George B. Agnew, Oct. 18, 1906 (quote); Woodruff to Agnew, Oct. 25, 1906, Agnew Papers; *Ithaca Daily Journal,* Oct. 26 (quote), Nov. 2, 1906; *Yates County Chronicle,* Oct. 10, 1906; *Nation* 83 (Oct. 4, 1906): 276; Roosevelt to Woodruff, Oct. 11, 1906 (quote), Oct. 14, 1906, *LTR,* V; Woodruff to Roosevelt, Oct. 13, 1906, Roosevelt Papers, LC; Roosevelt to Hughes, Oct. 12, 1906, Hughes Papers, LC; Roosevelt to Parsons, Oct. 14, 1906, Oct. 16, 1906; Parsons to Roosevelt, Oct. 15, 1906, Parsons Papers.

11. *Trib.,* Nov. 7, 1906 (quote); *Manual* (1907), pp. 814–15.

12. New York City, *The City Record,* Jan. 1907; Edward M. Shepard to Herman A. Metz, Nov. 10, 1906, Shepard Papers; Horace White to Andrew D. White, Feb. 13, 1907, Horace White Papers; Irwin Yellowitz, *Labor and the Progressive Movement in New York State, 1897–1916* (Ithaca, 1965), p. 213; Wesser, *Charles Evans Hughes,* p. 100.

13. *Trib.,* Nov. 8, 1906; James W. Wadsworth, Jr., to George B. Agnew, Nov. 13, 1906; Agnew to Wadsworth, Nov. 16, 1906, Agnew Papers; Yellowitz, *Labor and the Progressive Movement,* pp. 209–15; Martin L. Fausold, *James W. Wadsworth, Jr.: The Gentleman from New York* (Syracuse, 1975), pp. 44–55.

14. The Appendix discusses the choices of offices used in the analysis of ticket-splitting; the mean percentage shown in Figure 6 is weighted according to county size.

15. Frederick C. Tanner, "Reminiscences," pp. 41–43, COHC; F. X. Salzman to James S. Sherman, Oct. 26, 1906, Sherman Papers; Elihu Root to Whitelaw Reid, Nov. 23, 1908, Root Papers, LC.

16. *NYT,* Nov. 8, 1906; *Nation* 83 (Nov. 8, 1906): 383; *Trib.,* Nov. 7, 1906; *Ithaca Daily Journal,* Nov. 7, 1906; *SLP,* Nov. 13, 1906; *Literary Digest* 33 (Nov. 10, 1906): 661–62, (Nov. 17, 1906): 701.

17. Herbert Hillel Rosenthal, "The Progressive Movement in New York State, 1906–1914," Ph.D. diss., Harvard University, 1955, pp. 123–27; Herbert Parsons to Charles Dewey Hilles, July 24, 1907, Parsons Papers; Hilles to Arthur I. Vorys, Sept. 16, 1907, Hilles Papers; Timothy L. Woodruff to William Loeb, Jr., Feb. 6, 1908, Roosevelt Papers, LC; Henry L. Stoddard to George B. Cortelyou, May 18, 1908, Cortelyou Papers; J. O. Hammitt, "An Awakening in New York State," *Independent* 65 (Oct. 1, 1908): 758–61 (quote 760); Robert Emmett O'Connor, "William Barnes, Jr.: A Conservative Encounters the Progressive Era," Ph.D. diss., SUNY at Albany, 1971.

18. Schurman, ed., *Addresses and Papers,* pp. 32–33 (quote); Robert Fuller, "Governor Hughes and the Bosses," typescript, Hughes Papers, NYPL; William Barnes, Jr., to Hughes, Nov. 26, 1906, Hughes Papers, LC; Hughes to Barnes, Dec. 3, 1906, Hughes Papers, NYPL; Charles D. Hilles to Arthur I. Vorys, July 5, 1907, Sept. 23, 1907, Hilles Papers; Timothy L. Woodruff to Hughes, April 2, 1908; Hughes to Woodruff, April 4, 1908; George E. Dunham to Hughes, April 5, 1908, Hughes Papers, LC; J. Sloat Fassett to Woodruff, Feb. 7, 1908; Woodruff to William Loeb, Jr., Feb. 12, 1908, Roosevelt Papers, LC; Jacob Gould Schurman to Hughes, March 28, 1908, Schurman Papers; Pusey, *Charles Evans Hughes,* 1: 184, 193, 196, 238; Rosenthal, "Progressive Movement in New York State," pp. 71–72, 76; Wesser, *Charles Evans Hughes,* pp. 146–47, 176–77, 200, 221–22.

19. Parsons to Hughes, Dec. 26, 1906, March 14, 1907; Hughes to Parsons, March 18, 1907, Parsons Papers; Schurman, ed., *Addresses and Papers,* p. 30; Danelski and Tulchin, eds., *Autobiographical Notes,* pp. 136, 138; Wesser, *Charles Evans Hughes,* pp. 114–23, 253–56; Pusey, *Charles Evans Hughes,* 1: 188–89 (quotes 189); Fausold, *James W. Wadsworth, Jr.,* pp. 60–61.

20. James W. Wadsworth, Jr., handwritten autobiographical materials, Wadsworth Papers; Parsons to Robert H. Fuller, April 1, 1907, Parsons Papers; Charles D. Hilles to Arthur I. Vorys, July 24, 1907, Hilles Papers; Roosevelt to Root, Aug. 3, 1908 (quote), Aug. 8, 1908, Sept. 5, 1908, Root Papers, LC; Horace White to Andrew S. White, Feb. 3, 1909, White Papers; *Auto. TCP,* pp. 464–65; Lloyd C. Griscom, *Diplomatically Speaking* (Boston, 1940), pp. 332–33.

21. Fuller, "Governor Hughes and the Bosses," pp. 3–4; see also a typescript on Hughes and the Republican party, undated and unsigned, but probably by Robert H. Fuller, 1909, Hughes Papers, NYPL.

22. Speech by Hughes at the City Club, Feb. 25, 1908; speech by Hughes at the Middlesex Club of Boston, Feb. 12, 1907, Hughes Papers, NYPL; Danelski and Tulchin, eds., *Autobiographical Notes,* p. 132; Schurman, ed., *Addresses and Papers,* pp. 36, 47, 231–32, 157–58, 162, 215–16; Robert H. Fuller to Herbert Parsons, April 2, 1907, Parsons Papers; Charles Evans Hughes, *Conditions of Progress in Democratic Government* (New Haven, 1910), pp. 59–123.

23. Schurman, ed., *Addresses and Papers,* p. 157; Hughes to J. Sloat Fassett, May 10, 1907, Hughes Papers, LC; Hughes to Barnes, Dec. 3, 1906, Hughes Papers, NYPL.

24. Schurman, ed., *Addresses and Papers,* pp. 157–62 (quotes 159, 160).

25. Schurman, ed., *Addresses and Papers,* p. 32 (quote); Jacob Gould Schurman to Hughes, Oct. 14, 1907; Hughes to Schurman, Oct. 15, 1907, Schurman Papers; Fuller, "Governor Hughes and the Bosses," pp. 3–4; speech by Hughes at the Amen Corner Dinner, Feb. 9, 1907; speech by Hughes before the West Side Republican Club, March 17, 1908; Hughes to Barnes, Dec. 3, 1906, all in the Hughes Papers, NYPL.

26. Wesser, *Charles Evans Hughes,* pp. 27, 104; Hughes's speech before the New England Dry Goods Association, March 10, 1908, Hughes Papers, NYPL; Hughes, *Conditions of Progress,* p. 71; Hughes to Barnes, Dec. 3, 1906, Hughes Papers, NYPL.

27. Pusey, *Charles Evans Hughes,* 1: 181; Danelski and Tulchin, eds., *Autobiographical Notes,* pp. 135–36; Parsons to Charles D. Hilles, July 24, 1907, Parsons Papers.

28. Pusey, *Charles Evans Hughes,* 1: 185 (quote), 194–96, 202–7, 229–30, 262–63; Wesser, *Charles Evans Hughes,* pp. 161–63, 183–84, 204–6; Fuller,

"Governor Hughes and the Bosses," pp. 13–14; Hammitt, "An Awakening in New York State," p. 759 (quote).

29. Fuller, "Governor Hughes and the Bosses," pp. 11 (quote), 12, 17.

30. Woodrow Wilson, "The Study of Administration," *PSQ* 2 (June 1887): 197–222; Frank J. Goodnow, *Politics and Administration* (New York, 1900). Among the most useful historical treatments of the development of administrative government are: Robert H. Wiebe, *The Search for Order, 1877–1920* (New York, 1967), pp. 164–95; and Martin J. Schiesl, *The Politics of Efficiency: Municipal Administration and Reform in America, 1880–1920* (Berkeley, 1977), pp. 68–87.

31. Schurman, ed., *Addresses and Papers*, p. 22 (quote); Hughes, *Conditions of Progress*, p. 38 (quote); *P.P., 1908*, p. 46 (quote); Schurman, ed., *Addresses and Papers*, pp. 121–22 (quote).

32. Wesser, *Charles Evans Hughes*, pp. 124–45; Pusey, *Charles Evans Hughes*, 1: 191–94, 197, 215, 225–26; Danelski and Tulchin, eds., *Autobiographical Notes*, pp. 137–40; the Horace White Papers contain extensive correspondence reflecting diverse Republican points of view on the Kelsey matter. J. Ellsworth Missall, *The Moreland Act: Executive Inquiry in the State of New York* (New York, 1946), pp. 9–23.

33. Schurman, ed., *Addresses and Papers*, pp. 113 (quote), 276–77 (quote); Hughes, *Conditions of Progress*, pp. 46 (quote), 50, 98, 108 (quote), 118.

34. Hughes, *Conditions of Progress*, pp. 42 (quote), 44 (quote); Schurman, ed., *Addresses and Papers*, p. 103 (quote); *P.P., 1908*, p. 46 (quote); Danelski and Tulchin, eds., *Autobiographical Notes*, p. 145.

35. Hughes, "Some Aspects of Our Democracy," June 30, 1910, Hughes Papers, NYPL; Schurman, ed., *Addresses and Papers*, p. 227.

36. Frank S. Black, *Addresses of Frank S. Black* (n.p., n.d.), p. 281; Parsons to Hughes, Feb. 18, 1907; Parsons to Robert H. Fuller, April 1, 1907, Parsons Papers; Barnes to Hughes, Nov. 26, 1906, Hughes Papers, LC; *NYT*, March 1, 1907 (quote); Wesser, *Charles Evans Hughes*, p. 257.

37. Fassett to Roosevelt, Aug. 2, 1908; Elon R. Brown to Roosevelt, Aug. 1, 1908; Roosevelt to Root, Aug. 8, 1908, Root Papers, LC; *Barnes v. Roosevelt* contains correspondence on the party leaders' view of Hughes in 1908: Barnes to Roosevelt, Aug. 21, 1908 (quote), Aug. 24, 1908; Parsons to Roosevelt, Aug. 24, 1908, Aug. 28, 1908; Roosevelt to Parsons, Aug. 27, 1908. Wesser, *Charles Evans Hughes*, pp. 226–31.

38. Roosevelt to Root, Sept. 5, 1908, Root Papers, LC; William Stiles Bennet, "Reminiscences," p. 155, COHC; Parsons to Charles A. Dana, April 13, 1908; Barnes to Parsons, May 9, 1908 (quote); Parsons to Barnes, May 12, 1908, Parsons Papers; Parsons to Hughes, Oct. 5, 1908, Hughes Papers, LC; *FC*, June 17, July 29, Aug. 19, Sept. 16, Oct. 21, 1908; *Yates County Chronicle*, Sept. 30, 1908. On the passage of the gambling law, see Wesser, *Charles Evans Hughes*, pp. 189–208.

39. Roosevelt to Barnes, Aug. 21, 1908 (quote), *LTR*, VI; Roosevelt to Root, Aug. 3, 1908, Aug. 8, 1908, Sept. 5, 1908, Root Papers, LC; Roosevelt to John A. Sleicher, Aug. 29, 1908, Hughes Papers, LC; Republican State Committee, *Facts and Figures Concerning the Conduct of the Government of the State of New York by Republican Officials during Seven Administrations* (1908), pp. 1–4; Wesser, *Charles Evans Hughes*, pp. 231–38; Rosenthal, "Progressive Movement in New York State," pp. 110–15; O'Connor, "William Barnes, Jr.," pp. 79–83.

40. *Manual* (1909), pp. 789–91, 794–95; *NYT*, Nov. 4, 5 (quote), 1908; *Ithaca Daily Journal*, Oct. 28, 1908; *Yates County Chronicle*, Nov. 4, 1908; *Malone*

Paladium, Nov. 12, 1908; *SLP,* Nov. 10, 1908; Elihu Root to Whitelaw Reid, Nov. 23, 1908, Reid Papers; Wesser, *Charles Evans Hughes,* pp. 250–51.

41. Chauncey M. Depew, letter addressed "My dear Governor," (probably to Frank S. Black), Nov. 16, 1908, Depew Papers, LC; Hughes's actual margin of victory was 69,000.

42. Bruce William Dearstyne, "Railroads and Railroad Regulation in New York State, 1900–1913," Ph.D. diss., Syracuse University, 1974, pp. 86–89; *P.P., 1907,* p. 32; *Trib.,* Sept. 27, 1906; *SLP,* April 9, 1907; Wesser, *Charles Evans Hughes,* p. 154; Pusey, *Charles Evans Hughes,* 1: 200.

43. *P.P., 1907,* pp. 29–35; Thomas M. Osborne, "The Public Service Commissions Law of New York State," *Proceedings of the American Political Science Association* 4 (1908): 290–97; Wesser, *Charles Evans Hughes,* p. 155; Pusey, *Charles Evans Hughes,* 1: 201–2; Dearstyne, "Railroads and Regulation," pp. 90–92.

44. William S. Opdyke to Malby, March 21, 1907; Opdyke to David Willcox, March 9, 1907, Delaware and Hudson Railroad Corporation Papers; Dearstyne, "Railroads and Railroad Regulation," pp. 94–113; Wesser, *Charles Evans Hughes,* pp. 158–59; Pusey, *Charles Evans Hughes,* 1: 202; Danelski and Tulchin, eds., *Autobiographical Notes,* pp. 141–42.

45. Albert H. Harris to Frank W. Stevens, April 25, 1907, Corporate Records of the New York Central Railroad Company; William S. Opdyke to A. I. Culver, April 23, 1907, Delaware and Hudson Papers; see also: Opdyke to Culver, April 24, 1907; Opdyke to Lewis E. Carr, March 9, 1907, March 25, 1907, March 29, 1907, April 2, 1907, April 8, 1907, April 23, 1907, May 13, 1907; Carr to Opdyke, March 28, 1907, April 9, 1907; Opdyke to George R. Malby, March 18, 1907, April 15, 1907; Malby to Opdyke, March 16, 1907, April 13, 1907, April 16, 1907; Opdyke to George F. Brownell, March 29, 1907, April 15, 1907; Brownell to Opdyke, March 30, 1907, April 26, 1907 (2 letters, with inclosures), Delaware and Hudson Papers.

46. See Schurman, ed., *Addresses and Papers,* pp. 100–146, for Hughes's speeches at Utica (April 1, 1907), Glens Falls (April 5, 1907), Buffalo (April 18, 1907), and Elmira (May 3, 1907), quoted pp. 131, 141; *P.P., 1907,* p. 32; George R. Malby to William S. Opdyke, April 13, 1907, Delaware and Hudson Papers; Dearstyne, "Railroads and Railroad Regulation," pp. 113–17, 212–13; Wesser, *Charles Evans Hughes,* pp. 161–63, 169; Pusey, *Charles Evans Hughes,* 1: 202–7.

47. Hughes's Elmira speech provides the best example; Schurman, ed., *Addresses and Papers,* pp. 133–35, 143–44; J. Sloat Fassett to Hughes, May 4, 1907, Hughes Papers, LC; Pusey, *Charles Evans Hughes,* 1: 206.

48. Pusey, *Charles Evans Hughes,* 1: 206–7 (quote); Horace White to Francis Hendricks, March 14, 1907, White Papers; Dearstyne, "Railroads and Railroad Regulation," pp. 117–22; Wesser, *Charles Evans Hughes,* pp. 166–70.

49. Augustus Cerillo, Jr., "Reform in New York City: A Study of Urban Progressivism," Ph.D. diss., Northwestern University, 1969, pp. 228–53; Dearstyne, "Railroads and Railroad Regulation," pp. 131–232.

50. Schurman, ed., *Addresses and Papers,* pp. 129–32, 137 (quote); Osborne, "Public Service Commissions Law," pp. 303–4; Bruce W. Dearstyne, "Regulation in the Progressive Era: The New York Public Service Commission," *New York History* 58 (July 1977): 331–47.

51. *P.P., 1908,* pp. 21, 45; *P.P., 1909,* pp. 42–43; *P.P., 1910,* pp. 28, 236–37; Andrew Colvin to Horace White, April 10, 1909, White Papers; Elihu Root to

Timothy L. Woodruff, March 19, 1910, Root Papers, GARL; *P.P., 1907,* pp. 88–91; *P.P., 1908,* pp. 93–95; William S. Opdyke to Lewis E. Carr, May 27, 1907, Delaware and Hudson Papers; Pusey, *Charles Evans Hughes,* 1: 208; Wesser, *Charles Evans Hughes,* p. 180.

52. *P.P., 1907,* pp. 310–11; *P.P., 1908,* pp. 17–20, 241–81; Wesser, *Charles Evans Hughes,* pp. 184–88; Pusey, *Charles Evans Hughes,* 1: 211.

53. *P.P., 1908,* pp. 31, 44, 50, 233–34; *P.P., 1909,* pp. 287–332; *P.P., 1910,* pp. 35–37; Wesser, *Charles Evans Hughes,* pp. 322–25; Pusey, *Charles Evans Hughes,* 1: 211–12.

54. *P.P., 1909,* p. 34; *P.P., 1910,* pp. 36, 235–36; Wainwright to Hughes, June 22, 1910, Wainwright Papers; Danelski and Tulchin, eds., *Autobiographical Notes,* p. 153; Wesser, *Charles Evans Hughes,* pp. 314–21; Yellowitz, *Labor and the Progressive Movement,* pp. 109–12; James Weinstein, *The Corporate Ideal in the Liberal State, 1900–1918* (Boston, 1968), pp. 40–61. While the liability and compensation measures were by no means the only labor laws of the Hughes years, they were certainly the most important ones. Not until after the Triangle Shirtwaist Company fire of 1911, in which 146 workers died, did New York State significantly revise its labor legislation. Indeed, the tragic fire and the resulting investigation played a similar role in relation to factory legislation as the life insurance inquiry did in regard to corporation regulation.

55. Don C. Sowers, *The Financial History of New York State: From 1789 to 1912* (New York, 1914), pp. 322–23; *Annual Report of the Comptroller* (Albany, 1906–11).

56. *P.P., 1908,* pp. 28–29, 37–38; *P.P., 1909,* pp. 51, 78 (quote); *P.P., 1910,* pp. 38–41 (quote 39); Pusey, *Charles Evans Hughes,* 1: 260.

57. *P.P., 1908,* pp. 37–38; *P.P., 1910,* pp. 40–41 (quote 41); Schurman, ed., *Addresses and Papers,* pp. 222–26 (quote 224); Hughes's speech at the State Fair, Sept. 14, 1910, Hughes Papers, NYPL.

58. For estimates of presidential-year voter turnout from 1824 to 1968, see U.S. Bureau of the Census, *Historical Statistics of the United States: Colonial Times to 1970,* 2 vols. (Washington, D.C., 1975), 2: 1071–72.

59. One excellent study of the Socialist party in New York City is Arthur Goren, "A Portrait of Ethnic Politics: The Socialists and the 1908 and 1910 Congressional Elections on the East Side," in Joel H. Silbey and Samuel T. McSeveney, eds., *Voters, Parties, and Elections: Quantitative Essays in the History of American Popular Voting Behavior* (Lexington, Mass., 1972), pp. 235–59. The literature on the rise of public opinion in the early twentieth century is thin, but one starting point is Stow Persons's chapter "Democracy and Public Opinion," in *American Minds: A History of Ideas* (New York, 1958), pp. 363–81.

60. In 1905 William Travers Jerome's election as district attorney in Manhattan, in spite of a ballot format that rewarded straight-ticket voting, served to renew interest in ballot reform; *Trib.,* Nov. 10, 1905; *Buffalo Commercial,* Nov. 21, 1905; Syracuse *Evening Herald,* Nov. 10, 1905. For Hughes's ballot-reform proposals, see *P.P., 1907,* pp. 25–26; *P.P., 1908,* pp. 23–24. Wesser covers the battle over direct nominations in detail; *Charles Evans Hughes,* pp. 252–301.

61. *P.P., 1907,* pp. 28, 144; *P.P., 1908,* pp. 24, 47–48; *P.P., 1909,* p. 37 (quote); H. D. Hadlen to Robert H. Fuller, Sept. 19, 1908, Hughes Papers, LC; *NYT,* Sept. 27, 1908; *Ithaca Daily Journal,* Nov. 5, 1907; Hughes's speech before the Hughes Alliance in New York City, Jan. 22, 1909, Hughes Papers, NYPL. The

rise of rural and small-town interest in direct nominations may be traced in *FC*, Dec. 6, 13, 27, 1905, Jan. 10, 31, Feb. 7, 14, May 16, June 6, 13, 20, 27, July 11, 1906, April 10, June 19, July 10, Dec. 4, 1907, Feb. 26, April 1, May 6, 13, 1908.

62. *P.P., 1909*, pp. 36–41; *P.P., 1910*, pp. 28–35, 91–93, 94–97, 149–52; Arthur Ludington, "The New York Direct Primaries Bill of 1909," *APSR* 3 (Aug. 1909): 371–81; "Governor Hughes' Plan for Direct Nominations," an undated, unsigned typescript in the Hughes Papers, NYPL, probably by Robert H. Fuller.

63. Wesser gives the compromise interpretation; *Charles Evans Hughes*, pp. 259–64 (Wadsworth quote 264).

64. Hughes's speech at the Academy of Music in Brooklyn, April 15, 1909; Hughes's speech at Convention Hall in Buffalo, March 27, 1909; see also Hughes's speeches at New Rochelle (March 29, 1910) and Binghamton (May 9, 1910), all in the Hughes Papers, NYPL. For other defenses of the Hinman-Green bill on the grounds of its establishment of responsible party leadership, see Frederick M. Davenport, "Reminiscences," pp. 47–48, COHC; Direct Primaries Association of the State of New York, *Direct Primary Nominations. Why Voters Demand Them. Why Bosses Oppose Them* (New York, 1909); Danelski and Tulchin, eds., *Autobiographical Notes*, pp. 150–53; and speeches by Frederick M. Davenport at Olean (Oct. 12, 1909) and Rochester (Oct. 18, 1909), Hughes Papers, NYPL. Wadhams to Fuller, May 13, 1909 (quote); Fuller to Wadhams, Aug. 7, 1909, Hughes Papers, NYPL.

65. The literature opposing the direct primary produced by New York State Republicans was voluminous; for some representative tracts, see: John C. Ten Eyck, *The Representative System of Party Government vs. Mandatory Direct Primaries* (n.p., 1909); Timothy L. Woodruff, *Direct Primary Nominations: Speeches of Hon. Timothy L. Woodruff* (New York, 1909); Charles H. Young, *Direct Primary Nominations* (New York, 1909); Jacob Gould Schurman, "Direct Primary Nominations," an address before the One Hundred Club of Utica, Feb. 5, 1909, Schurman Papers; and Edgar T. Brackett, "The Advantages of the Convention," *Proceedings of the Academy of Political Science* 3 (1912–13): 220–28. Horace White to Paul D. Paine, March 20, 1909 (quote), White Papers; Fausold, *James W. Wadsworth, Jr.*, pp. 72–81; O'Connor, "William Barnes, Jr.," pp. 83–90.

66. *AEJ*, Jan. 6, 1909; Barnes to Nicholas Murray Butler, Jan. 9, 1909; Butler to Barnes, Jan. 11, 1909; Butler to James W. Wadsworth, Jr., March 1, 1901; Wadsworth to Butler, March 2, 1909, Butler Papers; Thomas J. McInerney, "The Election of 1912 in New York State," Ph.D. diss., University of Denver, 1977, pp. 89–125.

67. Hughes, "Some Aspects of Our Democracy."

68. "Report of the Joint Committee of the Senate and Assembly of the State of New York, Appointed to Investigate Primary and Election Laws of this and Other States," *Senate Documents*, No. 26 (Albany, 1910); typescript of the senate debate on the Hinman-Green bill, April 15, 1909, Hughes Papers, NYPL. For thorough treatments of the legislative history of the measure in 1909 and 1910, see Wesser, *Charles Evans Hughes*, pp. 256–75, 288–301; and Rosenthal, "Progressive Movement in New York State," pp. 128–55, 172–75, 236–43.

69. McInerney, "Election of 1912 in New York State." For Roosevelt's speeches on behalf of direct democracy in 1910–12, see *The Works of Theodore Roosevelt: Memorial Edition*, 24 vols. (New York, 1923–26), 19: 10–481. Direct-primary laws were finally enacted in New York in 1911 and 1913, but in 1921 the direct

primary was abolished for statewide offices; see Charles Edward Merriam and Louise Overacker, *Primary Elections* (Chicago, 1928), pp. 64, 98. The initiative and referendum were not enacted.

70. The best account of national politics in 1910 remains George E. Mowry, *Theodore Roosevelt and the Progressive Movement* (Madison, 1946), pp. 120–56.

71. "Proceedings of the Senate in the Matter of the Investigation Demanded by Senator Jotham P. Allds," *Senate Documents,* No. 28 (Albany, 1910); Oswald Garrison Villard, *Fighting Years: Memoirs of a Liberal Editor* (New York, 1930), pp. 201–15; Wesser, *Charles Evans Hughes,* pp. 275–88; Rosenthal, "Progressive Movement in New York State," pp. 155–69, 212–24.

72. Handwritten notes by Robert H. Fuller concerning a conference between Lloyd C. Griscom, Governor Hughes, President Taft, and others, Feb. 12, 1910; handwritten notes on further meetings, Feb. 13, 1910, Hughes Papers, NYPL. Statement released by Governor Hughes's office, March 10, 1910, Hughes Papers, NYPL; Root to Woodruff, March 19, 1910, Root Papers, GARL; Woodruff to Root, March 26, 1910, Horace White Papers; Root to Hughes, March 25, 1910; Hughes to Root, April 13, 1910, Hughes Papers, LC; Roosevelt to Henry Cabot Lodge, Sept. 15, 1910, Sept. 21, 1910, *LTR,* VII; Wesser, *Charles Evans Hughes,* pp. 290–91.

73. Mowry, *Theodore Roosevelt and the Progressive Movement,* pp. 134–42, 148–56; Rosenthal, "Progressive Movement in New York State," pp. 244–324; Herbert H. Rosenthal, "The Cruise of the Tarpon," *New York History* 39 (Oct. 1958): 303–20.

74. "Speech of Acceptance of Henry L. Stimson, Republican Candidate for Governor, Delivered at the Republican Club Tuesday, October 4th, 1910"; Arthur E. Blauvelt to Stimson, Oct. 15, 1910; George Roberts to Felix Frankfurter, Oct. 15, 1910; William H. Wadhams to Stimson, Oct. 26, 1910, all in the Stimson Papers. For a regular Republican assessment of Stimson's tactic of playing down his Republicanism, see Chauncey M. Depew to E. H. Butler, Nov. 9, 1910, Depew Papers, Yale. Typescripts of Stimson's speeches in the campaign of 1910 may be found in four scrapbooks in the Stimson Papers.

75. *Manual* (1911), pp. 748–49, 752–53.

76. Samuel P. Huntington, *Political Order in Changing Societies* (New Haven, 1968), pp. 93–139.

9. From Realignment to Reform in New York

1. Platt to Lemuel E. Quigg, May 7, 1908, May 14, 1908, Quigg Papers, N-YHS; Harry M. Glen to Platt, May 20, 1908; Platt to Glen, May 27, 1908, Platt Papers, Yale; *FC,* May 27, 1908.

2. New York *Press,* March 7, 1910; New York *Morning World,* March 7, 1910; New York *Evening Post,* March 7, 1910. These and other articles on Platt's death are gathered in a scrapbook in the Platt Papers, private. See also *Outlook* 94 (March 19, 1910): 606.

3. Note that Figure 7 is based on total adult male population, including unnaturalized immigrants. Figure 8 is based on turnout estimates by Walter Dean Burnham in U.S. Bureau of the Census, *Historical Statistics of the United States: Colonial Times to 1970,* 2 vols. (Washington, D.C., 1975), 2: 1071–72.

4. On turnout and ticket-splitting, see Walter Dean Burnham, "The Changing Shape of the American Political Universe," *APSR* 59 (March 1965): 7–28; *idem,*

Critical Elections and the Mainsprings of American Politics (New York, 1970), pp. 71–134; and Jerrold G. Rusk, "The Effect of the Australian Ballot Reform on Split Ticket Voting, 1876–1908," *APSR* 64 (Dec. 1970): 1220–38. Among the state and local studies describing the rise of interest-group organizations are: Richard M. Abrams, *Conservatism in a Progressive Era: Massachusetts Politics, 1900–1912* (Cambridge, Mass., 1964); Herbert F. Margulies, *The Decline of the Progressive Movement in Wisconsin, 1890–1920* (Madison, 1968); Carl V. Harris, *Political Power in Birmingham, 1871–1921* (Knoxville, 1977); and Mansel G. Blackford, *The Politics of Business in California, 1890–1920* (Columbus, Ohio, 1977). On public opinion, see Lowell, *Public Opinion and Popular Government* (New York, 1913); Stow Persons, *American Minds: A History of Ideas* (New York, 1958), pp. 363–81; and Warren I. Susman, "'Personality' and the Making of Twentieth-Century Culture," in John Higham and Paul K. Conkin, eds., *New Directions in American Intellectual History* (Baltimore, 1979), pp. 212–26.

5. James Willard Hurst, *Law and Social Order in the United States* (Ithaca, 1977), pp. 33–36; *idem, Law and the Conditions of Freedom in the Nineteenth-Century United States* (Madison, 1956), pp. 71–108; Grover Huebner, "Five Years of Railroad Regulation by the States," *AAAPSS* 32 (July 1908): 138–56; Richard Hofstadter, *The Age of Reform: From Bryan to F.D.R.* (New York, 1955), pp. 213–69; Gerald D. Nash, *State Government and Economic Development: A History of Administrative Policies in California, 1849–1933* (Berkeley, 1964); Robert H. Wiebe, *The Search for Order, 1877–1920* (New York, 1967), pp. 145–95.

6. I have developed this point at more length in "The Discovery That Business Corrupts Politics: A Reappraisal of the Origins of Progressivism," *AHR* 86 (April 1981).

7. This paragraph is based on an analysis of the yearly summaries of state legislation reported in New York State Library, *Index of Legislation* (Albany, 1904–9). Also useful was the accompanying *Review of Legislation* (Albany, 1904–9).

8. David P. Thelen, "Social Tensions and the Origins of Progressivism," *JAH* 56 (Sept. 1969): 323–41; David P. Thelen, *The New Citizenship: Origins of Progressivism in Wisconsin, 1885–1900* (Columbia, Mo., 1972); David P. Thelen, *Robert M. La Follette and the Insurgent Spirit* (Boston, 1976).

9. Samuel T. McSeveney, *The Politics of Depression: Political Behavior in the Northeast, 1893–1896* (New York, 1972); Walter Dean Burnham, "Party Systems and the Political Process," in William Nisbet Chambers and Walter Dean Burnham, eds., *The American Party Systems: Stages of Political Development* (New York, 1967), pp. 277–307; Burnham, *Critical Elections*; Walter Dean Burnham, Jerome M. Clubb, and William H. Flanigan, "Partisan Realignment: A Systemic Perspective," in Joel H. Silbey, Allan G. Bogue, and William H. Flanigan, eds., *The History of American Electoral Behavior* (Princeton, 1978), pp. 45–77. For some important reservations about realignment theory, see Allan J. Lichtman, "Critical Election Theory and the Reality of American Presidential Politics, 1916–40," *AHR* 81 (April 1976): 317–51; and J. Morgan Kousser, "History – Theory = ?," *Reviews in American History* 7 (June 1979): 157–62.

10. E. E. Schattschneider, *The Semisovereign People: A Realist's View of Democracy in America* (New York, 1960), pp. 78–85; Burnham, *Critical Elections*, pp. 71–90, esp. p. 84; Paul Kleppner, "From Ethnoreligious Conflict to 'Social Harmony': Coalitional and Party Transformations in the 1890s," in Seymour Martin Lipset, ed., *Emerging Coalitions in American Politics* (San Fran-

cisco, 1978), pp. 58–59; Jerome M. Clubb, "Party Coalitions in the Early Twentieth Century," in *ibid.,* pp. 71–73.

11. Schattschneider, *Semisovereign People,* pp. 80–82; Burnham, Clubb, and Flanigan, "Partisan Realignment," pp. 71–75 (quote 71); Burnham, *Critical Elections,* p. 10 (quote); Benjamin Ginsberg, "Critical Elections and the Substance of Party Conflict: 1844–1968," *Midwest Journal of Political Science* 16 (Nov. 1972): 603–25; Benjamin Ginsberg, "Elections and Public Policy," *APSR* 70 (March 1976): 41–49; Michael R. King and Lester G. Seligman, "Critical Elections, Congressional Recruitment and Public Policy," in Heniz Eulau and Moshe M. Czudnowski, eds., *Elite Recruitment in Democratic Polities: Comparative Studies Across Nations* (New York, 1976), pp. 263–99; Jerome M. Clubb and Santa A. Traugott, "Partisan Cleavage and Cohesion in the House of Representatives, 1861–1974," *Journal of Interdisciplinary History* 7 (Winter 1977): 375–401.

12. The index of competitiveness used here is adapted from Paul T. David, "How Can an Index of Party Competition Best be Derived?" *Journal of Politics* 34 (May 1972): 623–38. It is based on the mean percentage of the total vote received by the two major parties for the several offices used in the analysis for each year (see Appendix) and is calculated as follows:

$$\frac{\text{mean minority party \% of the total vote}}{\tfrac{1}{2}\,(\text{mean minority party \% + mean majority party \%})} \times 100$$

The county-level figures plotted on the graph are means of the individual county indices of competitiveness.

13. My article "The Party Period and Public Policy: An Exploratory Hypothesis," *JAH* 66 (Sept. 1979): pp. 279–98, presents a more general version of this argument concerning periodization.

14. Samuel P. Hays, "The Politics of Reform in Municipal Government in the Progressive Era," *Pacific Northwest Quarterly* 55 (Oct. 1964): 157–69. Martin J. Schiesl accepts Hays's view that municipal reformers and party bosses supported competing systems of municipal politics and public decision making, but Schiesl persuasively denies that the reformers' conception of politics was inherently any less democratic than the partisan system; *The Politics of Efficiency: Municipal Administration and Reform in America, 1880–1920* (Berkeley, 1977).

15. Angus Campbell et al., *The American Voter* (New York, 1960), pp. 143–45; V. O. Key, Jr., *The Responsible Electorate: Rationality in Presidential Voting, 1936–1960* (Cambridge, Mass., 1966), pp. 91–104; Burnham, *Critical Elections,* pp. 122, 128, 130.

16. Laws of 1890, chap. 321; Laws of 1895, chap. 810; Laws of 1908, chap. 521; Walter Dean Burnham, "Theory and Voting Research: Some Reflections on Converse's 'Change in the American Electorate,'" *APSR* 68 (Sept. 1974): 1004–13. The constitutional amendment, adopted in 1894, separating local from state and national elections may actually have had a greater effect on voter turnout than did registration requirements. In many counties in northern and western New York, where off-year turnout dropped sharply beginning in 1897 (when only local offices were contested), gubernatorial-year turnout began to fall five years later, in 1902. It seems likely that, after a time lag, the loss of the voting habit in the odd years began to take a toll on participation at state elections too.

17. Burnham's "Changing Shape of the American Political Universe" article brought forth replies by Rusk ("Effect of the Australian Ballot Reform") and

Converse ("Change in the American Electorate," in Angus Campbell and Philip E. Converse, eds., *The Human Meaning of Social Change* [New York, 1972], pp. 263–337). All three men carried the issues further (and all retreated somewhat from their earliest positions) in the *APSR* 68 (Sept. 1974): Burnham, "Theory and Voting Research," pp. 1002–23; Converse, "Comment on Burnham's 'Theory and Voting Research,'" pp. 1024–27; Rusk, "Comment: The American Electoral Universe: Speculation and Evidence," pp. 1028–49; and Burnham, "Rejoinder to 'Comments' by Philip Converse and Jerrold Rusk," pp. 1050–57. Thoughtful as these articles are, the debate among the three authors is somewhat discomforting because the "institutional" thesis, as narrowly framed by Rusk and Converse, does not really provide an alternative to Burnham's bold and broad, if diffuse, account of a new political universe. The phrases quoted in the paragraph are from Burnham, "Theory and Voting Research," p. 1012; Converse, "Change in the American Electorate," p. 298; and Burnham, "Rejoinder to 'Comments,'" p. 1054.

18. Burnham, "Changing Shape of the American Political Universe," pp. 22–28; *idem,* "Party Systems and the Political Process," pp. 298–301; but see *idem,* "Theory and Voting Research," p. 1022.

19. Wiebe, *Search for Order,* pp. 111–32; Samuel P. Hays, *The Response to Industrialism, 1885–1914* (Chicago, 1957), pp. 48–70.

20. Kolko's works have focused on federal, rather than state, legislation; see *The Triumph of Conservatism: A Reinterpretation of American History, 1900–1916* (New York, 1963); and *Railroads and Regulation, 1877–1916* (Princeton, 1965).

21. Stanley P. Caine, *The Myth of a Progressive Reform: Railroad Regulation in Wisconsin, 1903–1910* (Madison, 1910), finds a pattern similar to the one described here; see also Bruce W. Dearstyne, "Regulation in the Progressive Era: The New York Public Service Commission," *New York History* 58 (July 1977): 311–47. For a critical summary of recent studies of regulation, see Thomas K. McCraw, "Regulation in America: A Review Article," *Business History Review* 49 (Summer 1975): 159–83.

22. McCormick, "The Discovery that Business Corrupts Politics."

23. Besides the works by Wiebe and Hays cited above, see Louis Galambos, *The Public Image of Big Business in America, 1880–1940: A Quantitative Study in Social Change* (Baltimore, 1975); and for a sympathetic introduction to the work of the "organizational" school, see Louis Galambos, "The Emerging Organizational Synthesis in Modern American History," *Business History Review* 44 (Autumn 1970): 279–90.

24. Indeed, one result of the new election laws was to secure for the major parties the legal recognition of their preeminent role in the nominating process; for a contemporary critique of this development, see William Mills Ivins, *On the Electoral System of the State of New York* (Albany, 1906).

25. Among the writings that have thoughtfully addressed the issues raised in these paragraphs are: Grant McConnell, *Private Power and American Democracy* (New York, 1966), pp. 30–50; Theodore J. Lowi, *The End of Liberalism: Ideology, Policy, and the Crisis of Public Authority* (New York, 1969), pp. 3–97; and Robert D. Marcus, *Grand Old Party: Political Structure in the Gilded Age, 1880–1896* (New York, 1971), pp. 251–65.

26. Hays, "The Politics of Reform in Municipal Government," makes this point persuasively.

Appendix

1. U.S. Department of the Interior, Census Office, *Statistics of the Population of the United States at the Tenth Census* (Washington, D.C., 1883), p. 647. U.S. Department of the Interior, Census Office, *Report on Population of the United States at the Eleventh Census* (Washington, D.C., 1895, 1897), pt. 1, p. 775; pt. 2, pp. xvi–xviii. U.S. Census Office, *Twelfth Census of the United States: Population* (Washington, D.C., 1901), pt. 1, pp. 991–92. U.S. Department of Commerce, Bureau of the Census, *Thirteenth Census of the United States: Population* (Washington, D.C., 1913), vol. 3, pp. 227–37.

2. U.S. Bureau of the Census, *Historical Statistics of the United States: Colonial Times to 1970*, 2 vols. (Washington, D.C., 1975), 2: 1071–72.

3. Richard Jensen, *The Winning of the Midwest: Social and Political Conflict, 1888–1896* (Chicago, 1971), pp. 34–57; Walter Dean Burnham, "Theory and Voting Research: Some Reflections on Converse's 'Change in the American Electorate,'" *APSR* 68 (Sept. 1974): 1017–18; Howard Allen, "Vote Fraud and the Validity of Election Data," paper presented at the annual meeting of the Organization of American Historians, April 7, 1977.

4. *TDT*, Nov. 3, 1894; *FC*, Nov. 2, 1898; *SLP*, Oct. 31, 1900; Benjamin B. Odell, Jr., to George Lincoln Burr, Nov. 2, 1898, Burr Papers; J. F. Parkhurst to Thomas C. Platt, Nov. 10, 1900, Platt Papers, Yale.

Index

Index

Index

From Realignment to Reform

Designed by Richard Rosenbaum.
Composed by Eastern Graphics
in 10½ point Times Roman, 1½ points leaded,
with display lines in Times Roman.
Printed offset by Thomson/Shore on
Warren's Olde Style, 60 pound basis.
Bound by John H. Dekker and Sons, Inc.
in Holliston book cloth.

Library of Congress Cataloging in Publication Data

McCormick, Richard L.
    From realignment to reform.

    Bibliography: p.
    Includes index.
    1. New York (State)—Politics and government—1865–1950.   I. Title.
    F124.M14   320.9747   80-69824
    ISBN 0-8014-1326-5